PARADIGM WARS

PARADIGM WARS

Indigenous Peoples' Resistance to Globalization

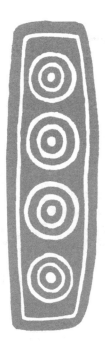

EDITED BY
Jerry Mander and Victoria Tauli-Corpuz
International Forum on Globalization

SIERRA CLUB BOOKS
SAN FRANCISCO

THE SIERRA CLUB, founded in 1892 by John Muir, has devoted itself to the study and protection of the earth's scenic and ecological resources—mountains, wetlands, woodlands, wild shores and rivers, deserts and plains. The publishing program of the Sierra Club offers books to the public as a nonprofit educational service in the hope that they may enlarge the public's understanding of the Club's basic concerns. The point of view expressed in each book, however, does not necessarily represent that of the Club. The Sierra Club has some sixty chapters throughout the United States. For information about how you may participate in its programs to preserve wilderness and the quality of life, please address inquiries to Sierra Club, 85 Second Street, San Francisco, California 94105, or visit our website at www.sierraclub.org.

Published by Sierra Club Books
85 Second Street, San Francisco, CA 94105
www.sierraclub.org/books

Produced and distributed by
University of California Press
Berkeley and Los Angeles, California
University of California Press, Ltd.
London, England
www.ucpress.edu

Book and cover design by
Daniela Sklan, Hummingbird Design

Cover photo by Rodrigo Buendia/AFP/Getty Images

Library of Congress Cataloging-in-Publication Data
Paradigm wars : indigenous peoples' resistance
  to globalization / edited by Jerry Mander and
  Victoria Tauli-Corpuz.
      p. cm.
"International Forum on Globalization."
Rev. ed of: Paradigm wars. San Francisco,
Calif. : International Forum on Globalization,
2005.
  ISBN-13: 978-1-57805-132-8 (alk.paper)
  ISBN-10: 1-57805-132-0 (alk. paper)
  1. Indigenous peoples—Economic conditions.
  2. Indigenous Peoples—Social conditions.
  3. Culture and globalization. 4.Globalization. 5.
Anti-globalization movement. 6. Environmental
degradation. I. Mander, Jerry. II. Tauli-Corpuz,
Victoria. III. International Forum on Globalization.

GN380.P37 2006
303.48'2—dc22   2006044289

Printed in the United States of America on New Leaf Ecobook 50 acid-free paper, which contains a minimum of 50 percent post-consumer waste, processed chlorine free. Of the balance, 25 percent is Forest Stewardship Council certified to contain no old-growth treesand to be pulped totally chlorine free.

10 09 08 07 06
10 9 8 7 6 5 4 3 2 1

Acknowledgments

THE EDITORS OF THIS BOOK EXTEND OUR DEEPEST THANKS to all the people who have helped with this project since we began work on it in 2000. The entire staffs of the International Forum on Globalization (IFG) in San Francisco and the Tebtebba Foundation (Indigenous Peoples' International Centre for Policy Research and Education) in the Philippines contributed in countless ways over the last several years, researching, communicating, and helping organize the project. We would also like to thank the other organizations who participated in our early mapping project, including Amazon Watch, Arctic Peoples Alert, the Cultural Conservancy, the European Center for Ecological and Agricultural Tourism, Greenpeace-U.S., Indigenous Environmental Network, Pacific Environment, Project Underground, Rainforest Action Network, White Earth Land Recovery Project, U'wa Defense Project, and Pachamama Alliance.

Originally published as a Report of the International Forum on Globalization's Committee on Indigenous Peoples, the project was first launched at the United Nations in Geneva in 2005, receiving an enthusiastic reception. Now that Victoria Tauli-Corpuz has been elected chair of the UN Permanent Forum on Indigenous Issues, we look forward to further engagement with UN agencies, so as to move the ideas in this book forward.

This new expanded edition from Sierra Club Books, as well as the initial IFG report, was designed by Daniela Sklan, Hummingbird Design;

we are so very grateful to her for its elegance and aptness. We would also like to give special thanks to Elizabeth Berg of Sierra Club Books, who did the overall masterful fine-tuning and edit in the last stages of preparation for this edition. Useful copy editing help at earlier stages came from Marcella Friel, Stephanie Marquardt, Pam Mandell, and E. Koohan Paik. Finally, we greatly appreciate the unflagging help, ideas, and support we steadily received from Helen Sweetland and Danny Moses of Sierra Club Books.

The research director for the project was Suzanne York of the IFG staff, with additional research by Victor Menotti, Antonia Juhasz, and Elizabeth Connor. Additional writing was contributed by Shannon Biggs, now of Global Exchange, and Rebecca Robbins.

Finally, we most gratefully acknowledge the important financial support we received at various stages from the Lannan Foundation, which has been a partner in this project since the very beginning. We also received significant and timely help from the Solidago Foundation, Christensen Fund, C.S. Fund, and Wallace Global Fund, all of whom have helped make this project possible.

Victoria Tauli-Corpuz
Tebtebba Foundation
Baguio City, Philippines

Jerry Mander
International Forum on Globalization
San Francisco, United States

Contents

PART ONE

Culture Clash

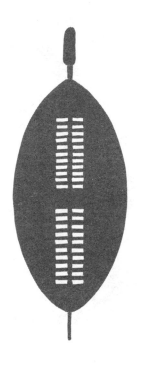

A Cree girl near James Bay, Quebec, during the epic, successful struggle to prevent the construction of giant dams that would have flooded an area of Cree traditional lands nearly the size of France. The World Bank has funded thousands of huge dam projects on native lands on every continent, despite fierce opposition by local communities seeking to retain ancestral hunting and fishing grounds and local livelihoods.

CHAPTER 1

Introduction: Globalization and the Assault on Indigenous Resources

Jerry Mander
International Forum on Globalization

NO COMMUNITIES OF PEOPLES ON THIS EARTH have been more negatively impacted by the current global economic system than the world's remaining 350 million indigenous peoples. And no peoples are so strenuously and, lately, successfully resisting these invasions and inroads.

It is the first purpose of this book to describe the nature, breadth and ferocity of the assaults upon native societies that are ongoing today, and the global institutions and corporations that drive them, while desperately seeking access to their own lifeblood—the planet's fast disappearing resource supply.

But it is also our purpose to convey the impressive energy, scale, and clarity of purpose of a global indigenous resistance. It is growing increasingly broad, powerful, well organized and effective in both domestic and international contexts. Indigenous peoples are demanding respect, recognition and codification of their "prior rights" to live where they have always lived, in the manner they choose, and with control over all decisions about their ancestral lands, and what is on them and in them.

Here is the basic problem: Economic globalization, and the corporations and bureaucracies that are its driving forces, literally cannot survive without an ever-increasing supply of oil, natural gas, forests, minerals of all kinds, fish, freshwater, and arable lands, among other crucial needs. They also require supportive infrastructures—new roads, pipelines, dams, electricity grids, airports, seaports, etc.—to take the resources from the often pristine places where they are found and carry them across vast terrains and oceans to markets.

In fact, the ultimate success of global corporations, and the entire economic model they sponsor and promote, is built upon a highly rickety platform requiring never-ending exponential economic growth, itself dependent upon never-ending resource supply to feed the growth. In the long run, of course, such never-ending growth is impossible on a finite planet. By now we already see a clear, sharp decline in availability of the most basic resources—certainly the most accessible and cheapest resources—leading to fierce contention over the remainder, even wars, as in Iraq over oil, and elsewhere on a smaller scale, over water.

Corporate growth and expansion are the primary bases of most short-term corporate profits. They also determine rates of investment and loans, shareholder value, and executive salaries. These factors, which are all intrinsic to the economic model, mandate that the global economic system continue its ever more needy exploration for the last resources in nature, wherever they may be, to feed into the voracious maw.

Alas, a high percentage of these last resources are found today on lands where native peoples thrive, as they have for millennia. And so we have the roots of serious conflict: invasions, double-dealings and forced removals, cultural and political assaults, and very often, extreme violence, as we will see in these pages. You could call these resource wars. But more precisely they are world-view wars; *paradigm* wars, actually, deeply based in opposite understandings of how human beings should live on the earth. This book is dedicated to amplifying that main point.

THE CENTRAL IRONY

As my colleague and co-editor on this project, Victoria Tauli-Corpuz, and several other authors within this document will repeat, it is no small irony that the very reason that native peoples have become such prime targets for global corporations and their intrinsic drives is exactly because most indigenous peoples have been so very successful over millennia at maintaining cultures, economies, worldviews and practices that are not built upon some ideal of economic growth or short-term profit-seeking. They do not seek to mine ever more of the natural world they live within for individual benefit, nor do they ship vast mountains of resources, like logs, copper or oil, across oceans to foreign markets. So, in a world where the resource base is in dangerous decline, a high percentage of the native peoples of the planet continue to live in natural areas of significant abundance.

Indigenous societies have achieved this—and the point is true of native peoples in all parts of the world, even those who are otherwise quite different from one another—by tending toward a formula that includes such shared primary values as reciprocal relationships with nature, economies of limits and balance, the central importance of community values and collective ownership, and their integration into and equality with the natural world. These values are mostly opposite to those of the dominant society. So even after millennia of living in a place, the resources are still there, though they call like sirens to voracious corporate actors, whose existence depends upon maximizing short-term growth and profit. Faced with these aggressions, native peoples are now actively resisting.

Right now, there are still an estimated 5,000 distinct indigenous societies on earth, living in varying degrees of autonomy or integration with respect to the larger society. A substantial number of these societies in Central and South America, Southeast Asia and Africa, as well as in the northernmost regions of the world, still have cultures and economies that are largely intact. All of these societies are eager to retain as much of their ancestral lands, sovereignty, governance systems and economic, cultural and spiritual practices as they can. Most would love to see invader societies leave their ancestral territories altogether and let them be. Yet all now face this latest iteration of an historic colonial advance—the highly accelerated drive by global corporations seeking access to land and resources.

And so, in the Amazon jungles and the mountains of the Andes; in the tundras of the far north, the forests of Canada, Siberia and Indonesia; the small islands of the Pacific, and the agricultural lands of the Philippines, Guatemala, Mexico and the United States; and in the grasslands and deserts of Africa, we now find native peoples facing grave threats to their lands, forests, wildlife, minerals, water, and themselves.

Remarkably, though, because of the strength of their convictions, and with the support of important new collaborations among indigenous groups of different regions and the help of indigenous and nonindigenous organizations within domestic and international venues, they are trying to reverse this tide. They are fighting for confirmation of their rights to sovereignty, self-governance and collective ownership and processes; they seek protections for their languages, cultural and religious practices and artifacts, and their traditional knowledge and science. Arguably their most important demand is control over all decisions about their ancestral lands, and the right to determine when, if ever, resource removal or any other intrusion is to be permitted, and under whose terms—the right of "free, prior and informed consent," presently denied in most parts of the world. This single issue is the basis for hundreds of struggles in domestic and international contexts.

It will be obvious throughout these texts that the problems that native peoples face today are huge. And of course they did not begin in this century. In many parts of the world they go back thousands of years, and in North America at least five hundred. But as we will see, the new global economic forms, which are enforced by the trade and investment rules of such global corporate instruments as the World Trade Organization (WTO), the World Bank, and the International Monetary Fund (IMF), among others, combined with spectacular new technologies of resource exploitation and militarism by which economic powers in the modern world further their interests, have conspired to bring assaults that are larger, faster and more powerful than ever before. So, the effectiveness of the indigenous resistance, especially in such places as the countries of South America, where indigenous peoples have made such significant advances, is all the more impressive, and becomes a further testament to the viability of indigenous ways and views.

The chapters that follow this one in Part One of this book are devoted to amplification of some of the underlying ingredients within native cultures that have sustained them so well for thousands of years, despite the aggressions they face. In the following chapter, "Our Right to Remain Separate and Distinct," Victoria Tauli-Corpuz begins with a description of traditional economic practices of her Igorot people, which have put them into conflict with the economic globalization juggernaut, and labeled them "obstacles to progress." It's a kind of "progress," however, that depends upon the destruction of her and other peoples' lands and resources, even to the very genetic materials of human beings and plants. She goes on to a full discussion of how these assaults play out through global bureaucracies, and what is being done to reverse this trend.

Fortunately for us all, in 2005 Tauli-Corpuz was unanimously elected chair of the UN Permanent Forum on Indigenous Issues—the one major international body with 50 percent indigenous representation—where she is in a good position to further the cause within that and other international venues. Among other recent advances for indigenous peoples, her accession to that role was very significant in itself.

In Chapter 3, "Aspects of Traditional Knowledge and Worldview," indigenous activists Winona LaDuke, Leslie Gray, and John Mohawk explore further teachings, practices, and language of indigenous peoples concerning land and economic practices that have sustained them, while causing hostility from the forces of colonialism and globalization. And then we excerpt from an article by the late Oxford University radical anthropologist Darrell Posey, who discusses native environmental values in conflict with the dominant Western system.

The last two chapters of Part One concern traditional community values and forms of education. Okanagan writer and educator Jeannette

Armstrong weaves an amazing mosaic of teachings about language, ancestry, and the deeply rooted connections with land and community in her chapter, "Community: Sharing One Skin," which is revelatory of the processes and understanding that keep native communities so internally strong and maintain a deep sense of connection among the people, their ancestors and their lands.

Finally, Quechua political leader Luis Macas, who is also the director of CONAIE, the powerful affiliation of all native groups of Ecuador, describes the profound importance of work now proceeding in Ecuador toward establishing a bilingual indigenous university (teaching in Quechua and Spanish) that explores, celebrates and preserves traditional indigenous forms of science, thought, education and practice.

"WTO LITERACY"

This book was first published in 2005 as a Report of the International Forum on Globalization. The initial intention of the report was to be a kind of "primer" digging deeply into the specific rules of economic globalization, the WTO, World Bank and IMF, so as to quickly demonstrate how and why it is possible for global corporations to so freely enter, exploit and destroy global resource lands, specifically indigenous lands. Because of the draconian rules of the WTO, and other major global institutions, which invariably give dominant power to global corporations, even nation-states are being prevented from stopping or regulating these incursions. It has taken a very long time for most countries, especially the smallest and poorest ones, to learn that the rules they signed onto perhaps a decade earlier were a hoax. Though they were advertised as benefiting poor countries, they do not, and were never designed to. They benefited only the most powerful countries, and global corporations, while destroying nature, communities, local businesses, the rights of the poor, control

over resources, and the welfare of the indigenous peoples of the planet. The awareness of these negative outcomes has lately taken hold particularly strongly in South America. There, a considerable opposition has developed, often led by indigenous peoples, against all outside global trade institutions, even leading to the rejection of President George W. Bush as he vainly tried, in November 2005, to persuade South America to join the Free Trade Area of the Americas (FTAA). His efforts completely flopped.

But as we worked on this project, we decided to go beyond the original "primer" concept and expanded the project to include the very many other forces and ways that globalization is harming native peoples and the ways they are resisting, and that is what you find in most of this book today.

Nevertheless, Part Two of this document is still sharply focused on the original detailed explanations of the dire global Rules of the Game, the "primer" on global institutions, and their implications and effects. So in Part Two you will find an outstanding article by Victor Menotti of the IFG on the rules of the WTO. Debra Harry of the Indigenous Peoples Council on Biocolonialism and Vandana Shiva of the Navdanya project in India also write about global rules, particularly as part of the Trade-Related Aspects of Intellectual Property Rights Agreement (TRIPS) of the WTO, which permits corporate ownership and patenting of local indigenous seeds, as well as new genetically engineered versions of them. They also discuss the horrifying practice of corporate scouring of indigenous landscapes for genetic samples from plants and human beings that can be patented, genetically engineered, and marketed.

Finally, Victoria Tauli-Corpuz contributes a riveting chapter on the deadly role of the World Bank's Structural Adjustment Programs (SAPs). Each of these articles goes into great detail about specific ingredients of the governing rules of the global economy as promoted by the WTO, the

World Bank, and the IMF. These articles concretely explain how certain rules and policies directly impact the situation of native peoples, with respect to their rights of sovereignty and their ability to sustain and preserve their environments, cultures and traditional livelihoods. In prior times native peoples mainly had to deal with individual colonizing nation-states that invaded and stole native lands and suppressed indigenous sovereign rights. Now, however, those same nation-states often find themselves subordinated to WTO policies and rules, so native people need to find ways to fight their local battles also on a global scale. That, of course, is where we can join the fray.

It is a difficult task. Most of us are not conversant with arcane economic concepts, or with the highly complex rules by which global institutions smooth the pathways for their corporate clients. Neither is it simple to see exactly how such rules—written in forbidding economic jargon—serve commercial interests while degrading landscapes and resident cultures. One could argue that the very complexity of the language of the global rules excludes meaningful public participation in debates over these issues and leaves the terrain to the usual "experts," who are often in the pay of corporations and bureaucracies. (In one famous incident, the U.S. nonprofit Public Citizen offered a $10,000 prize to the charity of choice of any U.S. congressperson who could correctly answer ten questions about the details of the North American Free Trade Agreement before voting on it. None succeeded.)

But if we are to resist current trends, it will be useful to develop some degree of "WTO literacy," as it were. We should all become better acquainted with the intricacies and trappings of the General Agreement on Trade in Services (GATS), the Agreement on Agriculture, and the Trade-Related Intellectual Property Rights Agreement (TRIPS), among many others, as the devil is in the details. All such agreements within the WTO, as well as the rules of the World Bank and the International Monetary Fund (IMF), are designed to empower a short list of theoretical concepts that form the structural model of economic globalization. Here's a very abbreviated summary of those central concepts:

▲ Free Trade: Requires countries to eliminate all taxes or other domestic barriers, including environmental, labor or health laws, that may slow the free movement of corporate products and services across national boundaries, as well as to free access to resources.

▲ Privatization: Transfers to corporate ownership such "public commons" as freshwater, forest lands, energy resources, and even the genetic structures of plants and humans; also public services such as water delivery, education, transportation, health services and sanitation, public broadcasting, welfare services, etc.

▲ Deregulation: Lifts all controls on corporate behavior, responsibility, and liability.

▲ Structural Adjustment: World Bank and IMF rules that require as conditions for loans and other benefits that nations remodel their economies—including social welfare and environmental policies—to fit a single universal model that better suits corporate growth.

▲ Export-Oriented Growth: Deliberately favors large-scale export industries over small-scale, local economic activity—small farms, local artisans and markets, small businesses—thus replacing often thriving local economies with trade-oriented systems.

▲ Free Movement of Capital: Removes restrictions on global investors so they may move their money in and out of countries and markets without any restrictions despite the often destabilizing effects, as in Thailand, Russia, Mexico and elsewhere.

Those are the basic theoretical concepts that we are all meant to live by. And the system of global rules that underpins these concepts is meant to assure that corporations have full access to resources, labor, and markets. Together these concepts and rules are designed to create an homogenized global system where all countries—even with cultures as different as, say, Brazil, Sweden, South Africa and Canada—are supposed to adopt exactly the same economic system and, with it, identical political values, cultural values, consumption values, and lifestyles. Everyplace should be like everyplace else, thus serving global corporate efficiency. Global monoculture!

Advocates of globalization say that the combination of these concepts and the rules governing all countries—which will be amplified in Part Two—was created to eventually bring a kind of economic utopia. As corporations grow and profit, the benefits would "trickle down" to all of us. The homily became, "A rising tide will lift all boats." Unfortunately, the twenty years since the model became dominant have not brought prosperity; instead they have greatly increased the separation between wealthy and poor within nations and among them; they have concentrated corporate power as never before, thus diminishing political and economic democracy everywhere; and they have devastated the environment and accelerated global problems like climate change. The model does not lift all boats, only yachts. It was (and is) a fraud.

In retrospect, we can see that the model was never actually designed for the common good; it was inherently doomed to fail in the long run. No economy based on an ever increasing supply of resources, ripped from a finite planet, could last very long. Now we are seeing the limits of the process and the desperate strivings for its last bounties. The whole design is for exclusively short-term gain for a small number of institutions at the hub of the process. And unfortunately their targets for resources are all too often on native lands.

FROM THE ARCTIC TO THE AMAZON

Parts Three and Four of this book deal with an array of direct consequences that indigenous people are now facing because of economic globalization. Part Three reviews some of the "macro" effects of the model, such as the report by Sheila Watt-Cloutier of the Inuit Circumpolar Conference on the severe climate change that is rapidly altering the environment of native peoples of the far north. This is preceded by a report from Amazon Watch on the effects of the massive infrastructure developments in the Amazon basin that are harming tens of thousands of Indians throughout the region. A shocking article by University of Queensland (Australia) professor Zohl dé Ishtar presents a devastating report on the half century of U.S. military experimentation on the Marshall Islands in the Pacific and their people, beginning with the atomic testing at Bikini and Enewetok a half century ago, to the present-day Star Wars missile testing experiments on Kwajalein. These Star Wars programs forced removal of thousands of islanders to a lesser island, Ebbeye, where they now live in slum conditions. This story has not gotten the attention it deserves.

There are also articles on current battles over the world's remaining freshwater, much of it on Indian lands, and the pollution of Mayan corn in southern Mexico by the uncontrollable spread of imported genetically engineered varieties from the United States. In each of these cases there are extremely active resistance campaigns among the affected peoples, with the aid of highly effective non-Indian NGOs.

More subtle effects of globalization are also discussed, including the theft and global marketing of sacred objects that are at the heart of indigenous culture, as indigenous attorney Terri-Lynn Williams-Davidson describes. A chapter from E. Koohan Paik examines the impacts upon—and now the impressive recovery of—one nearly extinct native language, Hawaiian. Great efforts are now under way among indigenous peoples globally to reverse both of these negative trends.

Two other subjects also get some rare attention. Both have to do with controversial efforts of ecology-minded northern organizations to "protect" environments where native peoples live. The first is "ecotourism," which is supposed to benefit native peoples because it is a way they can earn some cash income without destroying and selling off resources from their environments. In fact, however, the process has far more subtle and arguably equally devastating effects on cultures thus put on display, as if they lived in culture zoos. The second has to do with the forced removal of indigenous people from ancestral lands because huge outside conservation NGOs such as Conservation International have determined that indigenous lands would be better preserved if the people who lived in them for millennia—keeping the lands and wildlife in a healthy condition—were removed and turned into "conservation refugees," as Mark Dowie reports. Both of these latter problems are now subjects of intense controversy between environmentalists and indigenous peoples, two communities that should be working together.

In Part Four, the focus goes to extractive industries and their effects on native peoples. The section contains briefings on situations caused by oil and natural gas exploration, gold mining, nuclear waste disposal and other mining activities in Africa, Southeast Asia, the Philippines, Central America, and the United States. It closes with a formal declaration from a conference of indigenous peoples demanding to be included in all stages of decision making about policies concerning extractive industries.

Part Five explores some positive turns of events. It begins with a report by Beverly Bell on an important convergence of indigenous peoples of South America toward joint activity. Then Suzanne York focuses on the startling uprising of indigenous peoples in Bolivia, in opposition to the World Bank's water privatization programs there, and also the plans to export Bolivia's natural gas to the United States. This is yet another case where the global economy was poised to benefit the rich by virtually giving away a prized natural resource from a very poor country. The Bolivian uprisings have succeeded in reversing national policy on both matters. Water has now been pulled into the control of the Indians and *campesinos* who led the opposition. In fact the president was forced to resign as a result of the uproar, leading soon after to the overwhelming election of Bolivia's first indigenous president, Evo Morales. It remains to be seen how this revolution will ultimately work out, given the mounting pressure from the United States and global energy interests, but it is a promising demonstration of the power of a well-organized indigenous community.

Meanwhile, in the United States, indigenous activist Winona LaDuke reports on a "positive and sustainable future" on the verge of realization among Indian tribes of the U.S. Great Plains states. That's an area that has been exploited for energy development—coal, oil, uranium—for more than a half century, leaving environmental devastation, lung disease, nuclear waste dumps, and pollution of many kinds, while providing scandalously little income for the native communities whose lands are gutted for these purposes. The region is the site of some of the strongest and steadiest winds in the world—they're calling it the "Saudi Arabia of Wind." Suddenly tribes are seeing their future in the development of renewable wind energy. This may lead to a spectacular reversal of fortunes, at the same time as it creates a new model for environmental protection among Indian nations and the larger society as well.

An article by Canada's First Nations activist Arthur Manuel proposes a new creative legal strategy which asserts that nonrecognition of indigenous rights to land and sovereignty qualifies as an "illegal export subsidy" under WTO rules. Manuel's organization has succeeded in placing that argument into the offical WTO deliberations on the U.S.-Canada Softwood Lumber dispute, with possible major ramifications in other cases.

The book concludes with articles by Victoria Tauli-Corpuz and me. She closes with a wrap-up report on the vast array of activities being undertaken by indigenous activists among international and national agencies and bureaucracies, especially within the United Nations. While this work can be slow going, Tauli-Corpuz shows that significant progress has been made in the last decade toward internationial recognition of indigenous rights of economic self-determination, "prior, informed consent," political sovereignty, and collective human rights. She remains extremely active in agencies that may have the power to enforce new protections and standards in dealing with indigenous sovereignty issues. She is optimistic that a unified message of indigenous peoples is making headway.

My own final comments are directed less to indigenous peoples than to communities of scholars, activists, and journalists who have thus far focused primarily on such issues as the environment, human rights, social justice, and democracy, and to suggest to them that indigenous struggles embody all of these issues. In more

ways than one, indigenous issues are the frontier issues of our time. They deal with geographic frontier struggles where the larger, destructive globalization process attempts to suck up the last living domains on the planet—its life forms, its basic resources, its peoples—in the empty cause of short-term wealth accumulation. And it is also a frontier struggle in conceptual terms: What are the values that can sustain us for the future? What are the worldviews that can keep the earth alive? How are we to live on behalf of coming generations of human beings and the larger community of beings and creatures?

It is increasingly clear to me that indigenous peoples of the earth have the answers to many of these questions, if we would listen. Our job is to work to dismantle the institutions that now lead the world in the opposite direction, and to join forces in all efforts to replace those institutions with a hierarchy of values and standards that serve the earth and the communities who simply want to live their lives in peace and stability, in a traditional manner, on their own ancestral lands with control of their livelihoods and resources.

So, my personal plea is that all communities of activists should recognize that their own particular issues will only be benefited if they include the indigenous struggles as part of their own and permit the interests of indigenous peoples to share the front burners of their causes.

About 150,000 of Mexico's indigenous population rallied in Mexico City's Zocalo in March 2001, protesting economic globalization. Some had walked from as far away as the Zona Maya in Chiapas to oppose Mexico's willingness to undermine the "ejido" system of collective farms to suit NAFTA trade rules and to allow cheap subsidized U.S. corn into Mexico. They also demanded new guarantees for indigenous land, cultural and economic rights. Similar demonstrations have taken place throughout South America and elsewhere, and are increasing.

CHAPTER 2

Our Right to Remain Separate and Distinct

Victoria Tauli-Corpuz

(Igorot)

Tebtebba (Indigenous Peoples' International Centre for Policy Research and Education)

I SPENT MY CHILDHOOD in my ancestral home-town of Besao, among the Igorot peoples of the Philippines. It was a world barely touched by industrialism. There was no electricity; the only motor vehicles we saw were the two buses that arrived in the late afternoon from the only city in our region. We raised our own food—rice, vegetables, taro, chickens, and pigs.

Igorots possess a highly sophisticated knowledge of agriculture. Many communities produce ten or more traditional rice varieties, and our rice terraces, found high up in the mountains, feature complex irrigation systems, testifying to Igorot expertise in hydraulics and engineering.

Wet rice production for domestic use still remains the main preoccupation of most Igorots who live in traditional villages. The agricultural cycle revolves around the phases of rice production, from seedbed preparation to harvesting. Interspersed between these are hunting and food gathering from forests and rivers, and the planting of crops like beans, sweet potatoes, and cassava. As a child, I used to join my cousins and aunts to work in the *payeo* (ricefields). During planting and harvesting, we practiced *ug-ugbo*, a

traditional form of mutual labor exchange. We formed ourselves into groups with neighbors and friends, set out before sunrise, and collectively planted or harvested one field, moving on to other fields until the sun set. In the evening we all gathered to celebrate finishing the work. Sunday was market day, when people from neighboring villages came to trade or sell their wares.

Igorot cultural rituals are linked to the phases of the agricultural cycle and the life cycle (births, weddings, and deaths). The Igorots do not consider ourselves the owners but the stewards or trustees of ancestral lands. Land is the source of our identity and it provides the material and spiritual link between past, present, and future generations.

We were raised as Christians, but our lives were also rich in our own traditional culture and rituals: the *begnas* before planting rice and after harvest; *dadawak* during weddings; rituals for the newly born and the dead, and so on. At a very early age our parents and elders taught us basic values deemed *gawis* (good): respect for nature and ancestors, honesty, collectivity, community solidarity, reciprocity, and love for Mother Earth. The most important lesson is *innayan*. This

Kankanaey-Igorot word can be translated as "don't do it," or "exercise caution," or "have limits." But *innayan* is more than that. It is a principle and a value system that guides our behavior and relationships with other human beings, creation (animals, plants, micro-organisms), the spirit world, and nature, and governs our relationship to technology. A closely related term is *lawa*, which means taboo, forbidden, holy, or sacred. *Lawa* and *innayan* underpin the traditional religion of the Igorots. Adherence to these values is crucial for our identity and our continuing existence as a people. Though life was hard, it never occurred to me that we were "poor" or "underdeveloped."

At age twelve, I passed a scholarship test for secondary school and went to study in Manila. I was thrown into culture shock, into a totally different world: there was electricity; countless vehicles zoomed through the streets; and you needed money for everything. However, what shocked me most was the way my classmates and teachers regarded me and other Igorot as backward and savage. I got into numerous fights because I couldn't agree that my Manila classmates were more "civilized" than my people, especially when I saw so much poverty and violence in Manila society.

Years later, when I became a student activist in the early seventies, I understood why such discriminatory mind-sets existed. In the early days of colonialism, the Spaniards needed to portray us as headhunting savages in order to justify their violence. Later, the U.S. colonizers shipped our ancestors to be displayed in a sort of circus sideshow at the St. Louis Exposition in 1904, to show Americans what heathens we were and to justify President McKinley's "Benevolent Assimilation" policy.

Learning the history of our colonization made me realize that the Igorot traditions—cultural, economic, cosmological, judiciary, and so on—must not be undermined or destroyed. The more

I see the decline of Western civilization and the role science and technology play in that decline, the more I am convinced that the wisdom and knowledge of indigenous peoples can help lead humanity forward. The continuing survival of humanity will largely depend on how diverse cultural and biological systems coexist and flourish.

INDIGENOUS WORLDVIEWS: OBSTACLES TO "PROGRESS"?

Now we face economic globalization, an outgrowth of the colonization that indigenous peoples have suffered for five hundred years. In the past, colonizers used swords and guns to quell my ancestors' resistance to colonization. Colonial and postcolonial governments and their satellite institutions of churches, schools, and media tried to teach us to despise ourselves and our cosmologies, traditions, customary laws, and lifeways. They trained indigenous peoples, including my parents and myself, to look at the world through the eyes of the colonizers. Today, the promoters of economic globalization, the neocolonizers, use the overwhelming pressure of homogenization to teach us that indigenous political, economic, cultural, and knowledge systems are obstacles to their "progress." Industrialized peoples look upon the principles that guide indigenous peoples' daily lives as backward, unrealistic, or hopelessly romantic. In response, we have had to consciously reclaim and relearn our traditional worldviews and religions to strengthen our bid for our rights to our identity, our culture, and our territories.

Many indigenous peoples are still awed by the magic of the cosmos and the mystery of life. Our rituals, worldviews, belief systems, and stories affirm our surrender to this mystery and magic. Among the most important to us are our understanding and reverence of nature, our experience of living in community and reciprocity with the spirits of the natural world, our respect for the sacredness of all life, our sharing of work and burdens, and our solemn mandate to protect Mother Earth's gifts for future generations. Industrialized culture regards our values as unscientific obstacles to modernization and thus worthy of ridicule, suppression, and denigration. The industrial world also views our political, social, and land-tenure traditions as dangerous: our collective identities; our communal ownership of forests, waters, and lands; our *usufruct* system of community sharing; and our consensus decision making are all antithetical to the capitalist hallmarks of individualism and private property.

The mechanistic worldview of industrialization and globalization regards humans and other living beings as machines that should be manipulated to function with ever increasing efficiency and productivity. Nature, in this view, is inert, dead, manipulable matter that has value only as a commodity. Microorganisms, plants, animals, and human beings are nothing more than biological commodities to be exported and trafficked in world markets. The genetic engineering of sheep like Tracy to enable them to secrete marketable drugs in their milk is an example of this. Trade must be liberalized, in the mechanized worldview, so that cheap, highly subsidized wheat or canola oil can travel thousands of miles from Europe and North America to Asian countries that, in turn, produce and export rice and palm oil. Concepts like "productivity," "competitiveness," "efficiency," and "engineering" dominate the discourse and practice of global economics and science.

If this logic continues to dominate the mind-sets of policy makers, then there will be no place for indigenous values such as subsistence agriculture, which mainly produces for local or domestic consumption. Invisible in the calculation of the gross national product is nature's contribution in ensuring soil fertility and nurturing biodiversity, and women's unpaid work in caring for the family and community. How can such conflicting worldviews possibly coexist?

For indigenous peoples, keeping our territorial or ancestral lands is the most important thing. This is what determines our identity. This is where our ancestors walked and where they learned everything they left to us. Our land is where we forge our relations with Mother Earth and create social bonds with each other. It is no wonder, then, that rapidly increasing so-called ethnic conflicts in the world are really pitting indigenous peoples, asserting our rights over our territories, against the global institutions that want to *separate* us from our land. Globalization policies and activities play a huge part in inflaming these conflicts by erasing borders and erasing identities that are inextricably linked to our rights as indigenous peoples.

PRESSURE FOR INDIGENOUS RESOURCES

In December 2000, Tebtebba Foundation hosted the International Conference on Conflict Resolution and Indigenous Peoples in the Philippines. Around one hundred indigenous peoples' organizations from all over the world—Latin America, Africa, Asia—attended and shared their experiences.

All our stories, though different in place and circumstance, are essentially the same: Competition over lands and resources because of globalization has led to conflagrations worldwide. These include the U'wa in Colombia, who are fighting oil development on their lands; the Pygmies in Rwanda and Burundi, who are battling against logging concessions in their forests; the Igorot, Mangyan and Lumad peoples in the Philippines, who are resisting incursions of mining corporations into their ancestral lands; the Penans of Sarawak, the Cree of Canada, and the Mapuche of Chile, who are all fighting World Bank dam projects. And these are only a few examples.

Now that national governments are liberalizing laws and regulations to match WTO rules, corporations are aggressively moving into new communities seeking to exploit the world's last remaining natural resources, most of which are found on indigenous peoples' lands. We have been fighting such exploitation for ages, so naturally the places where the resources are left are the places where indigenous peoples have been the most successful in resistance.

However, our minerals, logs, and biodiversity are not enough for them. They also need our collective knowledge about plants and even our human genes. The Aceh people from Indonesia reminded everyone at the conference that their fight is not really an "ethnic conflict," as the colonizers like to describe it; it's about the oil on their land. And although they were once successful in stopping ExxonMobil, globalization policies now make it easier for corporations to invade and usurp land and resources, and so the oil company is trying to return. In addition to benefiting from liberalized government policy, corporations also strategize with paramilitary groups to terrorize and destroy the peoples who assert their rights to their homelands.

The Myth of "Sustainable Development"

Unfortunately, most governments adhere to the dominant worldview of infinite economic growth through a globalized market economy. Even "sustainable development," which is supposed to represent the antithesis of economic globalization, has been subsumed under this model.

In fact, the term *sustainable development* has come to mean sustainability of the global market economy, not environmental sustainability or the sustainability of communities. In a global market economy, only economies of scale can survive, and they in turn can only survive through cheap labor, mass-production capacity, government subsidies and ever-increasing access to resources. Every decision is determined by the most efficient means of production at the lowest possible labor cost, so goods can be sold cheaply to world markets. The country that subsidizes production

and exports so it can flood foreign markets with its products gains the so-called "comparative advantage." Economic and political systems are being harmonized—in other words, homogenized—via the regulations of the World Trade Organization, the World Bank, and the International Monetary Fund. Negotiations focus more on minimizing environmental regulation than they do on addressing the negative consequences of economic growth on the environment and the people. This leaves no room on the planet for *genuinely* sustainable development that supports local economies, respects traditional livelihoods, or nurtures the land.

In the same duplicitous spirit, modern science, such as genetic engineering, is now regarded as a tool for sustainable development, since it does not produce the same kinds of pollution as industrial machine and pesticide-intensive agriculture, though it produces new problems. Even the mining industry is trying to sell the concept of "sustainable mining," which is nothing but a crude attempt to greenwash mining activity. Clearly, the goal of reconciling environmental integrity and developmental imperatives is becoming increasingly confused and unreachable.

So, where does this leave the 80 percent of indigenous peoples who still live in communities that are not completely ruled by global market logic—communities that still practice successful subsistence agriculture, hunting, and fishing? Does it mean that our only chance of surviving is to forget our traditions and assimilate into capitalist thinking and practice?

Sometimes indigenous farmers do try to convert their traditional farming into cash-crop production for exports. It doesn't usually work out. For example, in one province in my region, many people stopped growing their own food and shifted into growing potatoes and other temperate vegetables, which are not indigenous. Suddenly, due to import liberalization—that is, the lifting of protections against foreign imports—our market was flooded with prepackaged, ready-to-fry, dried potatoes subsidized by the United States and Canada and sold at half the price of the potatoes we grew ourselves. Approximately fifty thousand potato farmers were put out of a job because of the entry of these cheap, highly subsidized potatoes coming from thousands of miles away. Fortunately, because of that terrible experience, the people have returned to producing their own food crops, which removes them from the ups and downs of a global market that is well beyond their control.

Since the Philippines joined the WTO, many of the domestic laws established to protect small farms and industries are being destroyed. For example, the 1998 Indigenous Peoples' Rights Act is being undermined by new laws—consistent with global rules—that provide incentives to attract foreign corporations and investments. The Philippine Mining Act of 1995 allows mining companies to enter the country and to own up to eighty thousand hectares of mineral lands for fifty to seventy-five years. They are allowed investments with 100 percent equity using no local partners. They are allowed to take all their profits out of the country rather than reinvest them. They are free to remove people from their lands. They have water rights and timber rights. So if they want to deforest our land to build their own infrastructure, they are free to do so, with no government regulation or oversight. Such a law is completely consistent with "free trade" ideology as promoted by the World Bank, IMF, and WTO (*See Box A, page 54.*)

Fortunately, many people are now resisting these incursions, and a strong anti-mining movement is growing in the Philippines and spreading to Indonesia, Malaysia, the Solomon Islands, and other parts of Asia and the Pacific. In the Philippines, four foreign companies—Rio Tinto Zinc (United Kingdom), Western Mining Corporation (Australia), Newcrest (Australia), and Mt. Isa (United States)—have all recently left the country because of massive resistance from indigenous peoples and other local communities.

Privatization and SAPs

The Structural Adjustment Program rules (SAPs) propagated by the World Bank and the International Monetary Fund have been important in expediting the invasion of global corporations into Third World nations. These new rules help privatize public services, utilities, and land resources such as forests. Now the big push is for the privatization of water, which is taking place throughout the Philippines with the same aggressiveness experienced by Bolivia in 2000. Not surprisingly, the indigenous peoples of Bolivia led huge demonstrations protesting water privatization in Cochabamba. (*See chapter on Global Water Wars, page 109.*) And the same is beginning in the Philippines.

Indigenous peoples see no reason to hand over control of water to private industry. Why should we relinquish our traditional water-management practices to a national bureaucracy? This totally alien concept is intended to destroy efficient indigenous water-distribution mechanisms already in place. As global institutions continue to push for privatization, more strife of the kind we saw in Bolivia can be expected.

Privatization of forest resources is also predictably disastrous for indigenous peoples. In most traditional communities, forests are considered communal. The concept of land ownership is completely absurd to us. But more to the point, once these huge land concessions come in with the "legitimacy" to log, we are stripped of our very culture and sustenance.

BIOPIRACY OF INDIGENOUS KNOWLEDGE AND RESOURCES

Indigenous peoples' resistance to colonization and globalization has been instrumental in retaining our indigenous knowledge, sciences, and technologies. Now, with modern medicine desperately seeking new treatments for diseases, indigenous knowledge of plant life is being sought as yet another new commodity. Ironically, it is because we have been so successful in protecting the earth's precious biodiversity that our lands have become such magnets for corporations and governments not only for the minerals, forests, and waters of our land but also for our knowledge about the properties and benefits of the plants that grow there—and even our human genes.

Corporations are prospecting throughout native lands for seeds we have developed and for our knowledge of the cosmetic and pharmaceutical properties of forest plants. They take our seeds and our knowledge home—usually without our permission—and patent our plants. This biopiracy reaches inside our bodies to our gene structures: They are surreptitiously collecting blood samples from our people without telling us why. Scientists call it the Human Genetic Diversity Project, but we call it the Vampire Project. Biopiracy is legitimized under the WTO's Trade-Related Aspects of Intellectual Property Rights Agreement (TRIPS), which confirms the rights of individuals and corporations to patent life forms in defiance of our traditional beliefs and practices. The TRIPS agreement is pushing all countries to allow corporate scientific institutions to search for and patent indigenous plant varieties that have beneficial properties.

Our traditional *usufruct* system retains common community ownership and control over all plants and their properties—without patents. WTO-style patent laws are not even in place yet, but corporate biopiracy is already flourishing. Four plants from our territories in the Philippines have already been patented, including the bitter gourd (*ampalaya*) and another plant, called *sambong*, that we use for treatment of asthma. A perfume company, Yves St. Laurent, has patented a plant we call *ilang-ilang* for its beautiful fragrance.

TRIPS is clearly the imposition of alien Western legal regimes, which are incompatible with indigenous peoples ways of thinking and behaving. It contradicts indigenous peoples' customary laws, worldviews and values for retaining community ownership and control over plants and their properties. TRIPS threatens our capacity to ensure that our collectively evolved knowledge will remain under our control and use. By establishing a universal practice of patenting life forms, TRIPS insults the ethics of regarding life as sacred. (*See chapter on biocolonization, page 71.*)

Tourism also plays a critical role in bioprospecting. Whereas the obvious negative impact of conventional tourism on indigenous peoples is the way it commodifies and destroys traditional indigenous cultures by turning them into commodities, its less obvious effect is the way it facilitates the hidden entry of bioprospectors. Ecotourism, which is promoted by some environmental organizations, brings "researchers" to our communities who then collect plants, soil, insects, and other materials from our lands and forests. (*See chapter on ecotourism, page 133.*)

Our rights over our lands, resources, knowledge, culture, and genes are all interconnected. Protecting biodiversity means not just protecting biological resources but also protecting cultural diversity and respecting our rights to our territories. Local sovereignty by distinct groups of peoples seeking control over their resources must be protected; this is the foundation for our political lobbying.

Indigenous peoples are being pressured to permit conversion of our economic systems into the capitalist framework of high productivity and profitability, which are not primary values that we share. If we go along, it means losing control over our territories, knowledge and resources. Why should we allow foreign or national mining corporations to lease our lands for seventy-five years when we know fully well that what will be left for us will be polluted and devastated lands and the disappearance of waters? Why should we be forced to share our knowledge over seeds, medicinal plants and resource management with corporations who claim ownership, simply because they can wave a patent in our faces? What will the world gain if our diverse and sustainable ways of living are destroyed so we can fit into the cogs and wheels of the globalized capitalist world?

SIX CRUCIAL STEPS FORWARD

Our ancestors told us that land is sacred, that animals and plants are our relatives, and that it is our duty to ensure that they are defended for the next generations. Our resistance to the efforts to homogenize us must be supported, including the affirmation of our right to self-determination, and our right to be allowed to remain different and diverse. Legal instruments that conflict with our indigenous values, cosmologies, lifestyles, and customary laws should not be imposed on us from any outside body. These are not decisions for the WTO or the IMF or the World Bank. We fight for the right to define ourselves and to maintain our continued existence as indigenous peoples on our own ancestral lands.

What are the challenges and strategies we should pursue to ensure that our indigenous ways of thinking and doing will not be obliterated? What policy recommendations are being proposed? Here are six important standards and policies we should push for:

First, it should be recognized that our role in promoting truly sustainable development lies in our ability to continue practicing our indigenous systems of production. This means allowing us to have control over our ancestral territories, upon which these practices can survive, and not denigrating the cosmologies that underpin these practices. We demand that governments and financial institutions like the World Bank and other regional banks allow our indigenous economic,

cultural and socio-political systems to co-exist with other systems. They should not force us to be assimilated or integrated into the mainstream if it means the destruction of our diverse world-views, diverse ways of producing and consuming, diverse cultures and governance systems.

In spite of colonization, and now globalization, many of our sustainable practices, whether in the area of agriculture, forestry or health, have persisted. In fact, it is a miracle that these practices persist to this day, given the incursions and destruction that have taken place in the form of assimilation and integration policies. This persistence is a major testimony to the viability of indigenous societies.

Recently, I wrote a paper on our agriculture practices and concomitant belief systems and cultural rituals. I used as a major reference a paper written by my uncle in 1954. I was struck that, after almost fifty years, not much has changed in how we grow food and the linkage between this and our traditional religion. This convinced me even further of the viability of our ancient production systems, which have weathered a litany of perverse development impositions, not the least of which was the Green Revolution.

Second, it is urgent that the roots of the unrest in indigenous peoples' territories be addressed by governments and the international community. The conference on conflict resolution and indigenous peoples, which I mentioned earlier, presented the Manila Declaration. The Declaration highlighted the need to deal with the root causes of conflicts, which in many cases are the appropriation of indigenous lands and resources and the denigration of viable indigenous economic, political and cultural systems.

The threats to the very existence of indigenous peoples—especially those whose populations have been reduced to mere hundreds—are very serious. We are talking about the U'wa in Colombia, the Batwa in Burundi and Rwanda, and the Shor peoples in Siberia, among others. Their representatives in the Manila conference appealed to the international community for support in their fight for survival.

If the United Nations is not able to play its role in peace-building, other mechanisms should be built to address conflict situations. One resolution at the conference was the creation of an International Independent Commission of Indigenous Peoples for Mediation and Conflict Resolution. Its mission is to promote and defend the rights of indigenous peoples, especially in conflict situations, and to mediate between conflicting parties for the resolution of the conflict and the achievement of a just and lasting peace.

Third, institutions that claim that they are promoting sustainable development, whether this be the United Nations and bodies like the UN Development Program (UNDP), the World Bank and other regional banks, or governments, should be informed about what indigenous peoples want. There is a need to sensitize those involved in development and environment work to indigenous peoples' vision and practices.

Let's face it: The survival of authentic indigenous tradition is diametrically opposed to economic globalization. One is based on true sustainability through a nuanced harmony with Nature's cycles; the other values nothing other than how natural resources translate to the bottom line. One benefits the community and stretches far into the future; the other benefits only a few, and only until resources are depleted. Because of these profound paradigm differences, we must remain active and vigilant against the distortion of authentic indigenous beliefs by institutions claiming to promote sustainable development.

Fourth, case studies, reviews and assessments of how mainstream development has destroyed or distorted indigenous models of sustainable development should be undertaken. If such were done, the results could be widely disseminated. Assessments of policy guidelines on indigenous peoples made by the World Bank, other regional banks, UN bodies, the European Union, etc., both in terms of substance and how these could be implemented, should also be undertaken. There have been initial efforts made in this direction, but they do not ensure the direct participation of indigenous peoples themselves and are in need of expansion.

Fifth, efforts should be expanded to ensure that our issues and concerns are addressed in a holistic manner. We have recently had some successes on this point in international agencies. For example, for many years we urged the UN to set up a Permanent Forum on Indigenous Peoples because we were frustrated that our issues were always being addressed in a fragmented manner. It was unworkable. We were tired of being told that we could discuss our rights as peoples only in the Commission on Human Rights. We were forced to present our attempts at preserving our peoples and nations in reductionist arguments about environment or biodiversity. We sought a mechanism within the UN that would be at a higher level within the UN hierarchy, thus allowing us to address environment, economic and social development, health, culture, and human rights as one comprehensive issue, consistent with our own views. Finally, the UN agreed to establish the Permanent Forum on Indigenous Peoples, with indigenous peoples sitting as equal partners in all discussions.

Sixth, the assertion by indigenous peoples of our rights to self-determination and to "free, prior and informed consent" to all development plans affecting us should be recognized and promoted, not only by the governments and the UN, but also by society at large.

These rights are essential for us to pursue our political status and our economic, social and cultural development. Our assertion of such rights, even in the face of state and corporate violence, has enabled us to maintain our indigenous systems and our sciences and technologies. Recognition of these rights by governments and the broader society is crucial if we are to save whatever is left of the planet's cultural and biological diversity. *(In Chapter 26, at the end of this book, I will go into greater detail on the specific steps international agencies and governments must take.)*

Indigenous peoples have come a long way in asserting our identities and rights. However, there is still much to be done. There are still indigenous peoples in many parts of the world who are in danger of extinction. This would mean the loss of the diverse knowledge and cultures that they embody. Actions from civil society are as crucial as those from governments and international institutions. Indigenous peoples have shown, time and again, the viability and sustainability of their economic and socio-cultural, political, and indigenous knowledge systems. Whatever is lost is a loss for the entire world, not for indigenous peoples alone.

FRANS LANTING/MINDEN PICTURES

Throughout the world, indigenous peoples share very similar world views, values, knowledge and practices, often in contradiction to those of the larger society. They are expressed through art (as here by the Aborigines) and by teachings about relationships with other humans, land, and the creatures of the earth, as well as natural limits and reciprocity with the natural world. Indigenous philosophies and practices have successfully protected places that now have come under increased threat from a global economic juggernaut that answers to another call.

CHAPTER 3

Aspects of Traditional Knowledge and Worldview

Following are four excerpts that reveal fundamental issues putting traditional/native world views into conflict with the dominant global economic model. The first two authors are the well-known Indian activists and thinkers Winona LaDuke (Anishinaabeg), who directs the White Earth Land Recovery Project in Minnesota, and John Mohawk (Seneca), who directs the American Studies Program at the University of Buffalo. Their statements are excerpted from talks they gave at the International Forum on Globalization's seminar, Indigenous Peoples and Globalization, in July 2001. The comment on "holy land" is from a speech by Native American psychologist Leslie Gray of the Woodfish Institute, at Bioneers 2003 in San Rafael, California.

The fourth set of excerpts is from the late Oxford University anthropologist Darrell Posey, taken from his article "Cultural and Spiritual Values of Biodiversity" published by the United Nations Environment Program, 1999.

The People Belong to the Land

Winona LaDuke
(Anishinaabeg)
White Earth Land Recovery Project

THE TEACHINGS OF OUR PEOPLE concerning our relationships to the land are deeply embedded in our language. For instance, in Ojibway, *nishn-abe akin* means "the land to which the people belong." This implies an entirely separate paradigm for property rights from that contained in discussions held in the U.S. courts. *Nishnabe akin* doesn't mean "the allotment to which the people belong," nor does it mean "the land that belongs to the people." It means that we belong to the land. This concept is accompanied by many teachings, one of which is that our relationship to the land is just that—a relationship. Not a bargaining of rights versus responsibilities. In a relationship with the land, responsibilities are already implicit.

Another phrase that we hear quite a bit in our language is *dinawaymaaganinaadog*, which means "all our relatives"—not just those with two legs, but also those with four legs, or wings, or fins. Our teachings are filled with stories about *dinawaymaaganinaadog*, such as how the bears taught us medicine or how the wolves taught us child-rearing.

We also have many teachings about trees, and our communities are known for our excellent birch bark canoes and houses. But the recent decline of birch trees in our area may be attributed to the neglect of our teachings and the neglect of our relationship with those trees. Instead of respectfully managing the gifts of the birch, we have come to prefer plastic, throwing off the relationship between the people and "all our relatives."

Again, the concept of "relationship" is not only central to our philosophy in the broadest sense but absolutely crucial to the health of our immediate environment.

So you see, our language, our teachings, and our cultural practices are one. This is why it is paramount in our communities to ensure the vitality of our languages, and to ensure the viability of the cultural teachings that are imparted by those languages. Without our languages, we are simply wandering—philosophically, spiritually, economically. To preserve our languages we need to protect our lands and our historic practices.

When you discuss the "property rights" of our communities, you must point out how our traditional land tenure system, particularly our traditional collective ownership, has been seriously infringed upon. Today, in GATT or the WTO or these other trade agreements, we see the culmination of hundreds of years of imposition of alien concepts about land ownership. As far back as the time of the papal bulls in the fifteenth century, edicts from the pope proclaimed that only Christians could own land. This essentially became the mandate for colonialism, the "Manifest Destiny" argument for the righteousness of Christians above all other peoples. It made a vast and historic impact from which we have never recovered. To this day, we are fighting in courts that remain prejudiced against non-Christians, courts created by papal law.

Whereas colonization favored the Christian god, today's globalization model favors the gods of money and technology. It is a logic equally distant from reality, brutally imposed by one group of self-proclaimed monarchs. This time, they're not Christian; they're just rich. But the tyranny is the same.

The logic of the global market has justified innumerable violations against our and every other community, whether land tenure issues and the allotment processes or deforestation by Weyerhauser, the destruction of the buffalo herd or the diversion of water affecting our wild rice. But yet, in spite of that, we retain an immense and viable subsistence economy. We are able to feed ourselves, because our ecosystem and our relatives have somehow been able to adapt. Our reservation in northern Minnesota is still populated with all the creatures that were there before, minus the buffalo and the sturgeon. Fortunately, we're now seeing the sturgeon recover, and we're working on the buffalo. That's a pretty good testament to the resilience of an ecosystem. So that has been the work we have undertaken in the last fifteen years in our community; how do we restore and strengthen all that in the face of these broader impacts? And how do we increase and generate local wealth, whether it is the wealth of subsistence—just making sure that you can feed yourself—or the wealth that comes from the cash economy, which is now so dominant.

The opposing paradigms—money/market/technology versus subsistence—are expressing themselves on many levels. Most apparent is our fight against globalization's relentless pressure to clearcut our forest lands for exports, which is straight out of the tradition of the papal bulls.

The conflict between the two paradigms pervades less obvious aspects of life as well. Today, we grapple with these issues, particularly in terms of a couple of things that we produce for our larger economy. Our organization, White Earth Land Recovery Project, produces wild rice and maple syrup, raspberries, strawberries, hominy corn and some other products. We produce it for both local food and sustenance, and sell the surplus. The issues that we face today—the impacts of globalization and the impacts of new technologies, for instance, in production of maple syrup—raise the question of how we keep our trees standing rather than clearcut. And there's the issue of technological choice. Increasingly, maple syrup producers are using PVC pipes and pumps to suction sap out of trees at a higher level of production, with no need for human labor. But we have teachings about maple syrup. They tell how, long ago, pure maple syrup—not sap—came out of the trees. But we got lazy; in trying to save labor, we experimented with a technique that backfired, causing the trees to no longer produce syrup. Now, trees produce only sap, and forty gallons of sap produce only one gallon of syrup, for only part of the year. Our teachings direct us to examine the hidden price of labor-saving shortcuts, which is why we choose to avoid them. Who knows, they might backfire so that it takes a hundred gallons of sap to make one gallon of syrup! True, collecting sap by hand is economically inefficient in the eyes of the market, and yes, it is impossible to compete with certified organic producers who use PVC pipes, which produce 30 percent more sap. But what are the long-term costs? How will these PVC producers fare in thirty or forty years, sucking those great quantities out of the trees, year after year? The money/market/technology paradigm never addresses such questions.

Perhaps the essence of the conflict between the two paradigms is captured in the treatment of rice. Wild rice is at the core of our being. The Creator gave us wild rice—incredibly, a different variety for nearly every lake on our lands—as part of our original instructions. These instructions teach us how to live sustainably, in an intricate relationship with all living things. Currently, the University of Minnesota is studying the genome of the rice for "lessons" of their own, although we have never asked them to do so. The university has been fooling with rice for thirty years now, making paddy rice that is now grown in California at far higher levels of production than in our

area. Three quarters of the total rice crop now comes from California, and I happen to know that Uncle Ben's did not get that rice from the Creator. The university is now renewing its interest in messing with the rice crop; they're talking about more genetic manipulation. Our communities are very concerned about the impact on wild crops of genetically manipulated rice—if it will affect them, if these varieties will somehow overshadow our own varieties, which are very biologically diverse. This is a huge issue in our community, and it has much to do with these issues of globalization. The idea of tampering with this wild crop, so sacred, unique and central to our culture, has inflamed even the most conservative institutions in our communities. It worries all of the people in our community. Questions about genetic manipulation and patenting express the essence of the conflict between these two paradigms. The respect for all life and creation versus the universities' and corporations' rights to "legally" own, commercialize and globalize that creation. But this is the nature of the globalization model: its self-proclaimed domination over all peoples in the service of money and technology.

For us, rice is a source of food and also wisdom. For the globalizers, it is just a commodity to be exploited for profit. The paradigms are at loggerheads.

So that is the struggle in our community. The dialogue that I am interested in is that within our communities about which direction we're going in, as well as the dialogue about how to bring our voice to the broader communities. That philosophical, spiritual and cultural dialogue needs to be deepened in our own communities, because it's in our hands to determine the future.

Subsistence and Materialism

John Mohawk
(Seneca)
University of Buffalo

INDIGENOUS OR NATIVE PEOPLE bring a unique argument to the world stage. They don't have armies or navies, they don't have national currencies, they don't have any of the attributes that Western nations think make up nationhood. And yet they propose that their continued existence is a moral imperative: that they have a moral right to continue to live as a distinct community and in the manner they have for millennia. They aren't asking for a military, they don't want a currency or international trade agreements. All they are asking is to be able to maintain the life they have been living in the environment they found, where they became conscious of themselves as Peoples and Nations. But today, we are up against vastly different worldviews.

Let me illustrate with an example. Let's say you have three people who approach a tree. One's a *socialist* materialist, one's a *capitalist* materialist and one's a traditional native person. The capitalist materialist will explain to you that he has to cut the tree down because this is in the best interest, not only of himself but also of society; that it is a kind of destiny; that by cutting the tree down, he will rationally distribute the materials from the tree and he'll do the most good for the people. A socialist person approaching the tree will also tell you to cut the tree down, because after cutting the tree down you can distribute it equally to everybody and it's going to do the most good for the world that way. But a native person looking at the tree will say that the tree, in its unharmed, original form, has a value that's greater than anything the others are proposing. So far, however, the materialist-destiny-capitalist argument has prevailed.

For the last 180 years, we have confronted such fundamentally conflicting arguments every day, except we haven't been taught to categorize them. The materialist arguments now clearly dominate the university, but there's been an underlying, pervasive argument around destiny that we haven't really talked much about in the West. In the nineteenth century, however, the colonization of the West was spoken about as a destiny: Manifest Destiny. On the basis of that destiny, it was okay to go in and steal people's resources; okay to steal their waters; okay to kill them; okay to move them; okay to do whatever had to be done in order to achieve the destiny. You can justify anything when you think you are acting in line with destiny and that you have the capacity to create a utopia. The Christians who marched on Jerusalem had such a plan. So did the Nazis who marched on Europe, and we saw it again in Serbia and lately in Iraq. Almost everywhere, you can find people displacing people, seizing people's resources, even abusing or murdering people in the name of some sort of mandate of state, religious destiny or utopian vision.

What has opposed that, historically, are arguments around *morality*: Does a people have a right to come and steal another people's things, destroy their culture, steal their children, ruin their languages, do all these other things? Do they have a right to do that? These acts are justified in the name of predicted benefits from capitalist intervention, but that argument is shortsighted. For example, a recent *New York Times* article quoted U.S. government officials saying that by denying the people in Africa the right to genetically modified foods (GMOs) we're essentially harming them. Mind you, they didn't complain that they're being harmed; in fact, most African nations are refusing GMO foods. Really, it's the people who want to sell them the biologically modified foods who are proposing that they are being harmed. And of course there is the other argument—popular among even the liberal people in the North—that indigenous peoples shouldn't be allowed to maintain themselves and their cultures as they exist now; to do so denies them the access to such wonderful Western inventions as television and video games and all those technological things that our kids must *really* want too. There's been this projection in the name of what could be called a vision of a "Technological Utopia."

The materialist argument boils down to who can make the best argument about the best, fastest and most efficient use of the world's resources. The point of the best, most efficient use of the world's resources in the capitalist mind is that it concentrates the wealth in the hands of someone who has the best technology and the best business plan and the best political inroads—and who can mobilize them. If we think that way, then we're just caught in the socialist versus capitalist paradigm. But we want to have a different kind of discussion; we want to talk about "subsistence."

Subsistence living has nothing to do with materialism. People who live a subsistence life don't think of it as, "Oh, I got seven pounds of fish today; I'm therefore materially well off." They *are* materially well off, but they don't see the world that way. They see themselves living in the world and in a relationship to the world in which not only does the world nurture them, but they have a reciprocal obligation to nurture it. They're here to maintain its survival as a coherent thing. That's what subsistence really is about. Subsistence isn't an economic exchange. It's a cultural, spiritual, social exchange that's intended to go on for generations. In fact, it's the most *moral* relationship with nature that humans have ever devised. It's a way of dealing with that which is greater than we are in a respectful and coherent and sane manner. We're not going to use it up; we're going to sustain it for the next generation and the generation after that.

We're not going to win the materialist argument. And the destiny arguments, as we've seen, are

deadly. Those are arguments that originate out of nationalism or religious fervors, and they are dangerous to people, to cultures and to the planet. The health of the earth depends on our ability to effectively articulate a new way. In many ways, it is the indigenous cultures' relationship to the earth that represents the only real hope for the long-term survival of people on any scale in the world.

Indigenous people are here to maintain survival as a plausible goal. I think what we need to do is to try to get everybody under one psychological tent. We need to adopt a strategy so that the voices of indigenous people can lead the way to a moral relationship with the planet. So how do we do this? What is it that motivates people to protest in front of a corporation? What gets them out there? For the most part, what really gets people—natives and others—mobilized in the culture that we're in is moral outrage that something's happening that has to be stopped. And that's what we need to trigger. Young people will gravitate to that. But while we're doing that, we need to support the integrity of our own communities. And when we meet and work with other peoples, we still need to support the integrity of our own communities. We need to sustain the clarity that exists in our world about what we're really doing. We're really not arguing over whether we should get 40 percent of the board-foot value of the wood. That's not what we're doing. Subsistence means that there's a forest here today, and we find a way to make a living here. Then tomorrow, there's still a forest here. That's subsistence.

As far as the Europeans who first landed here, it must be said that they saw their problems very differently than we did and still do. In Europe, the biggest problem was that they couldn't produce enough food to eat. They were hungry, and there was always the threat of famine. When they got to the Americas, suddenly there was plenty to eat; in fact, a big piece of the reason they came here was that Americans had so much to eat. They came and found a first-rate edible landscape, which they set out to destroy. You bring a bunch of sheep and cows and cut down all the trees for a couple of hundred years and you don't have an edible landscape anymore.

At work on the European side was a willingness to battle nature. They tried to outsmart nature—that's what all their technology is about, that's what biotechnology in particular is about. The idea was to get what you want out of nature—resources, food—without nature's help. But for the Indians, the question was not how to make war on nature but how to cooperate with nature. So Indians asked the question, "Okay, what happens if we try to go along with nature?" Instead of trying to plant blueberries down by the lake where they always get flooded, why don't we plant more blueberries where nature already put blueberries in the already existing blueberry patch?

So when you look at what happened between Indians and Europeans, the Indians were taking care of the land so there would be grass to feed the deer. The deer and the buffalo were our domesticated animals. The Indians were right on top of it; they knew just what they wanted; they had a very sophisticated system of food management. But it was cooperative with nature. They also raised some basic questions of fundamental fairness. The Indians raised the question of fairness not about human to human; they asked about human to land, human to animal, human to everything. And they tried to get Europeans to see that.

The attitude in Indian country was essentially one of respect, and the question was, How do we actually live that out? If you read a lot of the literature from Columbus's arrival until now, you see that the Indians were constantly imploring the Europeans to rethink their relationship with nature. "You've got it wrong," we said. "You've got to be fair." But the European answer was to find the best possible outcome for themselves, which is, "I make money." And that's more or less still where it is.

The Whole Planet Is the Holy Land

Leslie Gray
(Oneida)
The Woodfish Institute

A BASIC QUESTION I invite students to ask themselves is: Where is the Holy Land? It can sound very strange to an Indian person to hear non-Indian people refer to the Middle East as the Holy Land. *This* is the Holy Land. This is where Onondaga is; the sacred counsel fire burns at Onondaga still. This is where the Black Hills are, the traditional vision questing place of Black Elk, Lame Deer and many others. This is where pilgrims crawl on their knees to be healed at Chimayo. This is where the spiritual city at Chaco Canyon was constructed with every point in alignment with the heavens. This is where Blue Lake is. This is where Big Mountain is. *This is the Holy Land.* Of course, all over the planet you will find sacred sights that were honored and preserved by the indigenous people of that bioregion. And of course, everywhere you step, you step on the sacred bones of ancestors. So the whole planet is the Holy Land.

Why is it important to feel the sacredness of the land you are on? Because at the dawn of the twenty-first century people are still going to war over the idea that one spot in the Middle East is the Holy Land. Another way to say it is that it is still possible for a few people interested in domination and power to bamboozle the many, who only see as sacred one place and one religion based on the spiritual story of that place. And here in the United States, where the prevailing culture clings to a narrow conception of a distant Holy Land, the public is easily bamboozled into war for control of distant natural resources. So there is a high cost for failing to acknowledge the whole earth as sacred.

If you meet Native American people who sustain their world view and preserve their traditions, they had to work very hard to do it, and maybe that's the thing to take away from this.

Non-Indians need to stuggle in a similar way: Don't participate in the myth of whiteness; there is no such thing. Every single person in the world has an ethnicity. Ethnic does not mean colored or being a person of color. Ethnicity is your culture, and it's your culture as it relates to a particular place on earth, a particular bioregion, and a particular land. Everyone can trace those roots back for themselves. The most radical thing you can do is to start thinking of yourself as having come from someplace in this land. That thought alone is going to be a huge contradiction to the prevailing models.

Indigenous Ecological Knowledge

Darrell Posey
Oxford University

TRADITIONAL LIVELIHOOD SYSTEMS embrace principles of sustainability that, across cultures and regions, generally emphasize the following values: cooperation; family bonding and cross-generational communication, including links with ancestors; concern for the well-being of future generations; self-sufficiency and reliance on locally available natural resources; rights to lands, territories and collective and inalienable (as opposed to individual and alienable) resources; restraint in resource exploitation; and respect for nature, particularly sacred sites.

Two Native American scientists, Raymond Pierotti and Daniel R. Wildcat, have said: "Living with nature has little to do with the often voiced 'love of nature,' 'closeness to nature,' or desire 'to commune with nature' one hears today. Living with nature is very different from 'conservation' of nature. It is crucial to realize that nature exists on its own terms and that nonhumans have their own reasons for existence, independent of human interpretation. Those who desire to dance with wolves must first learn to live with wolves."

Pierotti and Wildcat also point out that the concepts of "biodiversity" and "conservation" are not indigenous and, indeed, are alien to indigenous peoples. This does not mean they do not respect and foster living things, but rather that nature is an extension of society. Biodiversity is not an object or idea to be conserved, it is an integral part of human existence. This is why the conservation and management practices of indigenous peoples are highly pragmatic; for them, this traditional knowledge emanates from a *spiritual* base.

For the Haudenosaunee (Iroquois) people, Onondaga Nation Chief Oren Lyons has said, "all living beings are kin." Many indigenous peoples believe they once spoke the language of animals, and their shamans still have this ability. Biodiversity, therefore, is actually the "extended family." The Hawaiian concept of *lokahi* (unity) covers the "nurturing, supportive and harmonious relations" linking land, the gods, humans and the forces of nature. Thus, when outsiders (environmentalists, developers, scientists, etc.) see themselves as working with elements of nature, indigenous peoples may view these same activities as meddling in the internal affairs of the "extended family."

Whereas scientific and economic forces assume that traditional communities must change to meet "modern" standards, indigenous and traditional peoples believe the opposite must occur: science and industry must begin to respect local diversity and the delicate balance between life, land and society. With its quantum mechanics methods, Western science and technology are at a loss to address the universe as a whole, so we are left with an isolated, linear logic setting international policies.

❧   ❧   ❧

Two of the most damaging aspects of international trade policies are these: first, market prices of natural resources are determined only by the external corporate system and do not reflect the true costs, environmental and social, of those resources; and second, despite the sustenance diverse natural resources provide for native populations (food, shelter, medicine, etc.), indigenous peoples' knowledge and care of these resources are ascribed no value; they are free for the taking. This "intellectual *terra nullius,*" or "empty land" concept, allowed colonial powers to expropriate "discovered" land for their empires. Corporations and states still defend this morally vacuous concept because it supports "biopiracy" of local folk varieties of crops, traditional medicines and useful plant and animal species.

Scientists have been accomplices in these raids by publishing data that is released into the public domain and gleaned by "bioprospectors," such as pharmaceutical companies seeking new products. It is also commonplace for scientists to declare areas and resources "wild" through ignorance, or negligence, without even the most basic investigations into archaeological, historical or actual human management practices.

This is more than semantics. "Wild" and "wilderness" imply that these landscapes and resources are the result of "nature" and, as such, have no owners: they are the "common heritage of all humankind." This has been a convenient way for corporations seeking resources to target such places, because it suggests that local communities have no tenurial or ownership rights, and thus their lands, territories and resources are "free" for the taking. For this reason, indigenous peoples have come to oppose the use of terms like *wilderness* and *wild* to refer to the regions in which they live. As far as they're concerned, their source of sustenance—physical, societal and spiritual—is not "up for grabs." It is little wonder indigenous groups in the Pacific region have declared a moratorium on all scientific research

until protection of traditional knowledge and genetic resources can be guaranteed to local communities.

By defining useful local plants as "wild" and entire ecosystems as "wilderness," scientists have not only perpetuated the *terra nullius* concept but also ignored knowledge of ecosystems that have been molded, managed and protected by humans for millennia. Indigenous, traditional and local communities have sustainably utilized and conserved a vast diversity of plants, animals and ecosystems since the dawn of *Homo sapiens*.

Western society may have invented the words *nature, biodiversity* and *sustainability*, but it certainly did not initiate these concepts. One hundred thousand years before the term *sustainable development* was coined, aboriginal peoples were trading seeds, dividing tubers and propagating domesticated and nondomesticated plant species. For millenia, human beings have molded environments through conscious and unconscious activities to create "sacred sites"—what anthropologists call "anthropogenic" or "cultural landscapes." These "sacred sites" or "cultural landscapes" express a merger between Nature and culture so complete it is impossible to separate the two.

In resistance to the construction of the Tellico Dam in Tennessee Valley, one Cherokee asserted, "If we were to make our offerings at a new place, the spiritual beings would not know us. We would not know the mountains or the significance of them. We would not know the land and the land would not know us. . . . We would not know the sacred places. If we were to go on top of an unfamiliar mountain we would not know the life forms that dwell there."

For the Cherokee, when a dam floods the land, it also destroys the medicines and the knowledge of the medicines associated with that land. The sacred site tradition creates conservation areas of all kinds. Water sources are considered holy, and so the areas around them are shielded from disturbance; individual plant and animal species are protected by restricting human access. Wellsprings are the "soul of the Hopi people," representing their very identity, and for the Masai and Fulani pastoralists, oases are sacred; their lives are dependent on the protection of these crucial resources.

Another example of a "cultural landscape" is the "forest island" (*apete*) created in savannas by the Kayapo of Brazil. The Indians have used detailed knowledge of soil fertility, microclimate, and plant varieties to plant and transplant non-domesticated species into wooded, useful concentrations. Historically, these *apete* have been considered "natural" by botanists and ecologists, even though they would not exist without the skill and management of the Indians. These sites are integrated so seamlessly into the ecosystem that outsiders often cannot recognize them during land-use planning exercises. Another case in point is the Ontario resource managers who cannot detect the anthropogenic wild rice (*manomin*) fields of the Ojibway. The most common type of sacred site or cultural landscape is the sacred grove. The "dragon hills" of Yunan Province in China are kept intact specifically because of their sacred nature. Likewise, Ghjanan groves are linked to burial grounds and spirits of the ancestors who protect the forests that surround them. Similar groves are reported in Côte d'Ivoire, Benin and Ghana and throughout North America. In India, sacred groves are extensive and well known.

The balance of vegetation and wildlife is maintained by these refined systems of indigenous technologies. Many so-called pristine landscapes are in fact either created by humans or modified and cultivated by human activity, such as controlled fires. Tragically, however, the failure of Western economic and scientific forces to recognize sacred and other cultural landscapes has blinded them to the management practices of indigenous peoples and local communities. Aboriginal peoples, for instance, have been centralized into settlements; as fire management has disappeared, not only have sacred sites and the indigenous knowledge associated with them been neglected, but mammal populations and plant species have visibly declined as well.

Many ancient indigenous agricultural and land management systems survived until the colonial period. These systems were based on complex ecological knowledge and understanding, and were highly efficient, productive, and inherently sustainable. The raised bed systems used for millennia by traditional farmers of tropical America, Asia and Africa are classic examples. Known variously in Meso-America as *chinampas*, *waru waru*, and *tablones*, these were extremely effective for irrigation, drainage, soil fertility maintenance, frost control and plant disease management. In India, peasants grow over forty different crops on localities cultivated for more than 2,000 years without a drop in yield, yet remarkably free of pests.

Agro-biodiversity is the foundation of all agriculture, both modern and traditional. Whereas modern science depends on gene bank collections to support diversity, traditional farmers combine, select and screen planting materials and thus have successfully maintained agro-biodiversity for thousands of years. The importance of foraging to traditional cultures also supports biodiversity, since wild foods are gathered from managed land areas rather than agricultural plots. Traditional systems and management strategies, such as the Brazilian practice of integrating agriculture with fishing techniques, strengthen the network of living things.

Local traditional knowledge plays a major role in medicines and health systems as well. According to the World Health Organization, up to 80 percent of the nonindustrial world's population still relies on traditional forms of medicine. A fundamental concept in traditional health systems is that of balance between mind and body, given that both are linked to community, local environments and the universe. Ayurvedic and traditional Chinese medicines define disease as "breaking of the interconnectedness of life." Above all, healthy ecosystems are critical to healthy societies and individuals, because humanity and nature are one, and not in opposition to each other.

To reverse the devastating cycle that industrialized society has imposed on the planet, we will have to relearn ecological knowledge and earnestly deal with the tough question: "Can sustainable practices harmonize with growth of trade and increased consumption?" We will have to sustain an ecologically powerful argument to offset deforestation, soil erosion, species extinction and pollution; a global environmental ethic, implacable enough even for global and economically powerful institutions, will have to be implemented and enforced. These undertakings may be daunting, but the wisdom of traditional and indigenous peoples continues to guide us. As Bepkororoti Paiakan, a Kayapo chief from Brazil, puts it: "We are trying to save the knowledge that the forests and this planet are alive—to give it back to you who have lost the understanding."

"The Okanagan teach that each person is born into a family and community. You belong. You are them. Not to have community or family is to be scattered or falling apart. The bond of community and family includes the history of the many who came before us and the many ahead of us who share our flesh. Our most serious teaching is that community comes first in our choices, then family, and then ourselves as individuals. . . . We also refer to the land and our bodies with the same root syllable. This means that the flesh that is our body is pieces of the land come to us. The soil, the water, the air, and all the other life forms contributed parts to be our flesh. We are our land."

CHAPTER 4

Community: "Sharing One Skin"

Jeannette Armstrong
(Okanagan)
Director, En'owkin Centre

I AM FROM THE OKANAGAN, a part of British Columbia that is much like most of California in climate—very dry and hot. Around my birthplace are two rock mountain ranges: the Cascades on one side and the Selkirks on the other. The river is the Columbia. It is the main river that flows through our lands, and there are four tributaries: the Kettle, the Okanagan/Smikanean, the San Poil, and the Methow.

My mother is a river Indian. She is from Kettle Falls, which is the main confluence of the Columbia River near Inchelieum. The Kettle River people are in charge of the fisheries in all of the northern parts of the Columbia River system in our territories. The Arrow Lakes and the tributaries from the Kettle flow south through the Columbia Basin. My great-grandmother's husband was a salmon chief and caretaker of the river in the north.

My father's people are mountain people. They occupied the northern part of British Columbia, known as the Okanagan Valley. My father's people were hunters—the people in the Okanagan who don't live in the river basin. They were always a separate culture from the river people. My

name is passed on from my father's side of the family; it is my great-grandmother's name. I am associated with my father's side, but I have a right and a responsibility to the river through my mother's birth and my family education.

So that is who I am and where I take my identity from. I know the mountains, and by birth, the river is my responsibility: They are part of me. I cannot be separated from my place or my land.

When I introduce myself to my own people in my own language, I describe these things because it tells them what my responsibilities are and what my goal is. It tells them what my connection is, how I need to conduct myself, what I need to carry with me, what I project, what I teach and what I think about, what I must do and what I can't do. The way we talk about ourselves as Okanagan people is difficult to replicate in English. Our word for people, for humanity, for human beings, is difficult to say without talking about connection to the land. When we say the Okanagan word for ourselves, we are actually saying "the ones who are dream and land together." That is our original identity. Before anything else, we are the living, dreaming Earth pieces. It's a second identification that means human; we identify ourselves as separate from other things on the land.

The word *Okanagan* comes from a whole understanding of what we are as human beings. We can identify ourselves through that word. In our interaction, in our prayer, we identify ourselves as human as well, different from birds and trees and animals. When we say that, there is a first part of the word and an *s*; whenever you put an *s* in front of any word, you turn it into a physical thing, a noun. The first part of the word refers to a physical realm.

The second part of the word refers to the dream or to the dream state. *Dream* is the closest word that approximates *Okanagan*. But our word doesn't precisely mean "dream." It actually means "the unseen part of our existence as human beings." It may be the mind or the spirit or the intellect. So that second part of the word adds the perspective that we are mind as well as matter. We are dream, memory and imagination.

The third part of the word means that if you take a number of strands, hair or twine, place them together and then rub your hands and bind them together, they become one strand. You use this thought symbolically when you make a rope and when you make twine, thread and homemade baskets, and when you weave the threads to make the coiled basket. That third part of the word indicates we are tied into and part of everything else. It refers to the dream parts of ourselves forming our community, and it implies what our relationships are. We say, "This is my clan," or, "This is my people. These are the families that I came from. These are my great-grandparents," and so on. In this way I know my position and my responsibility for that specific location and geographic area. That is how I introduce myself. That is how I like to remember who I am and what my role is.

One of the reasons I explain this is to try to bring our whole society closer to that kind of under-

standing, because without that deep connection to the environment, to the earth, to what we actually are, to what humanity is, we lose our place, and confusion and chaos enter. We then spend a lot of time dealing with that confusion.

When we Okanagan speak of ourselves as individual beings within our bodies, we identify the whole person as having four main capacities that operate together: the physical self, the emotional self, the thinking-intellectual self, and the spiritual self. The four selves have equal importance in the way we function with and experience all things. They join us to the rest of creation in a healthy way.

The physical self is one part of the whole self that depends entirely on the parts of us that exist beyond the skin. We survive within our skin and inside the rest of our vast "external" selves. We survive by the continuous interaction between our bodies and everything around us. We are only partly aware of that interaction in our intellect, through our senses. The Okanagan teach that the body is Earth itself. Our flesh, blood and bones are Earth-body; in all cycles in which Earth moves, so does our body. We are everything that surrounds us, including the vast forces we only glimpse. If we cannot continue as an individual life form, we dissipate back into the larger self. Our body-mind is extremely knowledgeable in that way. Okanagan say the body is sacred. It is the core of our being; it permits the rest of the self to be. It is the great gift of our existence. Our word for body literally means "the land-dreaming capacity."

The emotional self is differentiated from the physical self, the thinking-intellectual self, and the spiritual self. In our language, the emotional self is what connects to other parts of our larger selves around us. We use a word that translates as heart. It is a capacity to form bonds with particular aspects of our surroundings. We say that we as people stay connected to each other, our land, and all things by our hearts.

The thinking-intellectual self has another name in Okanagan. Our word for thinking/logic and storage of information (memory) is difficult to translate into English because it does not have an exact correlation. The words that come closest in my interpretation mean "the spark that ignites." We use a term that translates as "directed by the ignited spark" to refer to analytical thought. In the Okanagan language this means that the other capacities we engage in when we take action are directed by the spark of memory once it is ignited. We know that in our traditional Okanagan methods of education we must be disciplined to work in concert with the other selves to engage ourselves beyond our automatic-response capacity. We know too that unless we always join this thinking capacity to the heart-self, its power can be a destructive force both to ourselves and to the larger selves that surround us. A fire that is not controlled can destroy.

The Okanagan teach that each person is born into a family and a community. No person is born isolated from those two things. You are born into a way of interacting with others. As an Okanagan you are automatically a part of the rest of the community. You belong. You are them. You are within a family and community. You are that which is family and community; within that you cannot be separate.

All within family and community are affected by the actions of any one individual, so all must know this in their individual selves. The capacity to bond is absolutely critical to individual wellness. Without it the person is said to be "crippled/incapacitated" and "lifeless." Not to have community or family is to be scattered or falling apart.

The Okanagan refer to relationships with others using a word that means "our one skin." This means that we share more than a place; we share

a physical tie that is uniquely human. It also means that the bond of community and family includes the history of the many who came before us and the many ahead of us who share our flesh. We are tied together by those who brought us here and gave us blood and place. Our most serious teaching is that community comes first in our choices, then family, and finally ourselves as individuals, because without community and family we are truly not human.

The Okanagan perception of the self and of the dominant culture has to do with the "us" that is place: the capacity to know we are everything that surrounds us, to experience our humanness in relation to everything else and thus to know how we affect the world around us.

The Okanagan word for "our place on the land" and "our language" is the same. We think of our language as the language of the land. This means that the land has taught us our language. The way we survive is by speaking the language that the land offered us as its teaching. To know all the plants, animals, seasons, and geography is to construct language for them.

We also refer to the land and our bodies with the same root syllable. This means that the flesh that is our body is pieces of the land come to us through the things that the land is. The soil, the water, the air, and all the other life forms contributed parts for our flesh. We are our land/place. Not to know and celebrate this is to be without language and without land. It is to be displaced.

The Okanagan teach that anything displaced from what it requires to survive in health will eventually perish. Unless place can be relearned, all other life forms face displacement and ruin.

As Okanagan, our essential responsibility is to bond our whole individual and communal selves to the land. Many of our ceremonies have been constructed for this. We join with the larger self and with the land, and rejoice in all that we are. We are this one part of the earth. Without this self and this bond, we are not human.

❀ ❀ ❀

The discord that we see around us, in my view from inside my Okanagan community, is at a level that is not endurable without consequences to the human and therefore to everything that the human influences. A suicidal coldness is seeping into and permeating all levels of interaction; there is a dispassion that has become a way of life when facing illness and other forms of human pain. I am not implying that we no longer suffer for each other as humans but rather that such suffering is felt deeply and continuously, and cannot be withstood, so feeling must be shut off.

I think of the Okanagan word used by my father to describe this condition, and I understand it better. Translation is difficult, but an interpretation in English might be "people without hearts."

Okanagans say that "heart" is where community and land come into our beings and become part of us because they are as essential to our survival as is our own skin. By this bond, we subvert destruction of other humans and of our surroundings and ensure our own survival.

The phrase "people without hearts" refers to collective disharmony and alienation from the land. It refers to those who are blind to self-destruction, whose emotion is narrowly focused on their individual sense of well-being without regard to the well-being of others in the collective.

The results of this dispassion are now on display, as large nation-states continuously reconfigure economic boundaries into a world economic disorder to cater to big business. This is causing a tidal flow of refugees from environmental and social disasters, compounded by disease and famine, as people are displaced in the rapidly expanding worldwide chaos. War itself becomes continuous as dispossession, privatization of lands, and exploitation of resources and a cheap labor force become the mission of "peace-keeping." Finding new markets is the justification for the westernization of "undeveloped" cultures.

Indigenous people, not long removed from our cooperative, self-sustaining lifestyles on our lands, do not survive well in this atmosphere of aggression and dispassion. I know that we experience it as a destructive force, because I personally experience it so. Without being whole in our community, on our land, with the protection it has as a reservation, I could not survive.

The customs of extended families in community are carried out through communing rather than communicating. I want to illuminate the significance of communing and point out that through its loss we have become dehumanized. To me, communing signifies sharing and bonding. Communicating signifies the transfer and exchange of information. The Okanagan word close in meaning to communing is "the way of creating compassion for." We use it to mean the physical acts we perform to create the internal capacity to bond.

One of the critical losses in our homes in this society originates in the disassociation we experience as a result of modern "communications" technology. People associate emotionally more with characters on television than with people in their lives. They become emotional strangers to each other and emotional cripples in the family and community.

In a healthy, whole community, the people interact with each other in shared emotional response. They come together emotionally to respond to crisis or celebration. They "commune" in the everyday act of living. Being a part of such communing is to be fully alive, fully human. To be without community in this way is to be alive only in the flesh, to be alone, to be lost to being human. It is then possible to violate and destroy others and their property without remorse.

With these things in mind, I see how a market economy subverts community to where whole cities are made up of total strangers on the move from one job to another. This is unimaginable to us. How can a person be human while continuously living in isolation, fear, and adversity? How can people twenty yards from each other be total strangers? I do see that having to move continuously just to live is painful and that close emotional ties are best avoided in such an economy. I do not see how one remains human, for community to me is feeling the warm security of familiar people like a blanket wrapped around you, keeping out the frost. The word we use to mean community loosely translates to "having one covering," like a blanket. I see how family is subverted by the scattering of members over the face of the globe. I cannot imagine how this could be family, and I ask what replaces it if the generations do not anchor to each other. I see that my being is present in this generation and in future ones, just as the generations of the past speak to me through stories. I know that community is made up of extended families moving together over the landscape of time, through generations converging and dividing like a cell while remaining essentially the same as community. I see that in sustainable societies, extended family and community are inseparable.

The Okanagan word we have for extended family is translated as "sharing one skin." The concept refers to blood ties within community and extends the instinct to protect our individual selves to all who share the same skin. I know how powerful the solidarity is of peoples bound together by land, blood, and love. This is the largest threat to interests wanting to secure control of lands and resources that have been passed on in a healthy condition from generation to generation of families.

Land bonding is not possible in the kind of economy that surrounds us, because land must be seen as real estate to be "used" and parted with if necessary. The separation is accelerated by the concept that "wilderness" needs to be tamed by "development," and this is used to justify displacement of peoples and unwanted species. I know what it feels like to be an endangered species on my land, to see the land dying with us. It is my body that is being torn, deforested, and poisoned by "development." Every fish, plant, insect, bird, and animal that disappears is part of me dying. I know all their names, and I touch them with my spirit. I feel it every day, as my grandmother and my father did.

I am pessimistic about changes happening: the increase of crimes, worldwide disasters, total anarchy, and the possible increase of stateless oligarchies; borders are disappearing, and true sustainable economies are crumbling. However, I have learned that crisis can help build community so that it can face the crisis itself.

I do know that people must come to community on the land. The transience of peoples crisscrossing the land must halt, and people must commune together on the land to protect it and all our future generations. Self-sustaining indigenous peoples still on the land are already doing this, and they are the only ones now standing between society and total self-destruction. They present an opportunity to relearn and reinstitute the rights we all have as humans. Indigenous rights must be protected, for we are the protectors of Earth.

I know that being Okanagan helps me have the capacity to bond with everything and every person I encounter. I try always to personalize everything. I try not to be "objective" about anything.

I fear those who are unemotional, and I solicit emotional response whenever I can. I do not stand by silently. I stand with you against the disorder.

Protesting Ecuadoran indigenous peasant farmers force their way through a police cordon outside the National Congress building January 21, 2000 in downtown Quito, Ecuador. At least 1,500 antigovernment protesters were joined by a handful of military officers and occupied the Congress to press their successful demand for the resignation of Ecuadoran president Jamil Mahuad, and then later, President Lucio Gutierrez. These events in Ecuador are typical of indigenous uprisings over the past decade throughout Latin America over cultural, educational, political and economic issues.

CHAPTER 5

Amautawasi Quechuan University

Luis Macas

(Quechua)
Confederation of Indigenous Nationalities of Ecuador (CONAIE)

The following remarks are translated from an October 2005 speech given in Spanish by Luis Macas, president of the Confederation of Indigenous Nationalities of Ecuador (CONAIE). The occasion was the annual meeting of the National Network of Grantmakers, a group of progressive U.S. funders. (Recording by Moving Images, Seattle, WA. Info@movingimages.org. Translation by Victor Menotti, IFG.)

GOOD AFTERNOON. Meetings like this with people such as yourselves help to nourish us and give us energy to continue work in our communities. They revive our spirits to continue the struggle to recover our rights, to recover our knowledge, and to express our ways of thinking.

For the past twelve years, we have been working continuously to establish a university based on our own indigenous issues, methodologies, and languages. We begin with the recognition of the diversity of our peoples. We don't believe in a homogeneous culture, as governments have tried to impose upon indigenous peoples. We believe in our own special cosmologies and in our own logic.

And so, to the Ecuadorean government, to the Bolivian government, and to the Peruvian gov-

ernment, our people have asserted that "we are separate states." But of course, we indigenous peoples are not "states," as in "nation-states." We are states composed of many nations. Many governments consider our saying this to be a subversive act. They say we are trying to undermine their authority.

We began this work many years ago, but in the 1990s, after meeting with some of our great indigenous friends here in the north, we began to make ourselves more visible as indigenous peoples in our own national context. The whole time before, since the start of the colonial era in 1492, we had been invisible. A lot of people did not even believe that indigenous peoples were still alive. The whole world was saying, as our anthropologist colleagues were saying, that "the Indians, the Incas, the forest peoples are now something one visits only in the National Museum. It's a shame they don't exist anymore." But of course they were saying this because we didn't have our own voice at that time to speak as our own nations, as our own nationalities, as our own peoples. And so began the struggle in Ecuador, Colombia, Peru, Bolivia, and

Venezuela, for recognition of our own states of cultural diversity. This was our first "subversion." This was our first effort to put our stamp on the state.

But now people ask, "What do the Indians want now? And why do we have to recognize each of their nations if we are all really Ecuadoreans? Or Peruvians? Or Colombians?" And we reply, "I'm not only Ecuadorean; I am also from the Quechua Nation, which existed thousands of years before Ecuador was even created."

Indigenous people were not taken into account when the state of Ecuador was constructed some two hundred years ago. We did not participate in that process, and indigenous peoples continue to be excluded today. There could be a way out, however. We need to begin building a society in which we can grow by sharing culture and knowledge in a context of rights, in which indigenous peoples can contribute to a harmonious society. Our proposals for intercultural dialogue and the construction of a plurinational state do not mean dividing the state into a lot of micro-states, but fully respecting diversity and recognizing that all cultures have a role in society.

Initially, we engaged in a struggle for our territory, for our traditional homelands. And we will continue the struggle to recover our lands—the autonomous lands of each of our peoples. But we also recognize the need to establish our own indigenous systems of thought and education. So, I want to talk mainly about that today.

OUR FIGHT FOR AN INDIGENOUS EDUCATION

Today we think a lot about our education. Indigenous peoples say we are going to educate ourselves, but how and where will we do it? And with which materials? These were our original questions when we started this struggle for our own Quechua education.

In 1989, our peoples first institutionalized bilingual education. We have thirteen indigenous nations in Ecuador, and we established that each nation will have education in its own language, not just Spanish but bilingual. We managed to do this, but some Ecuadorean people asked, "Why do the indigenous peoples need bilingual education when they must integrate into our national society?" We replied that we did not want to integrate into a society that has corrupted itself into a society of decadence. But we also said that we would contribute to the construction of a new society, a different society, if it was to be a society for everyone. Then, in 1990, we organized a huge uprising, with tens of thousands of people peacefully filling the highways and city plazas and saying to the government, "If you do not accept our demands, then we will not allow any office in this country to function." The good news is that the Ecuadorean people and civil society supported us.

That's how we began our fight for indigenous education, an education that begins precisely within each of our peoples. And this year (2005) we are opening our first university for our people.

My own education was at a classic university where one studies in only one language. I studied anthropology and law. I had that opportunity because my community financed my studies, and they supported me so that I could become what I am today. And even this moment, I know I belong to my community; I am not just an individual. That's why we fight for our collective rights and not just for the rights of an individual citizen. We demand rights for a collective society. Today, because of the struggle of our peoples, this right is fortunately recognized in our national constitution, but it was not so before. We used to be only Ecuadoreans, and to be a "good" Ecuadorean, one had to forget being an Indian.

When we began the construction of our university, we asked, "What kind of a university?" Ecuador is a very small country, with only 13 million inhabitants. The country already has around twenty universities. We had to decide if this would become simply Ecuador's twenty-first university or a totally different university. We decided not to become simply the twenty-first. Instead we decided to become the first indigenous peoples' university with indigenous thinking, indigenous methodologies, and our indigenous languages.

We are in a fight to recover our original philosophies and our sciences, from thousands of years ago, philosophies and sciences that have been undermined, held back by colonization. Colonization still persists today. It's no longer Spain but others that colonize our peoples now. We have to free ourselves from them, because if we don't we're surely going to disappear. That's why we say that we are willing to resist physically and, above all, to resist in the struggle of ideas, to rescue the paradigms of our indigenous wisdom.

We call our intercultural university Amautawasi, or "the house of wisdom." It is a project that both originates from and focuses on our peoples' communities. The strength of this university is that it is decentralized; that's why the government had such a hard time understanding our idea. They thought there would be a huge building, a big campus to house the people, to centralize the knowledge, and to locate the university in one place. But our university is decentralized, reaching out toward the communities.

We don't have an infrastructure yet for this university; we are starting new this year. But we begin with four centers: one on the Pacific Coast, two in the Andes Mountains, and one in the Amazon region. The intellectual base of this university will not be in the cities but in the indigenous communities, to serve our communities, to address the problems of our communities from within each community. That's why the government didn't want to authorize the permit for the functioning of our university and why, for twelve years now, we had to battle them for it. In 1994,

thousands of us had to again march in the streets all the way to the capital, Quito, to say, "Very well, if the government does not allow our university to work, then neither will we allow the government to work!" And that's the way we won our education. Today we have already enrolled around eight hundred students in this university from the indigenous villages.

Also, in 1994 we confirmed bilingual education for the university, one of our biggest steps. We had to make four attempts before we were approved by Ecuador's National Council of Universities. Four times we had to modify our proposal, but we did it. Our faculty includes nonindigenous people, as well as non-Ecuadoreans; we have, for example, a British person and a German who have been living in Ecuador for thirty years. We are showing in practice how intercultural cooperation can work.

SOME ELEMENTS OF OUR WORLDVIEW

We want to recover our cosmography, the way we see the world, because it is totally different from Western society's view.

We are rapidly recovering our ancestral knowledge and talking about many dimensions of our collective beliefs as Quechuas, as Shuar, etcetera. Quechua nations stretch from the north of Argentina and Chile, through Peru, Bolivia, Ecuador, and to southern Colombia. It's a huge area with millions of men and women. We are recovering not only our territories and our land rights but more importantly, our traditional ways of thinking.

We don't want to only repeat the same theories that have always been taught in all the other universities. In our teachings, consideration of three basic dimensions are absolutely necessary: the space of "macrocosmos," the space of the "microcosmos" (of the present), and the space of the past (which gives us profound meaning). As I try to describe this, the translation from Quechua may be a little difficult and inexact but we continue to look for the words that can give a true translation.

What is the purpose of our relationships, either with nature or with other humans, as far as being human? We come from a society that is collectivist. That's why we value so much what we call in our world the "complementary duality," which is our understanding of interdependence—that one person or one expression cannot exist without the other. It's not like the Western worldview, which has an absolutely different conception, which is individual, unique, and unilateral. In the Ecuador government's schools we were taught only the Western worldview, which is monotheistic; it is a worldview of social and cultural homogeneity, which extends even to peoples' behavior toward one another.

For us it's important to always include an idea of "complementary duality." We maintain in our community what we call "reciprocity." Ours is a world not of individuals but of communities and living in reciprocity. We are responsive to each other within our communities. "Proportionality" is another fundamental principle in our community, which of course provides the basis for equity in our communities. For us, complementary duality is ongoing and permanent; this is our worldview.

For a community to sustain itself, we require recognition of three types of "being": the cosmic or spiritual being, the corporeal or material being, and the communitarian being. All are necessary. Awareness of both the communal/collective being and the individual human is an indispensable condition for our communities to function. Our conceptions of time and space cannot be separated; how we view what is the past, the present and the future is intimately related to our perception of space and directionality.

Our communities are also defined by our understanding of what we call "directionality" or the four directions: above and below, left and right. These directionalities run in pairs, vertically and horizontally. Even within this concept of directionality, the idea of complementary duality is present. These dimensions cannot be ignored by our communities because this perspective is always present in our minds.

The four directions not only define our view of space but also four other important dimensions of our lives. The first dimension, coming from above, is about "knowing," called *yachay*. The second dimension, *ruray*, from below, is about "doing." From the left, we have the third dimension, *ushay*, which means the soul, the will, or the energy. From the right comes the *munay*, which is to want, love, and desire. Together these four dimensions form what we call the good life. These things cannot be separated; one cannot have separate or parallel dimensions. To know, to do, to be able to, and to want—they all go together to define quality of life and wisdom in our communities. Maybe these concepts are a little difficult—not only is it hard for some people to understand it is also hard for me to explain to you! But we must try. Our teachings and our university are centered in these concepts.

Along with the four directions, there are also for us four natural elements that are fundamental to life. Related to *yachay* is the air, which is an essential element if we are "to know." What we "do" after birth is of *ruray*, the land Mother Nature possesses. Water is, obviously, something we must have in life in order to have the energy to survive, like *ushay*. And then there is fire, like *munay*. Air, land water, fire: these four elements are not outside of the dimensions or directions of our world or our community.

CHALLENGES

What are the challenges we face in our university? The foremost challenge is intercultural misunderstanding, when one society does not recognize the other. As indigenous peoples, we respect the diversity and cultural differences of all peoples. We must do this completely, so that we can recognize not only other indigenous peoples but also those of the larger society. We have to look for the complementarity in each other, and not just for competition. We must also cultivate complementarity within our communities. This is essential if we are to recognize ourselves as indigenous communities. But we must see ourselves also in relation to Western society. We must define how we view ourselves within that larger context.

We must be careful that one cosmology is not imposed on top of another's, where one culture is subordinate and another one dominates. We believe another challenge in our university is to avoid becoming a ghetto and cutting ourselves off from other societies.

Technology is another major challenge. We must carefully try to take advantage of our understanding of how technology may help our communities improve. We cannot isolate ourselves when there are so many opportunities now to unite with our counterparts elsewhere. We will not save ourselves simply by staying off the train of history. We have to work in that dimension too so that we do not restrict our own possibilities. Even though we are not the same, we are equal but from another culture.

There is also the challenge of how we talk about the living world; human beings are one part of a web of all living beings. Human beings are not on top, as there are many other kinds of living beings that complement humanity. Ours cannot be a society that dominates nature, because all these elements give us life. For us, traditional knowledge is different from Western knowledge because we're creating not isolation but integration, so that we are part of a universe where we share intercultural experiences. We want the best of Western knowledge but through a process based on our own wisdom.

We need a way for all to learn communally, to be part of the community, and to define how to act in the community. This is important for our youth in the university. To arrive at this state we need to learn a lot of things, such as recovering how to think communally; we need to recognize what we know and what we don't know, so that we know what we must still learn and relearn.

In my case, for example, if I had not begun with such a deep relationship with my community, I might have gone to any university and pursued any career solely for myself as a "good professional." This may be a temptation for many people, but not if we are to relearn the ways from our elders and our grandparents about what we had in our communities, about the initiatives of our communities, the facts of our history. And so these are the levels of learning we want in our system of higher learning: intercultural knowledge and shared wisdom. We can't only be subjects of the government's education programs. Of course, we'll have subjects like economy, anthropology, and government studies, because people think the state is a monster but do not understand it well. However, we will maintain our own methodologies and ways of shaping our learning, and we'll share these with others. We have close professional colleagues who will support us, not only doctors and postgraduate specialists but also the village elders. We will use our own communal calendar, not only the one imposed by the state, so that we can continue working by our own perceptions of time.

We will construct an educational form based on the traditional ways we learned in our communities; this will be a fundamental part of learning in our university. Though we hope the government supports us, our university has to be something we use to help ourselves.

Thank you very much.

PART TWO

Globalization:
Rules of the Game

In 1982, the World Bank was teamed with a brutal dictatorship in Guatemala known to be waging a war of annihilation against Maya communities. The village of Rio Negro stood in the way of the Bank's plans to construct a hydroelectric dam. After villages refused to relocate from their ancestral lands, the Bank averted its eyes when the army massacred some four hundred Maya, mostly women and children.

CHAPTER 6

World Bank and IMF Impacts on Indigenous Economies

Victoria Tauli-Corpuz

(Igorot)

Tebtebba (Indigenous Peoples' International Centre for Policy Research and Education)

FOR MOST INDIGENOUS PEOPLES, their introduction to the World Bank occurs when controversial World Bank–funded projects suddenly appear in their territories. A look into the history of infrastructure building in indigenous territories shows that many such projects are funded through loans, either by the World Bank or by regional multilateral banks, such as the Asian Development Bank and the Inter-American Development Bank. Recently, other banks such as the U.S. Export-Import Bank (Ex-Im Bank) and the Japan Bank for International Cooperation (JBIC) have also been issuing loans for such projects. Many of these have been undertaken in indigenous peoples' territories, without their consultation or consent. Inevitably, the banks and the International Monetary Fund (IMF) have become targets of criticism.

The impacts of the World Bank and the IMF on the lives of indigenous peoples come not only from bank-funded development or infrastructure projects. Structural adjustment programs (SAPs), which heavily influence the economic and social policies of debtor governments, also shape the direction of development or "maldevelopment" in indigenous communities.

As will be repeated many times in these chapters, a basic right of indigenous peoples is the right to have control over their territories and the resources found therein. Another is the right to determine how any desired development should take place. The building of dams, roads, mines, and other facilities on indigenous lands, with World Bank support, has displaced tens of thousands of indigenous peoples from their own ancestral territories. Worse, activists and leaders of protests against such projects have been arrested, tortured, and killed. The declared objective of such World Bank projects is to reduce poverty, but in most cases its projects have created more poverty and social problems, not less.

FROM CHICO RIVER TO CHICO MENDES

In a series of hearings conducted in 1983 by the U.S. House Subcommittee on International Development Institutions and Finance, indigenous peoples and our advocates had a chance to speak up. The National Congress of American Indians, through spokesperson Rudolf Ryser, said, "The economic and development policies of states . . . and international banking institutions like the World Bank have profound and frequently disastrous effects on the peace and well-being of more than 500 million indigenous peoples throughout the world."

From the 1960s to the present, indigenous peoples from various parts of the world have undergone so-called development projects funded by the World Bank. In the Cordillera region in the Philippines, for example, we had the infamous Chico River Dam Project in the 1970s. It never came into being because of the sustained protests of the Igorot peoples of the region. However, the lives lost and human rights transgressed cannot be forgotten.

Even though the dam construction was aborted and the Igorot were not displaced, the proposed project created internal refugees because of the militarization that accompanied its attempted imposition. This struggle was cited during the U.S. Congress hearing on multilateral development banks in 1983, and it gained worldwide attention. It was a key factor in pushing the World Bank to develop a policy on resettlement in 1980 and, eventually, a policy on indigenous peoples.

Stories such as the Chico River Dam, however, have been repeated all over the world. In another tragic case, the World Bank lent $443.4 million to the Brazilian government from 1981 to 1983 for the Polonoroeste road-building project and agriculture colonization scheme. The loan went to pave 1,500 kilometers of dirt track to connect Brazil's south central region with the northwest tropical rainforest. The project affected an intact rainforest almost the size of France, inhabited by forty tribal groups of some ten thousand Amerindians, some of whom had never set foot outside of that area.

With the highway built, colonists were brought in to develop cocoa and coffee plantations. The arrival of half a million settlers led to further deforestation, increasing to 16.1 percent in 1991

from 1.7 percent in 1978. The project also caused serious health problems. More than 250,000 people, settlers and indigenous people alike, were infected with malaria. High infant mortality rates—from 25 to 50 percent—developed among the indigenous peoples due to measles and influenza epidemics. The public health disaster prompted the World Bank to provide another $99 million loan to spray 3,000 tons of DDT (a banned pesticide in the United States and Europe) to kill mosquitoes.

Further land conflicts erupted among the rubber tappers, indigenous peoples, cattle ranchers, and colonists. The increase in violence led to deaths of labor activists, peasants, human rights activists, and indigenous peoples, the most famous of whom was the leader of the rubber tappers, Chico Mendes, who was killed in 1988. The struggle against the Polonoroeste road project, however, was not in vain. Because of it, the World Bank issued its first Bank Policy Guideline, called "Tribal Peoples and Economic Development." It also created an environment department and pushed for the formulation of an Environment Assessment Policy.

Of course, the fundamental problem with Polonoroeste and other such projects is that they have nothing to do with what the people in the affected areas have identified as their needs. Had they been consulted, they would have chosen smaller, more appropriate projects that they themselves could manage and sustain. Unfortunately, when the financier is a huge bank whose framework does not include funding small projects that are not guaranteed to generate adequate profit for the investments poured into them, the indigenous need is ignored.

Worse yet, the politicians and bureaucrats of debtor governments usually have no qualms in justifying development models that serve the majority. The minority (which in most cases includes indigenous peoples) is asked to sacrifice for the majority so that "national development" can be achieved. In the case of the Chico River Dam Project, the Igorot, who would have been dramatically affected, could no longer accept the sacrifice of minorities in service to majorities.

POPULATION TRANSFER SCHEMES

Aside from loans for infrastructure projects, the World Bank has funded numerous population transfer schemes, uprooting indigenous peoples from their lands, which are the basis of their identities and cultures. One example is the Transmigration Program of the Suharto government in Indonesia. The bank loaned the government some $630 million from 1976 to 1986 for a resettlement project that moved millions of poor Indonesians from Java, Lombok, Bali, and Madura to West Papua, Kalimantan, and Sumatra. This move had two stated purposes: first, to ease increasing population pressure and unemployment in the congested inner islands; and second, to use these millions of people to grow agricultural export crops, particularly cacao, coffee, and palm oil. West Papua (renamed Irian Jaya when Indonesia forcibly annexed it from the Dutch in 1969) has a land area of 417,000 square kilometers; it is one of the world's richest reservoirs of biological and cultural diversity. Before transmigration, it had a population of 800,000 tribal Melanesians speaking 224 languages. By 1990, an additional 300,000 Javanese were jammed into the region.

This transmigration project can be clearly identified as the root cause of the long years of conflict that have followed. The outer islands that had to receive these transmigrants once contained 10 percent of the world's last remaining tropical forests; they are also the ancestral lands of numerous indigenous peoples. The massive influx of Javanese caused great damage and deforestation due to cash-crop plantations, mining operations (such as those of the giant global corporation Freeport-McMoran), and indiscriminate logging by World Bank–favored logging companies.

In this case, the World Bank is not the only institution that bears responsibility. Other bilateral financial institutions, including German, Dutch and U.S. Overseas Development Assistance (ODA), and multilateral bodies, such as the Asian Development Bank, United Nations Development Programme and World Food Program, hold a share of the blame.

Though the stated objective of transmigration was to alleviate poverty, the results show the opposite. In fact, poverty increased under transmigration. In the World Bank's own 1986 report, "Indonesia Transmigration Sector Review," leading Indonesian academics concluded that "the project had redistributed rather than alleviated poverty at an enormous cost—30 to 40 percent of the entire economic development budget of the outer islands in some years—and with widespread environmental destruction and social conflict as a bonus." The World Bank review revealed that 50 percent of the households in resettlement areas were living below the poverty threshold, and 20 percent below subsistence level.

The Bank takes the position that small-scale subsistence production, which characterizes many indigenous economies, does not contribute to economic growth. Economic growth only comes about, according to the Bank, if subsistence lands are rapidly converted into large-scale, capital-intensive, export-oriented commercial production. This takes the form of huge agricultural monocrop plantations, commercial mines, and/or plantation forest projects, all of which drive people from their lands by the millions. In a 1990 report, the World Bank itself admitted that from 1960 to 1980, around 28.4 million people were uprooted in Brazil due to the modernization and industrialization of agriculture.

The forced displacement of indigenous peoples is a logical consequence of many World Bank–funded projects. In spite of the existence of a Bank resettlement policy, there is no success story to tell. A U.S. Congress Human Rights Caucus hearing held in September 1989 could not cite a single project that showed a successful transfer program. Subsequent reports stated that by the early 1990s World Bank projects had displaced around two million people. This was the number of those directly dislocated by the projects; it does not include the people uprooted by the shift from subsistence agriculture—by which local farmers fed local communities—to commercial, export-oriented production of luxury foods for wealthy countries.

The World Bank blames the borrowing governments for the failure of transfer programs. In the Bank's view, the governments did not want to incur even more debt to pay for resettlement and rehabilitation of small farmers driven off their food-producing lands. And sometimes the intended funds ended up in the pockets of corrupt politicians and bureaucrats. However, the Bank shares equal responsibility, because Bank staff tend to turn a blind eye to the nonimplementation of the resettlement policy just to get the project completed. In any case, the shift from subsistence agriculture to export monoculture has proven disastrous everywhere.

HOW SAPS HURT THE POOR

Privatization efforts under Structural Adjustment Programs (SAPs) have had tragic results not only for indigenous peoples but also for the environment. The rationale used for privatizing government-run public services, from water delivery to education to social services, is that most state corporations are inefficient and corrupt. When these services are transferred to the private sector and operated on the basis of market rules, they run more efficiently, and consumers receive better services. Furthermore, income is generated that can help alleviate poverty.

The reality of SAPs shows that, as usual, the primary beneficiaries are transnational corpora-

tions that buy out state agencies. There is little indication that poverty is reduced, the environment protected, or services improved. The main goal of the Climate Convention, which was signed at the Earth Summit in Rio de Janeiro in 1992, was to reduce greenhouse gas emissions. Under the convention, governments of developing countries were given lead time to "develop their economies" before they reduced their emissions, while rich countries were required to reduce their emissions immediately. The United States did not sign the convention. President George H.W. Bush justified this, saying that "the American lifestyle is not up for negotiation." Instead of cooperating in a global plan to reduce pollution, the North transferred to the South their energy-intensive industries and supported the building of more fossil-fuel power plants to provide the energy they need. The World Bank facilitated the whole scheme.

To accomplish this transfer, the energy or power sector was quickly privatized. During the 1990s, in Orissa, a state in northeast India, the state offered its government-operated coal mines to the private sector through a SAP. World Bank incentives such as loan guarantees, low-interest loans, and guaranteed access to international markets made the sale possible.

Although the Bank did not provide the majority of the new investments for energy development in Orissa, it played a major role in arranging financing with the private sector and overseas development agencies. Thus, private coal-industry development in Orissa was financed both by the Bank and the G7 countries.

The return on investment was huge. Lawrence Summers, then undersecretary of international affairs at the Treasury Department (and now president of Harvard University), said in his testimony to the U.S. Congress in 1995 that for every dollar the U.S. government puts in the

World Bank's coffers each year, it gets $1.30 in procurement contracts for U.S. transnational corporations.

But what did the people of Orissa get? For the indigenous peoples who make up 25 percent of the population, as well as for other marginalized sectors, such as the farmers and fisherfolk, their lives worsened after this energy-intensive, toxic industrial development. To give some examples:

▲ Industrial pollution and mine tailings in the Brahmani River destroyed the subsistence economies of the tribes of the region. Ground-water in the coal production region of Talcher-Angul and Ib Valley was dramatically decreased, which meant that people had to turn to polluted river water for cooking, drinking, and irrigation —indeed, for their very lifeline;

▲ Health problems ranged from fluorosis (skin disease and brittling of bones and teeth) due to excessive fluoride, a by-product of aluminum smelting to bronchitis, skin and lung infections, and cancer brought about by coal dust and other toxic effluents from mining;

▲ People were displaced from their communities to make way for coal-fired steel mills and bauxite, coal and chromite mines, and they were displaced from their jobs because of the shift to open cast or strip mining;

▲ Power rates increased by 500 percent after privatization, way beyond the means of the majority of the population. Only 4 to 20 percent of the population can now afford power;

▲ Human rights violations increased against workers protesting the loss of their jobs and against tribes that want to maintain their traditional livelihoods.

On top of all this, the environment suffered because greenhouse gas emissions multiplied several times over. Orissa's industries and coal-fired power plants are expected to emit 164 million tons of carbon dioxide annually by the year 2006. This is about 3 percent of the projected growth of global man-made greenhouse gases for the next decade. Other toxic and potent global-warming agents such as tetrafluormethane and hexafluouroethane (from aluminum smelting), equivalent to eight million tons of carbon dioxide emissions, will be produced, causing irreversible damage to the earth's atmosphere.

Tragically, this story is not unique to Orissa. There are many Orissas in India, and many more throughout the world.

CONCLUSION

In the meantime, the World Bank and the G7 countries with their transnational corporations continue pledging to bring about "sustainable development" while funding unsustainable projects and businesses. At the end of the day, these powerful countries and corporations must ensure, as Larry Summers did, that business goes on as usual. The returns on their investments must be guaranteed, even if the lives of the world's poor continue to deteriorate and the environment is further destroyed. Structural adjustment programs restructure the economies of nations and peoples to ensure that they meet these goals. This means that subsistence economies, which sustained generations of indigenous peoples all over the world and protected the environment for millennia, have to go.

It is imperative that indigenous peoples fully understand and respond to the negative roles played by the Bank and the Fund in undermining their self-determination.

Box A: Eight Impacts of IMF/World Bank Structural Adjustment Programs

	1. FINANCIAL AND INVESTMENT LIBERALIZATION
IMF/WORLD BANK: REQUIREMENTS FOR AID	Countries must allow entry of foreign investment capital Countries must remove controls on currency speculation and permit investors to expropriate profits rather than reinvest locally Countries must allow foreign investors to increase their equity from the current 40% to 100% ownership, driving out local control
BENEFITS FOR THE ELITE (Corporations, Investors, G7 Countries)	Global transnational corporations (TNCs) can purchase and own increased amounts of land TNCs can purchase or start enterprises more easily and drive out local competitors Foreign investors are allowed to remove unlimited amounts of money rather than reinvest it Governments are required to change mining acts and forestry laws to allow for foreign ownership of lands and resources; countries compete for foreign investments by offering tax breaks, lowering labor and environmental standards, creating free trade zones
IMPACT ON THE POOR AND ON INDIGENOUS PEOPLES	Violation/undermining of ancestral land rights Displacement of indigenous peoples from their lands to make way for foreign entry Transfer from First World of highly polluting, energy-intensive industries to Third World or indigenous peoples' territories; inability to regulate corporate behavior Erosion/destruction of indigenous subsistence economic systems in favor of cash-crop monocultural production; massive extraction of natural resources for export Decapitalization of nations with volatile capital flow Loss of control of entire sectors of the economy to foreign TNCs Diminished enforcement of laws that promote local and indigenous peoples' rights
	2. CUTS IN SOCIAL SPENDING
IMF/WORLD BANK: REQUIREMENTS FOR AID	Countries must reduce public expenditures on health, education, social services, etc.
BENEFITS FOR THE ELITE (Corporations, Investors, G7 Countries)	More rapid payment of national debts to the World Bank/IMF and other private banks
IMPACT ON THE POOR AND ON INDIGENOUS PEOPLES	Less access to education, health, and human services for poor and indigenous people Deteriorating health conditions; rising illiteracy rates; degeneration of quality of life

	3. TRADE AND IMPORT LIBERALIZATION
IMF/WORLD BANK: REQUIREMENTS FOR AID	Countries must dismantle tariffs and regulations that protect local products and abolish laws limiting entry of foreign agriculture and manufactured products and commodities
	Countries must remove supports for local food production for local communities, but increase incentives to agribusinesses to produce export crops for foreign markets rather than for domestic consumption
	Countries should encourage manufacturers to focus on assembly operations (textiles and garments) or labor-intensive, low-value-added industries (electronics, computer chips) rather than support local industrialization and development for long-term stability
BENEFITS FOR THE ELITE (Corporations, Investors, G7 Countries)	Facilitates "dumping" of highly subsidized cheap agricultural products from the North into the Third World
	Encourages dumping of surplus manufactured commodities into Third World markets
	Increases foreign or hard currency to buy imported products and to pay foreign debts
	Eliminates local competition for TNCs
	Makes cheap labor more readily available
IMPACT ON THE POOR AND ON INDIGENOUS PEOPLES	Increases competition with TNCs; erodes subsistence economies of indigenous peoples who produce for domestic consumption
	Increases competition with cheap, subsidized, imported goods
	Bankrupts local firms and farms
	Increases use of best lands for cash crops and poorer land for food crops, thus reducing food production
	Brings overexploitation of forests and mineral resources, leading to environmental destruction and displacement of indigenous peoples
	Threatens food security; poor countries become net-food importers; women relegated to gathering food while men work for cash
	4. GUARANTEE OF PROPERTY RIGHTS OF CORPORATIONS
BENEFITS FOR THE ELITE (Corporations, Investors, G7 Countries)	Corporations gain same legal rights as humans and are treated as "persons"; may legally assert "human rights" to pursue their businesses
IMPACT ON THE POOR AND ON INDIGENOUS PEOPLES	Increases conflicts between indigenous peoples' traditional land rights and claims of corporations

(continued)

	5. PRIVATIZATION OF GOVERNMENT AGENCIES AND ASSETS
IMF/WORLD BANK: REQUIREMENTS FOR AID	Countries must sell state agencies to private sector
BENEFITS FOR THE ELITE (Corporations,Investors, G7 Countries)	Stimulates creation of private monopolies or competitive systems that serve only those with money Increases opportunities for government officials and cronies to acquire state assets at bargain prices Increased TNC control over construction and development activities Concentrates resources increasingly in hands of global corporations
IMPACT ON THE POOR AND ON INDIGENOUS PEOPLES	Massive job losses as private corporations re-engineer former state-run agencies Exclusion of poor and indigenous people from education, health care, and other services they can no longer afford
	6. CURRENCY DEVALUATION
BENEFITS FOR THE ELITE (Corporations, Investors, G7 Countries)	Boosts export sector Raises value of foreign debt and debt service Raises prices of imports needed for production processes
IMPACT ON THE POOR AND ON INDIGENOUS PEOPLES	Intensifies pressure to export by increasing the amount of goods that need to be sold abroad to earn sufficient foreign exchange for debt service Increases costs for inputs to production; currency devaluated; wages reduced

	7. SHRINKING GOVERNMENT SIZE
IMF/WORLD BANK: REQUIREMENTS FOR AID	Countries must trim government payrolls and reduce services, infrastructure, and public investments Countries must remove subsidies or price controls on basic food products or agricultural inputs for local production
BENEFITS FOR THE ELITE (Corporations, Investors, G7 Countries)	Reduces regulatory oversight of foreign corporations
IMPACT ON THE POOR AND ON INDIGENOUS PEOPLES	Massive layoffs in countries where government is the largest employer Greater inefficiency in government offices Increased corruption
	8. INCREASE IN INTEREST RATES
IMF/WORLD BANK: REQUIREMENTS FOR AID	Countries must increase interest charged for credit
BENEFITS FOR THE ELITE (Corporations, Investors, G7 Countries)	Increases profitability for investment while reducing responsibility for negative consequences of investment
IMPACT ON THE POOR AND ON INDIGENOUS PEOPLES	Reduced chances for indigenous peoples to borrow money for their farms or other businesses Small farmers forced to sell lands; often end up as tenant farmers or move to urban slums

Palm oil plantation in Sabah, Malaysia. The 1997 fires that engulfed Southeast Asia in a cloud of smoke half the size of the U.S. were mainly caused by plantation companies that illegally use fire to clear forests to make way for palm oil plantations. WTO agricultural provisions have benefitted large palm oil exporters and encouraged expansion of plantations. Small farmers in Malaysia, however, have been decimated by WTO policies that give Northern agribusiness more access to the South.

CHAPTER 7

How the World Trade Organization Diminishes Native Sovereignty

Victor Menotti
International Forum on Globalization

WHILE INDIGENOUS PEOPLES around the world have been gaining political ground in recent years by asserting their sovereignty within nation-states, those same national governments have given away their own authority, including sovereignty over natural resources, to the World Trade Organization (WTO). Although indigenous peoples have been winning landmark domestic court decisions and capturing national elected offices, fundamental decisions as to who finally controls land, water, genes, and essential public services are now effectively being put under the authority of the WTO. The result is diminished powers for indigenous peoples in relation to other levels of government and vis-à-vis global corporations, whose rights are increasingly enforced by global trade bodies.

Indigenous peoples are demonstrating increased sophistication in using judicial and electoral processes to change national policies. For example, the Supreme Court of Canada agreed with the Haida people of British Columbia and declared that First Nations' land titles must be recognized by *sub-federal* governments (provinces, counties, municipalities, etc.) who manage natural resources. This landmark ruling could have enormous implications for export-based forestry in the province of British Columbia, where 90 percent of the logging is done on public, or *crown*, forests, which First Nations claim as their own. Meanwhile, indigenous peoples of Bolivia and Ecuador have played decisive roles in bringing to power new presidents.

However, in these and other cases, some leaders of *national* indigenous movements now understand that to truly resolve these issues, they must also address *global* forces beyond the borders of the nation-states in which they live. Though battles against various colonial monarchies date back centuries, today's drive for natural resources is increasingly determined by a single set of global rules created by the WTO. With these rules, the WTO has indirectly imposed a single regime over indigenous peoples everywhere. In response, native communities fighting for their sovereignty are recognizing this new arena of struggle, and indigenous organizations are unifying internationally to change those rules.

The purpose of this article is therefore to provide a practical guide and primer explaining specifically how key WTO agreements impact indigenous peoples and issues.

KEY WTO AGREEMENTS
AFFECTING NATIVE PEOPLES

The World Trade Organization was created in 1995 by national governments to establish a legally binding framework of rules for global commerce that all 148 member nations were obliged to follow. Local and national governments could still pass their own laws, but they were required to conform their laws to the WTO or suffer major trade penalties.

The WTO's central effort has been to reduce the role of individual governments in all economic matters, thereby also reducing national and popular sovereignty. The WTO essentially functions as if it were a world government, which was clearly among the intentions of its first director general, Renato Ruggiero, who termed it "global government for the new millenium." It passes laws that its members are obliged to follow, settles disputes in its own courts that member nations cannot override, and has major enforcement powers, primarily financial. WTO rules extend into nearly all functions and levels of the governance of member nations, but most fundamental is that it restricts how people can influence their governments to regulate aspects of commerce. The rules of the WTO are not confined to economic matters. Many cultural, health, and environmental standards are direct victims of WTO rulings. Under WTO rules (which comprise some thirty separate agreements), *sub-federal* governments, such as local, state, provincial, and tribal governments, are subordinated (i.e., restricted from exercising full autonomy over their own jurisdictions), including on tax policy, food safety measures, and natural resource management. This has profound direct effect on tribal sovereignty, and economic culture and self-determination. These are eight of the key agreements.

1. The General Agreement on Tariffs and Trade (GATT)

Established in 1947 after the Bretton Woods meetings (which created the World Bank and International Monetary Fund), GATT sets out the core principles of free trade. For almost fifty years, these rules were voluntary, until the creation of the WTO, with enforcement powers over member nations. The following are some of GATT's core principles:

▲ *Article 1, "Most Favored Nation," and Article III, "National Treatment."* These articles have similar intentions. The first requires that all member governments treat goods imported from one WTO member nation "no less favorably" than goods imported from any other member nation. This effectively makes it impossible for governments to restrict imports from countries on moral or ethical grounds such as horrendous human rights or labor standards, or environmental record, or because they are dealing in illicit trade of some commodities or are making war, and so on. Under this article, it would have been impossible to boycott South African goods under apartheid.

Article III requires governments to treat all imported goods "no less favorably" than locally produced goods. Free trade advocates claim this article prevents "discrimination," which is a lofty-sounding ideal, but that is definitely not the point. The real purpose of Article III is to prevent any government from favoring or protecting its own local industries, or farmers or cultures that might otherwise be overwhelmed by globe-spanning corporations bringing vast amounts of cheap imports that make local or indigenous economies nonviable. Foreign businesses and banks may buy up local producers or local banks and literally take over the economy of smaller, weaker nations. These rules also prevent countries from protecting jobs or local natural resources from accelerated exploitation, or local communities from being absorbed in the global economic juggernaut, as many agricultural communities already have been.

The combination of Article I and Article III directly affects indigenous peoples by endangering small local producers, especially in natural resource domains. For example, traditional wild salmon fishers in the U.S. Pacific Northwest now find themselves seriously undercut by very cheap, industrially farmed salmon imports from Chile. Meanwhile, Mayan corn farmers of Mexico are close to being wiped out by cheap, subsidized industrial U.S. corn exports. There are literally hundreds of such cases among indigenous farmers, forest peoples and fisherpeople around the world. Similar effects are found among indigenous peoples whose lands are exploited by foreign corporations for minerals, wildlife or genetic resources. Under Articles I and III, little resistance is possible.

▲ *Article V, Free Transit of Goods,* requires that governments promise to not physically block the transport of imports or exports at their borders. While this may sound harmless, it strips governments of the traditional right to regulate trade at their borders.

▲ *Article XI, Ban on Quantitative Restrictions,* prevents governments from limiting, via quotas or bans, how much of a good can go in or out of their country. This also prevents countries and local communities from protecting local resources, jobs, industries, or standards. For indigenous people, it means further loss of control over foreign competitors entering local markets with cheap imports.

▲ *Article XX, General Exceptions,* makes governments meet certain conditions and proofs if they are to protect plant, animal, or human health. Though free trade advocates say this provides "flexibility" for governments to exercise their sovereignty, it puts the onus on countries seeking to protect resources to "prove" that laws protecting clean air, endangered species, local culture, food safety, and other public goods should not be overturned by the WTO.

Together, these principles break down the barriers separating global, national and local economies, effectively forcing producers large and small,

wherever on earth they are located, into one hypercompetitive market. It also sets off a frenzy to control and develop the last remnants of the earth's natural resources, suddenly opened up for global corporate access. The net result is that nearly all goods (including forest products, fish, farm, fuel, mineral products and even freshwater) are forced into a new commodification process in a global market controlled by a few transnational corporations and global bureaucracies.

For the estimated 300 million indigenous people worldwide, these rules pose a historic challenge, since many of the earth's remaining resources are found on their traditional lands. The new trade rules shift the fate of most natural resources—even those that are on "sovereign" native lands, upon which indigenous communities depend—to the vagaries of the international trading system. For the last five hundred years, exploitation of natural resources, on native lands and otherwise, was determined mainly by the laws of national governments or their colonial sponsors. But the creation of GATT and the WTO brings natural resources within a single global process designed to concentrate corporate control over their ownership, use, and benefits.

2. The Agreement on Agriculture (AoA)

The AoA reduces the ability of governments—national, local, or tribal—in three main areas of farm policy:

▲ *Market access.* The agreement gradually eliminates the ability of governments to set tariffs (taxes) on imports, or quotas, or standards concerning the quantity or quality of agricultural imports. This means that countries or communities that now favor small local or indigenous producers by controlling the volume of imports from foreign competition will soon not be allowed to do that. So communities like the Maya of Mexico that had once lived off local corn varieties are now suffering increased competition from subsidized industrial corn from the United States. The same can be said of many rice-growing areas of Asia, vegetable producers in the Philippines, and Anishinaabeg wild rice harvesters in Minnesota. All are thrown into competition with global food corporations, who use machine and chemical intensive production with very little human labor to achieve much lower direct costs.

▲ *Domestic supports.* Governments will also be prevented from using a variety of supports and programs aimed at helping small farmers, including price supports, low-cost credit programs, subsidized seeds, and marketing assistance, which supported small producers.

▲ *Export subsidies.* Governments are also not permitted under AoA to provide subsidies for exporters of food products. In practice, however, governments find ways to continue export subsidies for larger growers, through indirect means like massive export advertising benefits, which further suppress viable options for local growers.

WTO rules on farming are essentially designed to "open up" foreign markets for large-scale luxury export producers. The rules therefore offer great incentives for nations to emphasize expanding and supporting export-oriented industrial agricultural production at the expense of small, traditional, indigenous producers who grow food for local markets and communities. Discriminating in favor of this kind of massive monocultural production—especially of exotic commodities not usually produced in a locale, such as export beef, luxury vegetables, soy, or exotic flowers—brings enormous environmental problems to lands that have often been occupied by indigenous peoples for millennia. Aside from the pollution from industrial-intensive production, large new infrastructure systems are required to bring the products from distant locations to seaports and airports and then across oceans. Very often these new roads, canals, pipelines, and ports are built directly on indigenous lands, without prior

approval, causing great conflict. In Brazil, for example, the Xavante people and other indigenous groups are now actively opposing the construction of a new industrial waterway for the shipment of industrially grown soy from the Brazilian interior. The proposed canal would run adjacent to the Rio das Mortes alongside the Xavante Reserve, which is an important source of Xavante food and water. And many other indigenous peoples are fighting dams, pipelines, roads, and so on.

In a very positive development, in reaction to the WTO rules, indigenous groups are now joining with nonindigenous farmer and fisher organizations, demanding WTO recognition of two key rights: 1) "food security," the right of people to access enough food to feed themselves; and 2) "food sovereignty," the right of traditional local producers to continue to grow food for local consumers, and of each community to continue to produce enough food to feed its own people. Under present WTO rules this is impossible.

The 1999 Indigenous Peoples' Seattle Declaration puts it this way:

> The WTO Agreement on Agriculture, which promotes export competition and import liberalization, has allowed the entry of cheap agricultural products into our communities. It is causing the destruction of ecologically rational and sustainable agricultural practices of Indigenous Peoples. Small-scale farming is giving way to commercial crop plantations, further concentrating ancestral lands into the hands of the few agri-corporations and landlords. This has led to the dislocation of scores of people from our communities who then migrate to nearby cities and become urban homeless and jobless.... [F]ood security and the production of traditional food crops have been seriously compromised. Incidents of diabetes, cancers, and hypertension have significantly increased among indigenous peoples because of the scarcity of traditional foods and the dumping of junk food in our communities.

By the time of the 2003 Cancun WTO Ministerial, indigenous communities were well organized to fight for food security and food sovereignty and to express their views on the WTO's rules for agriculture. (*See Box B.*) Indigenous organizations and small farmers' groups like Via Campesina combined to demand a ban on "dumping," a common practice of large producers. ("Dumping" in WTO jargon occurs when an exporting country delivers huge amounts of products far below actual cost because of various forms of export subsidy.) Meanwhile, Mayan communities, who produce corn for local consumption, spoke of the way free trade forced open Mexico's markets to subsidized corn from the United States, leaving indigenous farmers unable to sell their own corn. Even in small Mayan villages, one now finds tortillas mostly made from cheap imported corn, making it difficult for small producers to survive. Hopefully the new combined efforts of indigenous communities and peasant farmers will be able to change some WTO rules. At Cancun, the indigenous coalition partners declared their battle against the "*loss of livelihoods of hundreds of thousands of indigenous corn-producing peasants in Mexico because of the dumping of artificially cheap, highly subsidized corn from the USA, and the tens of thousands of indigenous vegetable producers in the Cordillera region of the Philippines because of dumping of vegetables*" (*Cancun Declaration, see Appendix*).

3. The Agreement on Sanitary and Phyto-Sanitary Measures (SPS)

SPS restricts what governments can do to protect food safety and to prevent the entry of harmful or invasive species or diseases inside their borders ("bioinvasion"). The United States and other big food exporters use the SPS rules to *prevent* other nations from regulating (even by simply requiring consumer information labels) the import of genetically engineered organisms, which may threaten native biodiversity and ecosystem balance with genetic pollution.

In Oaxaca, Mexico, genetically engineered (or transgenic) corn has been found growing near indigenous villages where the maize genome originates. It is not known exactly how transgenic corn arrived in so remote a place, but researchers note that the combination of a flood of U.S. corn imports and the Mexican authorities' virtually nonexistent monitoring system to control the entry of transgenic foods have made it almost impossible to stop. WTO rules on food safety severely limit what nations like Mexico can do to regulate or monitor imports of transgenic products. Aldo Gonzalez, an indigenous farmer and former mayor of the Oaxacan village where transgenic corn was first discovered in Mexico, explains that contaminating his peoples' traditional corn fields and seed banks with transgenic corn could pollute and even destroy what they have relied on for thousands of years. (*See also Chapter 18.*)

4. The Agreement on Subsidies and Countervailing Measures (SCM)

SCM outlines what kinds of subsidies governments are allowed to give to companies. WTO rules are supposed to be based on the *theory* of free trade, which includes the principle that governments may not subsidize private corporations. Though the WTO has detailed rules banning subsidies, they are filled with loopholes that allow big subsidies for global corporations but not local or small producers.

One of the largest subsidies that the WTO ignores concerns land that has been taken away from native peoples for natural resource exploitation. Though WTO vigorously enforces corporate rights, it usually fails to recognize indigenous property rights. This nonenforcement of indigenous rights even applies in cases where native lawyers have won compensation for lost property rights in *national* court decisions that confirm indigenous rights. WTO's failure to acknowledge these rights is itself a kind of subsidy for resource corporations who get free access to indigenous resources. Tribal fishing communities in India have had their traditional coastal areas replaced by massive foreign investor-driven shrimp farms, constituting an almost incalculable export subsidy that allows India to dump "endless shrimp" in the United States, displacing America's traditional shrimping communities. In Canada, First Nation leaders are calling for trade rules that recognize Canada's failure to compensate for indigenous property rights as an illegal export subsidy. They ask that softwood exports from native lands be subject to trade penalties. (*See also Chapter 25.*)

5. The Agreement on Trade-Related Aspects of Intellectual Property Rights (TRIPS)

TRIPS lays down explicit requirements for the kind of patent regimes nations must use to protect intellectual property, such as inventions and technological innovations. It also explicitly allows *patenting*—a legal claim of ownership—of plants, animals, and microorganisms but does not require that patent applicants declare the source of the genetic resources, which increasingly come from indigenous lands.

TRIPS rules have produced a major international battle of indigenous peoples and small farmers versus giant agriculture and pharmaceutical companies over what indigenous communities call "biopiracy." Biopiracy is the practice of privatizing and patenting biological or genetic resources that indigenous or traditional communities have traditionally owned, developed and used. Under TRIPS rules, biotechnology companies, particularly seed and drug companies, can *privatize* genetic resources by obtaining patents that allow them to legally exercise *exclusive* control over marketing the claimed material; this has been a major blow to local *usufruct* rights—by which communities, notably in India, have traditionally been recognized as collective owners of local resources and innovations—and of rights to the global commons.

Because indigenous peoples often reside in some of the world's most remote regions, which are still undisturbed by industrial exploitation, native lands contain the greatest biodiversity of plants and animals, making them favorite targets for *bioprospectors* who scour the earth looking for raw genetic material from which they can market new drugs and seeds, controlling them by patents.

Indigenous people are generally not opposed to sharing what they have to feed the hungry and cure the sick, but they do oppose outsiders who claim ownership over plants that indigenous peoples have always used. Moreover, TRIPS does not require patent holders to even compensate or "share benefits" (i.e., profits) with the indigenous communities where the genetic material originated.

Corporate appropriation of biological diversity extends beyond living beings and into the very knowledge that indigenous communities—particularly in South America and India—have collectively generated over millennia about how to use specific species for healing and farming. Field scientists often use indigenous knowledge to identify the most commercially valuable species, only to return home and file a patent claiming it was their "discovery." Using indigenous knowledge can save companies millions of dollars in research costs by narrowing down their search to those species already known by indigenous peoples to have some useful quality.

Examples of biopiracy include W.R. Grace's patenting of a pesticide derived from the *neem*, a tree that villagers in India, according to Dr. Vandana Shiva, "have used for millennia as a biopesticide and a medicine." (In March 2005, the European Patent Office revoked the patent.)

A California scientist filed for a patent on the psychoactive plant *hayahuasca*, which indigenous peoples throughout the Amazon use for spiritual rituals. Mexico's indigenous peoples are seeing an influx of bioprospectors descending on their lands, encouraged by the Plan Puebla Panama, whose cornerstone is the exploitation of the area's legendary biological wealth. Other examples include, in the Americas, *quinoa* and *sangre de drago*; in Asia, turmeric and bitter melon; and in the Pacific, kava.

The good news is that indigenous resistance against biopiracy is gaining ground by publicly exposing the "pirates," challenging national patent systems, and actively engaging in the international policy arenas where rules are set protecting indigenous rights, biological diversity, and intellectual property rights. Successful challenges against patents in various nations have, in some cases, caused patent holders to withdraw or even be denied their applications.

A new array of international peoples' movements, including indigenous rights and small farmers' groups, are pressuring trade ministers to change TRIPS to recognize the rights of indigenous peoples over biodiversity that were established in the UN's Convention on Biological Diversity. "No Patents on Life" has become the clear message from indigenous peoples active around the WTO. And in late 2003, a block of African nations submitted a formal proposal to the WTO calling for a change in TRIPS to make the patenting of life unacceptable. The U.S. position is that it would prefer to not change the patent system, but rather address disclosure and benefit-sharing through permits, contractual obligations and civil or criminal penalties. International campaigning will continue to "take out of WTO" biodiversity and other natural resources. (*See Chapter 8.*)

6. The General Agreement on Trade in Services (GATS)

GATS establishes rules for how governments regulate services, broadly defined as "anything you can't drop on your foot." GATS is currently being renegotiated in an attempt to expand privatization of such services as water treatment and delivery, education, health care and hospitals, broadcasting, advertising, culture, welfare and social security, insurance, and banking. A recent WTO ruling on Internet "gambling services" may have direct implications for Indian gaming in the United States.

The push to privatize fresh water has become one of the hottest issues in the globalization debate. Indigenous communities have been on the front line of this battle, fighting to maintain their traditional access to and communal management of what many regard as life's most precious resource.

In particular, Bolivia's indigenous peoples helped expose the emerging global water privatization schemes proposed in the WTO's General Agreements on Trade in Services. If the negotiations are successful, private water corporations could seize control of nearly all water "services," from free access to and direct management of fresh water resources to collection, purification, distribution, and reclamation.

Bolivia was only the first global flashpoint in the coming "water wars." In late 1999, Bolivia accepted a World Bank loan requiring that the government privatize the water system of its third largest city, Cochabamba. The region surrounding Cochabamba is inhabited by indigenous peoples who still live and farm the traditional way, using a communal catchment system that collects and distributes water to fields and villages.

After Bechtel Corporation was granted ownership of not only the pipes, pumps, and purification equipment that deliver water but also all facilities that gather and store water, they increased rates dramatically. The poorest users (minimum wage workers in Bolivia earn less than $100 per month) received water bills of $20 per month or higher. Water was shut off completely for others. A popular uprising ensued, martial law was imposed when people filled the streets, and pro-testers were shot dead. But Bechtel's contract was finally cancelled. (*See also Chapter 13 on water, and Chapter 23 on Bolivia's indigenous revolution.*)

In the run-up to the WTO's Cancun Ministerial, local Mayan communities worried they might be targeted for their unique systems of underground freshwater springs, called *cenotes*. They were con-cerned enough that they joined other peoples' movements in denouncing WTO plans to estab-lish global rules that would shift control over water resources from the traditional commons into the hands of a few global water corporations.

GATS also threatens indigenous peoples' ability to continue practicing traditional systems of health care or access Western-style health-care services. As mentioned earlier, traditional access to medicines derived from local plants and ani-mals is endangered by the privatization of genetic resources under WTO's intellectual property rights regime (TRIPS), which not only steals the resources that indigenous peoples have cultivated over millennia but can also restrict indigenous peoples' use of the same resources. In Thailand, for example, a national law designed to protect traditional medicinal uses of biodiversity was opposed by the United States because it might restrict the ability of foreign pharmaceutical companies to patent and monopolize Thai plants.

GATS also threatens indigenous peoples' ability to access Western-style health-care services when needed. The current push to expand GATS rules could privatize public health services. Many native peoples, especially in the United States, receive health services from state or public agen-cies. Private health service corporations may eliminate health-care services in remote regions that are expensive to serve, such as Indian reser-vations. No matter which way people get their health care, the WTO poses a threat.

7. (Proposed) Agreement on Non-Agricultural Market Access (NAMA)

Exporters are eager to use WTO rules to radically expand their *market access* in more foreign markets. Today most governments still impose *tariffs* (import taxes) on some goods to protect domes-tic producers against competition from cheaper imports. And nearly all governments have what the WTO calls *non-tariff barriers* (NTBs), which include any measure (for example, measures that require business licenses or health or environ-mental standards) that in some way diminishes market access for certain countries' goods. NAMA aims to eliminate *all* of these remaining *trade barriers*.

For example, the WTO is currently considering the elimination of tariffs on all wood products, which could increase logging in some of the world's most endangered forests, in Indonesia, Malaysia and Chile, which are still largely inhab-ited by indigenous peoples. If Indonesia succeeds in getting Japan and the United States to remove their tariffs on plywood, Indonesia plywood exporters will have greater incentive to log more trees for plywood. Also, eliminating tariffs lowers the price of products, directly increasing con-sumption. By lowering tariffs without any new protections, NAMA could have the effect of destroying the environmental habitat and resources of indigenous communities all around the world. In Indonesia alone, it could lead to displacement of the 40 million local and indige-nous peoples who depend on forest resources.

If passed, NAMA may also restrict the use of *eco-labels*, which some indigenous peoples, like the Maya of southern Mexico, use to show that their forest products have been certified as sustainably harvested. Because some nonsustainable wood exporters think eco-labels give their competitors an unfair marketing advantage, they want to use the WTO to ban them.

8. (Proposed) Agreement on Investment

Investment is a new theme for the WTO, which may soon begin negotiations to restrict the ability of all levels of governments to regulate incoming foreign investment. In Cancun, the WTO failed to expand its mandate to cover foreign investment, a major victory for protestors fighting for democratic control over global capital and restrictions on its free flow. But the investment issues could return soon through the WTO or the proposed Free Trade Area of the Americas (FTAA). This is very important to indigenous peoples, because "free investment" often is used to undermine indigenous ownership of resource-rich lands.

Indigenous peoples nearly everywhere are facing privatization by foreign investors of their traditional lands. While many resist the very concept of buying and selling communal property, some have opted (or had to settle) for partial forms of privatization. Though these policies are usually implemented through local or national programs, rich nations want to use the WTO to establish a new legal framework that frees and accelerates the privatization process, possibly prohibiting any restriction on who buys the land or how much they can buy.

While it is still not certain what elements would be included in any future WTO investment scheme, some of the critical issues are sure to be these:

▲ Restrictions against nations introducing investment "speed bumps." These are rules that countries have often used to slow down the rate at which investors can bring money in and take it back out, a practice that sometimes leaves local economies gutted. Such "speed bumps" have been successfully used to protect local resources in Chile, China, Russia and elsewhere;

▲ Restrictions against national requirements for a certain percentage of local ownership of investments, or that disallow the immediate repatriation of profits abroad—thus preserving some benefits for the local economies;

▲ Restrictions on the power of *sub-federal* governments—state, regional, county, city or tribal governments—to make their own rules regulating investments; and

▲ Requirements, like those in the North American Free Trade Agreement (NAFTA), that any loss of profits by investor companies because of above or other local or national rules be considered a "taking" against the corporation and be compensated.

All of these proposed WTO rules and others would negatively impact the ability of indigenous governments to control their resources and lands.

Rich nations are eager to establish in the WTO the right of foreign investors to directly sue national governments for cash compensation if that government enacts any measures that reduce the "planned profits" of a foreign investor. Such rules could force governments to pay foreign corporations for lost "extractive rights" on stolen land, or for restoring land damaged by industrial exploitation. This right currently exists in NAFTA, and it is already impacting indigenous peoples' land struggles. It would become globalized if introduced in the WTO or the FTAA.

The Haida people in Western Canada are now in a court battle with the provincial government of British Columbia over this issue. The Haida want to reclaim ownership of tens of thousands of acres of forests that were leased by British Columbia to U.S. timber companies for export logging. But the Canadian government has ruled that the First Nations have title to these lands, putting Canada into a dispute with British Columbia and the logging companies. Under

NAFTA, Canada could be sued for cash compensation because its recognition of native sovereignty rights would reduce the anticipated profits of foreign investors' logging leases.

CONCLUSION

Nowhere is the "clash of paradigms" between indigenous and industrial economies more clear than in the above rules governing world trade. Whereas the global industrial economy requires ever-expanding control over natural resources, indigenous economies are place-based and do not require physical expansion, instead finding ways to live within the ecological limits of their region. The WTO values commerce and corporate profits over humans and the natural world. As a result, almost every WTO ruling has been against the public interests of human health and the natural world.

Peoples' movements, which have become increasingly effective at using local and national governments to regulate corporate behavior, now must face the fact that corporations have created a powerful new global arena for rule-making. Indigenous rights organizations and trade activist groups must now unite to change these rules and subordinate trade considerations to the inherent rights of native peoples to sovereignty and self-determination.

We believe the whole philosophy underpinning WTO agreements and the principles and policies it promotes contradict our core values, spirituality, and worldviews, as well as our concepts and practices of development, trade, and environmental protection. Therefore, we challenge the WTO to redefine its principles and practices toward a "sustainable communities" paradigm, and to recognize and allow for the continuation of other worldviews and models of development. (Indigenous Peoples' Seattle Declaration; see Appendix)

Box B: Mayan Revolt at Cancun, 2003

When trade ministers met in Seattle in 1999 for the WTO's Third Ministerial, there were only a handful of indigenous organizations who had developed technical expertise on international trade policy. Although they were small in numbers, they had become increasingly effective in influencing government negotiating positions in WTO talks. Many of them gathered in Seattle and issued a strong and detailed declaration *(see Appendix)*. However, indigenous concerns were largely overshadowed by other issues and voices that were more visible on the streets of Seattle.

Things changed the next time the WTO met in a place where protest was permitted (Cancun, Mexico, September 10–14, 2003). Mayan communities near Cancun created a massive indigenous presence on the streets outside the WTO meeting, drawing world attention to the concerns of indigenous peoples everywhere.

Before the protests, WTO trade ministers had prepared to make binding decisions that would have expanded the WTO's power over indigenous peoples' lives by privatizing their communal land, water, and biodiversity, as well as essential public services. Ironically, only six months prior to the global economic summit, the local indigenous communities that surround Cancun had no information about the meetings or potential decisions that would affect their rights locally, as well as those of indigenous peoples worldwide.

But when Mayan leaders began working in concert with international NGOs, the full story started to be told, including the struggles against privatization of native communal property, the entry of large foreign investors buying up land, the increasing imports of subsidized corn that undercut local producers, and an expanding infrastructure for industrial tourism. All these issues were already impacting the Maya, who were battling Mexico's attempt to conform national policies to a global framework set by WTO.

For indigenous peoples, the importance of these issues first became vividly clear in 1994, at the time of the approval of NAFTA, when Mexico was asked by the United States and Canada to eliminate its *ejido* communal land ownership system. The creation of the *ejidos* was one of the great land reform victories of the Zapatista Revolution of the early 1900s, and formed the basis for the Mayan agricultural economy. But *ejidos* were thought by free traders to restrict investment opportunities, as foreign banks and corporations had no easy way to make large land purchases under a collective ownership scheme. So far, this scheme has been beaten back in the Zona Maya.

By the time of the Cancun meeting, however, Mayan community leaders were collaborating with members of the International Indian Treaty Council, Mexico's National Indigenous Congress, the Mexican Action Network Against Free Trade, the local peoples' Cancun Welcoming Committee, and the International Forum on Globalization. The leaders organized a Cancun preparatory meeting on June 14, 2003, in the historic Mayan pueblo of Tihosuco. A center of indigenous resistance against European colonists centuries ago in the Guerra de Castas, or Caste Wars, Tihosuco was chosen because of its "convocatory power." In the shadow of an enormous gutted colonial church, local leaders from a dozen key villages agreed to mobilize communities from the Zona Maya to go to Cancun for the WTO summit.

As trade ministers met in their luxury venues, indigenous peoples in the thousands convened their own international fora, participated in peaceful marches, issued a declaration *(see Appendix)*, and spoke at public rallies and to the international press. The Mayan mobilization in the streets set the tone for negotiating pressure in the suites, where trade ministers from poor nations, cognizant of the local opposition outside, united to stop the rich nations from globalizing their corporate agenda. The result was a collapse in the negotiations and another failed attempt to expand the WTO, as in Seattle four years earlier. Since Cancun, the involvement of indigenous peoples in popular resistance to WTO has continued to grow.

Botanical treatments for a variety of illnesses make up the local bounty from this small market in the tropics, where forests are the reservoirs of species diversity. WTO rules on intellectual property threaten the rights of traditional Indigenous forest communities to control or benefit from their botanical knowledge and use of local genetic resources.

CHAPTER 8

High-Tech Invasion: Biocolonialism

Debra Harry
(Northern Paiute)
Indigenous Peoples Council on Biocolonialism

FOR HUNDREDS OF YEARS, Indigenous peoples were exploited by outsiders, primarily Europeans, who saw Indigenous land, forests, water, animals, art, culture and other "resources" as items in a vast and profitable marketplace to which they were entitled. Indigenous lifestyles, knowledge, and traditions have also been a source of intense study for anthropologists, botanists, archaeologists and museums. Now there is a new wave of scientific inquiry fueled by the latest form of commercial greed. Science's leap into genetic engineering has inspired "bioprospecting" by pharmaceutical and agricultural corporations, who seek to privatize and monopolize the genetic structures and cell lines not only of native plants and seeds but of Indigenous peoples themselves.

INTRODUCTION

Today's planetwide search for genetic resources to use in commercial ventures has not only exacerbated the negative effects of scientific research on the lives of Indigenous peoples everywhere but has given birth to a new form of colonialism—*biocolonialism*—in the name of research and corporate "free trade" of genetic material and life processes.

Through the application of Western intellectual property law, namely patents, increasingly enforced by global trade agreements like the World Trade Organization (WTO) Agreement on Trade-Related Aspects of Intellectual Property Rights (TRIPS), corporations and other legal entities can claim monopoly ownership of human genes, the biodiversity of our lands and waters, and associated Indigenous knowledge.

When genetic resources become private property, they become alienable; that is, through patenting, genetic resources can be owned, bought and sold as commodities. Clearly, the commercialization of genes conflicts with Indigenous values and the collective nature of our customary management systems. Indigenous peoples have been consistent in our calls for *no patents on life forms*, as expressed in this declaration issued in 1995:

> *To negate the complexity of any life form by isolating and reducing it to its minute parts, Western science and technologies diminishes its identity as a precious and unique life form, and alters its relationship to the natural order. Genetic technologies which manipulate and change the fundamental core and identity of any life form are an absolute violation of these principles, and*

create the potential for unpredictable and therefore dangerous consequences. We oppose the patenting of all natural genetic materials. We hold that life cannot be bought, owned, sold, discovered or patented, even in its smallest form. (Declaration of Indigenous Peoples of the Western Hemisphere Regarding the Human Genome Diversity Project, available at www.ipcb.org.)

The profit motive in genetic research makes Indigenous peoples even more vulnerable to exploitation and to attitudes of racism, dehumanization, and oppression. Nearly everything that we hold collectively and value as peoples is at risk of appropriation and subject to the new global market in genetic resources, including Indigenous foods, medicines, and even our traditional knowledge developed and passed down from generation to generation over millennia.

This article gives some examples of the exploitation of human genes, plants, and knowledge as experienced by Indigenous peoples, and highlights some of the current debates taking place in international forums. Biocolonialism, left unchecked, could dominate and perhaps destroy Indigenous peoples' livelihoods and cultures. Protections can be instituted at the local level, and standards must be established at the international level that protect the human rights of Indigenous peoples to protect their genetic resources and Indigenous knowledge on their own terms and to live free from the threat and impacts of biocolonialism.

I. PRIVATIZATION OF HUMAN GENES

In 1984, a Seattle businessman, John Moore, filed a lawsuit claiming that his blood cells were misappropriated while he was undergoing treatment for leukemia at the University of California-Los Angeles Medical Center. His case had enormous implications for the efforts of universities and corporations to "mine" the human genetic resources of all people. During his treatment, Moore's doctor developed, *without*

Moore's consent, a cell line from his blood cells that proved valuable in fighting bacteria and cancer. The UCLA Board of Regents filed a patent claim on this cell line, from which they developed commercially valuable antibacterial and cancer-fighting pharmaceuticals. Moore claimed he was entitled to share in profits derived from commercial uses of these cells and any other products resulting from research on any of his biological materials. In a landmark 1990 California Supreme Court decision, the court established that patients do not have a "property right" in the tissues removed from their own bodies (*Moore v. Regents of the University of California*).

The *Moore* case set a dangerous legal precedent that allows for patenting of the DNA from individuals, with or without consent. It also highlights an inability to claim a "property interest" in DNA once it is removed from the body, making it extremely difficult to recover biological samples or to claim any rights or benefits from their use.

Indeed, there have been several well-known cases of attempts to patent cell lines derived from Indigenous peoples in the past. In 1993, the late U.S. secretary of commerce Ron Brown filed a patent claim on the cell line of a twenty-six-year-old Guaymi woman from Panama. Her cell line was of interest because some Guaymi people carry a unique virus, and their antibodies might have been useful in AIDS and leukemia research. International protest and action by the Guaymi General Congress and others led to the withdrawal of the patent claim by the U.S. secretary of commerce in November 1993.

The Hagahai peoples of Papua New Guinea were the subjects of a patent application filed by the U.S. National Institutes of Health (NIH) and an anthropologist named Carol Jenkins, who was doing research on the Hagahai. In 1994, the patent was granted, and later, in 1996, was abandoned.

Currently, Indigenous peoples are the subjects of a wide array of human genetic research projects because of the perceived uniqueness of our human gene pools. Over the past decade, we have seen extensive violations of human rights protections, including researchers who failed to obtain prior informed consent before taking genetic samples or who have allowed widespread unauthorized secondary uses or commercialization of those samples.

For instance, in 2002, the Nuu-chah-nulth tribe in British Columbia was outraged to find that samples taken for arthritis research at the University of British Columbia (UBC) in the early 1980s were still being used at Oxford University in England for unrelated research without the tribe's consent. When the researcher, Dr. Ryk Ward, left UBC in 1986, he took approximately nine hundred samples of Nuu-chah-nulth blood with him. He utilized the Nuu-chah-nulth samples in subsequent genetic anthropology-related research, resulting in hundreds of published papers and an appointment as head of the Institute of Biological Anthropology at Oxford University. In 2004, after Dr. Ward's death, Oxford University returned the blood samples and records to UBC. A Nuu-chah-nulth research ethics board will oversee any use of the samples in future research. Even though the samples have finally been repatriated, the Nuu-chah-nulth will continue to explore legal options to seek liability and compensation in this case of abject exploitation.

In March 2004, the Havasupai tribe of Arizona filed a $50 million lawsuit in Coconino County Superior Court against Arizona State University, the Arizona Board of Regents and three ASU professors. The suit claims that more than four hundred blood samples were taken from tribal members between 1990 and 1994 for diabetes research. Instead, the samples were used in research on inbreeding, schizophrenia and theories about ancient human population migrations to North America. If the Havasupai Tribe wins its suit, it will mark an important legal precedent where a tribe has successfully held an institution accountable for breaches of human rights protections in research and a landmark recognition of the collective rights of the tribe to protect its genetic materials.

Although many concerns stem from academic-based research, corporate interest in human genes is equally troubling. In November 2000, an Australian biotech company, Autogen Limited, announced that it had signed an agreement with the Kingdom of Tonga's minister of health to secure exclusive rights to the entire gene pool of the people of Tonga. In exchange, the company offered funding for research, royalties from commercial products generated from any discoveries that were commercialized, and free distribution of any new therapeutics to the Tongan people. Autogen hoped to use the DNA of Tongans in its hunt for profitable drugs to treat diabetes, cardiovascular disease, hypertension, cancers and ulcers. Tongan human rights activists condemned the agreement between the Tongan government and the Australian biotech company, and ultimately the proposed deal was abandoned.

II. PRIVATIZATION OF NATIVE PLANTS AND INDIGENOUS KNOWLEDGE

As the economic potential of genetic resources began to be realized in the early 1990s, access to genes became a key topic of discussion at the June 1992 United Nations Conference on Environment in Rio de Janeiro, commonly referred to as the Earth Summit. The Earth Summit resulted in an international treaty, the Convention on Biological Diversity (CBD), in which signatory Parties agreed to ensure the "conservation of biological diversity, the sustainable use of its components and the fair and equitable sharing of benefits arising from its utilization."

Today, much of the CBD's attention is focused on efforts to "elaborate and negotiate an international regime on access to genetic resources and benefit sharing." Indigenous peoples fear the international regime will simply result in mechanisms that facilitate the exploitation of genetic resources, while undermining the other two objectives of the CBD: sustainable use and conservation of genetic resources. This proposed regime, consisting of one or more instruments, is being elaborated in the CBD's Ad-Hoc Open-Ended Working Group on Access and Benefit Sharing (ABS) and may be negotiated at the eighth Conference of the Parties planned for 2006 in Rio de Janeiro, Brazil. The industrialized government parties' agenda is clear: facilitation of legal access to genetic resources and associated traditional knowledge. Meanwhile, the developing countries, primarily of the biodiverse-rich global South, are demanding fair and equitable benefit sharing, both in monetary and nonmonetary forms (i.e., training opportunities and technology transfer) from the utilization of genetic resources and their products and derivatives.

This focus on "benefit sharing" has the effect of promoting, rather than preventing, the commercialization of genetic resources. Although benefit sharing offers Indigenous people more than just outright biopiracy does, there are serious pitfalls as well. Benefit sharing entices Indigenous peoples to participate in the alienation of their genetic resources and knowledge. Even more problematic is the assertion that Parties to the CBD (i.e., national governments) are making sure that they have *absolute* sovereignty over genetic resources, without sufficient consideration of Indigenous peoples' territorial and human rights. Finally, in the current benefit sharing discussions, Parties only consider benefit sharing with Indigenous peoples for the use of our Indigenous knowledge, but not for the genetic resources originating in our territories. The experience of the San of South Africa in the patenting of the Hoodia plant serves as an instructive case model. *(See also Box D, "Whose Common Property?")*

In Africa, the San peoples, who, according to their tradition, do not eat while hunting, live around the Kalahari desert in southern Africa and use the stem of a cactus, called Hoodia, to stave off hunger and thirst on long hunting trips. South Africa's Council for Scientific and Industrial Research (CSIR) began looking for pharmaceutical profit potential in the Hoodia in the early 1960s based on the ethnobotanical knowledge of the San. In 1997 they secured a patent on the appetite-suppressing active substance of the Hoodia, called P57. CSIR licensed the development rights for Hoodia to Phytopharm, a company based in the United Kingdom. Phytopharm later sublicensed to Pfizer, the U.S. pharmaceutical giant, for development of an anti-obesity drug based on P57. While all of this research, patenting, and deal-making was going on, nobody bothered to inform the San nor obtain their *prior informed consent* for the use of their Indigenous knowledge. Phytopharm representatives later claimed they believed the San people who used Hoodia were extinct. In fact, the San number 100,000 across South Africa, Botswana, Namibia and Angola.

Finally, in 2003, the CSIR offered the San a benefit sharing arrangement, but only after CSIR and Phytopharm had been widely, publicly criticized for failing to obtain the consent of the San for the use of their knowledge. The San's share amounts to less than 0.003 percent of net sales, and that percentage only comes out of CSIR's share in the deal; Phytopharm's and Pfizer's earnings will go untouched. A disturbing aspect of the agreement rewards the San for their knowledge of Hoodia but explicitly prevents them from using that knowledge in any other commercial application. Thus, the ancient knowledge of the San has been silenced and alienated from their own use because it is now under the control of the patent regime.

It's difficult to see how benefit sharing agreements that allow for the monopolization and alienation of Indigenous knowledge and genetic resources in the guise of intellectual property protection can be of any meaningful benefit to Indigenous peoples. In the end, the benefits that come to Indigenous peoples are likely to be quite insignificant compared to those reaped by the pharmaceutical, agricultural or chemical companies and academic institutions with which they are dealing. (NOTE: *For further critique of benefit sharing, see Debra Harry and Le'a Malia Kanehe, "The BS in Access and Benefit Sharing," in* The Catch, *Beth Burrows, ed. [The Edmonds Institute, 2005], available at www.ipcb.org.*)

III. PROTECTION OF INDIGENOUS PEOPLES' RESOURCES & KNOWLEDGE

This new era of science and technology poses special challenges to the collective protection and management of genetic resources of Indigenous peoples. A lack of strong national protection laws requires Indigenous peoples to be proactive internationally and locally.

International Advocacy

In the international fora, Indigenous peoples have actively asserted their right of self-determination as the basis for our proprietary, inherent, and inalienable rights over our traditional knowledge and biological resources. This position is consistent with international human rights law, in particular, the right of permanent sovereignty over natural resources. For instance, in 1992, at the inception of the CBD, Indigenous peoples issued the Indigenous Peoples' Earth Charter, known as "The Kari-oca Declaration," at the Earth Summit. It states, in part,

We, the Indigenous peoples, maintain our inherent rights to self-determination. We have always had the right to decide our own forms of government, to use our own laws, to raise and educate our children, to our own cultural identity without interference. . . . We maintain our inalienable rights to our lands and territories, to all

our resources—above and below—and to our waters. We assert our ongoing responsibility to pass these on to the future generations.

Within the UN human rights arena, Indigenous peoples are actively asserting their inherent right to protect their cultural and natural resources as a part of the fundamental right of self-determination. A clear articulation of this assertion can be seen in Article 29 of the UN Draft Declaration on the Rights of Indigenous Peoples, which states, "Indigenous peoples are entitled to the recognition of the full ownership, control and protection of their cultural and intellectual property. They have the right to special measures to control, develop and protect their sciences, technologies and cultural manifestations, including human and other genetic resources, seeds, medicines, knowledge of the properties of fauna and flora, oral tradition, literatures, designs and visual and performing arts." (See Appendix.)

These calls for the recognition, respect and protection of our rights are repeated in international fora around the world, sometimes successfully, other times falling on deaf ears. Therefore, we must take proactive steps to defend and protect our peoples, territories, resources and knowledge under the traditional authority, Indigenous government, and at the community level.

Local Protection

Indigenous groups have now begun to assert their rights and to take proactive measures to protect themselves and their territories by actively controlling research. Several Indigenous nations, including the Navajo and Cherokee Nations, have established institutional review boards (IRB) modeled similarly to the human subjects review boards at major institutions. These tribal IRBs are designed to ensure that research projects uphold human rights protections, and to oversee other tribe-specific interests in relation to the research.

To support Indigenous nations that want to establish a legal mechanism to regulate research within their respective jurisdictions, the Indigenous Peoples Council on Biocolonialism (IPCB) developed the Indigenous Research Protection Act (IRPA). The IRPA serves as a model law to assist tribal governments in protecting their people and resources against unwanted research. The IRPA can be modified to meet specific cultural, political and legal situations, and includes a model research agreement. When an Indigenous group believes the research may be beneficial, the IRPA provides a regulatory framework to control the research process (*available at www.ipcb.org*).

CONCLUSION

The opposition by Indigenous peoples to a wide range of genetic research activity is founded on a critical analysis of the potentially negative impacts of genetic technologies on their lives and the natural world. Indigenous peoples worldwide have questioned the appropriateness of genetic engineering, denounced acts of biopiracy and asserted our rights to protect our communities and environments from gene hunters. Indigenous peoples' efforts and lifeways will continue to demonstrate a living alternative to an era of globalization that seeks to monopolize and commodify all of life's resources.

Box C: Code of Ethics of the International Society of Ethnobiology

One group of scientists that has acknowledged the damage that their own communities have inflicted upon indigenous peoples is the International Society of Ethnobiology (ISE). The following is their Code of Ethics, written in Belem, Brazil, in 1988, and meant to correct past performance and set out guidelines, processes and rules consistent with the desires of indigenous partners. Here is an edited version of their code.

PREAMBLE
It is acknowledged that much research has been undertaken in the past without the sanction or prior consent of indigenous and traditional peoples and that such research has resulted in wrongful expropriation of cultural and intellectual heritage rights of the affected peoples causing harm and violation of rights.

The ISE is committed to working in genuine partnership and collaboration with indigenous peoples, traditional societies and local communities to avoid these past injustices and build towards developing positive, beneficial and harmonious relationships in the field of ethnobiology.

The ISE recognises that culture and language are intrinsically connected to land and territory, and cultural and linguistic diversity are inextricably linked to biological diversity. Therefore, the right of Indigenous Peoples to the preservation and continued development of their cultures and languages and to the control of their lands, territories and traditional resources is key to the perpetuation of all forms of diversity on Earth.

PURPOSE
The Purpose of this Code of Ethics is:
 1. to optimise the outcomes and reduce as much as possible the adverse effects of research (in all its forms, including applied research and development work) and related activities of ethnobiologists that can disrupt or disenfranchise indigenous peoples, traditional societies

and local communities from their customary and chosen lifestyles; and

2. to provide a set of principles to govern the conduct of Ethnobiologists and all Members of the International Society of Ethnobiology engaged in or proposing to be engaged in research in all its forms, especially collation and use of traditional knowledge or collections of flora, fauna, or any other element found on community lands or territories.

The ISE recognises, supports and prioritises the efforts of indigenous peoples, traditional societies and local communities to undertake and own their research, collections, databases and publications. This Code is intended to enfranchise indigenous peoples, traditional societies and local communities conducting research within their own society, for their own use.

It is hoped that this Code of Ethics will also serve to guide ethnobiologists and other researchers, business leaders, policy makers, and others seeking meaningful partnerships with indigenous peoples, traditional societies and local communities and thus to avoid the perpetuation of past injustices to these peoples. The ISE recognises that, for such partnerships to succeed, all relevant research activities must be collaborative. Consideration must be given to the needs of all humanity, and to the maintenance of robust and vigorous scientific standards.

It is desirable that scientists, international citizens and organisations, and indigenous peoples and local communities collaborate to achieve the purpose of this Code of Ethics and the objectives of the ISE.

PRINCIPLES

The Preamble, Purpose and Principles ('the Principles') of the ISE Code of Ethics were adopted by resolution of the Annual General Meeting of the ISE held at Whakatane, Aotearoa/New Zealand on Saturday 28 November 1998.

The Principles of this Code are to embrace, support, and embody the many established principles and practices of international law and customary practice as expressed in various international instruments and declarations including, but not limited to, those documents referred to in Appendix 1 of this Code of Ethics. The following Principles are the fundamental assumptions that form this Code of Ethics.

1. Principle of Prior Rights This principle recognises that indigenous peoples, traditional societies, and local communities have prior, proprietary rights and interests over all air, land, and waterways, and the natural resources within them that these peoples have traditionally inhabited or used, together with all knowledge and intellectual property and traditional resource rights associated with such resources and their use.

2. Principle of Self-Determination This principle recognises that indigenous peoples, traditional societies and local communities have a right to self determination (or local determination for traditional and local communities) and that researchers and associated organisations will acknowledge and respect such rights in their dealings with these peoples and their communities.

3. Principle of Inalienability This principle recognises the inalienable rights of indigenous peoples, traditional societies and local communities in relation to their traditional territories and the natural resources within them and associated traditional knowledge. These rights are collective by nature but can include individual rights. It shall be for indigenous peoples, traditional societies and local communities to determine for themselves the nature and scope of their respective resource rights regimes.

4. Principle of Traditional Guardianship This principle recognises the holistic interconnectedness of humanity with the ecosystems of our Sacred Earth and the obligation and responsibility of indigenous peoples, traditional societies and local communities to preserve and maintain their role as traditional guardians of these ecosystems through the maintenance of their cultures, mythologies, spiritual beliefs and customary practices.

5. Principle of Active Participation This principle recognises the crucial importance of indigenous peoples, traditional societies and local communities to actively participate in all phases of the project from inception to completion, as well as in application of research results.

6. Principle of Full Disclosure This principle recognises that indigenous peoples, traditional societies and local communities are entitled to be fully informed about the nature, scope and ultimate purpose of the proposed research (including methodology, data collection, and the dissemination and application of results). This information is to be given in a manner that takes into consideration and actively engages with the body of knowledge and cultural preferences of these peoples and communities.

7. Principle of Prior Informed Consent and Veto This principle recognises that the prior informed consent of all peoples and their communities must be obtained before any research is undertaken. Indigenous peoples, traditional societies and local communities have the

Box C *(continued)*

right to veto any programme, project, or study that affects them. Providing prior informed consent presumes that all potentially affected communities will be provided complete information regarding the purpose and nature of the research activities and the probable results, including all reasonably foreseeable benefits and risks of harm (be they tangible or intangible) to the affected communities.

8. Principle of Confidentiality This principle recognises that indigenous peoples, traditional societies and local communities, at their sole discretion, have the right to exclude from publication and/or to have kept confidential any information concerning their culture, traditions, mythologies or spiritual beliefs. Furthermore, such confidentiality shall be guaranteed by researchers and other potential users. Indigenous and traditional peoples also have the right to privacy and anonymity.

9. Principle of Respect This principle recognises the necessity for researchers to respect the integrity, morality and spirituality of the culture, traditions and relationships of indigenous peoples, traditional societies, and local communities with their worlds, and to avoid the imposition of external conceptions and standards.

10. Principle of Active Protection This principle recognises the importance of researchers taking active measures to protect and to enhance the relationships of indigenous peoples, traditional societies and local communities with their environment and thereby promote the maintenance of cultural and biological diversity.

11. Principle of Precaution This principle acknowledges the complexity of interactions between cultural and biological communities, and thus the inherent uncertainty of effects due to ethnobiological and other research. The Precautionary Principle advocates taking proactive, anticipatory action to identify and to prevent biological

or cultural harms resulting from research activities or outcomes, even if cause-and-effect relationships have not yet been scientifically proven. The prediction and assessment of such biological and cultural harms must include local criteria and indicators, thus must fully involve indigenous peoples, traditional societies, and local communities.

12. Principle of Compensation and Equitable Sharing This principle recognises that indigenous peoples, traditional societies, and local communities must be fairly and adequately compensated for their contribution to ethnobiological research activities and outcomes involving their knowledge.

13. Principle of Supporting Indigenous Research This principle recognises, supports and prioritises the efforts of indigenous peoples, traditional societies, and local communities in undertaking their own research and publications and in utilising their own collections and data bases.

14. Principle of the Dynamic Interactive Cycle This principle holds that research activities should not be initiated unless there is reasonable assurance that all stages of the project can be completed from (a) preparation and evaluation, to (b) full implementation, to (c) evaluation, dissemination and return of results to the communities, to (d) training and education as an integral part of the project, including practical application of results. Thus, all projects must be seen as cycles of continuous and on-going dialogue.

15. Principle of Restitution This principle recognises that every effort will be made to avoid any adverse consequences to indigenous peoples, traditional societies, and local communities from research activities and outcomes and that, should any such adverse consequence occur, appropriate restitution shall be made.

Indigenous people and traditional farmers of the world have survived for centuries by protecting the biodiversity of their regions. This includes local knowledge of medicinal plants, and traditional seed varieties that have been passed through generations. Now, however, the WTO's Trade-Related Aspects of Intellectual Property Rights Agreement (TRIPS) is dealing a blow to these communities. Where small farms and indigenous peoples formerly enjoyed collective ownership of local biodiversity and knowledge—under various sui generis systems—TRIPS will open the way for global corporations to enter, steal and patent local seed varieties and plants for commercial purposes abroad. This erodes the rights of local producers to use this knowledge for community health and nutrition.

CHAPTER 9

TRIPS Agreement: From the Commons to Corporate Patents on Life

Vandana Shiva

Research Foundation for Science, Technology, and Natural Resource Policy

DURING THE NEGOTIATIONS on the General Agreement on Tariffs and Trade, the United States succeeded in forcing its own flawed patent system onto the world through the WTO. U.S. corporations had a major role, even admitting that they drafted and lobbied on behalf of the creation of the Trade-Related Aspects of Intellectual Property Rights Agreement (TRIPS). As a Monsanto spokesman said about the lobbying effort: "The industries and traders of world commerce have played simultaneously the role of the patients, the diagnosticians, and the prescribing physicians." By now, TRIPS has become the major "legal" means by which global corporations have been able to steal and patent the medicinal knowledge and the seeds of indigenous peoples throughout the world: global biopiracy.

TRIPS not only made U.S.-style intellectual property rights (IPR) laws global but also removed critical ethical and moral boundaries by including life forms and biodiversity as patentable subject matter. Living organisms and life forms that are self-creating, such as seeds, plants, herbs and animals were thus redefined as if they were machines and artifacts made and invented by the patentee; this despite the fact that the corporations made only minor genetic modifications in their labs—just enough to be redefined as "inventions." Intellectual property rights laws and patents then give the patent holder a monopolistic right to prevent others from making, using or selling these "inventions," even if the seeds were originally developed by local farmers. Seed saving by farmers was thus transformed from the sacred duty it had been for centuries to a criminal offense: stealing *corporate* "property." And all practices of *sui generis* ownership, that is, community-collective ownership of seeds and other forms of local biodiversity, were directly undermined. Article 27.3 (b) of the TRIPS agreement, which relates to patents on living resources, was established by the "Life Sciences" companies to confirm themselves as "Lords of Life."

Life Science corporations now claim patents on genes, plants, animals and seeds. Ciba Geigy and Sandoz have combined to form Novartis; Hoechst has joined with Rhone Poulenc to form Aventis (later acquired by Sanofi-Synthelabo); Zeneca has merged with Astra; Dupont has bought up Pioneer HiBred; and Monsanto now owns Cargill Seeds, DeKalb, Calgene, Agracetus, Delta and Pine Land, Holden, and Asgrow and

Seminis. Eighty percent of all genetically engineered seeds planted are Monsanto's "intellectual property." And Monsanto owns broad species patents on cotton, mustard, and soy beans—crops that were not "invented" or "created" by Monsanto but have been developed over centuries of innovation by farmers of India and East Asia working in close partnership with the biodiversity gifted by nature.

This process of patenting life forms is truly perverse—in many ways:

1. Ethical Perversion
Current IPR laws permit the claim that seeds, plants, sheep, cows, or human cell lines can be classified as "products of the mind" created by Monsanto, Novartis, Ian Wilmut or PPL. This ignores that living organisms have their own intrinsic self-organization. They make themselves, and hence cannot logically be reduced to the status of "inventions" and "creations" of patent holders. They cannot be "owned" as private property because they are our ecological kin, not just "genetic mines."

2. Criminalization of Saving and Sharing Seeds
Recognizing corporations as "owners" of seed through intellectual property rights actually converts the original farmers who developed the seed varieties into "thieves" when they save seed or share it with neighbors. Monsanto hires detectives to chase farmers who might be engaging in such "theft," and brings them to court, as they did the Canadian farmer Percy Schmeiser.

3. Encouragement of Biopiracy
Biopiracy is the term the global South now uses for the theft of biodiversity and indigenous knowledge through these patents. It deprives the South in three ways:

▲ It creates a false claim to novelty and invention, even when the knowledge of medicinal or other benefits of plants has actually evolved since ancient times. Biopiracy is intellectual theft, which robs Third World people of their creativity and their intellectual resources;

▲ It diverts scarce biological resources to monopoly control of corporations, depriving local communities and indigenous practitioners. Biopiracy is resource theft from the poorest two-thirds of humanity, who depend on biodiversity for their livelihoods and basic needs; and

▲ It creates market monopolies, excluding the original innovators from their rightful share of local, national and international markets. Instead of preventing this organized economic theft, WTO rules under TRIPS actually protect the powerful and punish the victims. In a dispute initiated by the United States against India, the WTO forced India to change its patent laws and grant exclusive marketing rights to foreign corporations on the basis of foreign patents. Since many of these patents are based on biopiracy, the WTO is in fact promoting piracy through patents.

Over time, the consequences of TRIPS for the South's biodiversity and southern people's—including indigenous peoples'—rights to their biodiversity will be severe. No one will be able to produce or reproduce patented agricultural, medicinal, or animal products freely, thus eroding the livelihoods of small producers and preventing the poor from using their own resources and knowledge to meet basic needs of health and nutrition. Royalties for the use of these patented items will have to be paid to the patentees, and unauthorized production will be penalized, thus further increasing the debt burden.

Indian farmers and traditional and indigenous practitioners all over the world will lose their market share in local, national and global markets. For example, the U.S. government granted a patent for the antidiabetic properties of *karela*, *jamun*, and *brinjal* to two nonresident Indians, Onkar S. Tomer and Kripanath Borah, and their colleague Peter Gloniski. The use of these substances for control of diabetes has been everyday knowledge and practice in India for ages. Their medical use was documented long ago in authoritative treatises like "Wealth of India," "Compendium of Indian Medicinal Plants" and "Treatise on Indian Medicinal Plants."

If there were only one or two cases of such false claims to corporate invention on the basis of biopiracy, they could be called an error. However, biopiracy is epidemic. *Neem, haldi, pepper, harar, bahera, amla, mustard, basmati, ginger, castor, jaramla, amaltas* and *new karela* and *jamun* have now all been patented. The problem is deep and systemic; it calls for a systemic change, not case-by-case challenges.

Some have suggested that biopiracy happens because native knowledge is not documented. That is far from true. Indigenous knowledge in India has been systematically documented, and

this in fact has made piracy easier. Even the folk knowledge, spread orally in local communities, deserves to be recognized as collective, cumulative innovation. The ignorance of such knowledge in the United States should not be allowed to convert corporate biopiracy into invention.

The potential costs of biopiracy to indigenous peoples and the Third World poor are very high, since two-thirds of the people in the South depend on free access to biodiversity for their livelihoods and needs. In India, 70 percent of seeds are saved or shared farmers' seed; 70 percent of healing is based on indigenous medicine using local plants. When corporations scour the earth to steal and control those indigenous genetic resources through patents, the poor are directly deprived.

To reverse this process means joining the international campaign for No Patents on Life, and demanding the cancellation of TRIPS.

Box D: Whose Common Property?

During the last negotiating round of the Convention on Biological Diversity (CBD), Ottawa 2002, global pharmaceutical and agricultural corporations strongly fought for the concept that biodiversity should be freely accessible for anyone, that it should be considered a "common heritage for all humankind." These resources should not be "locked-up" by the indigenous communities that nurtured and developed them.

This sounds altruistic until one considers that these are the same corporations that, once they have their hands on such resources, immediately move to separate them from the commons, to privatize, patent and monopolize them whenever they can, and to reserve all financial benefits to themselves. As for the medicinal benefits that might arise from these plants, now disembodied from the communities that nurtured them, they are

henceforth reserved for those people who can pay the commercial rates for them. *It would be hard to conceive of a more cynical stance.*

Indigenous and other traditional communities take the opposite view. These include millions of Third World farmers who have developed and shared useful seeds over centuries and continue to openly share them with each other via *sui generis* "community ownership," a true recognition and celebration of the values and practices of the commons.

Traditional farmers and indigenous peoples argue that the use of intellectual property rights regimes, such as the TRIPS (Trade-Related Aspects of Intellectual Property Rights Agreement) of the WTO, to legitimize the theft and expropriation of indigenous knowledge of

PART THREE

Diverse Impacts on Indigenous Peoples

Giant dam projects like the Tucurui in Brazil, which submerge hundreds of miles of indigenous lands, are only one kind of devastating infrastructure project now being built throughout the Amazon Basin to further resource development. Roads, canals, and oil pipelines are also being driven through native lands. Indigenous forests are being clear-cut to create giant new industrial agriculture projects—raising beef, soybeans, and other export crops grown by mega-agricultural corporations.

CHAPTER 10

Infrastructure Development in the South American Amazon

Janet Lloyd, Atossa Soltani, and Kevin Koenig
Amazon Watch

THROUGHOUT THE AMAZON, indigenous peoples are in the midst of undeclared resource wars, their lands either threatened or devastated by transnational corporations. Backed by complicit nation-states and the rules and pressures of the WTO, the IMF, and the World Bank, global corporate interests are driving new roads, pipelines, dams, and power lines deep into forest frontiers to exploit the remaining reserves of oil, minerals, and timber. The avalanche of industrial mega-projects in formerly inaccessible areas has increased significantly in recent years following the adoption of new, "relaxed" global trade and investment rules, which favor such options.

New infrastructure developments are being planned to link resource-rich forest frontiers to global markets. These projects snake through hundreds of miles of national parks, biospheres, and indigenous reserves, without consideration for the long-term consequences for the region's exceptional biodiversity, fragile ecosystems, and vulnerable indigenous cultures. Furthermore, much of the so-called development is accompanied by buildups of military and security forces that intimidate people who stand in the way and violate their basic rights.

Three decades of such large-scale industrial development projects in the Amazon have brought devastating consequences for the indigenous peoples of the region. In response, indigenous peoples are rising up in a battle for cultural, social, and economic rights. The U'wa people of Colombia, the Achuar and Shuar of Ecuador and Peru, and others are rejecting the interventions of economic globalization while demanding basic and universal rights: self-determination, land preservation, cultural integrity, and respect for the earth.

Shuar women will not die on [our] knees. We will die fighting until every last drop of blood is gone.
    —Shuar statement on resistance to oil companies,
August 24, 1999

We are seeking an explanation for this "progress" that goes against life. We are demanding that this kind of progress stop, that oil exploitation in the heart of the Earth is halted, that the deliberate bleeding of the Earth stop.
    —Statement from the U'wa people, August 8, 1998

IGNORING INDIGENOUS RIGHTS

When asserting their rights, indigenous peoples in the Amazon region point to the provisions enshrined in the International Labor Organization (ILO) Convention and in international doctrines such as the UN Draft Declaration on the Rights of Indigenous Peoples. These include the right to maintain their ways of life; to own, control and manage ancestral communal lands; to participate fully in decision-making; and to "free and informed consent" on projects that affect indigenous lives, culture, and lands. Though nearly all South American governments have ratified the ILO Convention, they often fail to enforce these rights.

What little consultation governments and corporations actually offer to indigenous stakeholders is often only informational in nature. For the most part, indigenous peoples cannot exercise the right to accept or reject a development project that affects even their legally titled lands. Meanwhile, governments usually exclude or ignore indigenous rights to subsurface oil or minerals and routinely grant them to private companies as concessions.

Traditional forms of indigenous authority are also ignored. Companies use divide-and-conquer tactics to pit communities against each other and weaken opposition to development plans. For example, companies operating Peru's Camisea gas development project flouted the jurisdiction of community authorities and negotiated with each community separately, thus weakening their collective bargaining power.

All too often, government and military representatives pressure indigenous leaders to sign development contracts under duress, knowing full well that the leaders have little information about project realities and even less experience in negotiating with powerful multinational companies.

In Ecuador in March 2001, the Italian company AGIP Oil signed an agreement with six Huaorani communities offering to compensate them with 50 kilograms of rice and sugar, a bag of salt, 2 footballs, 15 plates and cups, 34 cans of tuna and sardines, some medicines, a radio, a battery and solar panel, and $3,500 to build a schoolroom in return for building six oil wells on Huaorani lands. The agreement with AGIP Oil came after years of pressure from developers. The following Huaorani statement to Maxus, another oil company, shows how painful such decisions are for Amazon peoples:

> We Huaorani are a people who have lived in the Ecuadorian Amazon since the beginning; we cannot count for how long, since the world was born. In our home are the bones of our grandparents, and we do not want the company to come and destroy them. We are the land, subsoil and even the air. Everything is our home. Where there is wind we are breathing. Our home is like our body. If a tractor comes, it destroys the earth, and it destroys our skin. The earth hurts just like our skin. We have a good life, we are healthy, we have our culture. We do not need to negotiate with the company for its aid, we do not need the things that Maxus is offering us. We do not want to exchange our life for a school or a plane. We do not want to lose our territory.

The consequences of industrial development for the Amazon's ecology and peoples are predictable: loss of ancestral lands to colonists; deforestation, natural habitat degradation, and destruction; pollution and poor health; and social disruption and cultural breakdown of indigenous communities. Global consequences include climatic instability and irreversible loss of biodiversity. In the remote rainforest frontiers of Peru, Brazil, Ecuador, and Colombia, which house the Amazon's last isolated indigenous groups, threats from industrial activities such as oil exploration and logging are especially serious, given these populations' extreme vulnerability to disease epidemics.

In the following sections we present a brief run-down on some effects of this invasion.

IMPACTS ON TRADITIONAL CULTURE

Indigenous peoples' lands are inextricably linked to their cultural identity. When land and identity are bound together through cultural practices and beliefs, loss of land ownership can disintegrate cultural identity. At the Buenos Aires Biodiversity Convention in 1996, indigenous participants issued the following statement:

> The intimate knowledge about biological abundance that indigenous peoples have had through our ancient evolution forms part of our cultures. Therefore, an inviolable interdependency exists: nature is a vital element for the survival of our cultures; and these cultures have a vast knowledge about nature vital to the survival of biodiversity. Our cultural existence is empty, it becomes folklore, if our harmonious relationship with nature is broken; that is to say, if indigenous peoples are not recognised as part of biodiversity.

Among Amazonian indigenous peoples, ceremonial life is usually closely tied to agricultural and forest harvest cycles. Changes to agricultural practices often cause the loss of ritual traditions. Competition over increasingly scarce resources can exacerbate community divisions and erode social cohesion. Unnaturally high levels of sickness and death within a closely knit group with a strong sense of communal interdependency can cause grave psychological trauma and a disintegration of cosmological beliefs. Equally, community authority figures accustomed to managing crises within a group are often unable to respond adequately to impending threats. Therefore, the dissolution of social and political structures can occur, further weakening the ties that bind such people together.

In addition, forced contact with outside groups such as loggers and colonists can result in exposure to racial and cultural discrimination and possibly violent conflict. A sense of fear and intimidation among a group of people aggressively targeted because of their race and culture inhibits the continuing reproduction of a positive cultural identity.

The case of Ecuador's Tetete people is illustrative. By the 1980s, the impact of Texaco oil operations in the northern Ecuadorian Amazon had wiped out the Tetete. Disease killed many individuals, and the social and cultural consequences of the loss of lands and resources led remaining group members to disperse, abandoning their lands and identities.

Ecuadorian leader Valerio Grefa calls the assault on indigenous peoples and cultures by multinational companies and governments an assault on all life:

> We have come to talk on behalf of all the lives of the rainforest and the woods, but most of all on behalf of those that are no longer here: the beings of the waters, of fertility, of the crops, of abundance, of medicine. Of the gods who maintain the life of the rainforest, the rivers and the lakes, who have abandoned their world, where the trees and the plants disappear and do not appear again. We come on behalf of Life to end this centuries-old war that tries to finish off Nature. It is we who have preserved, conserved, and developed the biological diversity that now exists in abundance in our lands and territories. (Valerio Grefa, 1996)

> Our cultural principles include the defense of the right to a dignified life, respect for Mother Earth and the environment. These are essential and sacred elements that we should leave as an inheritance to our children, grandchildren, and their descendents. (U'wa Statement on Occidental Oil Company's Withdrawal, May 7, 2002)

LAND INVASIONS

Megaprojects, such as roads and pipelines, open up access to otherwise inaccessible forest frontiers, where vast resources fuel global corporate activity. Such access makes possible an influx of migrants who seek land and hope for a better life. Many come looking for work as laborers or wishing to sell their goods to the company's labor force. Access roads also bring loggers looking for valuable hardwood trees, as well as wildcat miners and wildlife poachers, who often increase violence, crime, and prostitution.

To construct a new pipeline, new access roads must be punched through pristine forests. After new roads are built, a new labor force that came to work on the projects settles in the frontiers, grabbing what they see as "empty lands." In the case of the Coari-Urucu gas pipeline in Brazil, the workers' camps consisted of nearly a thousand people. After construction finished in 1998, some seven thousand workers and vendors settled in and around the local towns.

These new migrants threaten the resource base and the very livelihood of indigenous peoples who depend on the forest for their survival. The result is depleted stocks of game, fish, and edible forest flora, and the destruction or contamination of local water supplies. Increased competition for agricultural lands and forest medicinal plants also jeopardizes the health of local populations. Inevitably, conflicts arise over use of land and resources. For example, gold miners seeking to extract resources from Yanomami lands have repeatedly attacked the people. In 1993, sixteen Yanomami died after being kicked, shot, and hacked with machetes in an assault by miners on the village of Haximu on the Venezuela-Brazil border.

Large landowners, cattle ranchers, and corrupt authorities who view indigenous people as an obstacle to their economic self-interest fuel these conflicts. Weak judicial and political systems in remote frontier areas foster a permanent atmosphere of tension, violence, and institutional oppression.

Human rights abuses inflicted on the Waimiri-Atroari peoples over the paving of the last section of the Manaus-Caracas road (BR-174) demonstrate how state representatives both tolerate and engage in abuses of indigenous rights when development projects are at stake. In the 1970s and 1980s, the BR-174 road passed through 120 kilometers of Waimiri-Atroari lands. The Brazilian army used intimidation tactics that included beating, torture, and killing of the Waimiri-Atroari. After the disappearance of two thousand individuals and the loss of 80 percent of their lands, the Waimiri-Atroari gave their approval on the understanding that an environmental protection plan would be implemented for their lands. The so-called compensation and protection plan was finally put into effect in the mid to late 1990s.

FORCED RELOCATION

Hydroelectric dam projects, principally in the Brazilian Amazon, have directly resulted in the forced relocation of thousands of indigenous and riverine peoples with devastating impacts on their health and cultures.

In the early 1980s, the Parakana people of the northeastern Brazilian Amazon were forcibly resettled on ten occasions to make way for the Tucurui Hydroelectric Scheme. Even before the Tucurui dam, the Parakana had experienced forced resettlement. In the initial stages of contact in the 1970s, the government ordered them to abandon large areas of their ancestral homelands after diseases introduced by workers building the Transamazonica Highway greatly reduced their numbers.

In 1977, a new resettlement scheme was developed to remove the Parakana from areas to be flooded by the Tucurui Hydroelectric Scheme. Chaotic management and lengthy delays in the resettlement process led to groups of Parakana being moved around to many locations. Disorganized relocation methods prevented the Parakana from carrying out normal subsistence farming activities, and the subsequent loss of food caused malnutrition and increased dependency. Meanwhile, delays in flooding the area brought migrant farmers and logging companies onto the abandoned lands. After flooding, these migrants pushed into the new Parakana lands, causing more land conflicts. Compensation funds destined for the Parakana were only partially released.

ILLNESS AND CONTAMINATION

Toxic pollution caused by oil production and mining has a devastating impact on the health of indigenous peoples who drink and fish from the rivers. The dumping of oil and chemically treated drilling wastes into rivers and aquatic systems results in prolific and persistent contamination. Concentrated levels of heavy metals and some carcinogenic hydrocarbons are dispersed throughout the food chain and the water supply of local inhabitants.

In the oil-producing regions of Ecuador's northern Amazon, thirty years of Texaco oil operations have left a dangerous toxic legacy for indigenous and *campesino* communities. Oil and toxic waste spills and seepages and toxic air pollution have caused deterioration of terrestrial and aquatic ecosystems. Indigenous peoples who live near, fish in, bathe in, and drink from the region's rivers report a high incidence of cancer, skin rashes and sores, stomach ailments, and respiratory problems.

Recent investigations indicate that cancer rates among indigenous and *campesino* communities living in Ecuador's oil-producing areas of Sucumbios and Orellana provinces are three times higher than the national average. For certain cancers, this figure rises dramatically: the risk of throat cancer is thirty times greater than the national average; the risk of kidney and skin cancer is fifteen times greater; and the risk of stomach cancer is five times greater.

This story is repeated throughout oil-producing areas of the Amazon. In October 2000, a Pluspetrol oil spill on the Marañón River in the Peruvian Amazon contaminated Peru's largest protected area, the Pacaya Samiria Reserve. The area's twenty thousand inhabitants, many from the Cocamas-Cocamillas people, suffered diarrhea and skin diseases and saw their food and water supply decimated by toxic pollution. Many medicines promised by Pluspetrol never reached affected communities, and food provided by the company did not meet basic needs.

The health impacts of large projects such as dams can be equally serious. The vast expanses of stagnant water that form Brazil's Tucurui Reservoir led to a plague of Mansonia mosquitoes and a dramatic increase in malaria among local peoples. Cases of waterborne diseases such as river blindness and schistosomiasis rose. Forced resettlement also had damaging consequences for human health. Formerly dispersed indigenous groups were forced to live in settlements where they were exposed to new diseases, such as intestinal infections and influenza, which thrive in dense populations. Poor levels of official health care, an irregular system of vaccinations, and unsuitable government-provided medicines led to many needless deaths among indigenous peoples of the Tucurui area.

For peoples living in voluntary isolation, the health impacts of industrial development projects are particularly severe. The introduction of diseases to which they have no immunity can be devastating. Throughout the Amazon region, there are many accounts of uncontacted populations being decimated by curable illnesses such as malaria, pneumonia, and smallpox. In the Camisea region of Peru in the mid 1980s, Shell Oil conducted preliminary exploration for oil and gas reserves. The exploratory work led to an influx of loggers. The contact from oil workers and loggers exposed the Nahua to whooping cough, smallpox, and influenza. An estimated 50 percent of the population died. Most of the rest of the group fled the area.

> We are unconditionally saying no to oil exploration on our land. Our rivers, our forests, which are the source of life for us, for our children, and for our children's children, cannot be bought. We are demanding that our right to develop our communities in a sustainable manner be respected.
>
> —Tito Puanchir, Shuar leader, Ecuador, 1999

> [Our] decision . . . is to not permit the penetration of oil, mining, or logging companies in our territory. . . . The Achuar have taken this radical decision because we have observed the environmental and social impact of twenty years of irrational oil exploitation in the north of our Amazon, and because we believe in the options for sustainable development.
>
> —Achuar organization FINAE, in a letter to the general manager of ARCO Ecuador, 1998

FORCED DEPENDENCY

Industrial development projects disrupt the traditional practices of indigenous peoples in myriad ways. When their natural resource base is reduced, indigenous communities are forced to abandon traditional economic activities and engage in the global economy to acquire food. As a result, they must either grow cash-crop exports to exchange for food or else engage in wage labor far from their communities.

When indigenous peoples can no longer rely on natural resources to sustain them, a vicious cycle of economic dependency ensues. Time spent on export-crop production for global markets leads to further neglect of normal subsistence activities such as agriculture, fishing, hunting, and gathering, which in turn further reduce economic independence.

Changes in economic activity lead to the reordering of indigenous society. With men spending greater amounts of time away from the community to acquire food, women must cope by themselves with all agricultural and domestic work. In addition, since some community members are more successful than others in managing the market economy, economic inequalities and social divisions appear in formerly egalitarian communities. Many indigenous communities complain that after infrastructure projects open up lands occupied by traditionally isolated peoples, their youth begin to desert the communities.

Megaprojects also bring sexual harassment and assaults upon indigenous women. After Shell ended its exploratory activities in Peru's Camisea area, a large number of teenage mothers were abandoned to raise workers' children alone. Child prostitution is also common around such projects, further adding to the degradation of traditional societies.

Contact with imported project workers introduces other social and environmental problems, such as alcohol abuse, into indigenous communities. The construction of the Bolivia-Cuiaba gas pipeline was a particularly egregious case: The impact on affected communities included disruption of communities by drunken workers, alcohol abuse, improper disposal of solid and liquid waste, illegal hunting, bioprospecting, logging, erosion, and destruction of drinking water supplies, among other dire results.

Traditional hunting in Inuit communities is being severely impacted by climate change. Where Arctic ice was once five feet thick, in many places it has been reduced to five or six inches, and in some places it has disappeared. Elsewhere in the north, a rapidly melting tundra is creating muddy conditions, causing homes to sink or slide. The survival of the northernmost communities is now threatened.

CHAPTER 11

Climate Change in the Arctic

Sheila Watt-Cloutier
(Inuk)
Inuit Circumpolar Conference (ICC)

Sheila Watt-Cloutier, Chair of the ICC, represents the interests of the 155,000 Inuit, whose peoples have lived in Alaska, northern Canada, Greenland, and Chukotka, Russia, for millennia. Her comments here are excerpted from testimonies before the U.S. Senate Committee on Commerce, Science, and Transportation hearings on climate change (chaired by Sen. John McCain) in spring 2004.

DISCUSSION OF CLIMATE CHANGE frequently focuses on political, economic, and technical issues rather than human impacts and consequences. But Inuit and other northerners are already experiencing the direct impacts of human-induced climate change, and we face dramatic problems and social and cultural dislocation in coming years.

For generations uncounted, Inuit have closely observed the environment and have accurately predicted weather enabling us to travel safely on the sea ice to hunt seals, whales, walrus, and polar bears. We don't hunt for sport or recreation, we hunt to put food on the table. Most of the world goes to the supermarket; Inuit go to the sea ice. Eating what we hunt is at the very core of what it means to be Inuit. When we can no longer hunt on the sea ice and eat what we hunt, we will no longer exist as a people.

RELOCATION

Several Inuit villages have already been so damaged by global warming that relocation, at a cost of hundreds of millions of dollars, is now our only option. The harm we have suffered from melting sea ice and thawing permafrost includes:

▲ Damage to houses, roads, airports, and pipelines;
▲ Eroded landscape, unstable slopes, and landslides;
▲ Contaminated drinking water;
▲ Coastal losses to erosion of up to one hundred feet per year; and
▲ Melting natural ice cellars for food storage.

In Shishmaref, Alaska, a small Inuit village on the Chukchi Sea, seven houses have had to be relocated, three have fallen into the sea, and engineers predict that the entire village of six hundred houses could be swallowed by the sea within the next few decades. Shishmaref's airport runway has almost been met by rising seawater, and its fuel tank farm, which seven years ago was three hundred feet from the edge of a seaside bluff, is now only thirty-five feet from the bluff. The town dump, which has seawater within eight feet, could pollute the nearby marine environment for years if inundated. Advancing seawater has contaminated Shishmaref's drinking water supply.

Similar changes to the environment have been documented in northern Canada. Residents of Sachs Harbour, a tiny community in the Canadian Beaufort Sea region, report:

▲ Melting permafrost causing beach slumping and increased erosion;
▲ Increased snowfall;
▲ Longer seasons during which the sea is free of ice;
▲ New species of birds such as robins, pin-tailed ducks, and fish-barn owls (Inuit don't have barns!) invading the region;
▲ Invasions of mosquitoes and black flies;
▲ Unpredictable sea ice conditions; and
▲ Glaciers melting, creating torrents in place of streams.

Plans are well under way to relocate certain communities. Climate change is not just a theory to inhabitants of the Arctic; it is a stark and dangerous reality. Human-induced climate change is undermining the ecosystem upon which Inuit depend for our physical and cultural survival. Emission of greenhouse gases from cars and factories threatens the ability of those who reside in the Arctic to live as we have always done—in harmony with a fragile, vulnerable, and sensitive environment.

ARCTIC HARBINGER

The Arctic is of vital importance in the global debate on how to deal with climate change; it is a barometer of the planet's environmental health. Following a 2002 trip to the Arctic, the UK environment minister pointed out that what happens in the world happens first in the Arctic. Inuit, the people who live farther north than anyone else, are the canary in the global coal mine.

Inuit hunters and elders have for years reported changes to the environment, which are now supported by American, British, and European computer models that conclude climate change is amplified in high latitudes.

Science has in recent years caught up with Inuit observations. In 2003, the Arctic Climate Impact Assessment (ACIA) released the world's most comprehensive regional climate change assessment. The ACIA was prepared by more than 250 scientists from fifteen countries and chaired by the United States. The following are two of its key conclusions:

1. Marine species dependent on sea ice—including polar bears, ice-living seals, walrus, and some marine birds—are very likely to decline, with some facing extinction.

2. For Inuit, warming is likely to disrupt or even destroy our hunting and food-sharing culture as reduced sea ice causes population decline or extinction of the animals we depend on. By 2070 to 2090, year-round sea ice will be limited to a small portion of the Arctic Ocean around the North Pole. The rest of the Arctic will be ice-free in summer.

Suicide rates among Inuit are the highest in North America. Many of our people have resorted to destructive behaviors as they attempt to make sense of the modern world. Those who find serenity often do so by going back, as we say, "onto the land," to be inspired by the wisdom of generations of Inuit who lived at peace with the land. If climate change takes that source of wisdom away from us, just as we are coming through our struggle with modernization, then I profoundly fear for my people. Climate change will be the last straw. To an outside eye, the Arctic environment seems harsh and unforgiving, but to us Inuit it has provided all we need to thrive sustainably. Yet, with these dramatic changes, the reverse is occurring, and the changes to our climate and our environment will bring about the end of the Inuit culture.

Climate change in the Arctic is not just an environmental issue with unwelcome economic consequences. It is a matter of livelihood, food, and individual and cultural survival. It is a human issue. The Arctic is not "wilderness" or a "frontier"; it is our home and homeland.

WHAT CAN WE DO?

What can Inuit do about this global situation? We refuse to play the role of powerless victim. Responses to climate change have split the nations of the world. Our plight and the Arctic assessment show the compelling case for global unity and clarity of purpose to avert a future that is not ordained.

We are not asking the world to take a backward economic step. All we are saying is that governments must develop their economies using appropriate technologies that limit significantly emissions of greenhouse gases. Short-term business interests won't accede to this unless governments around the world require it. Inuit and other northerners are at peril because some governments are taking a short-term view favored by some businesses. This must change.

What can Inuit do to convince the world to take long-term action, which will have to go far beyond Kyoto? How do we convince the major emitters, such as the United States, of the risks we face in the Arctic? How can we bring some clarity of purpose and focus to a debate that seems mired in technical arguments and competing economic ideologies?

We believe one route is to look at the international human rights regime that is in place to protect peoples from cultural extinction—the very situation facing Inuit. ICC is examining various regimes. We conclude that the 1948 American Declaration on the Rights and Duties of Man, supported by the Inter-American Commission

on Human Rights, may provide an effective means for us to defend our culture and way of life.

The commission can be invited to Alaska and northern Canada to speak with Inuit and other northerners to find out what climate change means in the Arctic. ICC believes it would be internationally significant if global climate change were debated and examined in the arena of human rights—an arena that many governments, particularly those in the developed world, take seriously.

Other steps include using the ACIA circumpolar assessment to educate governments and industry about the long-term consequences of climate change, and enabling indigenous peoples of the circumpolar Arctic and residents of the small island-states threatened by climate change in the Pacific, Caribbean, and elsewhere to develop political and public education strategies to persuade states to reduce emissions of greenhouse gases.

Inuit have lived in the Arctic for millennia. Our culture and economy reflect the land and all that it gives. We are connected to the land. Our understanding of who we are—our age-old knowledge and wisdom—comes from the land. It is our struggle to thrive in the harshest environment that has given us the answers we need to survive in the modern world. That outlook, a respectful human outlook that sees connection to everything, should inform the debate on climate change.

Inuit remain intimately connected with each other and with the land. Is it not to reestablish that connection that we are all here? Is it not because people have lost the connection between themselves and their neighbors, between their actions and the environment, that we find ourselves trying to come to grips with climate change? With the utmost humility, all I can say is that the world's decision makers should come to the Arctic and live with us for a while. We have a lot to teach the world about getting along together and respecting the land.

A recent launch (2002) of a U.S. Interceptor missile from Kwajalein atoll in the central Pacific, part of the "Star Wars" program. To make way for the tests, thousands of Indigenous islanders who made their livelihoods fishing within the wildlife-rich lagoon were forced off Kwajalein to the small, barely habitable island of Ebbeye. They now live there in crowded slum conditions, unable to go home. Star Wars testing is the latest iteration of U.S. policy in the Marshall Islands, which began over a half-century ago with the atomic tests at Bikini and Enewetak atolls, whose peoples have still not returned home and have suffered horrific illness from radiation and deprivation. By doing these tests in faraway Pacific islands, the United States has avoided media scrutiny and public outrage.

CHAPTER 12

A-Bombs to Star Wars—
The Sixty-Years War on Marshall Islanders

Zohl dé Ishtar
University of Queensland

LIVING ON SMALL ISLANDS in the middle of the Pacific Ocean, the Indigenous people of the Republic of the Marshall Islands have for decades borne the brunt of the U.S. drive to develop nuclear weapons. The islands' geographical isolation, far from the focus of the world's media and the majority of social justice movements, has given the United States a mantle of secrecy to develop its nuclear bombs, missile delivery systems, and, more recently, space warfare technology—"Star Wars." This nuclear playground has violated the health of the Marshallese people, contaminated their ancestral lands and waters, and robbed them of their political and economic freedoms.

The U.S. government has intentionally developed its nuclear arsenal in the Marshall Islands, hidden from world attention. Few people outside the Pacific region are aware that the Marshall Islands even exist, or that U.S. preparations for nuclear war and global domination are currently, and have long been, played out upon the lands and lives of this small, peaceful, matrilineal nation.

I. ATOMIC BOMBING OF BIKINI AND ENEWETAK

In the twelve years between 1946 and 1958, the United States detonated sixty-six nuclear bombs in Bikini and Enewetak atolls, small rings of islands in the northern Marshall Islands. In March 1946, in preparation for "Operation Crossroads," all 167 residents of Bikini were relocated from their resource-rich atoll to the solitary and infertile sandbar island of Rongerik. In May of that year, the residents of Enewetak, Rongelap, and Wotho atolls were also temporarily relocated. The operation began with two bomb tests on Bikini, each equal in size to the bomb dropped on Hiroshima. On June 30, 1946, the world's first post–World War II nuclear bomb was detonated on Bikini atoll.

One year later, in July 1947, the Marshall Islands (along with other Micronesian nations under U.S. colonization) became the United Nations' only Strategic Trust Territory under U.S. administration. The Trust obligated the United States to *"promote the development of the inhabitants of the trust territory towards self-government or independence as may be appropriate ... and to this end shall ... promote the economic advancement of the inhabitants ... encourage the development of fisheries, agriculture and industries; protect the inhabitants against the loss of their lands and resources."*

Yet, in December 1947, the U.S. government removed the people of Enewetak from their homeland once again and relocated them to Ujelang atoll. This cleared the way for Operation Sandstone, yet another series of three atomic tests.

Relocation and Radioactivity

In March 1948—nearly two years after their relocation to Rongerik—the Bikinians, on the verge of starvation, were finally taken off the island. They were relocated to Kwajalein and then to Kili, a single island with no protected lagoon or harbor, which made fishing impossible. Still more atomic tests were conducted on Enewetak in 1951 and 1952, including the detonation of the first hydrogen device. The hydrogen bomb was 10.4 megatons, or 750 times larger than the bomb dropped on Hiroshima. This test, known simply as "Mike," vaporized an entire island.

On March 1, 1954, despite weather reports indicating the wind was blowing toward inhabited islands, the United States detonated its first deliverable hydrogen bomb above Bikini atoll. The bomb, known as "Bravo," was one thousand times the strength of the bomb dropped on Hiroshima. Fallout ash covered Rongelap and Ailinginae atolls, and a fallout "mist" enveloped Utirik and other islands. U.S. meteorologists stationed on Rongerik were exposed to the fallout. The United States directed its naval ships out of the anticipated fallout zone prior to the test, but it was forty-eight hours before the Rongelap people were evacuated. By that time, they were suffering from nausea, vomiting, and rashes. The Utirik people, who were similarly affected, were not removed from their island until another twenty-four hours had passed. The islanders were taken to the U.S. naval base at Kwajalein atoll for

observation, where they began suffering from burns, hair loss, and other illnesses.

The U.S. Atomic Energy Commission (AEC) responded to media alarm by releasing a press statement announcing that some Marshallese had been "unexpectedly exposed to some radioactivity. There were no burns. All were reported well." On March 7, 1954, however, a secret medical study, the "Study of Response of Human Beings Exposed to Significant Beta and Gamma Radiation Due to Fallout from High Yield Weapons," published the results of an evaluation of the islanders' health.

In April 1954, the secret committee advised that the Rongelap people who had been exposed by the Bravo tests had been so heavily contaminated that they should never be exposed to beta or gamma radiation "for [the] rest of [their] natural lives." On April 29, a U.S. Department of Defense report calculated that the people of Ailuk atoll had received a significant dose of radiation, but advised the U.S. government against relocating them because of the difficulties of evacuating four hundred inhabitants. In May, the Utirik Islanders returned home after U.S. officials guaranteed that the Utirik islands were only slightly contaminated and safe for habitation.

Cash Payments

Seventeen more nuclear bombs, including several hydrogen bombs, were detonated on Enewetak and Bikini beginning in May 1956. In December of that year, the United States awarded compensation to the Enewetak people living on Ujelang for the contamination of their islands. The Enewetak Islanders were given US$25,000 in cash, and a US$150,000 collective trust fund. The Bikinians living on Kili were given $25,000 in cash and a $300,000 trust fund, yielding $15 per person per year. Neither atoll was safe for habitation. The islanders were exiled on inhospitable islands facing food shortages and starvation, struggling to maintain hope of returning to their ancestral lands.

In July 1957, despite lingering radiation, the United States declared Rongelap safe for habitation and encouraged the Rongelap people to return home. The Department of Energy's Brookhaven National Laboratory released an internal report explaining the logic behind its encouragement: *"Even though the radioactive contamination of Rongelap Island is considered perfectly safe for human habitation, the levels of activity are higher than those found in other inhabited locations in the world. The habitation of these people on the islands will afford most valuable ecological radiation data on human beings."*

Stillbirths and Cancer

In May 1958, an additional series of thirty-two tests began, including several hydrogen bomb tests. By August 18, 1958, when the United States exploded its last nuclear device in the Marshalls, the Rongelap people were experiencing increasing ill health due to radiation exposure. According to Suliana Sitwatibau of the Foundation of the Peoples of the South Pacific International and Rev. B. David Williams of the General Board of Global Ministries: "In 1958, the rate of stillbirths . . . and miscarriages . . . among Rongelap women rose to more than twice the rate of unexposed Marshallese women for the first four years following their exposure in 1954." In 1963, Rongelap people exposed to the 1954 Bravo test began to develop thyroid tumors and experience a higher rate of growth retardation among children born after Bravo was dropped. By 1966, 52 percent of children on Rongelap who were under ten years when exposed to the Bravo test, as well as 35 percent of the total population, had developed thyroid abnormalities.

In 1968, the AEC announced Bikini atoll was safe for human habitation. Despite assurances from the AEC that there was "virtually no radiation left" and no "discernible effect on either plant or animal life," in October 1972, the Bikini Council rejected the prospect of returning en masse to their homeland. Several families, however, did return to Bikini, and others followed. In November

1972, Rongelap's Lekoj Anjain died of myelogenous leukemia at the National Cancer Institute in Bethesda, Maryland. He was one year old when he was exposed to the Bravo test. In 1973, an AEC draft report, not publicly released, determined that Bravo fallout had contaminated eighteen atolls and islands, including Kwajalein and Majuro, the capital island. *That year, Brookhaven National Laboratory reported that 69 percent of Rongelapese children (twenty out of twenty-nine) under ten years old at the time of the Bravo test had developed thyroid tumors.*

Meanwhile, the same medical scenario was unfolding for Bikinians. In June 1975, the U.S. Department of the Interior reported that Bikini had "higher levels of radioactivity than originally thought." That August, the AEC reported that Bikini's ground wells were radioactive and prohibited consumption of local foods. Low levels of plutonium were found in the urine of Bikinians who had returned to their homeland, but the U.S. Department of Energy (DOE) did not consider this to be "radiologically significant." In October, the Bikinians filed a lawsuit demanding a complete radiological survey of Bikini and other islands. In 1976, the DOE repeated its medical survey of the Rongelapese, again with alarming findings. But once again, it did not alert the Rongelap people.

Cleanup

In July 1976, the U.S. Congress approved $20 million for a nuclear cleanup of Enewetak atoll. Beginning in May 1977, the cleanup scraped over 100,000 cubic yards of topsoil off the island. The soil, together with contaminated debris from the testing operations, was dumped in a bomb crater on Runit Island. The crater was then sealed with a dome of cement.

In June 1977, the DOE found that radiation ingested by Bikini inhabitants was excessive, yet 139 Bikinians continued to live on Bikini Island. According to Marshall Islands journalist Giff Johnson, the United States was unprepared to give up what it considered to be "the only global source of data on humans" regarding plutonium ingestion. The department advised that the Bikini residents be repatriated from the island "within 90 days." In August 1978, a DOE survey of the northern Marshalls found that in addition to Bikini, Enewetak, Rongelap, and Utirik, ten other atolls and islands had been contaminated by the larger detonations. In September 1978, Bikini residents were relocated from their homelands and returned to the site of their decades-long exile on Kili Island.

In March 1980, with the cleanup of Enewetak completed, the Enewetak Islanders began to return to the southern islands in the atoll. The northern islands were still considered too radioactive for habitation. In 1981, the DOE again found the contamination of the Rongelap people to be extreme. Again, the islanders were not informed.

The Rongelap and Bikini Islanders were not alone in their experiences with the U.S. nuclear program. In December 1984, following a five-year study, the U.S. National Radiological Survey reported that almost half the Marshall Islands had been contaminated by the U.S. nuclear weapons testing program. According to Sitwatibau and Williams, *"Radioactive contamination 130 times above normal levels is detected at a testing point 502 kilometers west of Bikini. A Japanese government-sponsored scientific team sampling ocean water and marine life reports that radioactive contaminants are found in the ocean from the northern Marshalls westward almost to the Mariana Islands, some 4,800 kilometers away."*

In May 1985, confronted with increasing rates of illness resulting from nuclear contamination of their islands, the Rongelap people decided to relocate themselves to small Mejatto Island in Kwajalein atoll. The move was an attempt to secure a future for their children. As Darlene Keju-Johnson said, "Their bottom line is: 'We care about our children's future' . . . Their children came first. They know that they are contam-

inated. They know that they'll be dying out soon. They are dying now—slowly."

In January 1994, U.S. representative George Miller wrote to then president Bill Clinton saying the Rongelap people believed they had been used as "guinea pigs" by the U.S. military. Miller added: "The findings of the thyroid survey are disturbing . . . even if only 50 percent of the survey results are verified . . . the incidence rate is still significantly higher, by a factor of one hundred, than the rate of thyroid cancer found anywhere else in the world."

II. "STAR WARS" ON KWAJALEIN AND EBEYE

The Rongelap people's exodus to the small island of Mejatto in Kwajalein atoll was an attempt to give their children a future. However, relocating to Kwajalein was like jumping out of the frying pan and into the fire. In 1958, when the United States moved its nuclear testing program away from the Marshall Islands to Kalama (a.k.a. Johnston atoll), Kwajalein atoll became "the primary [U.S.] range for testing the accuracy of intercontinental ballistic missiles and developing anti-ballistic missile systems."

The Marshall Islands occupy an unenviable position at the center of the Pentagon's arc of power, which sweeps across the vast northern Pacific. Kwajalein has been so essential to U.S. development of ballistic missile delivery systems that, according to Giff Johnson, it "may have contributed more to the arms race than any other spot on earth."

To make way for the elaborate infrastructure required by the weapons program, Kwajalein's "traditional" landowners were progressively displaced from their islands within the atoll and resettled on the small island of Ebeye. Though Ebeye was once home to only sixteen people, in 1988 English journalist Jane Dibblin reported: "There are now 9,500 people living on Ebeye, on sixty-six acres or one-tenth of a square mile of land. Britain would have to accommodate twice the world's population to achieve the same density."

Slums, Overcrowding, Poverty

The U.S. military has taken over Kwajalein Island, the largest island in the atoll. A fine slice of California lifestyle, Kwajalein Island now contrasts starkly with Ebeye, aptly described as the "slum of the Pacific" and a "biological time bomb that could go off at any time."

In an attempt to deal with increasing overcrowding and poverty, Ebeye Island was artificially extended during the 1990s. *Currently, however, over 12,000 people continue to live on less than one hundred acres.* An additional thousand people have been relocated to Enniburr, where the pattern of substandard housing and inadequate facilities has been repeated. According to Republic of the Marshall Islands (RMI) foreign minister Alvin Jacklick, "Ebeye and Enniburr have become the worst ghettos of the Pacific, and the conditions there are barely humane."

Over 90 percent of the Ebeye and Enniburr residents are unemployed. Only 1,200 Marshallese working as "domestic servants, cooks, maintenance workers and groundskeepers for U.S. personnel on Kwajalein Island commute by boat from Ebeye Island each day." According to Bank of Hawaii economist Wali M. Osman, foreign aid has been tied to development packages, which have proven unsuitable and have only exacerbated the problems.

Reagan to Clinton to Bush

The military importance of Kwajalein increased dramatically on March 23, 1983, when President Reagan announced his ambition to develop the Strategic Defense Initiative (SDI) or "Star Wars"— a space-based system designed as a total ballistic missile defense (BMD) to protect the United States from missile attacks. Overnight, the U.S. Army Kwajalein Atoll/Kwajalein Missile Range (USAKA/

KMR) became instrumental to U.S. space warfare ambitions. The tiny islands of Kwajalein and the Marshall Islands thus became a vital node in the U.S. government's ambition to be overlord of a new world order. This makes the Marshall Islands a place of great significance globally.

Absorbing more than $50 billion in research costs, the project suffered fifteen years of repeated failures, while the objective remained unattainable. Packaged as a move to "render nuclear weapons impotent and obsolete," it faced immediate global condemnation for being "technically impractical and politically dangerous." Nonetheless, the militarization of the atoll continued unabated, and on October 1, 1997, the Clinton administration restructured and revamped the program as the U.S. Army Space and Missile Defense Command.

Then, on May 1, 2001, President George W. Bush delivered a speech at the National Defense University in Washington, D.C., signaling his administration's unilateral withdrawal from the ABM Treaty. Reaffirming the U.S. commitment to developing a "layered" missile defense system that would extend Reagan's Ballistic Missile Defense system, Bush repackaged the antimissile system as a deterrent to a missile attack from a "rogue nation," such as Iraq or North Korea, or an accidental or deliberate missile launch by China or Russia. Going well beyond Clinton's ground-based interceptor system, Bush's program is not aimed at protecting the United States against an all-out nuclear attack. Rather, it consists of a plethora of weapons systems that, although still in the planning and testing stages, are being developed at great expense to U.S. taxpayers. The program has been estimated to cost $200 billion, but an ever greater expense is the threat of proliferating nuclear weapons.

In December 2001, following the Bush administration's withdrawal from the ABM Treaty, missile testing at Kwajalein Missile Range increased dramatically. In September 2002, Giff Johnson reported from the Marshall Islands: *"The Kwajalein range hasn't been this busy since the heyday of the Reagan Administration."*

The Bush administration initially intended to have the first elements of the system operational by 2005, but there have been consistent failures in its testing regime. Not least of the mishaps is the failure of two-thirds of the missiles fired from Kwajalein to intercept incoming missiles and actually hit their targets.

III. ECONOMIC DEPENDENCY

Over the course of its involvement in the northern Pacific, the United States incrementally extended its control by drawing the Marshall Islands into an ever-tightening trap of economic dependency. This dependency resulted in the signing of the Compact of Free Association, which secures the future of U.S. military facilities at Kwajalein.

The compact originated in the Soloman Report commissioned by President John F. Kennedy in 1963. The report advised that the Marshalls (indeed the entire U.S. Trust Territory of the Pacific Islands, consisting of the Marshalls, Palau/Belau, the Northern Marianas, and the Federated States of Micronesia) be flooded with money, technology, and personnel through a rapid Americanization program, while giving an appearance of self-government. Once the Micronesians were economically dependent on the United States, it would then simply be a matter of forcing them into an agreement that would bind them militarily to the United States. This covert doctrine of imposed economic dependency has been so successful that today the Republic of the Marshall Islands relies on the United States for 68 percent of its revenue.

The first Marshall Islands Compact was approved in 1985 by 60 percent of the voting Marshallese and came into effect on November 3, 1986. Although the majority of Marshall Islanders agreed to the compact, there was considerable

opposition to it. As Jane Dibblin explains:

> *All of the atolls most directly affected by the U.S. military activity ... voted overwhelmingly against: 70 percent on Kwajalein, 90 percent on Bikini/Kili and 85 percent on Rongelap. In all, ten out of twenty-four [island communities] voted against.... While the Compact promises independence ... it is in fact a virtual U.S. annexation of the islands for military purposes, a denial of self-determination and a shrugging off of responsibility for security and defense matter.... [T]he U.S. can veto any item of domestic or foreign policy or any business or trade agreement which it deems is threatening.... U.S. security interests overshadow every other consideration. Self-determination is a mere gloss.*

The 1985 compact also freed the United States from any responsibility for the consequences, present or future, of its nuclear testing program. The clause dismissed all court cases pending against the U.S. and prohibited Marshallese from seeking further compensation. A trust fund was set up with $150 million, which, once invested, would provide $270 million in compensation payments and medical care for the "four atolls" deemed by the United States to have been affected by the nuclear testing (Bikini, Enewetak, Rongelap, and Utirik).

By 2000, this trust fund proved to be woefully inadequate in meeting the needs of the Marshallese. The Marshall Islands' Nuclear Claims Tribunal did not have enough funds for compensation because *most* Islanders suffered personal injury as a result of the U.S. nuclear tests, nor did it have enough funds to compensate the loss of the use of their land due to contamination.

Although the current compact doesn't expire until 2016, a renegotiation process began on September 11, 2000, when the RMI government petitioned the U.S. Congress to provide adequate compensation for the health and environmental effects of nuclear testing. The RMI requested approximately $3 billion to enable it to fulfill its outstanding compensation obligations. Warning that its request was inadequate over the long term (although more realistic than the $150 million paid by the United States under the earlier agreement), the RMI signaled that it retained the right under the terms of the compact to ask the United States for further assistance, including cleaning up Bikini, Rongelap, and other atolls.

When the renegotiated compact was signed in 2003, however, the Bush administration had only increased its compensation funding to $800 million, less than one-third the sum estimated by the Marshallese as a minimum requirement. In response to a Marshallese request for increased rent on Kwajalein, the United States was determined to keep the facility past the 2016 expiration of the lease. The RMI government, for its part, was desperate not to lose U.S. aid. In April 2003, the RMI and U.S. governments signed "Compact II," an agreement that extended the lease on Kwajalein for fifty years, until 2066, with an option for an additional twenty years. The Pentagon has thus secured the Kwajalein Missile Range lease until 2086.

Just as they have consistently resisted Pentagon control over their lands, the Kwajalein landowners resisted the terms of the new compact extension. Giff Johnson reported that, although the Kwajalein Islanders did not want the United States to leave, they wanted a "new fifty-year lease that [would take] into account the real value of Kwajalein . . . [or] if the U.S. [was] not willing to negotiate a new, fair lease agreement, then the landowners want[ed] to discuss repatriation of the base now in preparation for the expiration of the current deal in 2016." In effect, they got neither. Kwajalein Negotiation Commission Chairman Christopher Loeak described the U.S. offer as "insufficient to provide for the people of Kwajalein," and as failing "to account for population growth and inflation." Even though Kwajalein is "the only facility available to the U.S. for targeting incoming missiles," the Marshallese had little negotiating power to wield against the military monolith. Since the Marshalls

were economically dependent, the United States clearly had the upper hand. The Marshallese were faced with no option but to accede to U.S demands.

The Marshallese have no word in their language for "enemy," but as the Republic of the Marshall Islands stated in its petition to the U.S. administration in 2000: *"The sixty-six atomic and thermonuclear weapons detonated in the Marshall Islands allowed the United States Government to achieve its aim of world peace through a deterrence policy. The Marshallese people subsidized this nuclear detente with their lands, health, lives, and future."* Whether the U.S. administration's intentions are or have ever been to achieve peace through nuclear weaponry is unclear. But from a Marshallese perspective, any objective continues to have the same devastating outcome.

❧ *This article was adapted from its prior publication in* The Pacific Ecologist, *Autumn-Winter, 2004. ©Zohl dé Ishtar. Among the key historical sources cited by the author are these:*

Alcalay, Glenn. "The Aftermath of Bikini." *The Ecologist.* December 1980, vol. 10, no. 10.

Aldridge, Robert. 1989. *Nuclear Empire.* Vancouver: New Star Books.

Atomic Energy Commission (AEC). 1968. *Report the Ad Hoc Committee to Evaluate the Radiological Hazards of Resettlement of the Bikini Atoll,* August 12.

Burgess, Hayden. 1982. "A Nation Betrayed." *Te Hui Oranga O Te Moana Nui A Kiwa.* Aotearoa/ New Zealand Pacific People's Anti-Nuclear Action Committee.

Conard, Robert A. 1975. *A Twenty Year Review of Medical Findings in a Marshallese Population Accidentally Exposed to Radioactive Fallout.* Upton, NY: Brookhaven National Laboratory.

dé Ishtar, Zohl. 1994. *Daughters of the Pacific.* Melbourne: Spinifex Press.

Dibblin, Jane. 1988. *Day of Two Suns: U.S. Nuclear Testing and the Pacific Islanders.* London: Virago Press.

Gerson, Joseph and Bruce Birchard (eds.). 1991. *The Sun Never Sets: Confronting the Network of Foreign US Military Bases.* Philadelphia: South End Press.

Hayes, Peter et al. 1987. *American Lake, Nuclear Peril in the Pacific.* New York: Penguin Group USA.

Heine, Carl. 1974. *Micronesia at the Crossroads. A Reappraisal of the Micronesian Political Dilemma.* Honolulu: University of Hawaii Press.

Hines, Neal O. 1962. *Proving Ground: An Account of Radiobiological Studies in the Pacific. 1946-1961.* Seattle: University of Washington Press.

Johnson, Giff. 1984. *Collision Course at Kwajalein: Marshall Islanders in the Shadow of the Bomb.* Pacific Concerns Resource Center, Honolulu, Hawaii. Available from www.pcrc.org.fj.

Johnson, Giff. "A Deal by Summer." *Pacific Magazine and Islands Business,* February 2002. Available from http://www.pacificislands.cc/pm22002/pmdefault.php?urlarticleid=0007.

Johnson, Giff. "How Much Is Kwajalein Worth To America? Unique Test Range Is Marshalls' Big Bargaining Chip." *Pacific Magazine and Islands Business,* September 2002. Available from http://www.pacificislands.cc/pm92002/pmdefault.php?urlarticleid=0006.

Jones, Peter D. 1988. *From Bikini to Belau: The Nuclear Colonisation of the Pacific.* London: War Resisters International, Available from www.wri-irg.org.

Republic of the Marshall Islands. 1996. *Nuclear Testing in the Marshall Islands: A Chronology of Events. Nuclear Testing in the Marshall Islands: A Brief History.* Micromonitor News and Printing Company, Available from www.rmiembassyus.org/nuclear/chronology.html, August.

Robinson, W.C. et. al. 1977. *Dose Assessment at Bikini Atoll.* Lawrence Livermore Laboratory (UCRL-51879, pt. 5), June 8.

Siwitibau, Suliana and B. David Williams. 1982. *A Call to a New Exodus: An Antinuclear Primer for Pacific Peoples.* Suva: Lotu Pasifika Productions, Pacific Council of Churches, Fiji.

Smith, Gary. 1991. *Micronesia: Decolonization and U.S. Military Interests in the Trust Territories of the Pacific Islands.* Canberrra: Peace Research Center, Australia National University.

Global scarcity of freshwater is creating geopolitical crises on a scale with the problems caused by the shortages of oil. Water is increasingly used as a political weapon, as here in Botswana where the government cut off water supplies to Gana and Gwi Bush families, in order to save it for tourist use. In many parts of Africa, South America and elsewhere, World Bank programs are causing indigenous freshwater supplies to be rapidly privatized, with corporations charging very high rates for continued usage. This has led to massive protests and contributed to a major uprising in Bolivia.

CHAPTER 13

Global Water Wars

Antonia Juhasz
International Forum on Globalization

WORLDWIDE, THE CONSUMPTION OF WATER is doubling every twenty years, at more than twice the rate of increase in the human population. According to the United Nations, by the year 2025, as much as two-thirds of the world's population will be living in conditions of serious water shortage, and one-third will be living in conditions of absolute water scarcity. For this reason, *Fortune* magazine stated, "Water will be to the 21st century what oil was to the 20th." And one World Bank report warned that "the next world war will be about water."

In the modern world, water is not only a necessity of life for human beings, it is also crucial for industrial enterprise. In fact, the two leading global consumers of freshwater are industrial agriculture (for irrigation) and the telecommunications industry (which requires huge amounts of pure water for chip manufacture). Consumption of drinking water by human beings is actually a distant third. Given the increased scarcity of water, a global race to privatize and commodify the planet's remaining water is already well under way, with billions of dollars at stake.

Fortune reports that water privatization is already a $400 billion global business. That is one-third larger than the global pharmaceuticals industry. In the United States alone, it is a $100 billion industry, dominated by some of the worst corporate citizens in the world, including Shell Oil, Bechtel, and Enron. As water becomes increasingly scarce, more corporate pressure is being applied to places where indigenous peoples have maintained their resources and traditional uses.

But the good news is that during the last few years, a tremendous wave of resistance to the privatization of water has emerged on every continent, with some very notable early successes, as we will see. Now we are also beginning to see promising changes in national policies, especially in parts of South America. We will come back to these at the end of this article.

THEFT OF INDIGENOUS WATERS

For centuries, the waters of indigenous peoples have been stolen through colonialism, imperialism, and globalization. As invaders entered and claimed land, they routinely took the most fertile and water-rich areas, leaving little for indigenous populations. Ages-old systems of water sharing and sustainable agriculture—utilizing barely a fraction of the water of industrialized agriculture—have been dismantled. For what was once their ancestral right, indigenous peoples are now forced to pay higher market prices for water or, more often, do without it.

This trend is still obvious today. For example, the Masai of East Africa are restricted to an ever-dwindling fraction of their former supply. After living with a communal land-tenure system in which everyone in an area shared common access to water and pasture—an arrangement typical of most native peoples—the Masai have been forced to move to the driest and least fertile areas, forcing them to abandon their traditional lifestyle. And in Brazil, in January 2002, the Guarani and Kaiowa Indians were served with a court order evicting them from their ancestral homelands. After the lands were taken from them, they were forced into a tiny area devoid of water or food. When they ventured out to find these necessities, they were served with a court order that is still pending today.

In February 2002, the Botswana government cut off water supplies to Gana and Gwi Bush families in the Central Kalahari Game Reserve, in the government's latest attempt to force Bush people off ancestral lands they have lived on for twenty thousand years.

The water-rich lands of indigenous peoples have provided billions of dollars in income to corporations and governments that have used it primarily for unsustainable, water-intensive industrial agriculture and environmentally destructive resource-extractive industries.

⚜   ⚜   ⚜

While the privatization of water for drinking and sanitation has taken place all over the world, it is most prevalent in developing countries, where the World Bank and the IMF have made water privatization a condition for granting loans and debt reduction. As a result, local and indigenous populations around the world have watched as water supplies commonly utilized by their people for centuries are sold to private corporations, who then charge high prices for their use. More often than not, the high water prices preclude their ability to pay, thus leaving the people dependent on polluted sources.

The privatization process has followed a similar pattern worldwide:

1. Under the World Bank and IMF Structural Adjustment Program (SAPs), countries are required to dismantle environmental, health, safety, and labor provisions, thereby invalidating regulatory frameworks.
2. Most government services are privatized, with water privatization a specific condition of many World Bank and/or IMF loans.
3. Multinational corporations are brought to countries to provide the water services.
4. The corporations contract with the IMF for a guaranteed rate of return on their investments.
5. The corporations fire workers or lessen pay scales and worker protections, raise prices, and cut off services to poor areas that are unable to pay.

This pattern played out particularly brutally in the now famous story of Cochabamba, Bolivia.

Water Wars

In 1999, the World Bank and IMF made water privatization of Cochabamba, Bolivia's third-largest city, a condition for continued receipt of loans. There was just one bidder on the privatization contract—Aguas Del Tunari, a subsidiary of the San Francisco–based Bechtel Corporation. After Aguas Del Tunari took over providing the city's water, it raised rates overall, as much as tripling them for the poorest customers. In a country where the minimum wage was less than $60 per month, many users received water bills of $20 per month and higher. All of the water supplies were privatized. As a consequence, people who had built and used community water wells or irrigation systems for decades had to pay Aguas Del Tunari for water. This portion of the story is common all over the world. What is surprising is how the citizens responded.

The people of Cochabamba—a majority of them indigenous—formed an alliance with farmers, peasants, workers, environmentalists, human rights activists, and community leaders to form La Coordinadora de Defensa del Agua y de la Vida (The Coalition in Defense of Water and Life) to take back their water. After attempts at negotiations with the government and the water company were ignored, and peaceful marches were met with violence, the people of Cochabamba—young and old, students and workers, city and country dwellers—shut down Cochabamba through coordinated nonviolent street protests, strikes, and blockades. The government declared a state of siege, arresting protest leaders in their beds, shutting down radio stations, and sending more than one thousand soldiers into the streets with live ammunition. A seventeen-year-old boy was killed, and dozens of others were wounded. Through weeks of confrontation, the "water warriors" refused to back down. On April 10, 2000, the government conceded, signing an accord to end its contract with Aguas del Tunari and Bechtel. The workers, citizens, and local officials of Cochabamba are now running the water system themselves—not perfectly, but far more equitably and universally than before. Their model, *usos y costumbres*, or "traditional or customary usage," is based on traditional water practices that contradict Bechtel's water-for-profit model. For its part, Bechtel Corporation has turned to the World Bank's International Centre for the Settlement of Investment Disputes to sue the Bolivian government for $25 million. But by January 2006, public outrage was so great that Bechtel dropped its lawsuit. *(See also Chapter 23 on Bolivia's Indigenous Revolution.)*

Other parts of the world are experiencing similar battles. Citizens in South Africa are battling to end a water privatization contract forced upon them by the World Bank. After KwaZulu-Natal South Africa privatized their water, those who were too poor to pay for their water had their supplies cut off. They were then forced to resort to using polluted river water, resulting in an outbreak of cholera that has already claimed thirty-two lives. This story is repeating itself all across Africa today. More than five million people worldwide, most of them children, die every year from illnesses caused by drinking unsafe water. Still, the push for water privatization is on the rise in the World Bank and the IMF, despite little evidence that privatization improves access to or affordability of water, especially for the poorest sectors of the population.

North America

The threat to indigenous peoples' water is not limited to the policies of the World Bank and the IMF. Across Canada, indigenous communities are fighting the North American Free Trade Agreement (NAFTA) and the proposed Free Trade Area of the Americas (FTAA) for the right to their water. These agreements give global corporations the right to export water from lakes, rivers, and streams to distant markets. The needs and views of indigenous communities, who depend on clean and accessible water, have not been considered in the drafting or enforcement of these documents.

In one case, the people of British Columbia were infuriated to learn that their government had signed a contract with a California company, Sun Belt Water, to export their water to California. The decision had been made without adequate public debate or input and without an environmental or social impact assessment to determine the impact on the area. The people responded by forcing their government not only to end the contract but to ban bulk exports of water altogether. Sun Belt is using NAFTA to sue Canada for $220 million, not only for the money it lost due to the cancelled contract, but also for future profits it could have reaped from the deal. Sun Belt's CEO, Jack Lindsay, explained, "Because of NAFTA, we are now stakeholders in the national water policy in Canada." The voices of the local populations are ignored completely as the debate over who owns the water is taken over by global corporations and institutions.

Today, trade and investment agreements are providing corporations with even greater access to water systems in both developed and developing countries than the World Bank and IMF provide alone. Corporations are using these agreements to gain ownership of the world's ever-dwindling water supplies so that they will become the suppliers of last resort.

In February 1999, the *National Post* called Canada's water "blue gold" and demanded that the government "turn on the tap." Its business columnist, Terence Corcoran, wrote, "The issue will not be whether to export, but how much money the federal government and provinces will be able to extract from massive water shipments. . . . Using the OPEC model, they will attempt to cartelize the world supply of water to drive the price up." In fact, the "cartelization" has already begun. The Global Water Corporation has signed an agreement with Sitka, Alaska, to export eighteen billion gallons of glacier water per year to China, where it will be bottled in one of that country's infamous free-trade zones to save on labor costs. Indigenous populations in Alaska, who are dependent upon this water for their survival, were never included in the negotiations. Corporations hope that NAFTA, the FTAA, and the WTO will force countries to grant them access to and ownership of the world's water supply regardless of the environmental, health, or social consequences.

An existing agreement in the WTO, the General Agreement on Trade in Services (GATS), is cur-

rently being expanded. One of the primary targets of discussion is the expansion of GATS to cover public services such as the provision of water. If this moves forward, water services in the United States, Canada, and other "wealthy" nations would be deregulated and potentially privatized.

THE RISING OPPOSITION

Though the WTO, World Bank and IMF are working hard to continue accelerating the pace at which they can force the privatization of freshwater supplies, a powerful and coordinated opposition is also rapidly gaining steam. The first and most impressive expression of this was in Cochabamba, where the indigenous-led movement not only succeeded in reversing water privatization, but has since gone on to major political victories in Bolivia.

While that sort of revolutionary achievement has not yet been duplicated elsewhere, uprisings are widespread, for example, in such places as in Argentina, South Africa, the Philippines and Trinidad. In Ghana, major protests successfully reversed a water privatization scheme. And the government of Tanzania—which was forced to privatize water after draconian threats of economic isolation by the IMF and World Bank—has now cancelled its contract with Biwater, citing the company's poor performance. This could prove a major setback for water privatization schemes in Africa. Even in the United States, there have been fiery debates over privatization in such cities as Atlanta, New Orleans, and Stockton, California, and several other cities have already rejected water privatization. (*For further information on the U.S. water situation, contact Public Citizen's Water for All: www.wateractivist.org*).

In India, meanwhile, a new campaign for Water Liberation (*Jal Swaraj*) has focused its efforts on the massive overuse of scarce groundwater by private corporations, notably Coca-Cola, for water bottling. Protesters have succeeded in closing down several Coca-Cola bottling plants. The movement is also directed at major water privateers such as Suez Degrement, which operates in India and many other countries. During 2004, New Delhi, India ,was the site of the first People's Water Forum, launching an ambitious international program of lobbying and activism in both national and international contexts.

On the political front, two countries in South America have now officially codified that water cannot be privatized. Venezuela has had this law for several years, and in 2004 the voters of Uruguay passed a constitutional amendment that labelled access to water a fundamental human right that cannot be privatized.

Recent meetings of the major water privatization industry groups at the World Water Forum in The Hague (2000) and Kyoto (2003) have been met with rising opposition demanding that access to water be recognized as a human right, that water privatization be ended, that the status of water as a "commodity" under global economic rules be rescinded, and that its prior official status as a "public commons" available to all be codified.

All of these groups and campaigns subscribe to basic principles first articulated by the indigenous people of Bolivia in their Cochabamba Water Declaration, which states, in part:

▲ Water belongs to the earth and all species and is sacred to life; therefore, the world's water must be conserved, reclaimed, and protected for all future generations and its natural patterns respected;

▲ Water is a fundamental human right and a public trust to be guarded by all levels of government; therefore, it should not be commodified, privatized, or traded for commercial purposes. These rights must be enshrined at all levels of government. In particular, an international treaty must ensure these principles are incontrovertible; and

▲ Water is best protected by local communities and citizens who must be respected as equal partners with governments in the protection and regulation of water. Peoples of the earth are the only vehicle to promote democracy and save water.

The "portrait mask" is traditionally used by Haida people for a variety of ceremonies, including the End of Mourning Ceremony, in which it is made to resemble the deceased person. Increasingly, in the global economy, such art objects and sacred ceremonial objects are surreptitiously removed and transported via underground black markets or traded to foreign collectors and museums. Often they are copied and put into mass production for tourist markets, which represent them as authentic. Such theft and trade can be deeply demoralizing to indigenous peoples for whom these objects play important ceremonial roles.

CHAPTER 14

Sacred Objects, Art and Nature in a Global Economy

Terri-Lynn Williams-Davidson

(Haida)

Environmental-Aboriginal Guardianship through Law and Education (EAGLE)

FROM AN INDIGENOUS PERSPECTIVE, "cultural property" is not limited to tangible objects such as those used in ceremonies or art objects, crafts, music, and the instruments of daily life. For us, discussions of cultural property, or of culture itself, cannot be separated from its integration with the natural world. For indigenous peoples, the Earth and all of its life form the fundamental context, the foundation and the ultimate source from which culture emerges. In this article, I suggest that the problems, which are accelerated by globalization, of the theft and alienation of tangible things of our cultures cannot be solved without also addressing a larger problem of protection of Indian lands and rights. They are intrinsically connected.

I. CAPTURED HERITAGE

Colonization over the last century has resulted in most of the cultural objects of indigenous peoples of the world being removed from those who created and integrated them into our lives and rituals. This has been profoundly detrimental to the sustainability of indigenous cultural heritage and of the cultures themselves.

The forms of removal have ranged from direct trade or sale, to unconscionable fraudulent negotiations, to outright theft and counterfeiting. But the net result has been export from their places of origin to museums, institutions, private collectors and speculators of the world, many of whom operate in a multimillion-dollar global "black market" for such objects. Most appalling, the prized targets for this illicit and immoral global trade activity are the most treasured cultural objects, those necessary for the continued conduct of ancient traditional ceremonies and knowledge.

In a traditional context, ceremonial and other cultural objects are handled via very strict rules and protocols for their use or display. These protocols are, of course, seriously violated by the handling, collection, shipping, display, sale or other activities that accompany their being lifted by unauthorized outsiders from their culturally embodied context. Indigenous peoples understand that we have a Sacred Trust with the Creator to protect cultural heritage and all its expressions and sources, and to uphold all traditional protocols; breaches of these protocols directly undermine this Sacred Trust and the ancient ceremonies that keep it alive.

It would be difficult to overstate the importance of the maintenance of ceremonies among indigenous peoples; they regulate and reaffirm the relationships between people—individuals, clans, communities and nations—as well as between people and the Earth, including the Earth's life forms. Ceremonies play an integral role in weaving the cultural fabric of indigenous peoples, particularly with respect to the education of the youth and the integration of the values and principles we need to live by. Without the maintenance of our ceremonies, our societies inevitably drift toward unrootedness and assimilation into the broader society. This is how the theft and removal of ceremonial objects can cause tremendous injury to the continuity of traditional culture and teachings. It is also why their return has become an issue of grave seriousness for many indigenous societies.

It is not only the recovery of the objects themselves that is so important. Also at stake is the entire scale of a cultural revitalization that is already under way among indigenous peoples throughout the world, which is also experienced in growing movements to recover language, arts, and lands. In many ways, the revitalization of the past half-century has been particularly fueled by the devoted activities of indigenous artists, who are working to renew and sustain the culture on a daily basis.

Art has always permeated all aspects of indigenous life and has been inseparable from daily life, so inseparable that many indigenous languages do not have a separate word for art. The making of traditional art objects has increased dramatically over the past few decades, bringing new generations of indigenous artists closer to traditional teachings and principles. This process has become very important in the revitalization movement in numerous cultures, notably the peoples of the northwest coast of Canada. It has also had significant economic benefits. Indigenous

artists have been able to create a thriving alternative economy that helps to counter the proposals for industrial-style development that are steadily served up by the larger society. An expanding market for indigenous art has also begun to employ indigenous peoples in a way that permits us to continue to create, while learning values integral to the culture.

However, just as the market has grown for these art objects, there has developed a downside: the market has also globalized and has led to a new global industry of imitation indigenous art. It has spawned a new class of nonindigenous entrepreneurs engaging the services of artisans in Third World countries, who reproduce art objects at high speed, on a nearly assembly-line basis and at a fraction of the cost of the original indigenous art. Frequently, one-of-a-kind objects are mass-produced without the consent or knowledge of the original artist, as for example, the reproductions of Northwest Coast Indian masks and other objects—reproduced in Third World countries like Indonesia—available for sale on the Internet at well below the cost of the original. Other familiar cases are the widespread imitations and reproductions of Native American weavings and jewelry, particularly Navajo and Pueblo art and jewelry, as well as the Japanese attempts to mass-produce sweaters of the Cowichan peoples in Canada.

One useful idea has been to develop a certification program that labels the bonafide indigenous art objects so consumers know they are supporting local artists rather than some assembly-line operation from abroad. This is already proving helpful, but it is not a complete answer.

Global reproduction of indigenous art can be extremely frustrating for local artists who cling to this opportunity for self-sufficiency. However, few indigenous artists can afford to obtain legal counsel to fight these reproductions and their entry into local markets. Even when legal counsel is retained, domestic copyright law prohibits the original artists from stopping mass production.

Matters are made still worse by the bureaucracies of globalization, such as the WTO and NAFTA, which make it difficult for any country to give preference to local producers of art (or anything else) over objects produced abroad and exported into domestic markets. Import controls or tariffs violate the rules of "free trade." So indigenous producers have little ability to protect the markets they have worked so hard to develop, especially from low-priced Third World "knock-offs." The net result of this situation is that native artistic production becomes less viable, and indigenous communities are increasingly pressured to accept proposals for industrial development, with the resulting long-term destruction of forests and other natural resources. *(See Chapter 7 by Victor Menotti on the rules of free trade.)*

Conversion to industrial-style development is, of course, a further assault on traditional cultures that have evolved for millennia in an integrated manner with the natural world and the biodiversity in their locales. The relationship is symbiotic: as culture changes, the earth is impacted; as the earth is impacted, local cultures are impacted, and a destructive spiral is accelerated.

The story becomes especially dramatic when you consider effects upon so-called cultural keystone species that are particularly important to individual cultures. For example, the buffalo of the central plains is a keystone species for cultures of those regions, with ceremonies, objects and art and rituals focused directly on them. Among the Haida people of the Pacific Northwest of Canada, a "cultural keystone species" is the western red cedar. Cedar, especially old-growth cedar, provides for much of the material, social, cultural and spiritual needs of the Haida. It provides raw materials for canoes, houses, hunting and cooking instruments, the tools for everyday life—even

for clothing and food. It also provides the monumental totem poles and mortuary poles (for burials), and the materials for ceremonial and art objects—masks, rattles, and other regalia. In addition, many medicines and other species with a high cultural profile are sustained by old-growth forests to which their fate is tied.

As the shift to globalization has opened global corporate access to revered western cedar forests, the Haida relationship with them has been injured. Haida access has been sharply restricted, and cultural and ecological devastation has resulted. The rapidly diminishing areas of monumental red cedar and old-growth forests in the Pacific Northwest have reached the point where full regeneration is questionable, and that is a serious setback for the regeneration of Haida culture as well. Thus, the recovery of control over the title and development of Haida lands, based on Aboriginal Rights, is as much a cultural necessity as an ecological and political one.

II. THE ARGUMENTS OVER ABORIGINAL TITLE

Arguably the most important cultural issue for indigenous peoples is the legal and political one: the urgency of campaigns to permanently confirm full legal title and ownership of traditional lands and all the resources thereon, since these lands are the wellsprings of indigenous life and vision, of art and religion. Right now, in many countries of the world, the matter is one of great debate, because the interests of narrow global investment and development corporations conflict profoundly with those of peoples on their own traditional lands.

Among countries descended from British colonial rule—Canada, United States, Australia, New Zealand—land tenure systems are largely derived from British common law. This holds that colonial governments obtained "crown title" to all lands and resources, but that such title is subject to the Aboriginal Title of the original inhabitants. Thus, the principle would seem to favor indigenous interests, especially where treaties have been concluded to confirm the situation. Unfortunately, however, this fundamental principle has not been respected. In Canada, for example, there remain very large areas of British Columbia, the Northwest Territories, and Quebec where treaties have not been concluded, and the matter of Aboriginal Title versus crown title has not yet been reconciled. The issues keep churning throughout the court system: Who owns the lands? Who has the rights to control or prevent development? Whose laws apply? What happens in the interim, before treaties are concluded or before Aboriginal Title litigation is completed? How do you preserve the subject matter of the disputes?

In British Columbia there are only a handful of treaties, leaving the vast majority of lands and resources still "encumbered" by Aboriginal Title. Negotiations between the original peoples and the federal and state governments have been ongoing for more than a century and are unsettled.

Complicating matters further is the fact that there is an effective dispute between the Canadian government and the province of British Columbia about Aboriginal Rights. As discussed elsewhere in this book, Canada's constitution officially recognizes, affirms and protects the rights of aboriginal, Inuit (Eskimo) and Metis peoples. *(See also Chapter 25 by Arthur Manuel.)* In addition, the constitution requires that Canada uphold a trust responsibility, or "fiduciary" relationship, encompassing all aboriginal lands that have not been surrendered through treaty or otherwise. Canadian courts have stated numerous times that the government is obligated to act in the best interests of Aboriginal and Treaty Rights holders. Most recently, Canada's highest court, the Supreme Court of Canada, held that the crown cannot "run roughshod" over the interests of the Haida, but must protect the Haida's interests—in particular, monumental cedar and Haida title—pending the reconciliation of crown sovereignty with Haida sovereignty.

On the other hand, the government of British Columbia has argued that in the absence of treaties or litigation confirming specific titles to specific places, the law remains unclear as to whether the province must wait for the Aboriginal Title to be "disencumbered" from crown title. Effectively, the BC government is suggesting it is okay, in the meantime, to conclude exploitation deals with timber and other resource companies to develop the land, even without the explicit permission of the indigenous communities.

Here, we have perfect conditions for raging conflict and for legal actions among all parties—the aboriginal communities, the provincial government, the national government, and the corporations. The situation has become so frustrating for the Haida, who see the forests of Haida Gwaii (Queen Charlotte Islands) being eliminated on a daily basis and who have pursued litigation for over a decade, that the Haida have recently begun to take direct action against logging companies like Weyerhaeuser Company. In an interesting development, local nonindigenous communities intervened in favor of the Haida Nation at the Supreme Court of Canada and have joined hands with the Haida in a joint effort to care for local communities and to curtail the globalization of Haida Gwaii's limited remaining forests. For example, in April 2005, the Haida put fishing boats in harbors and the islands' local people created peaceful checkpoints to blockade Weyerhaeuser barges and operations that were attempting to export Haida logs to Asian markets. This shows a new, powerful solidarity that, as we go to press, is ongoing.

III. THE GLOBALIZATION DIMENSION

Finally, it is necessary to include in the mix of factors affecting Haida land rights and culture the extremely negative role of international trade agreements, such as NAFTA and the WTO. Each has specific rules to prevent any member country of the agreement, such as Canada or any province of Canada (or any other country or state) from making laws that conflict with NAFTA or WTO rules. This prohibition specifically includes internal laws, internal agreements, or agreements with so-called "sub-governments" such as indigenous nations, if any of these have the effect of inhibiting the intentions of the trade rules. Recognition of aboriginal sovereignty, and Aboriginal Rights would certainly constitute a challenge to these global rules, but in such a case, according to the WTO's own rules, the WTO agreement trumps all local and domestic or sub-government arrangements or laws, thus effectively diminishing local and even national (Canadian) sovereignty and rights. The following are two such trade agreement stipulations, and some strategies for overcoming them.

Investor–State Mechanisms of NAFTA

This is the draconian rule found in Chapter II of the NAFTA agreement that holds that corporations may claim compensation for any lost profits from the "expropriation" of their development rights for a "planned but unrealized investment." This astounding provision for an international agreement basically argues that if a government or "subgovernment" (such as the Haida Nation), or local government, should act to prevent corporations from undertaking developments that were once deemed acceptable, then the corporations can sue for the profits they would have made, as if the project had really happened. Should we call this "virtual development"?

To try and counter the effect of this odd provision, the Haida Nation implemented a new legal strategy to give "formal notice" to any companies that entered Haida domain with designs to try and do business there that the Haida have the right to expropriate their investment at some future time, and that the company should henceforth proceed at its own risk. In the case of Weyerhaeuser, Canadian courts have held that Weyerhaeuser had full notice of the Aboriginal Title and Rights of the Haida. Providing such notice arguably would nullify any future reliance of the corporation upon the NAFTA investor-state mechanism to receive compensation for work and activity it had not actually performed.

"National Treatment" Clause of the WTO

Another problematic global rule that thwarts local control is the "national treatment" clause of the WTO. This makes it illegal for any country, province, or city to give preferred treatment to a local community, business, or investor over a foreign investor. All local laws, treaty rights, and constitutional protections for Aboriginal Rights would certainly be found to be illegal under the "national treatment" clause. Again, the WTO asserts that in case of disagreement over whose rules apply, the WTO rules must apply in the apparently higher cause of unfettered resource development.

But the most crucial question may be whether a country like Canada has any right to refuse to comply with international trade agreements when they conflict with internal laws. The WTO says not, and it has the power to enforce its rules by inflicting serious economic sanctions on any government that tries to protect its own laws. But the issue may not be as clear-cut as the WTO suggests.

For example, Article 46 of the Vienna Convention on the Law of Treaties admittedly does say that a state may not breach a treaty agreement such as the WTO just because it violates domestic internal laws. But the Vienna Convention also says that an individual country can refuse to honor an international agreement or treaty if it conflicts with "a pre-emptory norm of general internal law." "Pre-emptory norm" is further defined as a "norm accepted and recognized by the international community of states as a norm from which no derogation is permitted." A state is permitted to ignore international trade agreements if the trade agreement has the effect of invalidating an "internal law of fundamental importance," as would be "evident to any state conducting itself in the matter in accordance with normal practice and in good faith." In other words, if an internal law can be shown to be "fundamentally important," judging by normal standards of sovereign practice, then countries are permitted to keep the internal domestic law despite its WTO or other treaty commitments. That would certainly seem to be the case for the law of Aboriginal Rights now contained in the Canadian constitution, and the trust and fiduciary responsibilities attached to it. In fact, Canadian courts have several times clarified that wherever treaties have not been concluded internally with indigenous nations, governments must negotiate in "good faith to reach workable accommodations with Aboriginal Peoples." Given the constitutional protections that apply to them, protection of aboriginal interests is surely of "fundamental importance" in Canada.

It is our position that the Haida Nation now has a good opportunity to launch lawsuits against the Canadian government, with the claim that the government does not have the legal right to sign international trade agreements that provide corporations with unfettered access on lands where Aboriginal Title exists. Or, having signed such agreements, to remain as parties to them. If a trade agreement like the WTO infringes on Aboriginal Rights, which it certainly attempts to do, we believe it is illegal. We also believe that we have the legal right to prevent or regulate access to our forest or other resources as we see fit, as well as to prevent export of our traditional ceremonial objects and import of foreign art objects copied from Haida artists.

CONCLUSION

In a world of globalized markets, centralized economic bureaucracies, and the prevailing attitudes of the modern world, all things—sacred or otherwise—are seen as potential resources for commercial development. Perseverance and creativity are needed at every turn. For indigenous peoples, the issues are especially complex, since one aspect of life and nature is not separate from the others; all dimensions of culture, art and nature are intertwined. To save sacred ceremonial objects and our culture also requires turning away giant logging and other companies protected by obscure trade decisions thousands of miles away in Geneva. But indigenous peoples have always been adept at embracing opportunities, and we are rapidly learning how to uphold our Sacred Trust and deal with the situations we face. Certification schemes are helping to protect original artworks. New legal explorations on the international, domestic and provincial levels are buying us time. And we are seeking and gaining the strong support of public opinion. We are certainly at a critical turning point: while our forests, the natural world and also our culture is suffering from the commercial onslaught, we feel the powers shifting.

The Masai communities of Africa are among an estimated 600,000 indigenous peoples who have been forced to leave their ancestral lands in the name of "conservation" and land preservation. Big northern conservation NGOs like Conservation International and the Nature Conservancy have argued that biodiversity will be better served without people around, thus creating a giant international argument with native peoples who have lived with and cared for their lands and wildlife over millennia.

CHAPTER 15

Conservation Refugees

Mark Dowie
University of California, Berkeley

AS OTHER CHAPTERS OF THIS BOOK ATTEST, millions of native peoples around the world have been pushed off their land to make room for big oil, big metal, big timber, and big agriculture. But few people realize that the same thing has happened in the name of a much nobler cause: land and wildlife conservation. Today the list of culture-wrecking institutions put forth by tribal leaders on almost every continent includes not only Shell, Texaco, Freeport, and Bechtel, but also more respectable names like Conservation International (CI), the Nature Conservancy (TNC), the World Wildlife Fund (WWF), and the Wildlife Conservation Society (WCS). Even the more culturally sensitive World Conservation Union (IUCN) might get a mention.

In early 2004 a United Nations meeting was convened in New York for the ninth year in a row to push for passage of a resolution protecting the territorial and human rights of indigenous peoples. The UN draft declaration states: "Indigenous peoples shall not be forcibly removed from their lands or territories. No relocation shall take place without the free and informed consent of the indigenous peoples concerned and after agreement on just and fair compensation and,

where possible, with the option to return." During the meeting an indigenous delegate who did not identify herself rose to state that although extractive industries were still a serious threat to their welfare and cultural integrity, their new and biggest enemy was "conservation."

Later that spring, at a Vancouver, British Columbia, meeting of the International Forum on Indigenous Mapping, all two hundred delegates signed a declaration stating that the "activities of conservation organizations now represent the single biggest threat to the integrity of indigenous lands." These are rhetorical jabs, of course, but they have shaken the international conservation community, as have a subsequent spate of critical articles and studies, two of them conducted by the Ford Foundation, calling big conservation to task for its historical mistreatment of indigenous peoples.

"We are enemies of conservation," declared Masai leader Martin Saning'o, standing before a session of the November 2004 World Conservation Congress sponsored by IUCN in Bangkok, Thailand. The nomadic Masai, who have over the past thirty years lost most of their grazing range to conservation projects throughout eastern Africa, hadn't always felt that way. In fact, Saning'o reminded his audience, "we were the original conservationists." The room was hushed as he quietly explained how pastoral and nomadic cattlemen have traditionally protected their range: "Our ways of farming pollinated diverse seed species and maintained corridors between ecosystems." Then he tried to fathom the strange version of land conservation that had impoverished his people, more than one hundred thousand of whom had been displaced from northern Kenya and the Serengeti Plains of Tanzania. Like so many other peoples of Africa and elsewhere who have been pushed off their lands, the Masai have not been fairly compensated. Their culture is dissolving and they live in poverty.

"We don't want to be like you," Saning'o told a room of shocked white faces. "We want you to be like us. We are here to change your minds. You cannot accomplish conservation without us."

Although he might not have realized it, Saning'o was speaking for a growing worldwide movement of indigenous peoples who consider themselves "conservation refugees." Not to be confused with "ecological refugees," people forced to abandon their homelands as a result of unbearable heat, drought, desertification, flooding, disease, or other consequences of climate chaos, conservation refugees are removed from their lands involuntarily, either forcibly or through a variety of less coercive measures. The gentler, more benign methods are sometimes called "soft eviction" or "voluntary resettlement," though the latter is contestable. Soft or hard, the main complaint heard in the makeshift villages bordering parks and at meetings like the World Conservation Congress in Bangkok is that relocation often occurs with the tacit approval or benign neglect of one of the five big international nongovernmental conservation organizations, or as they have been nicknamed by indigenous leaders, the "BINGOs."

The rationale for "internal displacements," as these evictions are officially called, usually involves a perceived threat to the biological diversity of a large geographical area, variously designated by one or more BINGOs as an "ecological hot spot," an "ecoregion," a "vulnerable ecosystem," a "biological corridor," or a "living landscape." The huge parks and reserves that are created often involve a debt-for-nature swap (some of the host country's national debt paid off or retired in exchange for the protection of a parcel of sensitive land) or similar financial incentives provided by the World Bank's Global Environment Facility and one or more of its "executing agencies" (bilateral and multilateral banks). These are combined with offers made by the funding organization to pay for the management of the park or reserve. Broad rules for human use and habitation of the protected area are set and enforced by the host nation, often following the advice and counsel of a BINGO, which might even be given management powers over the area. Indigenous peoples are often left out of the process entirely.

PARKS VERSUS PEOPLE

Curious about a brand of conservation that separates nature from the people who have lived in it for millennia, I set out last autumn to meet the issue face to face. I visited with tribal members on three continents who were grappling with the consequences of Western conservation and found an alarming similarity among the stories I heard.

Khon Noi, matriarch of a remote mountain village, huddles next to an open pit stove. Brightly colored clothes identify her as Karen, the most populous of six tribes found in the lush, mountainous reaches of far northern Thailand. Her village of sixty-five families has been in the same wide valley for over two hundred years. She tells me I can use her name, as long as I don't identify her village.

"The government has no idea who I am," she says. They were here last week, in military uniforms, to tell us we could no longer practice rotational agriculture in this valley. If they knew that someone here was saying bad things about them they would come back again and move us out."

In a recent outburst of environmental enthusiasm stimulated by generous financial offerings from the Global Environment Facility (GEF), the Thai government has been creating national parks as fast as the Royal Forest Department can map them. Ten years ago there was barely a park to be found in Thailand, and because those few that existed were unmarked "paper parks," few Thais even knew they were there. Now there are 114 land parks and twenty-four marine parks on the map. Almost 25,000 square kilometers, most of which are occupied by hill and fishing tribes, are now managed by the forest department as protected areas. "Men in uniform just appeared one day, out of nowhere, showing their guns," Kohn Noi recalls, "and telling us that we were now living in a national park. That was the first we knew of it. Our own guns were confiscated ... no more hunting, no more trapping, no more snaring, and no more slash and burn. That's what they call our agriculture. But we call it crop rotation and we've been doing it in this valley for over two hundred years. Soon we will be forced to sell rice to pay for greens and legumes we are no longer allowed to grow here. Hunting we can live without, as we raise chickens, pigs, and buffalo. But rotational farming is our way of life."

A week before that conversation, in Bangkok, only a short flight south of Noi's village, six thousand conservationists attended the World Conservation Congress. Lining the hallways of that massive convention center were the display booths of big conservation groups, adorned with larger-than-life photos of indigenous peoples in splendid tribal attire.

But if delegates had taken the time to attend small panels and workshops, some of them held in a parking lot outside the convention center, they would have heard Khon Noi's story repeated a dozen times by Thai and foreign indigenous leaders who came to Bangkok from every continent, at great expense, to lobby conservation biologists and government bureaucrats for fairer treatment and to protest eviction. And they would have heard a young Karen father of two boys ask why his country, whose cabinet had ordered its environmental bureaucracy to evict his people from their traditional homeland, was chosen by IUCN to host the largest conservation convention in history.

The response of big conservation, in Bangkok and elsewhere, has been to deny that they are party to the evictions, while generating reams of promotional material about their affection for and close relationships with indigenous peoples. "We recognize that indigenous people have perhaps the deepest understanding of the Earth's living resources," says Conservation International chairman and CEO Peter Seligman, adding, "We firmly believe that indigenous people must have ownership, control and title of their lands." Such messages are carefully projected toward major funders of conservation, which in response to the aforementioned Ford Foundation reports and other press have become increasingly sensitive to indigenous peoples and their struggles for cultural survival. Financial support for international conservation has expanded well beyond the individuals and family foundations that seeded the movement to include very large foundations like Ford, MacArthur, and Gordon and Betty Moore, as well as the World Bank, its Global Environment Facility, foreign governments, USAID, a host of bilateral and multilateral banks, and, most recently, transnational corporations. During the 1990s USAID alone pumped almost $300 million into the international conservation movement, which it had come to regard as a vital adjunct to economic prosperity. The five largest conservation organizations, CI, TNC, and WWF among them, absorbed over 70 percent of that expenditure. Indigenous communities received none of it.

The Moore Foundation made a singular ten-year commitment of nearly $280 million, the largest environmental grant in history, to just one organization: Conservation International. And all the BINGOs have become increasingly corporate in recent years, both in orientation and affiliation. The Nature Conservancy now boasts almost 2,000 corporate sponsors, while Conservation International has received about $9 million from its 250 corporate "partners."

With that kind of financial and political leverage, as well as chapters in almost every country of the world, millions of loyal members, and nine-figure budgets, CI, WWF, and TNC have undertaken a hugely expanded global push to increase the number of so-called protected areas (PAs): parks, reserves, wildlife sanctuaries, and corridors created to preserve biological diversity. In 1962, there were some one thousand official PAs worldwide. Today there are 108,000, with more being added every day. The total area of land now under conservation protection worldwide has doubled since 1990, when the World Parks Commission set a goal of protecting 10 percent of the planet's surface. That goal has been exceeded, and over 12 percent of all land, a total area of 11.75 million square miles, is now protected. That's an area greater than the entire land mass of Africa.

At first glance, so much protected land seems undeniably positive, an enormous achievement of very good people doing the right thing for our planet. But the record is less impressive when the impact upon native people is considered. For example, during the 1990s the African nation of Chad increased the amount of national land under protection from 1 to 9.1 percent. All of that land was previously inhabited by what are now an estimated six hundred thousand conser-

vation refugees. No other country besides India, which officially admits to 1.6 million, is even counting this growing new class of refugees. World estimates offered by the UN, IUCN, and a few anthropologists range from 5 million to tens of millions. Charles Geisler, a rural sociologist at Cornell University who has studied displacements in Africa, is certain the number on that continent alone exceeds 14 million.

The true worldwide figure, if it were ever known, would depend upon the semantics of words like "eviction," "displacement," and "refugee." The larger point is that conservation refugees exist on every continent but Antarctica, and by most accounts they live far more difficult lives than they once did, banished from lands they thrived on for hundreds, even thousands of years.

AMERICAN HISTORY

The widespread policy and practice of removing people from protected areas may actually have originated in the United States in 1864, with the organized military expulsion of Miwok and Ahwahnishi Indians from their four-thousand-year-old settlements in Yosemite Valley. During the California Gold Rush, the valley and its native communities had been "discovered" by white settlers. One of them, a miner and wilderness lover named Lafayette Burnell, swooned over the lush beauty of the valley as he watched James Savage, commander of the notorious Mariposa Battalion, burn Indian villages and acorn caches to the ground—a first step to starving and freezing the Miwok into submission. Burnell approved of the torching. Fancying himself a passionate conservationist, he was determined to "sweep the territory of any scattered bands that might infest it." And swept it was, a process that lasted until 1969 when the last Miwok village was evacuated from the national park. Similar treatment was experienced by the Shoshone, Lakota, Bannock, Crow, Nez Perce, Flathead, and Blackfeet, all of whom at one time or another occupied and hunted in what is now Yellowstone National Park.

John Muir, a forefather of the American conservation movement, argued that "wilderness" should be cleared of all inhabitants and set aside to satisfy the urbane human's need for recreation and spiritual renewal. It was a sentiment that eventually became national policy in the language of the 1964 Wilderness Act, which defined wilderness as a place "where man himself is a visitor who does not remain," completely ignoring centuries of benign human presence.

The expulsion process has since been exported, and continues around the world to this day, albeit under less violent circumstances than the atrocious Miwok massacres. The government of India, which evicted one hundred thousand *adivasis* (rural peoples) in Assam between April and July of 2002, estimates that another two or three million will be displaced over the next decade. The policy is largely in response to a 1993 lawsuit brought by WWF that mandates an 8 percent increase in protected areas, requiring the relocation of almost five hundred *adivasi* villages. A more immediate threat involves the impending removal of several Mayan communities from the Montes Azules region of Chiapas, Mexico, a process that began in the mid 1970s and could still quite easily lead to civil war. Conservation International is deeply immersed in that controversy, as are a host of extractive industries.

Tensions are also high in the Enoosupukia region of Kenya, where two thousand members of the ancient Ogiek community were recently ordered to leave the Mau Forest, where they have thrived as hunter-gatherers for centuries. After the Ogiek villages were cleared, all structures were burned to the ground. And while the stated intent of the Kenyan government is "environmental," the Ogiek note that their land has been deeded over to powerful members of former president Daniel Arap Moi's Kalenjin tribe, and

that vast regions of the forest are being clear-cut. Kenya's deputy minister of environment, Wangari Maathai, has recently come to the Ogiek's defense. A lifelong environmental activist, Maathai remembers what the Mau Forest was like when the Ogiek lived there: no roads, no logging, plenty of biodiversity.

Meanwhile, over the past decade, each of the BINGOs and most of the international agencies they work with have issued formal declarations in support of indigenous peoples and their territorial rights. The Nature Conservancy's "Commitment to People" statement declares, "We respect the needs of local communities by developing ways to conserve biological diversity while at the same time enabling humans to live productively and sustainably on the landscape." After endorsing the UN's Draft Declaration on the Rights of Indigenous Peoples in 1984, the World Wildlife Fund (WWF) adopted its own statement of principles upholding the rights of indigenous peoples to own, manage, and control their lands and territories, a radical notion for many governments.

In 1999, the World Commission on Protected Areas formally recognized indigenous peoples' rights to "sustainable, traditional use" of their lands and territories. The following year the IUCN adopted a bold set of principles for establishing protected areas that states unequivocally, "The establishment of new protected areas on indigenous and other traditional peoples' . . . domains should be based on the legal recognition of collective rights of communities living within them to the lands, territories, waters, coastal seas and other resources they traditionally own or otherwise occupy or use." Tribal people, who tend to think and plan in generations, rather than weeks, months, and years, are still waiting to be paid the consideration promised in these thoughtful pronouncements.

Sadly, the human rights and global conservation communities remain at serious odds over the question of displacement, each side blaming the other for the particular crisis they perceive. Conservation biologists argue that by allowing native populations to grow, hunt, and gather in protected areas, anthropologists, cultural preservationists, and other supporters of indigenous rights become complicit in the decline of biological diversity. Some, like the Wildlife Conservation Society's outspoken president, Steven Sanderson, believe that the entire global conservation agenda has been "hijacked" by advocates for indigenous peoples, placing wildlife and biodiversity at peril.

Human rights groups, such as Cultural Survival, First Peoples Worldwide, EarthRights International, Survival International, and the Forest Peoples Programme, argue the opposite, accusing some of the BINGOs and governments like Uganda's of destroying indigenous cultures, the diversity of which they deem actually essential to the preservation of biological diversity.

One attempt to bridge this unfortunate divide is the "market-based solution," but the PR spin placed on this model has been misleading. BINGOs endorse ecotourism, bioprospecting, extractive reserves, and industrial partnerships that promote such activities as building nature resorts, leading pharmaceutical scientists to medicinal plants, gathering nuts for Ben and Jerry's ice cream, or harvesting plant oils for the Body Shop as the best way to protect both land and community with a single program. Global conservation Web sites and annual reports feature stunning photographs of native people leading nature tours, harvesting fair-trade coffee, Brazil nuts, and medicinal plants. But no native names or faces can be found on the boards of the BINGOs that are promoting these arrangements.

Market-based solutions, which may have been implemented with the best of social and ecological intentions, share a lamentable outcome. In almost every case, indigenous people are moved into the money economy without the means to participate in it fully. They become permanently indentured as park rangers (never wardens), porters, waiters, harvesters, or, if they manage to learn a European language, ecotour guides. Under this model, "conservation" edges ever closer to "development," while native communities are assimilated into the lowest ranks of national cultures.

Given this history, it should be no surprise that tribal peoples regard conservationists as just another colonizer—an extension of the deadening forces of economic and cultural hegemony. Whole societies, such as the Batwa, the Masai, the Ashinika of Peru, the Gwi and Gana Bushmen of Botswana, the Karen and Hmong of Southeast Asia, and the Huarani of Ecuador, are being transformed from independent and self-sustaining into deeply dependent, communities.

When I traveled throughout Mesoamerica and the Andean-Amazon watershed last fall visiting staff members of CI, TNC, WCS, and WWF, I was looking for signs that an awakening was on the horizon. The field staff I met were acutely aware that the spirit of exclusion survives in the headquarters of their organizations, alongside a subtle but real prejudice against "unscientific" native wisdom. Dan Campbell, TNC's director in Belize, conceded, "We have an organization that sometimes tries to employ models that don't fit the culture of nations where we work." And Joy Grant, in the same office, said that as a consequence of a protracted disagreement with the indigenous peoples of Belize, local people "are now the key to everything we do."

"We are arrogant," was the confession of a CI executive working in South America, who asked me not to identify her. I was heartened by her admission until she went on to suggest that this was merely a minor character flaw. Arrogance was in fact cited by almost every indigenous leader I met as a major impediment to constructive communication with big conservation.

Luis Suarez, the new director of CI in Ecuador, seems to be aware of that. "Yes," he said, "CI has made some serious blunders with indigenous organizations within the past four years, not only in Ecuador but also in Peru." And he admitted to me that his organization was at that very moment making new enemies in Guyana, where CI had worked with the Wai Wai peoples on the establishment of a protected area but had ignored another tribe, the Wapishana, whose six communities will be encompassed by the park.

HAPPY ENDINGS?

If field observations and field workers' sentiments trickle up to the headquarters of CI and the other BINGOs, there could be a happy ending to this story. There are already positive working models of socially sensitive conservation on every continent, particularly in Australia, Bolivia, Nepal, and Canada, where national laws that protect native land rights leave foreign conservationists no choice but to join hands with indigenous communities and work out creative ways to protect wildlife habitat and sustain biodiversity while allowing indigenous citizens to thrive in their traditional settlements.

However, in most such cases it is the native people who initiate the creation of a reserve, which is more likely to be called an "indigenous protected area" (IPA) or a "community conservation area" (CCA). IPAs are an invention of Australian aboriginals, many of whom have regained ownership and territorial autonomy under new treaties with the national government, and CCAs are appearing elsewhere around the world, from Lao fishing villages along the Mekong River to the Mataven Forest in Colombia, where six indigenous tribes live in 152 villages bordering a four-million-acre ecologically intact reserve. The tribes manage a national park within the reserve

and collectively own considerable acreage along its border. Before the Mataven conservation area was created, the indigenous communities mapped the boundaries of the land to be protected, proposed their own operating rules and restrictions, and sought independent funding to pay for management of the reserve, which is today regarded worldwide as a model of indigenous conservation. The Kayapo, a nation of Amazonian Indians with whom the Brazilian government and CI have formed a cooperative conservation project, is another such example. Kayapo leaders, renowned for their ferocity, openly refused to be treated like just another stakeholder in a two-way deal between a national government and a conservation NGO, as is so often the case with cooperative management plans. Throughout negotiations, they insisted upon being an equal player at the table, with equal rights and land sovereignty. As a consequence, Xingu National Park, the continent's first Indian-owned park, was created to protect the lifeways of the Kayapo and other indigenous Amazonians who are determined to remain within the park's boundaries.

In many locations, once a CCA is established and territorial rights are assured, the founding community invites a BINGO to send its ecologists and wildlife biologists to share in the task of protecting biodiversity by combining Western scientific methodology with indigenous ecological knowledge. And on occasion they ask for help negotiating with reluctant governments. For example, the Guarani Izoceños people in Bolivia invited the Wildlife Conservation Society to mediate a comanagement agreement with their government, which today allows the tribe to manage and own part of the new Kaa-Iya del Gran Chaco National Park.

But too much hope should probably not be placed in a handful of successful comanagement models or a few conservationists' epiphanies.

There are some respected and influential conservation biologists who still strongly support top-down, centralized "fortress" conservation. Duke University's John Terborgh, for example, author of the classic *Requiem for Nature,* believes that comanagement projects and CCAs are a huge mistake. "My feeling is that a park should be a park, and it shouldn't have any resident people in it," he says, including indigenous people. He bases his argument on research in Peru's Manu National Park, where native Machiguenga Indians fish and hunt animals with traditional weapons. Terborgh is concerned that they may acquire motorboats, guns, and chainsaws used by their fellow tribesmen outside the park. Then there's paleontologist Richard Leakey, who at the 2003 World Parks Congress in South Africa set off a firestorm of protest by denying the very existence of indigenous peoples in Kenya, his homeland.

And the unrestrained corporate lust for energy, hardwood, medicines, and strategic metals is still a considerable threat to indigenous communities—arguably a larger threat than conservation, though the lines between the two are being blurred. Particularly problematic is the fact that international conservation organizations remain comfortable working in close quarters with some of the most aggressive global resource prospectors, such as Boise Cascade, Chevron-Texaco, Mitsubishi, Conoco-Phillips, International Paper, Rio Tinto Mining, Shell, and Weyerhauser, all of whom are members of a CI-created entity called the Center for Environmental Leadership in Business. Of course if the BINGOs were to renounce their corporate partners, they would forfeit millions of dollars in revenue and access to global power without which they sincerely believe they could not be effective.

Fortunately, many conservationists are beginning to realize that most of the areas they have sought to protect are rich in biodiversity precisely because the people who were living there had come to understand the value and mechanisms of biological diversity without formal schooling in ecology, botany, or zoology. Some will even admit that wrecking the lives of ten million or more poor, powerless people has been an enormous mistake, not only a moral, social, philosophical, and economic mistake but an ecological one as well. Others have learned from bitter experience that national parks and protected areas surrounded by angry, hungry people who describe themselves as "enemies of conservation" are generally doomed to fail. As Cristina Eghenter of WWF observed after working with communities surrounding the Kayan Mentarang National Park in Borneo, "It is becoming increasingly evident that conservation objectives can rarely be obtained or sustained by imposing policies that produce negative impacts on indigenous peoples."

More and more conservationists seem to be wondering how, after setting aside a "protected" land mass the size of Africa, global biodiversity continues to decline. Might there be something terribly wrong with this plan? The Convention on Biological Diversity has documented the astounding fact that in Africa, where so many parks and reserves have been created and where indigenous evictions run highest, 90 percent of biodiversity lies outside of protected areas. If we want to preserve biodiversity in the far reaches of the globe, places that are in many cases still occupied by indigenous people living in ways that are ecologically sustainable, history is showing us that the most counterproductive thing we can do is evict them.

This article is adapted from its original publication in Orion *magazine, November/December 2005.*

A popular new strategy for the "protection" of indigenous people is to open their lands to ecotourism, thus bringing some cash income without requiring that forests be cut down or lands otherwise developed. However, the effects of large numbers of tourists passing through traditional communities has been less than benign, as natives are put in the position of curiosities and their artifacts are reproduced and commercialized, losing the aura of their original intent.

CHAPTER 16

Mixed Promises of Ecotourism

Suzanne York
International Forum on Globalization

TOURISM IS THE WORLD'S LARGEST service industry, and in the age of globalization, indigenous communities and peoples, their artifacts and their cultural heritage, are more and more sought after as new and unique "travel destinations." Tourism is hailed by global development agencies as a sure way to bring economic growth and prosperity, yet it is destructive in many ways, from pollution to unfair wages to land displacement. Ecotourism, on the other hand, is promoted as a more sustainable version of tourism, desirable to a niche tourist market of sensitive ecology-oriented adventure travelers. But for native peoples, ecotourism is just another form of often unwelcome development, an infringement on their lands usually without their consent, yet another threat to their rights and livelihoods, their culture, lands and environment.

Ecotourism is the fastest growing sector of the travel industry, with an average annual growth rate of 20 to 30 percent. It is promoted as environmentally friendly, culturally savvy, and sustainable. And it is also highly profitable. While there are no hard and fast numbers, a 2002 report by the United Nations Environment Programme stated that independent "nature tourism" companies in the United States and Canada handle well over one billion dollars in annual sales (ecotourism is considered a "specialty" segment of nature tourism).

The International Ecotourism Society defines ecotourism as "responsible travel to natural areas that conserves the environment and improves the well-being of local people." It promotes various activities, from bird-watching to adventure travel to conserving turtle habitat to visiting indigenous peoples—the more "primitive" the better. While ecotourism has successfully brought attention to some environmental conservation issues and occasionally enhanced cultural understanding, ecotourism in reality is not usually ecofriendly. Aside from the massive amounts of fossil fuel required for all forms of transportation, large numbers of tourists in pristine areas create a transient but continuing population problem in destination spots, bringing significant ecological damage. However sensitive the travelers, ecotourism inevitably harms the earth and the indigenous peoples who have lived off that earth for millennia.

Governments that promote tourism are hoping for the promised benefits of employment, infrastructure development, and foreign-exchange earnings. However, tourism has not fostered any meaningful sustainable development. Local populations, especially indigenous populations, rarely share in the benefits of tourism, including ecotourism, and are instead exposed to the negative impacts of the industry. Environmental degradation, loss of control of and access to local natural resources, social degradation, intrusion into traditional communities, human rights abuses, and commodification of cultures are the more usual outcomes. If jobs are created, they are at the lowest end of the spectrum—maids, busboys, porters and so on.

DOUBTFUL ECONOMIC BENEFITS FOR POOR COUNTRIES

According to the World Tourism Organization, 763 million people traveled to a foreign country in 2004, spending more than US$622 billion. Tourism represents approximately 7 percent of the worldwide exports of goods and services; international tourism receipts combined with passenger transport currently total more than $575 billion—making tourism the world's number one export earner, ahead of automotive products, chemicals, petroleum and food. *In 1993 the World Tourism Organization estimated that ecotourism roughly accounts for 20 percent of international travel in the Asia-Pacific region, and some areas, such as South Africa, have experienced a massive growth in visitors to game and nature reserves—over 100 percent annually.*

According to the World Bank, in 2001, $142.3 billion in international tourism receipts accrued to developing countries. Tourism is actually the principal export in a third of all developing countries and it is the primary source of foreign exchange earnings among the 49 Least Developed Countries. Unfortunately, however, much of that money leaves the country as fast as it comes in. *The World Bank estimates that 55 percent of international tourism income in the global South leaves the country via foreign-owned airlines, hotels and tour operators, or payments for imported food, drink and supplies.* Studies in individual coun-

tries have put the figure for "leakage" even higher—over 60 percent in Fiji. A study of tourism by the organization Sustainable Living found that "leakage" in Thailand was about 70 percent of all money spent by tourists. Estimates of leakage for other Third World countries range from 80 percent in the Caribbean to 40 percent in India. So it would seem that tourism may not be the panacea for global poverty that its advocates claim.

CULTURAL IMPACTS OF ECOTOURISM

Among the most degrading effects of ecotourism is the marketing of indigenous heritage, cultural identity, and sacred rituals. Ancient cultures are quickly reduced by this activity to another exotic product to be advertised and sold. Rituals, dances, and religious ceremonies are stripped of their deeper traditional spiritual value and made meaningless. Indigenous artifacts are valued only for their souvenir potential, and the indigenous people themselves tend to be valued only as a photo-opportunity. Local crafts are often crowded out of the market altogether, as corporations copy and mass-produce arts and crafts and clothing, marginalizing the local craftsperson and substituting cheap labor outside of the country. In Malaysia and Indonesia, for example, the fine art of batik, a dye-and-wax process that creates beautiful prints on natural fiber, is now mass-produced on synthetic materials in hundreds of factories in Southeast Asia. Traditional designs have been replaced by pop art.

The social effects on indigenous cultures are staggering. According to Deborah McLaren of the Rethinking Tourism Project, exposure to consumer culture makes locals regard themselves for the first time as "poor." As a community loses its self-reliance and has to turn to foreign companies for wages, necessities such as food and shelter become unaffordable. The globalization of the economy transforms local self-sufficient communities into consumer-oriented, dependent societies.

Take the case of the Masai of Africa, one of the earliest targets of "ecologically sound tourism." Since the 1950s, when big-game hunting started to become popular, the Masai have faced eviction from tribal lands, economic dislocation, assault on traditional values, and environmental degradation. Mainly pastoralists who used the land for their economic activities and traditional practices, the Masai were forced off their lands to make way for wildlife preserves, lodges, and campsites. Land disputes have arisen in resettlement areas, and the Masai have also experienced social and economic alienation, commercialization of their culture, prostitution, and the spread of AIDS. The rise in the number of tourists has had severe consequences for the environment, as increased deforestation and pollution have threatened the region's biodiversity and disrupted the ecological balance. In the Masai Mara National Park in Kenya and the Ngorongoro Conservation Area in Tanzania, forests bordering lodges and campgrounds have been cut down for firewood. Hotels have dumped sewage in Masai settlement areas, campsites have polluted rivers, and tourists and vehicles have destroyed grass cover, affecting plant and animal species. *(See also Chapter 15.)*

In Ifugao province in the Philippines, the Banaue Rice Terraces, declared a World Heritage Site by the United Nations Educational, Scientific, and Cultural Organization (UNESCO), have been sold by the government as a major tourist destination, to the detriment of the region's indigenous inhabitants. Tourism was advocated as the answer to the problems of one of the country's poorest provinces. The Ifugaos, the builders of world-renowned rice terraces, have subsisted for centuries off the crops planted in their terraces. The influx of ecotourists disrupted the traditional economic practices of the community, as people left indigenous subsistence farming for tourist-related businesses such as wood-carving and posing in traditional dress for tourist cameras. The wood-carving industry is depleting local forest resources. And a water shortage is occurring because the community has to share water with hotels and restaurants; now there is not enough water for the lower paddies of the rice terraces, leaving farmers unable to plant in these fields. Some have converted their rice paddies into residential lots where lodges and shops are built. Others have left farming altogether (harming Ifugao's tradition of cooperative farming) in favor of tourism-related jobs.

A study of the Philippines by the Tebtebba Foundation found that instead of improving their lives, tourism has made life harder for the Ifugao. They suffer from soaring costs brought about by the influx of tourists, and many are forced to seek better fortunes in cities. The pressure brought about by tourism will eventually kill the rice terraces, the main reason why tourists came to the area in the first place. The study concluded that the impetus for the tourist industry in Ifugao will soon be gone forever, leaving the people with whatever is left of their dignity, culture, and environment.

The United Nations proclaimed 2002 as the International Year of Ecotourism in an effort to encourage cooperation among governments, international and regional organizations, and nongovernmental organizations to promote sustainable development that protects the environment. Many indigenous groups are extremely concerned that the threats ecotourism poses to their societies are not being addressed by these organizations. The fundamental problems of the ecotourism industry, according to indigenous organizations, are: a lack of assessment of the nature of the ecotourism industry and its effects on the environment and people; disruption of local economies by displacement of activities that previously made possible self-reliant and sustainable community development; increasing damage to the environment and local communities as ecotourism grows; need to expand physical infrastructures to provide tourist access to remote areas; increased encroachment, illegal logging and mining; and plundering of biological resources. Governments are not prepared for ecotourism because they do not have frameworks to monitor and control ecotourism developments.

Indigenous peoples have a right to protect their lands and their heritage. They also have the right to determine what takes place on their lands and how it impacts their livelihoods. Only when indigenous peoples retain control over the development of tourism in their own communities, participating in planning and implementation, will negative impacts decline.

Box E: Toward an Indigenous Ecotourism

Recognizing the problems sometimes brought by ecotourism on indigenous lands, efforts are under way within many indigenous communities to create new guidelines and controls that will help ensure that some of the positive potentials of ecotourism can be realized, without the negative outcomes described above. In some places, communities are already running their own successful programs. At the heart of the matter are a few main considerations:

(1) Respect for the rights of indigenous communities to be fully informed of all proposed tourism activities by outsiders on their lands; the right to approve and regulate the activity; and the right to decline it.

(2) Intensive training within indigenous communities on the pros and cons of tourism and the best means to preserve and protect traditional values and practices.

(3) Protection of traditional land, economic base, and political control so indigenous communities can achieve viability and self-sufficiency without depending on any form of tourism or other economic activities that may not serve the community's long-term interests; development of locally based economic alternatives.

(4) Inclusion in the education curriculum of the wider society of units fostering a broader understanding of indigenous economic, political, and cultural values as deserving recognition equal to those of the nonindigenous society.

According to Indigenous Tourism Rights International, "prior informed consent" is crucial; its absence has been at the heart of most conflicts with indigenous communities facing advances from the outside world. This includes access to all information (negative and positive) concerning proposed economic activities, as well as access and participation in policy-making that affects indigenous communities; official support for tourism models developed by indigenous peoples; support for economic diversity within communities; and the absolute right to "say no."

In other words, indigenous peoples must participate directly in all phases of the planning, negotiation, approval, implementation and regulation of tourism activities that affect them. When this is achieved, positive results are possible. The following are a few examples of controls that led to good outcomes.

Toledo Ecotourism Association, TEA (Belize)

This is a community-based organization owned and operated by an association of Mopan, Kek'chi and Garifuna villages. The association enables the local people to plan, control and profit directly from "low impact" ecotourism.

The objective of TEA is to share the benefits of tourism as widely as possible in each participating village. Guides, food providers, and entertainers are rotated among seven to nine families in each village. Members vote on a board that oversees the running of the program, ensuring that guesthouses maintain standards and that tourism and its income is distributed as fairly as possible among the ten participating villages.

A parallel program is the Toledo Host Family Network/ Indigenous Experience Program, which arranges for tourists to stay in the homes of the villagers and participate in daily village life. Alternatively, the Mayan Guesthouse Program allows visitors to stay in guesthouses built by the villagers. In both projects the community provides food for their guests, sells their handicrafts, and acts as guides, while controlling activities.

RICANCIE: Indigenous Community Network of the Upper Napo for Intercultural Exchange and Ecotourism (Ecuador)

RICANCIE was founded in 1993 by several Quechua communities living in the Napo province of Amazonian Ecuador. Their goal is to improve the quality of life for nine Quechua villages via a community-based ecotourism project. The primary objectives have been the defense of the Quechua territory and rainforest from mining and oil development and also to improve the effects of tourism, which had been mainly negative. Prior to this, foreign travel companies arranged all tour groups. Most of the income generated by tourism left the villages and often led to conflict within the communities. RICANCIE has changed that by pursuing a self-determined development path. All decisions regarding events and strategies are made by a council whose members come from participating villages. The tourist infrastructure was built in accordance with the communal philosophy of the Quechua, and encourages all affected parties to participate in decision-making.

RICANCIE has created jobs and new sources of income for village members. Community-based ecotourism profits are used for projects in the participating communities. Other benefits are revitalization of cultural traditions and improved self-confidence among the Quechua communities. Additionally, community-based ecotourism has protected lands and offers an alternative to industrial agricultural practices, which lead inevitably to deforestation of primary rainforest.

Mutawintji Local Aboriginal Land Council, MLALC (Australia)

Mutawintji National Park, Mutawintji Historic Site and Mutawintji Nature Reserve in New South Wales were returned to aboriginal ownership in 1998 and are now run by the Mutawintji Local Aboriginal Land Council (MLALC). The organization is in charge of all tours to the national park, and guided tours are led by members of the council. The MLALC has also licensed its own tour operation, Mutawintji Heritage Tours, which supervises all nonindigenous tour operators.

Indigenous Tourism Rights International and the Central America Office of the International Indian Treaty Council (IITC)

Indigenous Tourism Rights International and the Guatemala-based Central America Office of the IITC have created a working relationship to engage indigenous community-based tourism projects in creating the Americas Indigenous Tourism Network and standards for indigenous ecotourism. The partnership focuses on indigenous communities in North America, Central and South America and the Caribbean.

The International Ecotourism Certification Movement

Indigenous Tourism Rights International (ITRI) is also working on promoting indigenous participation in ongoing ecotourism certification efforts in the Americas. Indigenous voices are often not heard in the ecotourism process; it is hoped that by engaging groups in meaningful consultation, their input will become part of the design process. ITRI has begun a collaborative process of establishing an Indigenous Fair Trade Tourism certification and association model.

In 2002, the Indigenous Peoples' Interfaith Dialogue on Globalization and Tourism conference, held in Chiang Rai, Thailand, reaffirmed the rights of indigenous peoples to control their traditional lands and values. At the event, Professor Luciano Minerbi of the University of Hawaii presented guidelines on how to minimize the negative impact of tourism on local communities. His paper, "A Framework for Alternative and Responsible Tourism: Eco Cultural Tourism," argued for a model of economic development that confirmed the primacy of indigenous land rights, traditional agriculture, traditional knowledge systems, cultural demarcation, new protection programs and devices, the promotion of the indigenous viewpoint among the public and government officials, and the acceptance and promotion of the viability of subsistence economic systems, among other points. These culturally and politically empowering steps could lead to acceptance of a controlled ecotourism that does not overrun its hosts.

From the sounds of a conch shell heralding a cultural renaissance to student video-graphers making films in the native Hawaiian language (as this film festival poster announces), Hawaiians are emerging from a century of colonial policy that included strict prohibition of all teaching in the Hawaiian language. Hawaiian immersion programs have become so popular and successful that they are the model for native language teaching around the world, taking an important place as part of broad new political and cultural expression among indigenous people in the Pacific, in North America, and elsewhere.

CHAPTER 17

The Fall and Rise of a Native Language

E. Koohan Paik

University of Hawaii, Kauai

A CENTURY BEFORE BRETTON WOODS codified plunder, corporate globalization had already devastated the Kingdom of Hawaii. By 1850, Kauai's lush sandalwood forests had been logged for a hungry Cantonese market; hardwoods had been razed to make North American railroad ties; New England goods were imported at a 400 percent markup; export crops like sugar and coffee supplied a booming Gold Rush market; a cheap labor force suffered grueling hours and many deaths; and the first book written in Hawaiian had been introduced—the Bible.

The fact that the Bible paved the way for the ultimate demise of the native language and culture wasn't noticed in the midst of the rapid advance of Christianity. Most Hawaiians were pleased to see a book published in their own language, albeit in the Roman alphabet. Reading, in both Hawaiian and English, was all the rage. In a handful of years, literacy skyrocketed to 90 percent, as missionary presses churned out 150 million pages of Hawaiian text to keep up with demand. During those years, the number of Hawaiian-language newspapers totaled around 150. The number of schools teaching in either Hawaiian or English jumped from virtually none to over a thousand. The *ali`i*, or nobility, saw bilingual literacy as a positive development in a changing economic landscape. What most of the *ali`i* did not foresee was that U.S. sugar companies would eventually use English as a shoehorn to systematically undermine the Hawaiian language, and how that would ultimately lead to the overthrow of the Hawaiian nation.

As corporate interests, and the English language, began to dominate the worlds of commerce and government, schools teaching in Hawaiian began to dwindle. In 1864, Matai Kekuanoa, appointed by King Kamehameha to head the board of education, issued a warning: "If we wish to preserve the Kingdom of Hawaii for Hawaiians, and to educate our people, we must insist that the Hawaiian language shall be the language of all our National Schools." But by 1880, schools teaching in Hawaiian had dropped from 1,500 to only 150. In 1886, teaching in Hawaiian was outlawed.

Meanwhile, English-speaking foreigners had persuaded the king to allow them to purchase land, leading to enormous foreign capital investments in sugar plantations, especially after the Reciprocity Treaty of 1876, which lifted all tariffs on Hawaiian sugar exports to the United States. As the sugar industry ballooned, cheap workers were imported by the thousands from all over Asia. Thus Native Hawaiians were increasingly without their language, their lands, and their livelihoods—a typical tale for colonized peoples. From there it was a short step to loss of their monarchy and nationhood, widely mourned among Native Hawaiians to this day.

COLONIZING THE MIND

A routine tactic in successful colonization is to colonize the minds of the people by killing the native language. Within language is an entire universe containing history, culture, pride, identity, and well-being. As Onondaga philosopher and chief Oren Lyons has put it: "Language is the soul of a nation."

To replace an indigenous language with a colonial tongue immediately puts the native at a disadvantage. As the colonized mind realigns to the worldview and universe embodied in the new language, it begins to rationalize the world through colonial eyes. Soon, the colonized people see all things native as inferior, including themselves, so they acquiesce to assimilation and exploitation. The phenomenon is known as "internalized oppression." Once the mental landscape has been conquered, the rest is easy.

The strategy is common. In 1492, Columbus's banner year, some three hundred languages were spoken in North America. According to the Society for Indigenous Languages, the number is down to 153 today, of which sixty-seven are nearly extinct, spoken by only a handful of people. This demise was largely due to the fact that, until 1990, it was illegal in the United States to conduct classroom instruction in Native American languages.

The problem was not confined to North America. Other examples include the Soviet Union, where Russian was the enforced language. So today, in Russia, 90 percent of the population speaks Russian, while seventy of the country's nearly one hundred other native languages (and cultures)

are nearly gone. When Nelson Mandela created "the new South Africa," he clearly understood the relationship between language, identity and diversity, and established as the country's eleven *official* languages Afrikaans, English, Ndebele, Sepedi, Sesotho, Swati, Tsonga, Tswana, Venda, Xhosa and Zulu.

Melissa Nelson and Philip Klasky of the San Francisco–based Cultural Conservancy have written: "We see two main strategies used to erase native cultures: quick, overt genocide through warfare, disease, starvation, *or* slow erosion through colonial assimilation and religious conversion. Survival meant adapting to the colonizer's ways. The killing of a language happens exactly as one would expect: the weak must speak to the strong in the language of the strong. The Darwinian way of the world bears some responsibility, globalization does the rest: movies, television, Reeboks, and the Internet."

During most of the hundred years after instruction in Hawaiian was banned, any student caught speaking Hawaiian was physically and emotionally punished. Talk to anyone with a drop of Hawaiian blood in them, and they'll tell you their family's own version of this painful history. Entire generations refused to utter Hawaiian in the presence of their own children, for fear of stygmatizing them as too "native."

In Hawaii, the mental relandscaping has been so complete that for most of the twentieth century, Hawaiians themselves supported the English-only policies. When the prestigious Kamehameha preparatory schools proposed Hawaiian language courses in the 1920s and 1930s, opposition from parents was so strong the project was abandoned. English, it was believed, was the passport to a good career and an identity as a full-fledged "American." However, this conversion to English (and the way of life that goes with it) has coincided with a precipitous decline in the health, welfare and education of the native people. Hawaiians have the shortest lifespan of any ethnic group in a state which touts the highest life expectancy in the United States. Native Hawaiians also have the highest incidence of heart disease, diabetes and cancer, the lowest median income among the four major ethnic groups, the highest proportion of the population in low-status occupations, and the highest unemployment. Passport to the good life? Not exactly.

What is unfortunate is that these statistics are often taken, even by natives themselves, as *proof* of native inferiority. It's an endless feedback loop of internalized oppression. To this day, many Hawaiians refuse to let their children learn the language, as if it might somehow lead to rejection, unemployment, and disease.

"THE LANGUAGE NESTS"

Nonetheless, resistance to cultural obliteration was never wholly crushed. In the early 1980s, a handful of Hawaiian-language educators shared a vision that Hawaiian could be revitalized as a daily language. To do so, it would have to be part of daily life from infancy. The language would have to be spoken at home and in the community, as well as becoming the medium of instruction from kindergarten to college. Parents would also have to learn Hawaiian and commit to speaking it at home. It was a tall order, considering that at the time, teaching any subject in Hawaiian was still against the law!

These thinkers were inspired by a native-language radio talk show that featured a different elder every week. Many of these elders were concerned that after they were gone, there would be no more native speakers, or *mnaleo*, a term that refers to mothers passing food to their babies through their lips, as birds do in the forest—a metaphor for the healthy transmittal of language. It was then that the group decided to take serious action.

They based their landmark program on the Maori preschool concept of *Kohanga Reo*, "the language nest," and named it in Hawaiian, `Aha Punana Leo, or "the Language Nests Organization." Today, thanks to `Aha Punana Leo, Hawaii's native language-medium education is among the most highly respected internationally.

One of the founders of `Aha Punana Leo, William "Pila" Wilson, ascribes the program's success to its philosophy of *mauli*, or life force. Hawaiian *mauli* allows for the continued existence of the Hawaiian people. `Aha Punana Leo sees academic achievement not as the end but as a means to the real goal—strengthening *mauli*. The program focuses on Hawaiian family experiences, behaviors, and values—the proper way to interact with adults and other children, actions toward food and animals, spiritual interactions, and the important role of music and dance.

HAWAIIAN IMMERSION INSTRUCTION

`Aha Punana Leo served only preschool students. Once toddlers were ready for kindergarten, there was no means to continue school in Hawaiian. That's when determined parents from all over the islands convened in Honolulu to *demand* that public schools offer Hawaiian as a medium of instruction. Finally, in 1986, the language ban was lifted. At the time of this writing, in 2005, there are well over one thousand *Hawaiian immersion* students enrolled across the archipelago.

Hawaiian immersion's development required recruitment of teachers capable of teaching in Hawaiian. `Alohilani Rogers was one such teacher. A soft-spoken scholar in her mid thirties, she recalls how her personal family history catalysed her passion for Hawaiian:

"When I was growing up, I always heard the story of my grandmother. She's pure Hawaiian, but she never spoke Hawaiian to us. And I always wondered, how is it that she's pure Hawaiian and never spoke Hawaiian?

"And then I heard the story of how she was taken away to an orphanage in Oahu where they beat her for speaking Hawaiian. I remember feeling how unjust that was, that my grandmother, pure Hawaiian, was never allowed to speak Hawaiian here in Hawaii.

"I would ask my grandmother to teach me, but she could remember very little. Anyway, it was considered detrimental to teach a child Hawaiian. It wasn't good to be Hawaiian, speak Hawaiian, dress Hawaiian, look Hawaiian.

"In high school, I decided that if I didn't learn it, that would be the end of the language. I needed to do something. By that time, Kauai High School offered a class in Hawaiian, but it didn't qualify as a foreign language for credit. So I had to take French. For two years of French class, I sat in the back and got Cs. When I was finally able to take Hawaiian, I sat at the front of the class and got As."

Now that Rogers is a veteran Hawaiian teacher, she still has to deal with wariness amongst parents: "They're not certain that learning Hawaiian will help their children succeed in life today: get a job, support their families, drive nice cars, that kind of thing. When I was in college, I got that question all the time—'How you gonna feed your family with Hawaiian language?' I would say, it's not about feeding my family; it's about making sure that I know who I am and where I come from. There's a Hawaiian proverb for that: *O ke kahua ma mua, ma hope ke kukulu.* Build the foundation first, and then on top of that build your house."

I personally first became deeply aware of the Hawaiian immersion renaissance through my work as a media literacy educator at Ho'ike, the Kauai, Hawaii, public access television station. The FCC mandates that public access television give voice to the otherwise excluded and disempowered. In view of this obligation, no voice was more deserving than the Hawaiian voice, whose tongue had been uprooted and grafted with another.

In that role we had the chance to organize an islandwide student film festival, with the first-ever category of *Hawaiian-language* student films. Not only would the festival give voice to the disempowered, it would also create a body of new media in Hawaiian. Students were asked to make films about their elders, *kupuna,* thus preserving family histories in Hawaiian. Equally important, the process would help develop media skills essential for expression in a democratic society in the modern world. Just as education in the written word democratized Europe in the Middle Ages, when only the ecclesiastical elite knew how to read and write, media education helps democratize our local population. It's as if Hawaii had come full circle, from the brief democratizing era when the written word was introduced to the long dark ages when the native language was outlawed to its recent revival, leading also to the language's new expression in video and other new media. Tools of communication would be back in the hands of the people.

THE NI`IHAU PHENOMENON

The film festival also brought into my life the luckiest anomaly in the history of the Hawaiian language, the Ni`ihau phenomenon. Ni`ihau is a small, isolated island to the west of Kauai that is almost entirely populated by Native Hawaiians. Ni`ihau eluded the language bans of the last century because it was, and still is, privately owned by ethnic Europeans; if it had been owned by Hawaiians, it would surely have been stolen or sold. But as a result, Ni`ihau became a kind of Noah's Ark for language preservation; its native population of less than 150 has been able to retain its Hawaiian fluency. In addition, about three hundred former Ni`ihauans now live on Kauai, where I was able to meet them. These first-language survivors are precious to the continued propagation of authentic Hawaiian fluency.

The sad irony is that these special people have always been the group to suffer the most socially. In a context that prizes English fluency, the

Ni`ihauans have been relegated to second-class citizenship. They have the lowest incomes and shortest life spans in the islands. As the most "native" of the natives, other Hawaiians sometimes ostracized them for being "different," and derided their language for its strange Tahitian-influenced dialect.

Lately, though, this has all begun to change. Ke Kula Ni`ihau O Kekaha (Ni`ihau School of Kekaha) is defying the statistics. A school serving Ni`ihauans in Kauai, Ke Kula boasts no drug problems, no graffiti, no fighting, and high performance. Math, science, traditional paddling, poetry, computer skills, and other subjects comprise the curriculum, which is taught entirely in Hawaiian.

This is not Hawaiian immersion. These students are already authentically fluent; they were born speaking Hawaiian. Numbering less than fifty, they are the heart of the effort to perpetuate Hawaiian language and culture on Kauai. It is within their fragile lexicons, rich in the subtleties and complexities of true fluency, that the future of the real language rests. Principal Haunani Seward believes that video can be a crucial tool in saving the spoken language, and so we have begun training her teachers in video production.

The joy that spills out of the open doors and windows of Ke Kula's bright, airy cinder-block schoolhouse contrasts starkly with the security guards and almost prison-like atmosphere at the island's "normal" public schools. A conch is blown to signal the start of class. *Hula*, song and poetry percolate spontaneously from voices, bodies and ukulele-strumming fingers. Because the kids are encouraged to be who they are, they are the purest embodiments of a lost culture. Now that they are videotaping each other, it is recorded for posterity.

One of my students at the Kauai Community College branch of the University of Hawaii is Eleanor Masuda, who is from Ni`ihau. She has told me how grateful she is to have been one of the few Hawaiians to grow up speaking her own language. But she is appalled by how it has been distorted by the outside world. In a paper on language, she discussed how the dominant culture has co-opted the word *aloha*:

"I'm disappointed how the Hawaiian language is used in advertising. For example, Safeway advertises that 'you can find *aloha* on the shelf' at their markets. I got upset. You can't find *aloha* on any supermarket shelf! It is in each individual person. *Aloha* has multiple meanings, such as Love and Welcome. But the action of the word *aloha* is powerful. '*Alo*' means space—the space in front of you—'*ha*' means breath. When you hug and kiss someone and say *aloha*, the words are the breath of love towards all people and nationalities."

The desecration of *aloha* sums up the colonial epoch in Hawaiian history. The land, the culture, the language—everything Hawaiian—have been taken and reworked to serve the invaders. In just a few generations, values based on generosity and abundance have been replaced by those of profit and scarcity. Pristine forests and beaches have given way to highways, parking lots and housing developments. Traditions have been twisted into a mockery of their true meanings, to be served up at hotel *lu`aus*. Hawaiians, no longer able to afford living in a pricey "paradise," are leaving at an alarming rate. And the word *aloha* is being used to hawk groceries packaged in New Jersey, in boxes printed in China, before being shipped thousands of miles across the Pacific to await their sale, which will ultimately profit a supermarket headquartered in California.

However, there are many people unwilling to "give up the ship" so quickly. These are, among others, the courageous parents who lobbied for Hawaiian immersion education, the `Aha Punana Leo visionaries, the children of Ni`ihau, and the young videomakers of Kauai. They are shining examples of positive action in the face of seemingly insurmountable odds. Because of them, Hawaiian is coming back home.

Mexico is the planet's "center of origin" for maize biodiversity; its gene pools feature more than five thousand varieties. This has not kept the Mexican government from permitting U.S. varieties of cheap subsidized corn to enter Mexican fields and markets, thus undermining traditional Mayan farming communities. The government claims it had no choice under the rules of the North American Free Trade Agreement and now the WTO. Some imported varieties are genetically modified and have spread into ancient varieties, causing anguish and consternation among traditional growers.

CHAPTER 18

Genetic Pollution of Mayan Corn

Suzanne York
International Forum on Globalization

THE INDIGENOUS PEOPLES OF MEXICO have cultivated corn (also called maize, or *maíz* in Spanish) for millennia. Mexico's five-thousand-year-old corn gene pool includes thousands of varieties and plant relatives specific to each region. They reflect not only tremendous biological diversity but also agricultural genius, as the varieties are adapted to soil, climate, pests, and other local conditions. Corn is the nation's most important food crop, and Mexico is the main global "center of origin" for maize biodiversity.

Indigenous peoples account for approximately 60 percent of Mexican corn growers. They cultivate the plant not only as a means of subsistence but also as part of a social, cultural, and religious process. Mayans, along with Zapotecs, Mixtecs, and other indigenous peoples, consider corn a gift from the gods, believing that humans are made from corn.

For all these reasons, the recent detection of genetically engineered (GE) corn in southern Mexico came as a particular shock to indigenous communities. However, it was made inevitable by the North American Free Trade Agreement (NAFTA) a few years before.

CONTAMINATION

In fall 2001, the Mexican government announced that scientists from the University of California at Berkeley had found that indigenous varieties of maize in Oaxaca were contaminated with genetically engineered corn varieties most likely imported from the United States. In fifteen of twenty-two tested communities, GE-contaminated maize seeds were discovered; these included some 3 to 10 percent of the total tested maize seed. Genetically engineered Bt, or *bacillius thuringiensis,* gene was one of the contaminants, and Berkeley scientists believe the native corn became contaminated through interbreeding with Bt corn. The Bt gene produces a pesticide toxic to many insects, but it can also harm insects that are beneficial to plants, such as ladybugs and lacewings, as well as harming insect-eating birds and damaging soil fertility. Though not approved for planting, biotech corn can be legally imported for use in food. The full extent of the contamination in Mexico is not yet known. But in January 2002, the Mexican ministry of the environment confirmed the initial tests and did a further study, which showed that in remote regions of Oaxaca and Puebla, 35 percent of tested maize varieties had GE contamination.

The introduction of GE corn in the plant's global homeland poses a long-term threat beyond Mexico, as the potential exists that contaminated maize varieties could spread to other traditional varieties, or even to wild relatives, with unknown consequences. It is also a threat to the survival of many other varieties developed by indigenous peoples over a millennium.

While the exact cause of the corn contamination has not yet been determined, most researchers suspect the dumping in Mexico of five million tons of U.S.-imported maize that contained transgenic material. In the United States, 35 to 40 percent of corn is genetically engineered. Since the corn is government-subsidized, it is considerably cheaper than nonsubsidized Mexican corn, so farmers buy and plant U.S. corn, thus spreading it across the country. As more Mexican farmers begin to plant the less expensive hybrid varieties of U.S. corn, the diversity of Mexico's corn will decline. There is significant concern in scientific communities that the dumping of GE crops could threaten vital gene repositories for Mexican domesticated corn, which are already declining at alarming rates.

In November 2004, a report written by a scientific panel of experts for the Commission for Environmental Cooperation (which was set up under NAFTA in part to address regional environmental concerns) concluded that GE corn from the United States posed a threat to Mexico, and that it should be limited or stopped. The panel recommended that the GE corn be labeled as such and milled before it is allowed into Mexico, to prevent the corn from being planted and from cross-pollinating with other plants.

The Mexican government had already banned the planting of GE crops in 1998 to protect the genetic integrity of indigenous maize. But by early 2005, despite the now clear threat of contamination, the Mexican government passed legislation authorizing planting and selling of GE crops. The so-called biosafety law (called the "Monsanto Law" by civil society activists) was very controversial, dividing the scientific community. It lifts barriers to the use, sale, farming, and import and export of GE crops; it also sets out rules on labeling some GE products according to guidelines put forth by the ministry of health. Under the law, approval for the planting and sale of GE crops will be decided on a case-by-case basis by CIBIOGEM (the Inter-Secretarial Commission on Biosecurity and GMOs), the national authority that oversees import/export, testing, and release of GE crops. This body is advised by scientists on the newly formed Biosafety Consultative Council. Opponents of the law have questioned the independence of this new council. They are also concerned about the lack of enforcement mechanisms and an inadequate process for informing local communities about the release of transgenics into the environment. Above all, opponents believe the bill makes it easy for industry to get approval for GE crops. Perhaps the most ominous aspect of this law, for indigenous and peasant farmers, is that it exempts companies from any liability for genetic pollution caused by their seeds.

The new law does not take into account the views of indigenous peoples and farmers, and many critics, including scientists, have spoken out against the law. Prior to final passage, a group of scientists and academics, including Dr. Ignacio Chapela, one of the biologists who discovered that native Mexican maize had been contaminated by transgenic corn varieties, called for a *continued* moratorium on the importation of GE maize. Now Chapela and others are concerned that Mexico will become a dumping ground for GE products by multinationals such as Monsanto, Sygenta, and Dupont.

THE ROLE OF NAFTA

The advent of NAFTA brought enormous problems to Mexico's indigenous farmers even before it was implemented and before any threats of GE contamination manifested. The United States demanded as a condition for Mexico's participation in NAFTA that it break up the traditional *ejido* communal land-ownership system that had been instituted after the Zapatista revolution in the early 1900s. Since the success of that revolution, virtually all indigenous farming was through *ejidos*, particularly Mayan corn growing in the Oaxaca-Chiapas region of southern Mexico.

After privatization of land ownership and elimination of the collectives, native corn farmers have not survived as they once did. Many of their lands have been lost to large growers or to plantation forest developers, leaving many Mayan corn growers landless and hungry. By breaking the back of the indigenous system, the Mexican government helped precipitate the uprising of the modern Zapatistas on New Year's Day 1994.

NAFTA had other important effects on indigenous corn producers. Mexico has gone from being a major corn producer to a major corn importer, with corn imports nearly tripling since NAFTA. Chapter VII of NAFTA required Mexico to open up its corn sector to imports in exchange for guaranteed access to U.S. and Canadian markets for horticultural products and other labor-intensive crops. So Mexico had to allow entry of cheaper subsidized corn imports from the United States and Canada, at prices far below what Mexican farmers had received before the free trade agreement. Unable to compete, Mexican farmers quit growing corn. Many *campesinos* and farmworkers migrated to large cities, leaving the country extremely dependent on corn imports from their NAFTA partners. Though corn prices for Mexican corn growers decreased, the price for consumers increased. (In 2008, under requirements of NAFTA, Mexico will eliminate remaining quotas on corn imports, which will open the gates even further to cheap GE American corn.)

Exacerbating the situation, again because of pressure from NAFTA, the Mexican government in 1998 ceased subsidizing tortilla mills and ended price controls on tortillas. This forced Mexican consumers to buy more expensive tortillas made from U.S. corn or buy no tortillas at all. This poses a grave danger to food sovereignty in Mexico. According to the Mexico-based Center for Economic and Political Investigations of Community Action, indigenous peoples and *campesinos* used to plant their corn, harvest it, save part of it for their own consumption, and sell the rest or keep it for the next harvest. Now they buy the seeds from a transnational company such as Monsanto, Novartis, or Cargill, produce many tons of corn at a low cost to the company, consume millions of dollars of agrochemicals, and later sell the product to buy packaged tortillas from the company to feed their families. Some indigenous corn growers finally stopped growing corn entirely, planting crops such as watermelon and cantaloupe for export, or gave up and migrated to the cities.

IS MAIZE CONTAMINATION SPREADING?

In fall 2003, a coalition of Mexican indigenous and peasant farming communities and civil society organizations released the results of their own studies of maize contamination in nine Mexican states (Chihuahua, Morelas, Durango, México DF, Puebla, Oaxaca, San Luis Potosí, Tlaxcala, and Veracruz). Among two thousand maize plants tested, samples from thirty-three communities in these states tested positive for GE contamination. Analyses found widespread contamination with Starlink maize, which is not approved for human consumption in the United States. Other evidence showed contamination of a single plant with as many as three GE types, all patented by transnational corporations.

Four unpublished Mexican government–sponsored studies to determine the presence of transgenes in maize have found varying levels of contamination in two or more states, corroborating the findings of the Berkeley scientists. Since the Berkeley scientists' evidence went public, the Mexican government and the scientific community have acknowledged that Mexico's traditional maize crop is contaminated with GE maize, despite the government prohibition at that time on planting GE seeds in Mexico; the moratorium has since been lifted.

A study done in August 2005 by Mexican scientists and U.S. researchers found no signs of contamination of native maize in one area of Oaxaca. (It should be noted that the editor of the study is employed by the Monsanto Laboratory of Washington University in St. Louis.) Civil society groups, including scientists, have taken exception to the study and to the assertions by agribusiness that contamination is not a threat to local maize varieties. They are concerned that it is a flawed study, used poor statistics, and sampled only a small geographic region, and as such is inapplicable to parts of Mexico where contamination has been found. The study also failed to include earlier results, by some of the report's authors, that found widespread contamination.

The coalition of indigenous and peasant farmers has demanded that the Mexican government publish the results of its studies on GE contamination, put a stop to all imports of GE maize, and implement a new legal framework that protects animal and human health from GE contamination.

An indigenous farmer from Oaxaca described government representatives coming to his community to tell him not to worry about contamination, since there is no evidence that GE crops are harmful to health. His response was, "We have ten thousand years of evidence that our maize is good for our health. To contaminate it with [GE]

maize is a crime against all indigenous peoples and farming communities who have safeguarded maize over millennia for the benefit of humankind."

DEFENDING CORN

However the GE-contaminated corn entered Mexico, it underscores the threat that GE technology and trade rules pose to indigenous agriculture. Ancient indigenous practices such as seed saving are under attack by multinational corporations and the World Trade Organization. Under the TRIPS agreement of the WTO, corporations can adapt and patent seeds that farmers have saved and exchanged for generations, making farmers dependent on corporations for the right to grow a crop they've grown for centuries and undermining their economic and cultural survival.

Taking matters into their own hands, an "in-defense-of-maize" community movement has arisen in Mexico, made up of farmers (indigenous and nonindigenous), civil society, academics, and ecologists. Two Forums in Defense of Maize have been held in the past several years, in which communities learn how to protect native maize varieties from contamination, detect contaminated maize, and carry out genetic testing. The forums also demanded re-institution of the moratorium on GE corn imports and called on international institutions to recognize the threat that contamination poses to biological diversity.

Indigenous farmers will not sit back and let the global trading system take over their lives and cultures. Indigenous leader Aldo Gonzales from Oaxaca has stated, "The pyramids could be destroyed, but a fistful of corn is the legacy that we can pass on to our children and grandchildren. Today we are being denied that possibility."

PART FOUR

Focus on Extractive Industries

This Ogoni man stands on the site of one of the best-known oil spills in Nigerian history, March 2001 in Ebubu, Nigeria. The massive 1970 oil spill and explosion in the Ogoni village of Ebubu killed his entire family, including his siblings and parents, and his best friends. Shell Oil, which owned the pumping station that went up in flames, promptly erected a wall around the explosion site, and government troops sealed off access to the area for almost thirty years, until 1999. The site has never been cleaned.

CHAPTER 19

Ogoni People of Nigeria versus Big Oil

Oronto Douglas and Ike Okonta
(Ijaw)
Environmental Rights Action

In February 2006, as this book was going to press, a group calling itself the Movement for the Emancipation of the Niger Delta attacked the huge Royal Dutch Shell oil production facilities in Nigeria, kidnapping nine people and causing some oil exports from the region to be suspended. The rebels are demanding increased community control of the delta's oil and other resource wealth, so that after decades of corporate and government intrusions, local people would finally share in the benefits and help determine their own future. This chapter was written before the 2006 uprising, but it gives details on the history of resource exploitation, massive land degradation, violence against local communities, and destruction of local livelihoods in the long run-up to the revolt.

ROYAL DUTCH SHELL has waged ecological and economic war against the peoples of the Niger Delta for over sixty years, in collaboration with successive Nigerian regimes that have violently and murderously sought to suppress their own peoples. In response, the Ogoni and other peoples of Nigeria are waging nonviolent resistance against Shell, one of the most powerful multinational corporations in the world, as well as against the International Monetary Fund and the oil-rich, corrupt Nigerian government—to reclaim our lands, our livelihoods, and our homes.

Oil production activities, such as gas flaring, oil spillage, construction of canals, and waste dumping, have already brought the ecosystem of the Niger Delta to near collapse. Shell degrades our private property but pays the affected communities little or no compensation. Nor do our communities receive a fair share of the oil royalties, the bulk of which are divided among Shell, the Nigerian government, and other oil companies. Shell's behavior is made far easier because it enjoys cordial relations with the military officers and politicians in power, in a symbiotic relationship sustained by their mutual desire to control the Niger Delta and exploit the oil. Shell maintains its own private police force, imports its own arms and ammunition, and has admitted making payments to the Nigerian military.

Trapped between a vicious and morally bankrupt government and an unscrupulous multinational, the indigenous communities of the Niger Delta have taken the path of nonviolent protest in a bid to protect what little remains of our endangered environment and our livelihoods.

THE NIGER DELTA

The Niger Delta is one of the world's richest areas of natural resources. There are extensive forests, abundant wildlife, and fertile agricultural land where rice, sugar cane, plantain, beans, palm oil, yams, cassava and timber are cultivated. The delta also has more freshwater fish species than any other coastal system in West Africa.

Before arrival of European traders in what is now modern Nigeria, the Niger Delta was inhabited mainly by the Ijo peoples who, with the other peoples of the delta, traded with the peoples of the hinterland, mainly the Igbo and Ibibio. The Ijo exported dried fish and salt to their neighbors in exchange for iron tools and fruit. The slave trade brought a stop to this flourishing commerce.

In spite of its considerable natural resources, the Niger Delta is one of the poorest and most under-developed parts of the country. Seventy percent of the inhabitants live a rural subsistence existence without electricity, piped water, hospitals, proper housing, or motorable roads. They are weighed down by debilitating poverty, malnutrition, and disease. Population is on the rise. This urbanization without genuine economic growth has produced the human ecologist's ultimate nightmare: a growing population that, in a bid to survive, is destroying the very ecosystem that should guarantee its survival.

At the root of the problem is the corporate exploration of the Niger Delta's substantial oil and gas reserves. Oil accounts for 95 percent of the country's foreign exchange earnings and represents about one-fourth of the gross domestic product. While Nigeria's wealth is squandered abroad, her people wither in poverty.

FROM AGRICULTURE TO OIL

At independence in 1960, Nigeria was virtually self-sufficient in food; agricultural products accounted for 97 percent of export revenue. Things took a dramatic turn in the 1970s, however, as international oil prices began to rise. Federal revenue surged to $2.5 billion in 1975 from a modest $295 million ten years earlier. Oil accounted for 82 percent of this activity, bringing great wealth to Nigeria's elite classes. By 1976, Nigeria was a member of OPEC and had become the seventh-largest producer of oil in the world, exporting two million barrels of crude a day. Virtually none of this wealth found its way to people in the delta. As agricultural exports declined and oil production soared, the federal government became more powerful and corrupt. Agricultural production slumped. Between 1970 and 1982, yearly production of the main Nigerian cash crops fell dramatically: cocoa by 43 percent, rubber by 29 percent, cotton by 65 percent, and groundnuts by 64 percent.

Nigeria became dependent on an oil industry that generated few jobs and had virtually no linkages with the other sectors of the national economy, which lapsed into the doldrums. Oil revenues peaked in 1980 at $24.9 billion, but because of extensive corruption, external indebtedness ballooned to $9 billion.

When the oil boom ended in the early 1980s, the country was in financial trouble. In mid-1985, the IMF offered Nigeria a bridging loan that amounted to almost $5 billion, but with a harsh Structural Adjustment Program that made Nigeria's monocultural economy even more vulnerable to Western imports and further impoverished the people. When President Buhari tried to resist this arrangement, a coalition of local and international oil and banking interests eased him out of power and, in August 1985, put General Ibrahim Babangida in his place. Babangida, under the guidance of the IMF, eliminated subsidies for key social services and set in motion the privatization of government-owned companies and agencies. Starvation and disease swept through the urban ghettos and the countryside, reaping a grim harvest.

THE RAVAGES OF SHELL

Shell operates the largest oil-producing venture in Nigeria. From 1986 to 1995 alone, Shell received approximately $2 billion in profit from its activities in the country. A report submitted to the World Conference of Indigenous Peoples on Environment and Development during the Rio Earth Summit in June 1992 by indigenous leaders of the Niger Delta told of the ecological consequences of Shell's activities in the region:

> *Apart from air pollution from the oil industry's emissions and flares day and night, producing poisonous gases that are silently and systematically wiping out vulnerable airborne biota and otherwise endangering the life of plants, game, and man himself, we have widespread water pollution and soil and land pollution that respectively result in the death of most aquatic eggs and juvenile stages of life of finfish and shellfish and animals. Agricultural lands contaminated with oil spills become dangerous for farming, even where they continue to produce any significant yields.*

Shell has also contaminated the delta's water supplies. In 1998, drinking water samples from five sites in the Niger Delta revealed that total petroleum hydrocarbon (TPH) in drinking water in all five Nigerian communities ranged from 250 to 37,500 times the legally accepted standard in the European Union.

Oil spills occur with disturbing regularity and enormity, because the bulk of Shell's pipelines are rusty, obsolete, and poorly maintained. Some Shell pipelines and sundry installations have not been replaced since they were put in place in the 1960s. Before resigning in 1994 in disgust and protest, Shell's former head of environmental studies, J.P. Van Dessel, said; "Wherever I went, I could see that Shell's installations were not working cleanly. They didn't satisfy their own standards, and they didn't satisfy international standards. Every Shell terrain I saw was polluted, every terminal I saw was contaminated."

THE ROLE OF THE OGONI

The Ogoni, a rural, closely knit community of farmers and fishers, have lived in the central part of the Niger Delta for millennia. Over the years the inhabitants had perfected the art of managing the resources of their environment in a sustainable way, so the land, rivers, and streams always yielded enough food for all. Indeed, Ogoni lands were once considered the food basket of the region. But all this was before the drilling rigs of Shell, in the words of the late Ogoni leader Ken Saro-Wiwa, "began to dig deep into the heart of Ogoni, tearing up farmlands and belching forth gas flames which pumped carbon monoxide and other dangerous gases into the lungs of my people."

In 1990, the Ogoni launched the Movement for the Survival of the Ogoni People (MOSOP), to put a stop to this regime of ecological devastation and economic exploitation. Led by Ken Saro-Wiwa, MOSOP provided an umbrella to a mass mobilization of Ogoni youth groups, women's associations, traditional rulers, churches, teachers, and professionals. On November 3, 1992, MOSOP issued a thirty-day ultimatum to all the oil companies operating on their land to either pay back rent, royalties and compensation for oil-devastated lands or leave.

The first real confrontation between MOSOP and Shell had taken place a few months earlier, on April 30, when a group of local farmers came out to challenge a Shell pipeline being laid on newly planted farmland in the village of Biara. The local farmers explained that they had not been paid any compensation for their land, nor had a proper environmental impact assessment been conducted, as stipulated by Nigerian law. A contingent of the Nigerian Army accompanying the oil workers responded by shooting into the protestors, killing one young man and wounding eleven others. However, Shell did pull out of Ogoni. News that the oil giant had been forced out of one of its oil fields in the Niger Delta sent shock waves through the country's security apparatus but did not end the story.

Shell received permission from Nigeria's government to import half a million dollars worth of weapons to arm the company's police guards. And a government memo recommended "ruthless military operations [to] smooth economic activities." A bloody showdown was unfolding.

In May 1995, four Ogoni chiefs were murdered, and Ken Saro-Wiwa and eight Ogoni activists were arrested. Military actions spread terror, torture, and death and turned thousands of Ogoni into refugees. Thirty Ogoni villages were reduced to rubble.

On November 10, 1995, despite enormous international protest, Ken Saro-Wiwa and his eight imprisoned companions—the Ogoni Nine—were hanged.

In December 1996, Shell admitted that it had invited the Nigerian authorities to help put down the "disturbance" in its Ogoni concession area. And Nigerian lieutenant colonel Paul Okuntimo later stated that he was paid by the company to "sanitize" the Ogoni and facilitate the return of Shell's five oil fields in the area.

Ken Saro-Wiwa and MOSOP have became heroes to the indigenous peoples throughout the Niger Delta. The massacres and executions have only hardened the resolve of the oil-producing communities to put an end to a system that has brought them so much pain, poverty, and death. Demonstrations, peaceful and well coordinated, are now a daily occurrence all over the Niger Delta.

THE WAY FORWARD

A simple cost-benefit analysis indicates that, rather than contributing to the social and economic well-being of communities, the oil industry as it presently operates in the Niger Delta is a net disbenefit. Among the direct costs are environmental pollution and degradation, destruction of the area's natural hydrology, concentration of lethal gases in the atmosphere, introduction of harmful acids into otherwise fertile soils, and pollution of groundwater by effluents. In addition, the Niger Delta is gradually sinking due to oil operations; it is estimated that 80 percent of the population will eventually have to move. Damage to property will be in the neighborhood of $9 billion. Shell's devastation of the environment has also left the available cultivable land gasping and devoid of nutrients and the creeks and rivers stripped of their fish population.

How do we stop this juggernaut from further damaging the area, threatening a people and their way of life? Nigeria's indigenous populations are speaking out, demanding self-determination and insisting on a new Nigeria informed by true federalism, equality, justice, and negotiated cooperation. The struggle in the Niger Delta is also a struggle for the soul of Nigeria and its future.

Dead fish scattered along the shore of the Boac River in the Philippines attest to the damage from a massive spill of copper mine waste by the Marcopper Mining Corporation in Marinduque Island. Scenes like this are increasingly common since the Philippine government passed the Mining Act of 1995, conforming to World Bank and Asian Development Bank prescriptions. The act opened the country to enormous new mining investments, free of traditional regulations that protect the environment and prevent currency speculation. Indigenous peoples are demanding new sets of rules that give them power to control investors on or near indigenous lands.

CHAPTER 20

The Philippine Mining Act of 1995

Tebtebba Foundation and the International Forum on Globalization

In an effort to liberalize the economy and create a favorable investment regime in the Philippines, the Asian Development Bank (ADB) pushed the Philippine government to adopt the Philippine Mining Act of 1995. The result has been a massive influx of foreign mining corporations into the country. Companies are now allowed to lease lands for seventy-five years and may repatriate to other countries 100 percent of their profits. Indigenous peoples, unable to resist the entry of open-pit mining companies, eventually lose their lands, their communities, and their seas and rivers to the pollution and devastation of the mining juggernaut.

THE PHILIPPINES IS A COUNTRY rich in mineral resources, and it is a major world producer of gold and copper. In the 1970s and 1980s, after a drop in mineral production due to the global recession, the ADB urged the Philippine government to open its economy for foreign investment, which ultimately led to the Philippine Mining Act. Under the act, only the government may grant mining rights to individuals and corporations. To attract foreign investors, the government may offer a package of fiscal incentives and investment guarantees, such as remittance of foreign loans and obligations from contracts, and freedom from expropriation. Mining companies, both foreign and local, are given rights to

use water and forest resources without permission from indigenous peoples living on the land being mined. And 100 percent foreign control over large-scale mining operations is allowed. In an attempt to respect the rights of indigenous peoples, the Mining Act does contain a pro forma provision on free and prior informed consent and token provisions on environmental safeguards.

Civil society organizations heavily criticized the Mining Act. By May 2002, at the Philippine National Conference on Mining, national, regional, and community-based peoples' organizations, including indigenous peoples and communities, gathered to discuss the adverse effects of mining. The impacts on these communities include the following:

▲ *Sham Consultation with Indigenous Peoples*
Companies have abused the principle of free and prior informed consent and used coercion, deception, and co-optation to gain the consent and participation of indigenous communities. In the Zamboanga Peninsula, the mining company Toronto Ventures, Inc., deceived the local Subanen people by having them sign a blank

sheet of paper, later using it as proof of endorsement of its mining project.

▲ Displacement from Ancestral Lands

Liberalization of the mining industry has resulted in legalized land-grabbing by mining corporations, which has deprived indigenous peoples of their ancestral domain rights. In Far South Mindanao, Western Mining Corporation's government-approved mining concession will cover 99,400 hectares and displace the Tagakaulo, B'laan, and Manobos indigenous peoples from their ancestral lands.

▲ Repression, Violence, and Militarization

Numerous cases of serious human rights violations against local communities have been reported to the United Nations Special Rapporteur on the Rights of Indigenous Peoples. Communities where Western Mining Corporation has mining claims have been terrorized. A fact-finding mission by the Philippine Peasant Movement (Kilsang Magbubukid ng Pilipinas, KMP), blamed the rights violations on militarization,

which intensified with the arrival of mining on the island. KMP accused the Philippine government and its military of acting as Western Mining's security guard. The military also assisted in organizing paramilitary groups, which stalked farmers who asserted their rights to land.

In Siocon, Zamboanga del Norte, military checkpoints appeared after Toronto Ventures Inc. (TVI) entered the indigenous Subanen's ancestral lands. The checkpoints were used to intimidate and harass the local community. TVI also hired "guards" and mobilized the police to intimidate traditional small-scale miners who had worked in the area before TVI's arrival.

It was clear from the testimonies of indigenous peoples at the conference that they are opposed to mining corporations and to any extractive industry on their lands. Instead of meeting the World Bank's goal of poverty reduction, the resulting ecological destruction, forced relocation, and loss of livelihoods and culture from mining has only worsened an already desperate situation.

This photo shows a tunnel built under Yucca Mountain in Western Shoshone territory in Nevada over the fierce objection of tribal leaders and the Nevada public. If finally authorized by the U.S. Congress, this will be the site of thousands of gallons of nuclear waste to be dumped here for perpetuity. Indian lands are favorite places for dumping the pollutants and effluents from industrial society because Indian economies are weak. But they are strenuously resisting, nonetheless, fearing eventual leakage and destruction of the desert water table.

CHAPTER 21

Briefing Reports

Tebtebba Foundation and the International Forum on Globalization

This chapter presents some briefings on the impacts of extractive industries and associated infrastructure developments—mostly oil, natural gas, and gold mining on indigenous communities—and the resistance by indigenous peoples to these projects. Such stories could fill a thousand-page book, but these are typical of situations around the world.

Oil Development and the U'wa

THE U'WA ARE AN INDIGENOUS COMMUNITY of approximately eight thousand people who have peacefully lived in the cloudforest of northeastern Colombia for thousands of years uncontacted by non-Indians until fifty years ago. Recent pressures on them to open their lands to oil drilling resulted in the U'wa issuing a startling communiqué in 1995. The U'wa vowed to commit collective mass suicide by jumping off a cliff if the oil drilling took place. They said it would be better to die by their own hands and will rather than see their sacred environment and culture destroyed. The president of the U'wa Traditional Authority stated, "We would rather die, protecting everything that we hold sacred, than lose everything that makes us U'wa." According to the U'wa, taking oil from the land would bleed the Earth dry, and "to take the oil is, for us, worse than killing your own mother."

The U'wa are acutely aware of what oil development has meant for other indigenous cultures in Colombia and the Amazon. Texaco's development of oil fields in the 1960s, and the resulting roads, buildings, pipelines, workers, and environmental contamination, displaced many indigenous communities, including the Inga, Kofan, and Siona, from their homelands. When Texaco eventually pulled out of the Ecuadorian Amazon, it left behind more than six hundred open-pit toxic waste sites.

In Colombia, human rights violations have historically gone hand in hand with development of oil fields. Indigenous peoples such as the U'wa have become caught in the ferocious crossfire between government forces and guerrilla factions. Colombia's left-wing guerrilla groups often attack oil industry installations and pipelines because they are viewed as strategic targets. To protect the pipelines and equipment, the government militarizes the area, which only exacerbates the situation. Occidental Petroleum's Caño Limon oil pipeline, in Colombia's Arauca department, brought not only pipeline attacks but also kidnappings, assassinations, illegal detentions, intimidation, and displacement of local residents. U'wa territory is also located in a high-conflict region, and there is every reason to believe that similar pipeline attacks would occur if oil drilling took place on their land.

Despite the U'wa's vows of suicide, the Colombian government, eager to develop and exploit potential oil concessions and bring in foreign investment, granted Occidental Petroleum the license to drill on U'wa land. The U'wa feared that the kind of oil spills that had occurred on previous Occidental drilling sites would poison and destroy their environment. Exploratory drilling began in 2000; roads were constructed, workers and equipment moved in, and the Colombian military forcibly removed hundreds of U'wa from the drill site. In response, the U'wa blockaded construction sites and, with support from Northern NGOs, conducted protest tours in the United States and lobbied U.S. legislators. They demanded that the company and Colombia's government respect the U'wa's right to determine the fate of their own ancestral lands and to deny any project on their homelands if they so desired. They also demanded legal title to their traditional lands and demilitarization of their territory.

An international campaign that was working with the U'wa to stop the drilling demanded that Occidental Petroleum pull out. The company had expected to reap billions of dollars from the oil field; it estimated that the site held 1.5 billion barrels. But the global campaign, using lawsuits, shareholder resolutions, writing campaigns, and demonstrations in front of Occidental's headquarters, eventually turned the oil project into a public relations nightmare for Occidental.

After its first exploratory well on U'wa land tested dry, Occidental announced at its May 2002 annual shareholder meeting that it would withdraw from the project and return its oil concession to government control. The victory was short-lived; in late 2002, Ecopetrol, a Colombian oil company, moved into Occidental's former concession and began drilling (bringing with them military protection). And so the cycle

begins again—the U'wa have renewed their vow of resistance and called on the Colombian government to cancel all oil projects on their territory, the government claims the need for development and investment, and the guerrillas and paramiltary forces see opportunities in the chaos. Meanwhile, international organizations such as Amazon Watch, Pachamama Alliance and U'wa Defense are continuing to mobilize in support of the U'wa's rights to self-determination.

Megaproject: Plan Puebla Panama

PLAN PUEBLA PANAMA (PPP) is a $10 billion, 10- to 25-year regional integration megaproject proposed by Mexican president Vicente Fox in 2001 and sponsored (via loans) by the Inter-American Development Bank (IDB), the Central American Bank for Economic Integration, and the World Bank. It involves all seven Central American countries and nine states in southern Mexico, and would open a region inhabited by nine million indigenous people to uncontrolled private foreign intervention and development.

The PPP calls for industrialization of agriculture, hydroelectric dams, oil pipelines, gas pipelines, dry canals, industrial corridors, *maquiladora* zones, superhighways, a regional energy grid, and high-speed rails that will run north-south and east-west from Puebla to Panama. The PPP's transportation infrastructure plan is already moving ahead and covers 9,450 kilometers of highway in Mesoamerica. The Pacific Corridor will create a series of roads and highways stretching from central Mexico to Panama, for a total of 3,150 kilometers. The Atlantic Corridor will extend the roads beyond the confines of the PPP, from Central America's Caribbean coast to the Mexico/Texas border. Tens of thousands of indigenous people will be forced off of the land to make way for development. The PPP is yet another plan that serves foreign investors at the expense of local communities, as corporations tap into the area's abundant resources and biodiversity, take advantage of cheap labor, and displace indigenous and rural communities in the way of projected dams, industrial farms, ranching, logging, mining, oil and bioprospecting.

The IDB has organized the PPP into eight "initiatives," including projects ranging from tourism promotion and energy interconnection to telecommunications development. The ultimate goal is to improve market access and exploit resources for export (mainly to the United States). The *maquiladoras* will be geared to export production, assembling consumer products using commodities imported from Asia. They will employ the poor *campesinos* who have been pushed off their lands and are unable to compete with the tons of heavily subsidized corn being dumped by the United States into the markets of Mexico and Central America.

The goal of the PPP's electrical interconnection component is to improve electrical generation and transmission capabilities, integrating the region's power grids with the United States and thereby facilitating the sale of electricity, also to the United States. The regional grid would be complemented by the building of numerous dams for the generation of hydroelectricity. Dams proposed for the Usamacinta River between Mexico and Guatemala would threaten not only the Mayan communities residing in the region but also Mayan culture, as they would flood the area's archaeological heritage.

The PPP may eventually extend beyond Panama. Colombia's President Uribe has enthusiastically called for integrating his country into the development project and is already advancing plans to merge its energy system with Panama's. Colombia has now been granted observer status in the Plan Puebla-Panama and hopes to use the PPP network to export electrical and hydrocarbon energy.

Grassroots organizations and indigenous groups were united in opposition to the PPP as soon as it was announced. Every year since 2001 there have been Mesoamerican forums held across the region to protest the PPP and to encourage citizens to discuss alternatives. Indigenous communities have blocked highways, ports and infrastructure projects throughout the region. In fact, civil society opposition to the PPP has already forced Mexico to attempt some downscaling and redesign of the plan and to try public relations to present it in a better light.

The Chad-Cameroon Pipeline and the Bagyéli

THE NEW CHAD-CAMEROON PIPELINE was created to transport crude oil from the oil fields of southern Chad to the coast of Cameroon, where it would be exported to international markets. The $3.7 billion oil project is Africa's single largest development investment. It was started by a consortium of multinational companies, including ExxonMobil, Chevron, and Petronas. Construction began in October 2000, after the World Bank agreed to provide $200 million in loans and to mobilize hundreds of millions of additional dollars from commercial banks. Fully operational in 2004, the project is expected to generate substantial revenues that the two governments will invest in poverty-reduction programs. In reality, the project seems likely to increase poverty, not reduce it. The pipeline cuts through Chad's most fertile agricultural region and Cameroon's Atlantic littoral forest, an area rich in biodiversity and home to the Bagyéli people. The Bagyéli practice subsistence agriculture linked to hunting and gathering and consider the forest their soul. The forest also enables the Bagyéli to earn some cash income from selling wildlife and other nontimber forest products. But following construction of the pipeline, the Bagyéli were forced to leave their traditional lands and move farther into the forest to look for game, radically altering their livelihood, their way of life, and their connection to their lands. They received no compensation for losing their territories.

The Bagyéli were not sufficiently prepared for the pipeline. In violation of World Bank guarantees, there was little effort to adequately explain the project and its risks to the community. The information campaigns used simple flyers, brochures, and posters; however, the Bagyéli people are 98 percent illiterate.

What little compensation the Bagyéli received for the destruction of their environment has been made meaningless by marginalization and discrimination in job recruitment. There is even concern that the Bagyéli's situation may exacerbate a growing dependence on their Bantu neighbors.

The Bagyéli have asked the World Bank to grant them confirmed land access. They seek support for their rights to their land and for access to their traditional hunting and fishing territories. Furthermore, a formal consultation process should be made permanent—between the community, the Bank and the developers—in which the Bagyéli have a decisive role in determining the ultimate uses of their land.

Oil and Natural Gas in Siberia and the Nenets

THE NENETS AUTONOMOUS OKRUG, located in southwest Siberia one thousand miles northeast of Moscow, is home to between five thousand and seven thousand of the Nenet people and approximately five thousand Koni. The area is also home to much of Russia's oil and natural gas industry; northwest Siberia produces 78 percent of Russia's oil and 84 percent of its natural gas.

The Nenet people have lived in the area for over a thousand years and are traditionally reindeer breeders, pasturing their herds on the tundra and in the forests. They depend on the land to sustain their traditional economy: animal herding, hunting, fishing, and harvesting of wild plants.

The oil industry that arrived in the 1970s is relatively new to the Nenets Autonomous Okrug. Aggressive short-term goals for increased production during the Soviet period left a legacy of pollution. Seventy percent of emissions in Russia are attributable to the oil industry, in part because of the continued burning of natural gas off the oil fields. After extraction, oil is transported through rusting pipelines that often break; these cause 8 to 10 percent of Russia's oil spills. One such disaster was the Komi oil spill, which released approximately 270,000 tons of crude (three times the amount spilled in the Exxon *Valdez* incident) onto the fragile lands.

In the 1990s, new oil and gas development began in the Nenets Autonomous Okrug. The Polar Lights Project, a joint venture between Conoco and the Russian company Arxangelskgeologiya, secured funding from the World Bank, the European Bank for Reconstruction and Development (EBRD), and the Overseas Private Investment Corporation (OPIC), among others. The project, located on the Ardelin oil field, has been producing oil since 1994 and averages 36,000 barrels per day. The oil is transported through forty-two miles of local pipeline before joining the Russian pipeline.

The Polar Lights Project, like all oil development in the fragile tundra regions, represents a severe threat to the ecosystem on which the Nenet and their reindeer depend. The pipelines and roads obstruct the path of migrating reindeer, and pollution and topsoil disruption destroy reindeer pasture, fish spawning grounds, fish and game habitats, and wild plants. Matters are worsened by the inferior pipeline technology of the region, and all these impacts are compounded by the incredibly slow recovery process of arctic tundra.

Oil exploration also threatens the social organization of the community. Hundreds of temporary workers who have no connection to or interest in conserving the land or respecting traditional values of the community descend on the area. Problems such as workers shooting reindeer and rampant drunkenness are increasing, as are assaults on women.

Despite these problems, the Nenet are not completely opposed to oil development. Some see it as a means to economic improvement, since oil workers provide a market for their reindeer products, and anticipate improved social conditions, but they demand participation in the way the development is undertaken.

On paper, Russian law recognizes the rights of indigenous peoples to their land, and since 1974 each reindeer breeding group has been officially granted breeding passage, where they can pasture and protect their herds. In reality, however, these rights have been largely ignored, resulting, at best, in very meager compensation for land taken for oil and gas exploration. Though some dialogues have been held between indigenous people, oil companies, and the local administration, no real changes have yet ensued. Meanwhile, the companies propose new drilling operations and pipelines that would have further adverse impacts on the region.

Nuclear Waste Dumps and the Western Shoshone Nation

THE NUCLEAR INDUSTRY is ready to install the world's largest nuclear waste dump underneath Yucca Mountain, part of the Western Shoshone national lands in the state of Nevada. The dump threatens everything the Western Shoshone have cultivated over thousands of years at this sacred place: their spiritual traditions, ecologically bound livelihoods, cultural identity, and sovereignty.

❁   ❁   ❁

International corporations such as British Energy, Cogema, Dominion, Southern Company, and Edison International have begun purchasing U.S. reactors and renewing operating licenses, despite the historically dismal performance of nuclear power. These relatively unknown giants are prepared to accelerate an atomic reality that will last for thousands of years as they merge, consolidate, and plan for expansion in the dawn of the new nuclear age of globalization. The merger wave spurred by deregulation began in the late 1990s. As the *Economist* magazine mused, "In the near future, today's 50 nuclear utilities will probably be reduced to a dozen." If atomic energy is to dominate the future, these will be the barons powering that energy source.

Internationally, the wealthy Group of Eight (G8) countries have been exporting more reactors than they erect domestically. Financing for these expensive ventures comes from the European Bank for Reconstruction and Development (EBRD), primarily operated by the G8, the U.S. Export-Import Bank (funded by taxpayer dollars) and the World Bank. As plants are built, the need increases for an international waste repository for the world's growing nuclear waste. Eventually, as global transport of nuclear products such as radioactive waste becomes a reality, the World Trade Organization (WTO) will likely regulate this traffic and undermine national radiation protection standards that hamper industry profits.

Both President Bush and Vice President Cheney have numerous personal ties to nuclear power and received large campaign contributions from industry heavyweights, many of whom served on the president's energy task force, including the industry's lobbying arm (and trade association), the Nuclear Energy Institute (NEI). Under the Bush energy plan, the nuclear industry stood to reap huge profits through generous tax breaks, incentives and massive subsidies. But first they needed to find a site to dump radioactive wastes. They decided on Indian land.

YUCCA MOUNTAIN, NEVADA

The U.S. Department of Energy (DOE) selected Yucca Mountain, Nevada, to be the sole repository for the 70,000 metric tons of highly radioactive nuclear waste generated at seventy-seven sites across the country; it was approved by Congress in 2002. Tens of thousands of shipments will travel through forty-three states to this site, located ninety miles northwest of Las Vegas. Though most media fail to report it, the Yucca Mountain site lies squarely within the traditional lands of the Western Shoshone Nation, which has been fighting this project since it was first proposed.

Yucca Mountain was the only site considered and studied by the DOE's team, despite its failing to meet technical and geological criteria. Seismic activity at Yucca Mountain ranks third after Alaska and California, making earthquakes an ever-present threat. Water flows deeply through the mountain, and the water's high mineral content threatens to corrode the storage casks, causing leakage. Under prime conditions, storage casks might last one thousand years; however, plutonium remains highly radioactive for 24,000 years, promising ecological disaster for future generations even if the casks expire naturally. Additionally, the mountain's natural formation does not meet Nuclear Waste Policy Act standards. John Bartlett, former director of the Yucca Mountain program, stated, "DOE retroactively changed the rules for site suitability in December 2001 after it had become apparent that the original rules could not be met for Yucca Mountain." In addition, NEI hired the same law firm that had been advising the DOE on the site's suitability. The firm was exposed for taking money from the nuclear industry to ensure the approval of the site, leaving data collected since 1992 tainted.

RADIOACTIVE RACISM

The Western Shoshone have inhabited Yucca Mountain and the surrounding land for thousands of years, long before the appearance of Europeans in the area. They contend that the selection of this site, despite its geologic unsuitability, is best explained as *environmental racism*. American Indians have long been targeted for unsavory nuclear activity that U.S. citizens want to keep far away from their own homes. The Office of Nuclear Waste has approached every federally recognized tribe in the country, even offering large sums of money for hosting nuclear activities, including dumps, on tribal lands. Almost all have refused.

The Western Shoshone believe they have been targeted because, like many other indigenous peoples, they are politically, culturally, and geographically isolated from the state within which they exist, and statistically they are among the poorest Nevadans. That no site other than Yucca Mountain was ever tested supports this belief.

The Western Shoshone Nation has long borne the brunt of the United States' nuclear experimentation. In fact, it is perhaps the most bombed nation on earth as a result of years of underground nuclear testing on tribal lands. Increased cancer rates and other conditions consistent with radiation exposure have been documented. The historic decision to dump nuclear waste at Yucca Mountain will only increase the ecological adversities visited upon the Shoshone.

SHOSHONE SOVEREIGNTY

The controversy is rarely couched as a sovereignty issue; however, that is what is at stake. The U.S. government recognized Western Shoshone sovereignty over ancestral territory, including Yucca Mountain, in the 1863 Treaty of Ruby Valley. By 1910, however, the United States was already claiming the area as public domain.

In 1946, the Indian Claims Commission was established, ostensibly "to settle finally and all legal, equitable, and moral obligations that the U.S. might owe to the Indians." In 1951, the commission found that Western Shoshone territorial title had been legally extinguished because of "gradual encroachment" by U.S. citizens into Shoshone territory, but the commission included sixteen million acres that had never been encroached upon in any way. The Washington firm representing the Indians nonetheless settled the case, *against* the express wishes of the Shoshone, for a proposed 1979 cash payment of $26 million, which was at the rate of fifteen cents per acre, or 250 times less than 1979 market value. To this day the Western Shoshone have not accepted the funds, nor do they recognize the ruling. By constructing the site, the United States is attempting to permanently settle the contested sovereignty over these lands. (*See also the following briefing on Gold Mining and the Western Shoshone.*)

HEALTH AND ENVIRONMENTAL IMPACTS

In August 2005, the Environmental Protection Agency proposed new public health standards at Yucca Mountain, setting a maximum dose level for the first 10,000 years and providing additional protection for up to one million years. These new standards would also require that the facility withstand the effects of earthquakes, volcanoes, and significantly increased rainfall while containing the nuclear waste during the one-million-year period.

In 1992, a 5.6 earthquake caused $1.4 million in damage to the DOE's Yucca Mountain field office. An earthquake of this magnitude would easily breach the casks, which could result in a plutonium explosion or dispersion along hundreds of miles of fault lines, threatening densely populated areas, agricultural land, and wildlife. Additionally, naturally corrosive groundwater

seeping deep inside the mountain would likely reach the casks in fewer than fifty years. The aquifer above the proposed dump site is the primary water source for hundreds of miles. If contaminated, the implications are grave for the indigenous inhabitants, who rely on it for drinking and for supporting their subsistence hunting and gathering lifestyle.

RELIGIOUS AND CULTURAL DESECRATION

All Western Shoshone land is considered sacred, and their existence as a people is tied directly to the land. Like many desert peoples, they consider water sacred and, in a desert environment, very precious. Exemplifying a need to care for the land and water in a way that is "spiritually responsible and environmentally sound," the balance with nature that they have cultivated over centuries is part of their national identity. Yucca Mountain itself is a traditional, holy gathering place containing thousands of documented cultural resources. The dump will forever desecrate this sacred site and the land that surrounds it. Fences will be erected, huge machines will bulldoze the land, and the mountain will be hollowed and filled with atomic decay. Even before the radiation inevitably escapes to kill the surrounding land, the way of the Western Shoshone will have been sacrificed.

In a related development, in September 2005 the Nuclear Regulatory Commission gave the go-ahead to a private corporation to establish a temporary nuclear waste site on the Goshute Indian reservation, roughly 45 miles from Salt Lake City. The waste site ultimately could store up to 44,000 tons of waste in steel containers. This has deeply divided the Skull Valley Band of Goshutes, a small Shoshonean-speaking tribe comprising approximately 124 members.

The Goshute Utah site is considered a layover for waste ultimately bound for the Yucca Mountain repository and, for the time being, a way around the stalemate in Nevada. Still, the battle for Yucca Mountain and for dumping radioactive nuclear waste is far from over. In early 2005, DOE disclosed that critical data supporting the Yucca Mountain project had been falsified by U.S. Geological Service scientists, raising new questions about the scientific data used by the government to build the repository. Energy Department officials claim Yucca Mountain will open as early as 2012, having pushed back the opening date several times. As this goes to print, the dump site has not yet been finally authorized, and opposition is mounting.

Gold Mining and the Western Shoshone

THE STORY OF THE WESTERN SHOSHONE is a long lesson in the many ways that law can fail indigenous people threatened by mineral interests. The ancestral territory of this Native American people encompasses an area stretching from southern Idaho through eastern Nevada to the Mojave Desert of California. Underneath this swath of over 240,000 square kilometers (over sixty million acres) lie billions of dollars worth of gold. Nearly 10 percent of the world's gold production and 64 percent of U.S. production comes from Western Shoshone land.

Prospectors hoping to strike it rich began entering Western Shoshone territory in the 1840s. Clashes with the Shoshone prompted the 1863 Treaty of Ruby Valley between the U.S. government and the Western Shoshone Nation. The treaty allowed settlers to mine, establish ranches, cut timber, and extract other natural resources from Shoshone lands, but it also recognized the Western Shoshone people as landowners and entitled them to royalties for the extractive activities. However, no royalties have ever been paid. (See also the following briefing on Cobell v. Norton.)

The gold rush continues today, but individual prospecting has been replaced by corporate mining, a practice that has proved far more destructive to Western Shoshone lands, sacred places, and scarce water resources.

Failure to pay royalties is a treaty violation, and the Shoshone have been attempting for decades to get the government to live up to its constitutional obligations. In 1979, the government tried to legislate a settlement that would have abrogated the treaty and awarded the Shoshone a one-time payment of $26 million, or roughly 15 cents an acre, in exchange for relinquishing title to their land. (See also preceding briefing on nuclear dumping.) The Shoshone refused the settlement, maintaining that the lands were never for sale in the first place. Even so, the federal government is acting as if it, rather than the Shoshone, were the landowner. Today, Shoshone ranchers are required to pay federal grazing fees to run cattle on their traditional lands, and the government continues to hand over huge tracts of Shoshone lands to mining companies. Among the beneficiaries are Newmont Mining, Placer Dome, and Barrick. Under the national mining law, which dates from 1872, corporations can purchase so-called public lands from the government for as little as $5 a hectare ($2.50 an acre), without owing a penny in royalties for the minerals they extract.

In December 2002, the Inter-American Commission on Human Rights, a part of the Organization of American States, found that the U.S. government was violating the fundamental rights of the Western Shoshone to property, due process, and equality under the law. But the government has ignored the ruling and is moving forward with legislation that would open the territory up to a major new form of extraction, geothermal energy, and to additional mining. In September 2003, the Shoshone filed suit yet again, reasserting their claim to their ancestral territory and demanding payment of the royalties owed them under the treaty.

A Landmark Legal Case:
Cobell v. Norton

AN EXTRAORDINARY CLASS ACTION lawsuit on behalf of 500,000 American Indians has been quietly wending its way through the U.S. court system for over a decade, though bitterly fought at every stage by the government. *Cobell v. Norton* charges that the United States Department of the Interior, and secretaries of the interior, including James Watt (under Ronald Reagan), Bruce Babbitt (under Bill Clinton), and Gale Norton (under George W. Bush), have grossly mismanaged Individual Trust Accounts held in behalf of Indian beneficiaries for as long as one hundred years. Federal District Judge Royce Lambert (a Republican) has been so appalled at the facts of the case, and the foot-dragging by the government, that he has called the Interior Department's handling of the case "egregious misconduct. . . . The gold standard for mismanagement by the federal government for more than a century." At various times, Judge Lambert has held both secretaries Babbitt and Norton in contempt of court, as well as thirty-seven other employees and lawyers of the Interior Department, and fined the government $600,000.

At issue are the monies that the government is legally obliged to hold in trust, manage, invest and distribute to the Indian beneficiaries in an orderly manner, based on treaty agreements over the past century and such acts as the Dawes Act of 1887, by which Indians were forced to give up much of their lands. The Indians were promised in return that certain financial benefits from the lands would accrue to them, from royalties for government-arranged leases for the extraction of oil, natural gas, copper, uranium, and other minerals, as well as the sale of timber and grazing rights, and in some cases outright sale of the lands.

Over the last hundred years almost none of this money has been paid to beneficiaries or their heirs. *(See also the briefing on gold and the Western Shoshone.)*

The Interior Department has stalled the case at every possible turn. In 1999 it was found that the Interior and Treasury Departments had destroyed "inadvertently" some 162 boxes of trust records but failed to notify the plaintiffs. Recently, Interior claimed it had lost relevant records concerning what happened to the money, resulting in contempt of court citations.

Indian plaintiffs and lawyers, however, led by a very determined Blackfeet banker named Elouise Cobell, asserted that a full accounting is still feasible, and that a conservative estimate based on the normal lease and sale rates for the pertinent times and places will show that the Indians are, by now, owed (with interest) over $130 billion in royalties. Other estimates are somewhat lower, but the total owed is certainly at least comparable to the cost of the Iraq War. It is little wonder that the U.S. government would not want to see the case resolved.

The U.S. District Court for the District of Columbia and the U.S. Court of Appeals have demanded that the government complete an accounting by 2007 of what has become of the money and create an acceptable plan for its disbursal. Astonishingly, however, the Bush administration placed a last-second rider on a federal spending bill in Congress that would have implemented the court's directives; the rider postpones all work on the accounting for at least one year.

Meanwhile, the Indian plaintiffs have made offers to end litigation via a negotiated compromise settlement. Thus far the government has rebuffed the offers. Apparently, the Bush administration prefers to keep the case in limbo for as long as possible, hoping, some say, that the plaintiffs will eventually die off or give up—or at least that the whole problem can be passed to the next president. Very few people close to the plaintiffs think they will ever give up, nor would their heirs—they are too furious over the government's arrogance and injustice. (NOTE: Just as we went to press, a federal appeals court overtuned a lower court ruling favoring *Cobell*'s demand for an accounting. The Indians immediately announced a new appeal, and the case seems destined to reach the Supreme Court.)

Gold in Borneo and the Dayak

KELIAN EQUATORIAL MINING (PT KEM) is 90 percent owned by the Anglo-Australian Rio Tinto Group and 10 percent by Harita Jayaraya of Indonesia. Since 1992 PT KEM has operated a large open-pit gold mine in Kelian, East Kalimantan, Indonesia, in the eastern part of Borneo, which is home to the indigenous Dayak community. Traditionally the Dayak have cultivated rice and vegetable crops and collected forest products for the community to use and sell.

The operations at the Kelian mine have a long history of social and environmental problems, including documented cases of human rights abuses, violence against women, and pollution from cyanide and acid rock drainage. In an attempt to avoid paying compensation for loss of livelihood, PT KEM claimed that there was no genuine community mining at Kelian. Locals were not allowed to participate in gold mining, agroforestry, or farming their lands around the mine site—no activities could take place on any part of PT KEM's mining concession. Dayaks were forcibly evicted from their lands by the military and police; chemicals were dumped into rivers; grave sites were destroyed; and cases of sexual harassment and rape were reported. Community protests began in 1988, and security forces were brought in by PT KEM; this was the start of numerous violations of the human rights of the locals by the company.

Negotiations took place between PT KEM and the Association for the Welfare of the Mining Community and Environment (LKMTL in

Indonesian), which represented the indigenous Dayak community and their demands for compensation. The negotiations deadlocked in 2000, and the community held large-scale demonstrations outside the mine site. Talks resumed in 2001, and a new deal was reached.

In preparation for the impending mine closure, PT KEM established a Mine Closure Steering Committee. The World Bank's Business Partners for Development scheme has been involved in developing the Kelian mine closure plan as a model of best practice. Negotiators were sent in to help settle differences between PT KEM and the community group LKMTL over compensation demands and human rights violations.

LKMTL has repeatedly asked Rio Tinto and PT KEM to take responsibility for the long-term environmental security and protection of the community's health, environment, and livelihood. They have requested guarantees, independent environmental monitoring, and free hospital facilities. The community has called for a moratorium on further mining and oil and gas projects until their human rights are secure.

In March 2003, the Mine Closure Steering Committee process at Kelian reportedly broke down, and local people blocked an access road to the mine to protest continuing abuses. LKMTL withdrew from the meetings, viewing the committee as only a token gesture that did not take community concerns and solutions seriously. They contended that acceptable weight had not been given to their grievances, which included fears of further environmental contamination from mine tailings and an insufficient compensation package for the community.

Civil society groups had been extensively involved in the World Bank's Extractive Industries Review consultation process. In the *Asia-Pacific Civil Society Statement of Withdrawal from the Extractive Industries Review*

Process (April 2003), member groups cited the World Bank's own leaked internal Operations Evaluation Department (OED) draft audit of January 21, 2003, which showed that closely associated with extractive industries are "long-term environmental damage with accompanying health consequences, the destruction of traditional (and more sustainable) economic foundations of local communities, involuntary displacements and property takings, economic dependence on such revenues and increased economic volatility, increased corruption, violence, and civil war."

The statement went on to say that "neither the World Bank Group nor the proceedings of the Extractive Industries Review to date have provided any evidence that Bank support for the extractive sector has promoted the Bank's mandate of poverty reduction. In fact, a wide range of evidence including that contained in the OED draft audit report indicates that the World Bank should pull out of oil, gas and mining since World Bank support for this sector has not reduced poverty."

Summary of Grievances and Demands of the Dayak

DAYAK GRIEVANCES WITH PT KEM'S KELIAN MINES:

Local people not allowed to carry out agro-forestry or to farm their customary lands, which lie within PT KEM's concession.

The community is gradually getting poorer because it was forced off its lands and prevented from mining within PT KEM's concession.

In 1991, twelve hundred drums of PT KEM chemicals fell into the river; local people believe they contained cyanide. Most of the community complained of itchy skin and sores. Other negative indications were mass fish deaths.

PT KEM's trucks and heavy equipment cause air pollution due to large amounts of dust they stir up when they pass people's homes on unpaved roads.

PT KEM's security guards harassed, beat up, and shot at local people around the Kelian River within the mine concession. This despite an edict by East Kalimantan's governor that allowed community mining within fifty meters of the banks of the river.

Local people have been evicted from their cultivated lands, homes, and small-scale mining sites without prior consultation.

Graves were destroyed when the main mine site and access road were established.

Local women and girls suffered sexual harassment and rape by PT KEM staff on and off the mine site.

THE DAYAK DEMAND THE FOLLOWING:

1. Compensation for land for which the company never paid;

2. Compensation for land where the company made inadequate payment;

3. Compensation for the loss of community miners' livelihood;

4. Compensation for homes and shelters that were destroyed with no payment;

5. Reduction of dust pollution caused by mine traffic along roads through settlements;

6. Measures to tackle environmental problems;

7. Redress for human rights violations;

8. Fulfillment of the promises made by PT KEM to the community regarding the provision of clean drinking water, electricity, and two hectares of land for cultivation and new housing.

Transmigration, Resources, Freeport McMoran, and Genocide in West Papua

WEST PAPUA, ALONG WITH PAPUA NEW GUINEA, is one of the most culturally and biologically diverse places on Earth. The island is home to one thousand different language groups (one-sixth of the world's total), with 250 found within West Papua's borders.

But since Indonesian takeover, West Papua's cultural makeup has changed significantly. The indigenous population of nearly 1.5 million now shares the territory with some 775,000 Indonesian migrants. Hundreds of thousands of migrants have been sponsored by the Indonesian government's discredited transmigration program. Others are spontaneous migrants, such as traders from the Indonesian island of Sulawesi. Year 2000 census figures for Papua showed a population of 1,460,846 indigenous people and 772,684 non-indigenous people. This represents a ratio of roughly two West Papuans to each non-Papuan.

The size of France, West Papua has the largest contiguous expanse of tropical rainforest outside the Amazon and among the largest numbers of endemic species on Earth. It is one of only three places in the world where glaciers exist in the tropics. Its snow-capped mountain chain—rising to more than 4,500 meters above sea level—is the highest between the Himalayas and the Andes. This beautiful land holds important cultural and spiritual significance for many Papuan indigenous communities. But alas, it is also rich in gold, copper, oil, and natural gas.

The largest mining company in West Papua is New Orleans–based Freeport McMoran Copper and Gold Inc. Freeport came to West Papua in 1967 after receiving the first mining contract issued by the Suharto government. Construction of the mine required moving millions of tons of earth from the top of Jayawijaya Mountain. Freeport's operations have grown from an initial 10,000 hectares to the more recent 2.6 million hectare mine at Grasberg. Freeport now operates the world's largest gold mine and third-largest copper mine. In 2001 it produced 1.4 billion pounds of copper and 2.6 million ounces of gold, with estimated reserves of 52 billion ounces of gold. But this production has cost the local people dearly in loss of land, environmental destruction and human rights abuses.

Large areas of rainforest were cleared to establish the mine and important rivers are being polluted by the 200,000 tons of tailing sand that is left by mine operations each day. By the time the mine ceases production, the adjacent Wanagong Valley will be filled to a depth of 450 meters, and the 114 hectare Carstenweid meadow will be covered with 250 meters of waste rock. Downstream the tailings cause severe flooding and erosion and the toxic minerals in the water contaminate fish and mollusks.

Large tracts of mangroves were cleared at the mouth of the Timika River to create the Amamapare seaport, and mine tailings now pollute nearby coral reefs. The Amungme people are deeply affronted by the destruction of Jayawijaya Mountain. In their cosmological beliefs, Jayawijaya is the head of their sacred mother. In their view, Freeport has already cut off their mother's head by reducing the top of the mountain to a plateau, and it is now digging into her heart.

West Papua contains 30 percent of Indonesia's remaining forests, and with the over-logging of Kalimantan and Sumatra, it is rapidly becoming the main source of Indonesian timber. By 2002, the Indonesian government had given out potential forestry concessions over 22 million hectares—30 percent of West Papua's land. Besides the areas where companies can officially log, there are many areas where illegal logging occurs. An estimated 70 percent of all timber exported from Indonesia is cut illegally; even though export of unprocessed raw logs was officially banned in the 1980s, unsawn logs are still exported from West Papua. The Asian Development Bank warned in May 2001, "Over-exploitation and poor management imperils Indonesia's forestry resources."

Under Suharto, tribal communities had no legal claim on their land, and logging concessions were entirely controlled by the government. Logging companies often employed the police and army to suppress local protests. The army itself and retired officers are heavily involved in running logging companies; one example is P.T. Hanurata, still jointly controlled by the Suharto family and Kopassus. In one notorious case in the early 1980s, people in the Asmat area were forced by the army to log trees without payment. More recently, Korean, Malaysian and Chinese logging companies have moved into the region. China is a major market for Papuan timber, as China is reducing its own logging because of its environmental crisis.

An Autonomy Law for West Papua specifies that any future use of customary land will require a permit from the affected community. However, as of 2004, the Autonomy Law has not been implemented.

Here is a summary of the impact of logging on the people and their environment:

▲ Local people are often forcibly removed and are rarely consulted or compensated for loss of their lands and forests.

▲ In January 2002, the head of West Papua's Social Welfare office stated that fifty-one nomadic tribes in the Waropen region were being pushed to extinction by excessive logging.

▲ Forced removal of West Papuans from forestry areas is often to poorer terrain, far away from traditional staple foods. Traditional hunting and fishing grounds are now out of bounds and any-one who returns can be charged with trespassing.

▲ Numerous rainforest bird species found only in West Papua are at risk of extinction because smuggling birds to Java and Singapore is a thriving business.

▲ Logging roads lead to substantial soil erosion and silting of rivers. Roads often cut through small streams, producing stagnant ponds where disease-carrying mosquitos breed.

▲ Bulldozers and other heavy machinery destroy trees and plants used by indigenous people for food and traditional medicine.

▲ Indigenous people get no long-term benefit from the infrastructure created for the workforce in mining and logging and have received rela-tively little employment from the projects.

(This briefing is excerpted from a much longer piece in Pacific Ecologist, *Winter 2004: "West Papua: Forgotten Pacific Nation Threatened with Genocide" by John Rumbiak and Abigail Abrash Walton.)*

Gold Mining in Papua New Guinea and the Lihir

NEARLY SEVEN HUNDRED KILOMETERS off the coast off Papua New Guinea lies Lihir Island, home to the open-pit gold mine of Lihir Gold Ltd. The raw gold produced from the mine is exported and turned into jewelry. Lihir is now one of the world's richest gold mines, producing approximately 600,000 ounces annually from an extinct volcano. In operation since 1997, the mine is expected to generate approximately 84 million tons of tailings and 300 million tons of waste rock, dumped into the sea, over its full seventeen-year life span. A satellite photo taken in 2000 shows that waste from the mine already covers an area of the ocean three kilometers wide.

Most of the island's 5,500 indigenous inhabitants are involved in subsistence agriculture. The mine has wreaked havoc on the Lihirians' traditional way of life, forced relocation of many villages, and brought a massive influx of outsiders who have caused social upheaval. Alcohol abuse, spousal abuse and failed marriages have increased. The Lihirian people's most sacred site was demolished because it was in the way of the developer. Other culturally important areas are being transformed into construction sites to support the mine. Traditional matrilineal ownership of land among the indigenous people of Lihir has been undermined.

The Multilateral Investment Guarantee Agency (MIGA), part of the World Bank Group, was an initial financier of the mine. In 2003 the World Bank commissioned an Extractive Industries Review of the project. A survey by the NGO Environmental Watch Group to determine if the local communities were aware of the World Bank's involvement in the project found that nearly 100 percent of those interviewed were unaware of any World Bank involvement in the Lihir mine; neither had they any idea what MIGA was. Clearly there was a lack of transparency in the review process and little information for residents about who to hold responsible for resulting environmental and social problems. Nonetheless, Lihir Gold is considering expanding the mine, due to promising reserves found on the island. This can only mean further environmental degradation and cultural destruction.

The World Bank's stated rationale for guaranteeing the Lihir mine project was that the export revenue earned from mining would trickle down to the community. However, the Lihirians say the effect is the opposite: increased hardship for the people. They now demand a full stop to the exploration and call on the Papua New Guinea government to put the people's needs ahead of mining revenue. The Lihirians argue that, had they been asked, they would have proposed a more realistic and sustainable project that might have relieved poverty and produced less negative impact.

The key proposals of the indigenous communities of Lihir and Papua New Guinea are:

▲ The World Bank must ensure that any review, development, or changes made to the mining law of Papua New Guinea and its management tools or regulatory framework be the business of every Papua New Guinean, including indigenous people;

▲ The Department of Mining and the World Bank team must make it their business to conduct public meetings in which changes of regulatory framework are fully discussed with as many people as possible and their approval sought;

▲ Changes in any legal framework must consider social, environmental, and economic concerns, from the viewpoint of the local people;

▲ The World Bank must support an independent environmental monitoring and research project for the Lihir mine. The Bank must fund research, and the monitoring team must stay with local people other than the Lihir Management Company; and

▲ No new mines must be encouraged until indigenous local communities are assured that basic rights have been respected and the industry is not going to put waste directly into rivers and oceans.

Box F: Indigenous Peoples' Declaration on Extractive Industries

(April 15, 2003, Oxford, United Kingdom)

Concerned with the threats to vital eco-systems from oil, gas, and mining development, indigenous peoples welcome the World Bank's Extractive Industries Review Initiative. The purpose of this process is to determine whether extractive industries can contribute to poverty alleviation and sustainable development. Such development should be based on environmental, economic and human rights. Indigenous peoples reject the idea that these industries could ever be sustainable—exploitation of natural resources only results in serious social and environmental problems. Among other effects, mining, oil, and gas development has led to the violation of basic human rights, invasion of lands and seizing of resources, forced relocation of communities, threats and intimidation to gain indigenous consent, and withholding of vital information from indigenous communities.

The Indigenous Peoples' Declaration calls on the World Bank's Extractive Industries Review to uphold their recommendations regarding indigenous rights and oil, gas, and mining development. Their ten key demands are:

1. A moratorium on mining, oil, and gas projects until indigenous human rights are secure; existing concessions must be frozen;

2. A ban on destructive practices such as riverine tailings disposal and open pit mining;

3. Prior to any future investments and projects, governments, companies, and development agencies must compensate damages and losses caused by past projects, which have despoiled indigenous lands and fragmented their communities;

4. International development agencies must require borrower countries and private sector clients to uphold human rights in line with their international obligations;

5. Recognition of their collective rights as peoples, to self-determination, including a secure and full measure of self-governance and control over indigenous territories, organizations, and cultural development;

6. Education and capacity building is needed so that indigenous communities can become trained and informed, thus allowing them to participate effectively and make decisions;

7. Negotiation of binding agreements between indigenous peoples, governments, companies, and the World Bank, which can be invoked in courts if dispute resolution or other means of redress fails;

8. Establishment of independent oversight mechanisms that are credible and accessible to indigenous peoples, to ensure compliance by all parties with agreed commitments and obligations;

9. Poverty alleviation must begin with indigenous peoples' definitions and indicators of poverty, and it must address the exclusion and lack of access to decision-making at all levels;

10. Above all, indigenous peoples demand respect for their rights to their territories, lands, and natural resources.

Indigenous peoples do not reject development but instead demand that development be determined by indigenous peoples themselves, according to their priorities. The Indigenous Peoples' Declaration calls for democratic national processes to review strategies and policies for extractive industries to achieve sustainable development.

PART FIVE

Turning Points

Indigenous demonstrators in La Paz Bolivia, during a public transport strike in June 2005. Their demonstration was part of an ongoing continentwide indigenous protest movement against neoliberal economic policies in South America, and for full recognition of indigenous rights. Beyond protest, however, the Indian communities of South America are organizing into huge new political coalitions (described in this chapter). They are seeking to take real power in many countries, and are succeeding in some, notably Bolivia, where an indigenous president, Evo Morales, was recently elected.

CHAPTER 22

Report from "The Heart of the Earth":
Second Continental Summit of Indigenous Peoples

Beverly Bell
Center for Economic Justice

"IN THE HEART OF THE EARTH, in the place where the sun shines directly..." So began the final declaration of the Second Continental Summit of Indigenous Peoples and Nationalities of Abya Yala, held in Quito, Ecuador, July 21–25, 2004. And there ended any allusion to a tranquil world. Five days of discussion and ceremony among eight hundred people from sixty-four indigenous nations and twenty-five countries, from Canada to Chile, demonstrated that a fierce and violent "second conquest" is occurring in that place. But the summit gave birth to new spaces and strategies for indigenous peoples to reclaim what is theirs and to live with peace and autonomy. It also became the latest expression that some of the strongest political mobilizations and the most developed plans for economic alternatives in Latin America today emanate from indigenous movements. Though the primary objective of indigenous peoples is to consolidate their autonomy, the new political and economic conjuncture brought on by globalization has forced them to engage in impressive new fights to defend their rights, lands, and self-governance.

GLOBAL CHALLENGES TO INDIGENOUS EXISTENCE

The Second Continental Summit in Quito took place in a climate of growing challenge to indigenous sovereignty and rights. Globalization has increased the risks for indigenous peoples who live on lands that contain strategic resources needed by global corporations: fresh water, oil, gas, forests, minerals, and biodiversity. Increased foreign investment—and increased profit—depend upon the exploitation of such natural resources. In Latin America, as elsewhere, the greatest concentration of unexploited resources sits on indigenous lands. Indigenous communities are therefore in grave danger from multinational companies, supported by the World Bank and the Inter-American Development Bank (IDB). Market-driven global processes are accentuating environmental deterioration and poverty in indigenous communities, while undermining sustainable communities and the viability of indigenous societies.

IMF- and World Bank–imposed structural adjustment programs in Latin America have pushed economies back to a reliance on raw material extraction by multinational companies. Latin American governments are negotiating the sale of natural resources with little concern about whether the landowners are indigenous, blacks, or peasants. Such negotiations, behind the backs of indigenous peoples, are in open violation of Convention 169 of the International Labor Organization, which says that indigenous peoples have the absolute right to be consulted about decisions that affect their territories or resources.

In the Amazon, wood, pharmaceutical, and oil extraction is rapidly increasing. *(See also Chapter 9.)* A huge free trade plan for Central America (Plan Puebla Panama), largely aimed at indigenous lands, has promoted the massive construction of highways and railroads, and the development of oil and electricity industries. Farther south, the highlands and eastern area of Bolivia are affected by gas and water projects. Two million hectares of the Ecuadorian Amazon have been ceded to oil companies, and 50 percent of the Colombian Amazon is considered by oil companies to be available for direct contracting. The felling of indigenous forests and their replacement by tree plantations owned by national and multinational corporations are intended to keep world paper prices low or continue lowering the price of vegetable oils used by transnational food companies. This, in turn, has converted entire indigenous regions previously dedicated to agriculture, like the Mapuche lands in Chile, or to sustainable forest harvesting, in places like Chajerado and Embera lands in Colombia, into areas devoted primarily to intensive forest production. Mining companies—gold, copper, ferro-nickel—have similarly transformed indigenous lands in Venezuela, Brazil, Colombia and Panama. There is virtually a permanent war by gold miners against indigenous communities residing on these and other rich lands (Yanomami, Curripaco, Baniva, Kuna).

INDIGENOUS MOVEMENTS RESPOND

In response to the new affronts, indigenous peoples are mounting new forms of resistance and organizing.

Throughout Latin America, indigenous movements are standing up for their rights to land, ethnicity, and culture. Indigenous peoples are resisting privatization or appropriation of their water, oil, gas, biodiversity, land, sacred coca leaf, food security, and traditional seed banks. They are joining with networks such as the Campaign of Struggle against the Free Trade Area of the Americas and Via Campesina to raise their voices against free trade pacts on the international arena. And they are doing this within a context of expanded struggles for ethnic recognition, autonomy, and self-government. The resistance and rebellion of indigenous people have, as one Latin American analyst said, "put hemispheric governability at risk." Here are a few examples of successful recent resistance and organizing:

▲ The first widely noted uprising was the famous Zapatista protests among the Mayan communities of Chiapas in 1994. These came about after Mexico modified its constitution to permit, for the first time, public sale of lands that had formerly been *ejidos* communally owned by the Mayan communities. Mexico did this to conform to NAFTA demands just coming into effect. The net result was destruction of Mayan communal corn farming viability. The protests succeeded to the point where five new autonomous zones have now been established under Mayan political and economic rule, without interference from Mexico.

▲ The indigenous peoples in southern Mexico and Central America—together with *campesino* movements—also launched a well-coordinated campaign at stopping Plan Puebla Panama *(see also page 164 about PPP)*. Their public education programs, popular mobilization, direct action, and international publicity were so strong that they forced governments to backpedal and dramatically decrease the scale of the program. (Some corporate investment and government plans continue in different forms.)

▲ In 2000 in Bolivia, the largely indigenous Coalition for the Defense of Water and Life organized such strong uprisings that the government was forced to renege on selling the nation's water to the Bechtel Corporation. More recently they led a highly successful opposition to the proposed export of natural gas to the United States. *(See also Chapter 21.)*

▲ In Colombia between 1997 and 2002, the U'wa peoples held demonstrations against a proposed Occidental Petroleum oil pipeline. They blocked highways and intensely lobbied in the United States and Europe to defend their sacred territory. Their actions ultimately forced Occidental to leave the area and return its oil concession to the Colombian state enterprise, Ecopetrol, and the struggle continues.

▲ In 2003 in Nicaragua, the Awas Tingni were able to get the Inter-American Human Rights Court to declare the government a violator of human rights for not recognizing their ancestral lands. Moreover, the court ordered the government to pay for damages incurred as a result of denying the Awas Tingnis' rights to property and adequate legal protection.

▲ The predominantly indigenous Forum for Cultural and Biological Diversity in Mesoamerica initiated and hosts annual seed exchanges, where indigenous and peasant farmers bring their non-GMO-tainted corn and other seeds to trade, thus expanding the protected stock.

It was in the context of these and other recent indigenous uprisings that the Second Continental Summit of Indigenous Peoples got under way in Quito.

CONVENING A CONTINENTAL SUMMIT

The gathering was organized by the Confederation of Indigenous Nationalities of Ecuador (CONAIE), the Organization of Quechua Nationalities of Ecuador (ECUARINARI), and the Coordination of Indigenous Organizations of the Amazonian Basin (COICA). Its location was significant, since the efforts of the Ecuadorian indigenous movement to gain a plurinational state giving equal weight to indigenous governments have been powerful reference points for indigenous peoples throughout the Americas. (The suppression of the human and political rights of Ecuador's indigenous people, even under an indigenous former president, Lucio Gutierrez, is unfortunately typical of relationships between state governments and indigenous citizenries.)

The workshops and plenaries exposed the enormity of assaults and violations facing indigenous communities today. Subversion of sovereignty, theft of land, expulsion from indigenous territories, extraction and privatization of natural resources, expropriation of indigenous knowledge and genetic material, environmental degradation, invasive biotechnology, loss of control of food sources and agriculture, militarization, fumigation, uncontrolled ecotourism, violation of human and political rights, criminalization of social protest, undermining of national and international treaties and laws, exploitative free trade pacts, growing foreign debt, attempts at cooptation of indigenous organizations, and destruction by corporations and international financial institutions are only a partial list of the aggressions under discussion.

The analysis emerging from the summit showed that, no matter how vast the dangers to indigenous peoples and their autonomy, they were no larger than the commitment to sustain social, economic, political, cultural, and spiritual integrity. This was evidenced in the plethora of proposals and commitments, as well as in the prayer, ceremony, and cultural celebrations that bracketed the discussions.

NEW ALLIANCES AND STRATEGIC PARTNERSHIPS

Among the major issues given attention were indigenous alliances with other social movements. The participants forcefully asserted that strategic partnerships are essential to defend indigenous rights and interests against neoliberal globalization and militarization. As Benjamín Inuca of the Federation of Quechua Peoples of the Northern Sierra of Ecuador said, "If we are not together, we are no more than a big meal." The timing of the summit, back-to-back with the First Social Forum of the Americas, created an important avenue into international spaces. After the closing ceremony, the crowd marched across town to join the inauguration of the Social Forum. Distinguished by dozens of traditional costumes and plentiful indigenous flags, and speaking on many different panels on a broad range of topics, indigenous people were a strong and visible presence at the event. This was a clear indication that indigenous peoples are crossing new bridges.

Another focus of discussion at the summit was the struggle for sovereign control of land and resources. Many adversaries were cited in the sessions, among them the International Monetary Fund, the World Bank, the Inter-American Development Bank, various national governments, the Global Environment Fund, NGOs like the Nature Conservancy and World Wildlife Fund, multinational corporations, and trade pacts such as the Free Trade Area of the Americas (FTAA). Demands included indemnity for environmental destruction, return of genetic materials and collective patrimony, control of food sources and agriculture, full knowledge of and participation by communities in all economic and development decisions and initiatives, and action to reclaim indigenous lands. The partici-

pants advocated a boycott of all multinational corporations involved in these activities, as well as the World Bank, IDB, and IMF. They also urged indigenous organizations to refuse grants from these institutions. Participants called for food sovereignty and a fight against biotechnology. The participants resolved that indigenous lands be left out of negotiations for market-driven development. They called for peoples to organize against the FTAA and other trade pacts, and to oppose free trade. And they called for a permanent space for exchange and communication to challenge neoliberal globalization.

INDIGENOUS KNOWLEDGE

Discussions of indigenous knowledge—a term preferred to "intellectual property"—also led to strong resolutions. The summit rejected patenting of indigenous knowledge and life forms, as well as intellectual property pacts proposed by the United States, and biogenetic prospectors. The summit demanded that national and international governments recognize and indemnify knowledge already taken. It demanded full and direct participation by indigenous peoples in the international fora where decisions regarding indigenous knowledge are made, such as the World Trade Organization and the UN Conference on Trade and Development. The group called, moreover, for adopting internal strategies to transmit and celebrate indigenous knowledge within families and communities.

Regarding other cultural and social rights, the summit affirmed the need for indigenous schools, transmission of indigenous languages, reclamation of traditional foods and medicines, re-adoption of ancestral economic customs based on reciprocity, reappropriation of stolen sacred sites and cultural resources, reclaiming and teaching of native history, research and protection of ancient cultures and traditions, and maintenance and dissemination of indigenous cosmic visions within the community.

Autonomy, diversity, and plurinationality were cross-cutting themes. Among other calls, the group demanded the ratification and application of Convention 169 of the International Labor Confederation and the Indigenous and Tribal Peoples Convention (which recognizes indigenous peoples, government, territories, and legal systems). It called for the Inter-American Commission on Human Rights and the International Court of Justice to uphold all conventions and treaties. However, the group also affirmed that for indigenous peoples, prior autonomous sovereign rights apply even in cases where legal elements such as treaties do not exist. "While there exist three thousand indigenous languages and cultures," commented one panelist, so far "only two hundred nations are recognized." The gathering urged full respect by all nations and international bodies for lands and rights, particularly for noncontacted peoples, and for political and judicial autonomy.

The eleven declarations, with their binding resolutions, contained many more commitments. These included: economic sovereignty; rejection of invasions, wars, and all forms of militarization; the release of dozens of indigenous peoples imprisoned throughout the hemisphere for defending their lands and rights; free transit of peoples; an indigenous international court; a network of communication and action of indigenous peoples; and support for the peoples of Venezuela and Cuba.

The final declaration concluded, "We possess our own models that guarantee the continuation of our peoples and nationalities in harmony with nature and based in our ancestral cultural heritage." The Indigenous Summit marked a new chapter in uniting indigenous peoples, as they equipped themselves with new strategies to defend and protect those models.

By thus refusing to be subject to a second colonization, indigenous peoples are organizing to assert their rights and autonomy. They are posing the greatest challenge to the plans of multinational corporations, international financial institutions, trade pacts, and local governments of any sector in Latin America. To quote indigenous rights activist Gustavo Castro Soto, "From here comes the greatest hope that another world is possible."

This article was adapted from its original publication in the Sharing Circle, *Fall/Winter 2004.*

Bolivia's Aymara Indians, two of whom are shown here blocking a highway near Cochabamba, are among hundreds of thousands of indigenous peoples who led the protests in that country against water privatization and against the export of natural gas to the United States, a classic case of a poor country exporting its wealth to the rich. The Indians demanded an end to neoliberal export and privatization programs and the replacement of Bolivia's president, and they won.

CHAPTER 23

Bolivia's Indigenous Revolution

Suzanne York
International Forum on Globalization

IN THE PAST FEW YEARS, a revolution against economic globalization has taken place in Bolivia, led by indigenous peoples and *campesinos*. It has been an impressive show of power by the poor, who are not benefiting from globalization and want a voice in how their nation's resources are used.

Until recently, Bolivia's poor had never wielded any significant political power. That changed suddenly in 1999 with the successful mass uprisings in Cochabamba against the privatization of water (*see also chapter 13*), and more recently in 2003, with the indigenous uprisings now known as the War on Gas. In the latter case, a proposed deal to export Bolivia's natural gas—its most abundant resource—to the United States was protested as yet another case where the rich become richer and the poor benefit little or not at all. The series of demonstrations that followed shook the Bolivian government, toppled three presidents, and by 2005 led to the election of Bolivia's first indigenous president, one of the movement's leaders, Evo Morales, creating a new atmosphere of hope and optimism.

Though the transition in power seemed to have happened very quickly, it was actually the culmi-

nation of a growing frustration and resistance among Bolivia's indigenous and *campesino* populations for at least two prior decades.

THE FAILURES OF NEOLIBERALISM IN BOLIVIA

Though indigenous peoples comprise a majority of Bolivia's population of 8.7 million (an estimated 56 to 70 percent, mainly Quechua and Aymara), they have been exploited and marginalized since the time of the Spanish conquest. In the 1980s, neoliberalism and the free-market system were advertised as being able to turn the situation around, yet today Bolivia remains one of the poorest countries in the Western Hemisphere. Nearly two-thirds of the population, many of whom are subsistence farmers, live in poverty and lack basic services such as electricity and running water. Most of these *campesinos* are indigenous peoples who speak one of twenty-three indigenous languages other than Spanish.

The chief architect of Bolivia's entry into the neoliberal free market experiment in the 1980s was Sánchez de Lozada, then the country's planning minister but later its president. Under great pressure from the United States, the World Bank, and IMF structural adjustment demands, Lozada rapidly privatized state-owned industries (oil, airlines, electricity, and mining), reduced public services, brought in foreign investors, and opened up the country to the global economy. In those years, the World Bank and IMF actually held up Bolivia as a model for other developing nations. The economic shock therapy did slow down runaway inflation for a time. But for the average Bolivian, the "economic austerity measures" brought growing disaster and resentment.

In order to meet IMF loan demands, the Bolivian government had agreed to impose harsh neoliberal economic policies on the people, including increases in personal income taxes and massive cuts in crucial social programs. These in turn produced tremendous unemployment, increased poverty, cuts to social services and pensions, and the negative outfall of enormous foreign debt. By 2001, Bolivia owed $4.4 billion in foreign debt and spent $340 million in annual debt payments. *This was the same amount the government spent on education, health, and other social programs combined.* Per capita income today is about $900 a year, down from $1,200 in 1974. Official Bolivian statistics on unemployment range from 8.7 to 11.6 percent. After two decades of such results, poor Bolivians were ready to actively resist. Their first opportunity came in 1999, with the privatization of the city of Cochabamba's water.

WATER WAR

The Bolivian government, pushed by the World Bank, awarded a forty-year concession starting in 1999 to Aguas del Tunari, a subsidiary of Bechtel Corporation, for the water and sanitation system of Cochabamba, Bolivia's third-largest city. Typically, the World Bank had threatened to cut its debt-relief program if Bolivia refused to privatize its water. Upon receipt of the contract, Aguas del Tunari immediately initiated price hikes of 200 percent, thus doubling or tripling the average consumer's water bill. Massive public

protests, strikes, and blockades followed the rate hikes. So powerful were these protests that Bechtel, a billion-dollar company, was forced to withdraw. (Bechtel, via Aguas del Tunari, then filed suit against the Bolivian government demanding $25 million in compensation for lost profits. But under public pressure it withdrew its suit in January 2006.)

During the Cochabamba water protests, a citizens' movement for indigenous peoples and campesinos was born: the Coalition in Defense of Water and Life (*Coordinadora Defensa del Agua y la Vida*). Members were both urban and rural and comprised farmers, the local factory workers union, progressive members of Congress, environmental groups, grassroots organizations, and huge numbers of indigenous people. This remarkable coalition included some of the poorest people on the continent, who came together to stand up to the military and resist martial law in their battle against economic globalization. The lessons they learned from the water battle later gave them the strength and organization to deal with the attempted giveaway of yet another natural resource—natural gas—that the government had decided to sell to transnational companies.

Cochabamba wasn't the only Bolivian city confronting World Bank–backed water privatization. The water systems of the adjacent municipalities of El Alto and La Paz were targeted for privatization in 1997 by the private consortium Aguas del Illimani, led by Suez Corporation of France. Ironically, the World Bank has a vested interest, as it owns 8 percent of shares in Aguas del Illimani, via its International Finance Corporation. Customer satisfaction with Aguas del Illimani was low. Pegging water rates to the U.S. dollar, the Bolivian-based Democracy Center reported that water prices had risen 35 percent since the company took over. New water and sewage hookups cost approximately $445 (half a year's income), and community water groups and even the government charged that the company had left more than 200,000 people without access to water because it failed to expand water infrastructure to the city's outskirts. Community groups began to mobilize against Aguas del Illimani in late 2004 with a citywide general strike, demanding that the city's water system be returned to public control. The Bolivian government finally decreed that the company wasn't serving the people and moved to cancel the water contract for both El Alto and La Paz.

GAS WAR: PHASE ONE

Bolivian government officials also proposed a huge natural gas pipeline, running across Chile to the ocean for export, as the solution to Bolivia's economic problems. Bolivia has South America's second-largest natural gas reserves, and the officials argued that the pipeline could revive the country's economy. However, the government's contract with a consortium of international gas companies, including Shell and British Petroleum, stated that only 18 percent of future profits from gas exports would go to Bolivia and 82 percent would go to international companies. To the average poor Bolivian, this looked like yet another giveaway to foreign interests—one more case of exporting an important natural resource (just as happened before with gold, tin, and coal) and leaving citizens with nothing. Opposition groups saw the pipeline project as another chance to air their grievances against the government and its failed free-market policies. Massive new protests began in La Paz in January 2003, and included a broad range of Bolivian society—miners, indigenous peoples, farmers, teachers, students, and even the National Police. The demonstrations led to clashes with the military that left thirty-three dead and around one hundred wounded in La Paz and other cities. In the face of mass demonstrations, Sánchez de Lozada backed down, scrapping the tax increase. Political momentum shifted to the protestors.

In August 2003, civil society groups, workers, farmers, and other organizations used the lessons learned from the prior water battles to form a fully coordinated national campaign to stop the exportation of Bolivia's natural gas to the United States and Mexico, calling it the National Coalition in Defense of Our Gas (*Coordinadora Nacional de Defensa del Gas*). The fact that the pipeline would run through Chile added to the deep national resentment because Chile had denied Bolivia its outlet to the sea in an 1879 war, which Bolivians have not forgotten. The protesting groups also demanded the release of jailed political leaders, prosecution for the deaths from the February protests, and the resignation of President Lozada, which was finally forthcoming in October 2003.

THE COCA FACTOR

Concurrent with the pipeline struggle, a U.S.-backed program to eradicate coca crops, used to make cocaine, sparked further bitterness and major domestic unrest. Thousands of Bolivians resent the crackdown on coca production, as it unfairly deprives poor and indigenous farmers—who grow coca for traditional non-narcotic uses—of their livelihood. For generations, Bolivians have used coca leaves for medicinal purposes, such as preventing altitude sickness or suppressing appetite. The Yungas region of Bolivia has been the site of legally produced coca since the beginning of the U.S. war on drugs. But with the imposition of World Bank and IMF structural adjustment policies in the 1980s, peasant farmers and other unemployed people were forced to migrate to the Chapare region and begin growing illicit coca. Ironically, the coca economy helped stabilize the currency by creating an income source for displaced peasants, as well as stimulating the overall national economy.

Bolivian- and U.S.-supported eradication almost wiped out coca in the Chapare, but a lack of viable alternative development programs led to protests, social unrest, and assertions that U.S.-funded counternarcotics forces were violating natives' human rights. Even U.S. economist Jeffrey Sachs, who was instrumental in getting the Bolivian government to adopt the neoliberal policies of the 1980s and 1990s, has stated that the United States hasn't provided many real options for coca farmers. He told the *New York Times* that U.S.-funded alternative development programs amount to a "ludicrously small investment" and cannot replace coca.

The coca growers, or *cocaleros*, who resisted eradication have become a political force in Bolivia, and their struggle has aided other social movements. Evo Morales, an Aymara Indian and congressman, and leader of the union of coca growers, has been a major force for the opposition in the protests over natural gas. In his first run for the presidency, in 2002, Morales narrowly lost to Sánchez de Lozada, but Morales's Movement toward Socialism party (Movimiento al Socialismo) gained one-third of the congressional seats. Lozada did not keep the presidency much longer; following nationwide protests in 2003, he fled the country for Miami, where he now lives. His vice president, Carlos Mesa, replaced him as president, though he did not last long either.

COALITION DEMANDS

By 2003, it was clear that poor Bolivians did not want to export natural gas, objected to global institutions and companies buying and selling their natural resources, and rejected neoliberal institutions, including the Free Trade Areas of the Americas (FTAA) agreement. The people wanted control over their resources; they wanted Bolivians to be the *first* to benefit, not the last. In the words of Bolivian indigenous leader Roberto de la Cruz, "We will no longer permit the transnational corporations to benefit more than Bolivians from our own natural resources" (*The Nation*, Oct. 22, 2003).

The National Coalition in Defense of Our Gas demanded establishment of a new government within the constitutional framework, and demanded:

▲ Derogation of Decree #24806 of August 1997, which permits transnational control of Bolivian gas;

▲ Immediate modification of the Hydrocarbons Law (created to promote foreign investment) to allow the Bolivian people to regain control of this resource;

▲ Immediate suspension of negotiations on gas and the Free Trade Agreement with Chile;

▲ Organization of a constituent assembly to restore participative democracy for the people.

Other demands include comprehensive land reform, higher wages, better pensions, transparency in government, political autonomy, and the right to grow coca.

In July 2004, Bolivia held a national vote on what to do with its natural gas resources. Voters approved an ambiguously worded five-point plan, submitted by the new president, Carlos Mesa, to develop the country's gas reserves. The next move was for the Bolivian congress to create a new oil and natural gas law, modify the Hydrocarbons Law, and establish how the reserves would be developed. Mesa argued against nationalization, reasoning that it would frighten off foreign investors. But for those wanting sovereignty over natural resources, nationalization is seen as the only way to end the exploitation.

Oscar Olivera, a leader of the earlier uprising against water privatization and now the leader of the National Coalition in Defense of Our Gas, has emphasized that the referendum would not, by itself, bring changes in the daily lives of working people. "The people are building their own horizon. The referendum ended today but the struggle continues; it's irreversible."

GAS WAR: PHASE TWO

Olivera was right; in spring 2005, Bolivia was again racked by protests and blockades led by indigenous groups frustrated at the government's lack of meaningful action on the nationalization issue. Protestors called for the renationalization of the natural gas industry and for rewriting the constitution to give more power to indigenous citizens. President Mesa, under pressure from indigenous groups, corporations, regional interests, and the IMF, tried to please all sides but could not negotiate a consensus. And as before, the failure to listen to the demands of the people resulted in the resignation of yet another president only twenty months after Lozada had been ousted. Carlos Mesa stepped down and was replaced on an "interim" basis by Eduardo Rodriguez, former head of Bolivia's Supreme Court. Rodriguez pledged to organize elections for a constituent assembly to rewrite the constitution, and to hold a referendum on regional autonomy, as demanded by the protestors.

Before the IMF had intervened to privatize Bolivia's petroleum industry, oil and gas revenues were split evenly between Bolivia and foreign oil companies. After Bolivia heeded the IMF's advice (based on the theory that more investment = greater oil production = more revenue), Bolivia's share of oil revenues declined to 18 percent. According to the Cochabamba-based Democracy Center, the government was supposed to receive a package of taxes and royalties to replace its former 50 percent share of oil and gas benefits. Instead, new petroleum taxes were passed on to Bolivian consumers in the form of taxes on domestic use and higher energy prices. By 2001, government gas revenues had fallen by $40 million and Bolivia's deficit was increasing. Bolivians hoped that this time the government would take their demands seriously.

Bolivia's congress passed a new Hydrocarbons Law in May 2005, pleasing no one. Though the new law raised taxes on foreign companies to 50 percent, it failed to return control of the nation's gas and oil reserves to the Bolivian people, thus igniting protests from social movements. Shortly after taking power, interim president Rodriguez put the congressional Hydrocarbons Law into effect. Large foreign investors reacted by putting investment plans on hold and threatening to go to arbitration if an acceptable accord was not reached.

As the struggle continues, regional divisions are gaining hold. The eastern half of the country, where the natural gas is located, is mostly non-indigenous and more prosperous than the poorer, indigenous-majority western half. The eastern departments are opposed to nationalization and welcome foreign investment. Still, the results of a nation-wide poll in June 2005 found 75 percent of Bolivians in favor of nationalization.

Even the World Bank recently concluded that although Bolivia's indigenous groups have increased their political influence, this has not yet resulted in an improvement in their living conditions. In a country where 64 percent of the population lives below the poverty line, half the population survives on less than $2 a day, and the richest 10 percent of Bolivians consume twenty-two times that consumed by the poorest 10 percent, is it any wonder the indigenous majority want to benefit from the natural resources surrounding them?

Bolivia's indigenous people take pride in their defiant demonstrations and are empowered by the recent success of their political activism, especially the election of President Morales. Bolivia's indigenous people are not alone in fighting the current economic system. As reported elsewhere in these pages, peoples' movements—frustrated with false promises of free markets and fed up with the Washington Consensus—are gaining ground throughout Latin America, particularly in Argentina, Brazil, Ecuador, Guatemala, Mexico, Paraguay, Peru, and Venezuela. Opposition in these countries is based on experience with what indigenous and poor *campesinos* see as the failures of privatization, deregulation, structural adjustment, and free entry of foreign investment. Indigenous peoples were promised that this new model would improve the economy and thus their lives. What they got instead was high unemployment, rising poverty, and recession. The indigenous opposition to the economic model was particularly stongly felt in November 2005, with the unified rejection of President Bush's advocacy of a new Free Trade Area of the Americas (FTAA).

Right now, the momentum is clearly with the indigenous peoples, who now have the opportunity to make their voices and ideas heard. In both phases of the gas wars, Bolivians called upon their government to use the natural gas first for in-country employment and income. If there is a surplus, it can be exported on terms favorable to Bolivia's people. According to new president Evo Morales, the question isn't whether or not to export but whether "the property of our oil and gas is going to belong to Bolivians or to the multinationals." (One ominous sign was that the United States reacted to Morales's statements and election by sharply cutting Bolivia's military aid, raising fears that a disgruntled military corps might revert to old behaviors and head a coup.)

Beyond control of gas and water, the indigenous people of Bolivia want not only a full say in how all resources of their country are used, but basic fairness, equality, and a chance to regain their dignity. While the long-range results of the Bolivian uprisings and elections are yet to be known, the immediate result has been to place new collective power and momentum in the hands of the indigenous peoples.

Box G: Venezuela's Constitutional Provisions on the "Rights of Indigenous Peoples"

In 1999, the newly elected National Constituent Assembly of Venezuela completed a new constitution, which included some of the most supportive language for indigenous rights of any country in the Western Hemisphere. The specific rights include protection from alienability of lands, the right to collective ownership and full consultation; recognition and respect for indigenous worldviews, languages and economic and political systems.

Despite such language, there remains some question about whether the commitments are being honored. At the 2006 America Social Forum in Caracas, huge protests by indigenous peoples focused on government plans to grant coal concessioins to energy corporations within collectively held indigenous lands along the northern border, *without* the promised prior consultations. As this book goes to press, negotiations with the government are about to begin.

Venezuela's indigenous population represents only about 1.5 percent of the country's population and is divided into twenty-eight ethnic groups, the largest being the Wayuu (or Guajira), numbering about 200,000, in the state of Zulia, near the Colombian border. Pressures for codification of indigenous rights began in the 1980s, when most of the indigenous peoples of Venezuela joined in the creation of the Venezuelan National Indian Council, opposing that government's neoliberal reforms, especially an IMF mandated oil price hike. Mass protest led to riots in Caracas. With the 1998 election of Hugo Chavez (himself partly Pumé) as president, and the formation of the new National Assembly, indigenous interests seemed to take a turn for the better.

Following is the partial text of Chapter 8, On the Rights of Indigenous Peoples, from the 1999 Venezuelan Constitution:

Article 119: The State recognizes the existence of indigenous peoples and communities, their social, political and economic organization, their cultures, practices and customs, languages and religions, as well as their habitat and original rights to the lands they ancestrally and traditionally occupy, and which are necessary to develop and guarantee their way of life. It shall be the responsibility of the National Executive, with the participation of the native peoples, to demarcate and guarantee the right to collective ownership of their lands, which shall be inalienable, not subject to the law of limitations and nontransferable.

Article 120: Exploitation by the State of the natural resources in indigenous habitats shall be carried out without harming the cultural, social and economic integrity of such habitats, and likewise subject to prior information and consultation with the indigenous communities concerned. Profits from such exploitation by the indigenous peoples are subject to the Constitution and the law.

Article 121: Indigenous peoples have the right to maintain and develop their ethnic and cultural identity, world view, values, spirituality and sacred places of worship. The State shall promote the appreciation and dissemination of the cultural manifestations of the indigenous peoples, who have the right to their own education, taking into account their special social and cultural characteristics, values and traditions.

Article 122: Indigenous peoples have the right to a full health system that takes into consideration their practices and cultures. The State shall recognize their traditional medicine and supplementary forms of therapy, subject to principles of bioethics.

Article 123: Indigenous peoples have the right to maintain and promote their own economic practices based on reciprocity, solidarity and exchange; their traditional productive activities and their participation in the national economy, and to define their priorities.

Article 124: Collective intellectual property rights in the knowledge, technologies and innovations of indigenous peoples are guaranteed and protected. Any activity relating to genetic resources and the knowledge associated with the same, shall pursue collective benefits.

Article 125: Indigenous peoples have the right to participate in politics. The State shall guarantee indigenous representation in the National Assembly and the deliberating organs of federal and local entities.

These extraordinary constitutional commitments have been celebrated as a model for other nations to follow, but now they are cited by indigenous Wayuu, Anu, Yukpa and Bori peoples demanding they actually be followed. The Indians specifically ask for recognition of their collective land rights to the disputed territory, and that all energy concessions be reversed. The ultimate outcome is not clear.

President Patrick Spears and Secretary Robert Gough of the Intertribal Council on Utility Policy are working on a project that may bring a reversal of fortunes for the Great Plains Sioux and other tribes of that region. Indian reservations have begun to convert the steady strong winds of the plains into new wind energy projects. Until now, Indian reservations in the United States have been exploited by energy companies for highly destructive coal, gas and uranium projects, which have left a legacy of pollution and disease. Conversion to an economy based on renewable wind energy may set an example for indigenous communities elsewhere and for the United States itself.

CHAPTER 24

Indian Country: "The Saudi Arabia of Wind"

Winona LaDuke
(Anishinaabeg)
White Earth Land Recovery Project

AT THE CLOSE OF THE LAST CENTURY, the so-called Indian Wars were over. The U.S. government had stolen the best Indian lands, carved the faces of its presidents in the sacred mountains, and forced the Lakota and other peoples onto seemingly barren reservation lands. But, on these lands once considered worthless, a grand new vision for a positive sustainable future is rapidly taking shape in native hands. The people of the Lakota Sioux Pine Ridge Reservation in South Dakota are transforming tribal economics and also America's energy future. The Lakota are starting work to harness the strong steady winds of the northern Great Plains (called *Taté* in Lakota) to power their communities toward a spectacular conversion; their goal is to build a new economy based on green power and to become the model for a renewable energy future—a profitable but sustainable future—among peoples who have been major victims of irresponsible energy development for a half century or more.

At Pine Ridge, the wind energy potential is immense, with the prospect of tapping 4,500 times more power than electrical consumers use on the reservation. The same possibility extends beyond Lakota Sioux territory, all across the Great Plains. On the Fort Berthold reservation in North Dakota, for example, the Mandan, Hidatsa and Arikara tribes possess 17,000 times more wind power potential than they can use. Similar projects are being explored throughout Indian Country, in Montana, Minnesota and Washington. People are already starting to call our lands "The Saudi Arabia of Wind."

The potential for renewable energy in Indian country is now well understood. In 2000, the U.S. Department of Energy released a report noting that "sixty-one Indian reservations appear to have renewable resources that might be developed" at a cost competitive with polluting power sources. In other words, cleaner renewable energy resources like wind can prove far more lucrative in the long run for Indian Country than the nonrenewable sources that have dominated tribal economies. We stand on the cusp of something very important. It is our choice to determine the legacy we leave for future generations.

FROM EXPLOITATION TO TRANSFORMATION

The irony of the situation is inescapable. Over the past fifty years, shortsighted U.S. energy policy and irresponsible management by the federal

Indian trust responsible for Indian resources have assaulted U.S. tribal communities with environmental and economic injustices, leaving pollution, uranium wastes, depleted water tables, lung disease, radiation sickness and extreme economic exploitation. For all that, we have very little to show. In a U.S. energy market valued at about $300 billion dollars, at least 10 percent (the approximate percentage of our overall resource contribution to America's energy supplies) should rightfully go to the tribes. But we receive a pittance, and Indian reservations have remained the poorest segment of American society. The Council of Energy Resource Tribes puts it this way:

> *The history of American electric power is a story of America's rise to world-wide economic preeminence, but for Indian tribes, it's a history of the abuse of power by the federal government and hostility to tribal economic interests by the states. In spite of treaties and the federal trust obligations, Indian resources were confiscated for the benefit of others at the expense of Indian people. No other group of Americans has suffered more from energy development.*

Even today some of the largest carbon dioxide–emitting utilities are burning Indian coal (or blowing it over the reservations). Thousands of abandoned radioactive uranium mine sites dot our reservation, and the largest hydropower dams on the continent have drowned tribal lands from the Columbia River to James Bay and Newfoundland. New proposals in Congress would exploit the Arctic National Wildlife Refuge for oil deposits at the expense of native livelihoods, and would dump nuclear waste at Yucca Mountain in the heart of the Western Shoshone nation.

Current national policies only stand to make things worse. According to the U.S. Department of Energy, coal accounts for half of U.S. electricity, a substantially higher portion than thirty years ago. That is not good news in Indian Country. Native nations in the United States, according to Joseph Kalt at Harvard University, hold the third-greatest coal reserves in the world. Cheap Bureau of Indian Affairs leases to big corporations have ensured that this coal gets to market but Indians get nearly nothing. The environmental cost, however, is high.

Of ten emitters of air pollution in New Mexico, four are coal outfits on the Navajo reservation: Four Corners power plant, San Juan generating station, BHP San Juan coal mine and BHP Navajo coal mine. (Coal mines contribute air pollution in the form of dust.) Another coal generator, the Colstrip complex at the Crow reservation, contributes a heavy dose of carbon dioxide, mercury, nitric oxides, sulfur oxides, and particulates into the Montana sky, and from there, of course, it blows east.

The consequences of coal power extend beyond any political jurisdiction. Inhabitants of the many Minnesota Ojibwe reservations throughout the Great Lakes and the Northeast have been advised to limit the number of fish they consume. Unhealthy levels of mercury and other heavy metals have been found in local fish stocks, and the culprit is suspected to be coal-fired power plants and incinerators. A number of northeastern states have filed suit against power producers in Ohio, Indiana, and Ontario, seeking to hold them accountable for acid rain, air pollution, and noncompliance with the U.S. Clean Air Act. Some of that pollution, however, may be coming from farther west, since the prevailing winds sweep eastward from the Great Plains.

Basin Electric Power, the mammoth utility serving nine states on the western plains, produces the most carbon dioxide per megawatt hour of electricity of any utility in the nation, according to a recent study by the Natural Resources Defense Council: "That is pretty much the dirtiest coal in the country." A couple of Basin's power plants are located just upwind from the Fort Berthold reservation, where they spew poisons directly onto some Mandan, Hidatsa and

Arikara communities—and to nearby lakes downwind. Further south, the Navajo have experienced similar fallout from regional power plants.

It's a dysfunctional economic and ecological feedback loop, which is one big reason why a move toward wind power is crucial: we're combusting ourselves to oblivion. The solution underway throughout Indian Country might provide the way out.

COMMUNITY DETERMINATION

On the million-acre Pine Ridge reservation—the second most populous in the United States, with more than 20,000 people—the plans to harness *Taté* reflect a community's determination to survive. Despite a host of hardships and the long history of failed government policies on the reservation, there is not only strength but amazing beauty and resilience here. A century after the 1890 Wounded Knee Massacre and the so-called Indian wars, indigenous singers are praying in their own languages as they have for a millennium. More than forty Sun Dances each year reaffirm the Lakota relationship to the Creation, as do other ceremonies. Buffalo herds, the lifeblood of traditional culture, amble across the prairie in growing numbers each spring. And there are more Lakotas every year. In Shannon County, squarely in the middle of the reservation, the population increased by 26 percent between 1990 and 2000, a number matched by population growth in other native communities in the region.

It is in this spirit of resilience and healing that the tribe has begun planning for its new wind turbines. In the 1980s, the White Plume Tiospaye secured—through sales and land agreements—enough reservation land to care for a large herd of buffalo and horses. Alex White Plume's family, descended from survivors of the Wounded Knee Massacre, leads the Big Foot Memorial Ride, a midwinter horseback ride hundreds of miles long meant to commemorate

and begin to resolve some of the sorrow left from the massacre. It is only natural that the family, like many others in Indian Country, would honor survival by turning its attention to future generations: a grand plan for economic revitalization through harnessing of the wind. *Taté* is a constant on the Pine Ridge reservation and others throughout the plains, bringing the remembrances of ancestors, the smell of new seasons, and regular reminders of human piety in the face of the immensity of Creation.

"We believe the wind is *wakan*, a holy or great power," explains Pat Spears, president of Intertribal Council on Utility Policy (COUP) and a member of the Lower Brule Tribe, from a reservation east of Pine Ridge. "Our grandmothers and grandfathers have always talked about [the sacredness of *Taté*], and we recognize that."

Alex White Plume echoes Spear's words when he talks about *Taté* as "the power of motion and transformation." According to Debbie White Plume, that motion has increasingly led tribes to seek a return to "the power the Creator gave us," not the power doled out by electric utilities and energy corporations. "*Taté*," she adds, "is a messenger for the prayers of the Lakota people."

Those prayers, combined with hard work and financial creativity, are beginning to pay off. In spring 2003, eighty miles east of the Pine Ridge reservation on the South Dakota-Nebraska state line, the Rosebud Sioux Tribe installed the first large-scale native-owned commercial wind turbine on tribal land in the United States. Amid gently rolling prairie, the 750-kilowatt three-blade NEG Micon propeller towers 190 feet above the ground in the heart of the Rosebud Lakota reservation.

The Rosebud turbine is a symbol of success in the face of complex obstacles. With a price tag for equipment of around $770,000, including installation and wiring to the grid, the Danish-made turbine was "turnkey ready." To purchase it, the Rosebud Lakota secured a one-time Department of Energy grant, plus a federal loan designed to electrify rural areas, as well as supplemental financing.

The tribe, with support from COUP, also negotiated a several-year contract to sell the turbine's electricity to nearby Ellsworth Air Force base at a profitable rate. When that contract expires, the two million plus kilowatt hours of annual wind energy from the turbine will supply half the energy for the tribe's casino and hotel complex.

On the heels of that success, the Rosebud Sioux Tribe is now planning an ambitious 30-megawatt wind farm with twenty to thirty turbines. Since the "load" on reservations like Pine Ridge and Rosebud is only about 10 megawatts, the tribe sees the excess power as potential income.

The Rosebud turbines, current and future, are just the beginning. COUP hopes they will set the stage for a broader plan by the tribes in the Great Plains region to bring 3,000 megawatts of power to market in the next two decades. "The wind energy that the tribes want to produce requires up to a $3 billion investment for building 3 gigawatts of wind turbines. The 'economy' around that is much greater!!" says Bob Gough of COUP. "After thirty years, you don't have a hole in the ground, the water is still clean, and you still have 100 percent of the resource."

It is amazing and particularly ironic that some of the windiest places in the country are Indian reservations. Go figure. The truth is, at the close of the so-called Indian wars, native peoples of the Great Plains were thought to be left with nothing. Their best lands were taken, their sacred Black Hills stolen for gold. In the mid-twentieth century, some of the best remaining lands and villages were flooded in the Pick-Sloan pork barrel irrigation project, which turned much of the Missouri River into a series of reservoirs.

In an area once thought to be nothing but desolate grassland plains, wind projects are now planned for Fort Berthold, Northern Cheyenne (Montana), Makah (Washington), and White Earth (Northern Minnesota) reservations. The economics make sense to tribes like the Assiniboine and Sioux of Fort Peck, Montana, who hope to bring on line a 660-kilowatt wind turbine that would produce an estimated two million kilowatt hours of power per year. That output alone would reduce the annual tribal electric bill by $134,000, and the savings could finance other programs. Having experienced decades of economic injustice in energy policy, these tribes are planning to own the turbines outright and to reap the economic benefits as part of a vision of tribal self-determination.

The benefits of this process would extend beyond those immediate communities. It is part of a strategy by native peoples across the Great Plains to move ourselves away from combusting the finite leftovers of the Jurassic Age, toward an era of renewable energy. According to National Renewable Energy Laboratory wind maps, the reservations on the Great Plains could provide enough wind power to meet more than one-third of present U.S. electrical consumption needs.

Sacred sites, Sun Dance circles, *hamblechi* (vision quest) areas, as well as ecologically sensitive areas would be exempted from turbines. But on the ranches and the vast stretches of tribal lands in the wind-rich region, there is a practical, accessible alternative to fossil fuels.

COST COMPETITION

This is how it starts. Using a wind-measuring device called an anemometer, native communities assess wind potential. The reading gives some sense of the appropriate type of turbine and viability of the project. The community then decides what size and how many turbines to put up and how to arrange financing. Unlike some farmers in Minnesota and Iowa who now lease out wind rights to major corporations for about $2,500 per turbine per year, the tribes would own their wind facilities outright. The average construction cost is $1,000 per kilowatt, so a 750-kilowatt turbine—enough to power about 250 homes—might cost $750,000. The most expensive part of the venture, and the area where communities need the most assistance, is building the turbines.

Jim Taulman, a renewable energy instructor at Pine Ridge's Oglala Lakota College and consultant for the Pine Ridge projects, points out that native wind projects would be connected to a massive grid that would cover much of the West and be linked to other grids nationwide. "It's distributed power production," Taulman explains. "Smaller, renewable-energy installations produce energy for local usage and send the excess to the utility grid." The devil's in the details, however, and the energy of the future is still competing by the rules of the past.

Since wind power is typically still more expensive than other sources, and since selling a turbine's excess energy to utilities is not yet financially viable, the tribes have had to rely on other ways to sell energy and finance new projects. One tool currently available is called a "Green Tag," used by the Rosebud project to finance almost 25 percent of its wind-turbine project. Green Tags are not sales of actual electricity. They are a separate salable product representing the environmental and social benefits of wind-produced energy. The purchaser of a wind-turbine's Green Tags—its environmental benefits—provides cash to the wind-energy producer. Think of it as a free-market subsidy provided by individuals, organizations, or even utilities.

Recent mandates in Massachusetts, Maine, New Jersey, Colorado, Iowa, Minnesota, and eight other states require utilities to buy a minimum percentage of their energy from renewable sources, and Green Tags are an accepted and convenient way to fulfill that obligation. While not a direct purchase of energy, it helps put cleaner, cheaper wind energy on the market.

The renewable-energy marketing firm Native-Energy (native-owned) has developed a novel way to purchase tribal projects' Green Tags. With a funding base of donors, it arranges to pay up front for a wind project's environmental benefits over the expected twenty-five-year life span of a turbine. Such a payment, coming in the critical early stages, provides much-needed startup capital.

While still expensive compared to most fossil fuels, the price of wind energy has dropped precipitously in the past twenty-five years thanks to increased technological efficiency. Wind is now cheaper than coal from a new plant, although not as cheap as coal from older, more polluting, facilities. The supply of wind is also stable, largely impervious to the supply fluctuations and regional politics that plague the fossil fuel market.

SUPPORT BY A CONSORTIUM OF CITIES

Some of the most promising initial customers for tribal wind power may be municipalities concerned about global warming. In October 2003, the mayors of 156 American cities pledged to honor the Kyoto Accord on greenhouse gas emissions, which the U.S. government refused to sign. In November, COUP invited those mayors to pledge support for native wind projects, and in March 2004, ten mayors agreed. The number of mayors has since reached thirty-six. Aspen, Colorado, has requested that native wind projects, not coal, cover hydropower shortfalls in its energy mix. If Aspen succeeds with this request, says Gough, other cities are likely to follow suit. Demand from the thirty-six cities could total hundreds of megawatts, a significant jump-start for the tribes.

Other nontraditional markets for wind energy are opening up as well. This summer, Michigan Interfaith Power and Light, a collection of a hundred religious congregations, signed an agreement with NativeEnergy to educate its members about buying Green Tags from the Rosebud wind farm and, over time, from other native wind energy projects in the Dakotas and beyond.

The biggest boost for wind power would come from a shift in government policy. The Apollo Project, an alliance of environmental groups and twelve labor unions, has called for an investment of $300 billion of federal money into renewable energy operations like Rosebud's. According to the project, that investment would stimulate an estimated $1.4 trillion in new Gross Domestic Product, and add 3.3 million new jobs. Renewable energy would also bring a new dynamic to the national political arena. Unlike oil, native wind power is not brokered by Halliburton or ExxonMobil and obviously does not depend on supply from distant places in a global economy.

The tribal wind program also provides an opportunity for native communities from the East and West coasts—including wealthy casino-operating tribes—to invest in some of the largest landholding, wind-rich tribes on the plains. This type of cross-tribal investment would help to restore the centuries-old trade relations that existed between indigenous nations.

Speaking with some of the largest casino-operating tribes at the United Southern and Eastern Tribes meeting in February 2003, Bob Gough of COUP laid out the financial potential of tribal investment partnerships, as well as the positive environmental impact from such partnerships. "We don't just want to be there when the blue-haired ladies put quarters into the machines," he told the audience. "We want to be there any time a light switch goes on." Several tribes in the Great Lakes and New England, including the Mohegans of Connecticut, who recently purchased hydrogen fuel cells to power their casino complex, have shown an interest in investing in Plains wind projects.

There is abundant opportunity, but making the Great Plains into the Saudi Arabia of wind energy will not be simple or easy. Remote tribal communities must wrangle with the "white tape" created by American industry. But in meeting after meeting, I've found that these communities are clear about their commitment and their history. It is as if they were declaring: "That was then, this is now." In the future we will not be cheated or stolen from. We intend to keep our spiritual agreements with the Creator, and hold onto our traditions, as we care for our mother the Earth.

Creating energy and harnessing the wind provides native people with an opportunity to recover one of our most important cultural traditions—adaptability. Tribes have constantly evolved and this is a time to recover dignity, integrity, and continuity through self-determination. Native communities have survived to inhabit the nuclear age. And native communities will live in the age of renewable energy. If things go as planned, with the power of *Taté*, we will help make it possible for everyone.

This article was adapted from its original publication in Orion *magazine, November/December 2004.*

This is a recent clear-cut on indigenous lands in the Great Bear Forest of British Columbia. The Canadian constitution recognizes Aboriginal Title to these and similar lands in places where treaties have not been concluded. But the Canadian government has been ignoring its constitution and permitting corporations to cut down trees for export without permission or compensation to the indigenous property owners. In the adjoining chapter, the author argues that this failure to defend Aboriginal Title amounts to a giveaway to corporations of valuable property, and qualifies as an illegal export subsidy under WTO rules.

CHAPTER 25

Indigenous Brief to WTO:
How the Denial of Aboriginal Title Serves
as an Illegal Export Subsidy

Arthur Manuel

(Secwepemc)
Indigenous Network on Economies and Trade (INET)

I. INTRODUCTION

IN 2002, THE WORLD TRADE ORGANIZATION took the extraordinary step of accepting *amicus curiae* briefs submitted by Canada's Interior Nations and the Indigenous Network on Economies and Trade (INET). This marked the first time *ever* that the WTO or any other trade bureaucracy officially accepted substantive indigenous submissions to a pending case, thus finally recognizing our legal standing, a significant breakthrough in itself.

The case in question concerned the highly controversial U.S.-Canada Softwood Lumber Dispute. At issue were high tariffs that the United States. unilaterally imposed upon Canada softwood lumber exports to the United States. The U.S. alleges that these exports were illegally subsidized—a violation of WTO rules—because Canada heavily subsidizes timber companies so they can sell far below true market value. The alleged subsidies enabled Canadian companies to

undercut U.S. producers, qualifying as an "unfair trade practice" under WTO rules. The U.S. assertion that these were illegal subsidies justified imposing countervailing duties on Canadian lumber. Canada appealed the U.S. ruling to the WTO, and since then the matter has been in the hands of WTO tribunals.

The indigenous submissions to the WTO tribunals focus on the fundamental point that *the subsidy is derived from the fact that nearly all of Canada's softwood exports are logged from indigenous lands without remunerating the indigenous proprietary interests.* Canada has given giant *free* logging concessions on these lands to corporations, although the Canadian constitution recognizes and affirms Aboriginal Title to all lands that have not been the subject of treaties between Canada and the Indian nations. No such treaties have been signed in British Columbia. The government of Canada and the province of British Columbia have *ignored* the Aboriginal Title, have acted as if the forest lands were owned exclusively by the government, and have not paid the indigenous peoples who own these lands; neither have the corporations, who have massively benefited from this exploitation. They have not even offered compensation for the direct damages to the land from their clear-cut logging. All of these factors clearly add up to a massive government subsidy to the logging industry, in violation of international trade law, as the United States has argued. And yet, the most aggrieved party is actually not the United States; it is the indigenous nations whose trees have been killed and stolen.

By ignoring the Aboriginal Rights of the indigenous peoples and relieving corporations from any need to pay for the indigenous property they are selling abroad, Canada is also ignoring its own constitutionally mandated trust obligations to indigenous peoples. In our submissions to the WTO, we have argued that when a government ignores its own laws recognizing aboriginal property rights and freely gives away such valuable goods as trees, it is really *theft*, in addition to qualifying as an illegal subsidy. Canada and the provinces are stealing indigenous property to offer it to corporations as financial contributions in the form of real goods that the corporation can then export across borders. Of course, the same argument could usefully be made about other resources, such as oil, minerals, fish, freshwater, and agricultural lands, which are constitutionally guaranteed to indigenous nations not only in Canada but in other indigenous territories around the world, where resources are also extracted virtually free by resource extraction corporations.

Another important point is: When the WTO accepted the indigenous submissions in this case, it set a precedent to recognize future submissions in similar cases, thus helping indigenous peoples everywhere strengthen our hold on our property rights, as recognized by international law and most constitutions in the

Americas. If so, we will have been able to use the rules of an otherwise dangerous bureaucracy against its own sponsors.

Perhaps recognizing the long-term implications of this case, the governments of Canada and India have argued that our *amicus curiae* submissions should be ignored, just as our rights have been.

II. "THE BRAZIL OF THE NORTH"

The economy of the western Canadian province of British Columbia has always been based on primary resource extraction. When the first settlers arrived in BC in the 1800s, they had already experienced deforestation in their respective homelands, and yet they did the same thing in the indigenous territories they invaded. For example, on the archipelago of Haida Gwaii (Queen Charlotte Islands), the Haida people had protected the magnificent cedar forests for thousands of years. They considered the trees of great spiritual, cultural, social, environmental and economic importance. But the new colonialists quickly began to deplete the forests to build shipping-related products—masts, hulls, and so on—while promoting to investors the glorious abundance of forest and fish resources. At first, indigenous people were allowed to trade and sell fish, but new government regulations soon excluded them from the industry. In the case of forestry, the big change came with major land tenure reforms after World War II. In the 1950s, the British Columbia government reallocated forest tenure toward large-scale, long-term licenses awarded to huge integrated wood-processing companies. This doomed smaller, more sustainable enterprises operated by local indigenous peoples.

Over recent decades, voracious development in British Columbia has brought extreme deforestation, damage to rivers and soils, and serious injury to the entire ecosystem of the region. Because of the scale of the destruction and the dependence of the British Columbia economy on natural resource exploitation, environmentalist Colleen McCrory of the Valhalla Wilderness Society, winner of the Goldman Environmental Prize, has called British Columbia the "Brazil of the North."

Indigenous peoples were the first to pay the full price for this environmental devastation, through the loss of our traditional economies, environments, and the cultural attachments to the biodiversity of the forests that are part of our tradition.

With the added acceleration of export-oriented trade agreements like the General Agreement on Tariffs and Trade (GATT) of the World Trade Organization and the North American Free Trade Agreement (NAFTA), the pressure to clear-cut forests for export timber and to extract other resources has become even greater, creating a desperate situation for the indigenous population of the region. All of this is in apparent defiance of Canadian law, and international law as well.

III. VIOLATIONS OF CANADIAN AND INTERNATIONAL LAW

The current behavior of the Canadian government with respect to indigenous peoples in British Columbia and across Canada not only violates WTO rules on subsidies, but also violates Canadian and international law. Here are a few examples:

Constitutional Protection for Aboriginal Land Title

Aboriginal Title is clearly recognized in the Canadian constitution as a real property right; in fact, it is the only such property right specifically protected by the constitution. In the 1992 Delgamuukw Decision, the Supreme Court of Canada affirmed that indigenous people can lose their Aboriginal Title and land rights only through treaty agreements with the federal government. In the case of the majority of the indigenous peoples of British Columbia, such

treaties have not been concluded. As a result, according to the Canadian Supreme Court, any "infringements" upon Aboriginal Title—such as the government granting concessions to logging corporations on aboriginal lands—can only be justified with the full knowledge and agreement of the aboriginal communities, after appropriate compensation is paid.

At this time, aboriginal peoples are not remunerated, no permissions have been granted, and the settlers have not obtained free and clear title, as Aboriginal Title has never been extinguished. Thus, according to the constitution, industry and government are legally required to respect and "accommodate" aboriginal ownership.

"Prior Informed Consent"

The rights of indigenous people to "prior informed consent" before any development takes place on their lands has been recognized and codified in numerous international agreements, including the International Labor Organization (ILO), the Convention on Biological Diversity (Article 8j) and the (pending) UN Draft Declaration on the Rights of Indigenous Peoples. Canada is officially a signatory or supporter of these agreements.

The Convention on Biological Diversity (CBD) says that signatory countries must all "respect, preserve and maintain knowledge, innovations and practices of indigenous and local communities embodying traditional lifestyles relevant to the conservation and sustainable use of biological diversity and promote their wider application with the *approval* and *involvement* of the holders of such knowledge, innovations and practices, and encourage the *equitable sharing* of the benefits arising from the utilization of such knowledge, innovation and practices" (emphasis added).

Clearly, Canada has not begun to live up to the CBD standards for informed consent. And, according to an independent assessment by the

Sierra Legal Defense Fund, neither has Canada managed its forests—including those on indigenous lands—in an ecologically sustainable manner. "Most of the nation's forests are still managed for timber, not important biodiversity values, such as wildlife or water," said the Sierra report. "Moves by some provinces to deregulate forest management responsibilities will further accelerate biodiversity losses." The report pointed out that many of these poorly managed lands were indigenous lands.

On issues related to free, prior and informed consent, the Supreme Court of Canada has affirmed the requirement in its well-known "Haida Decisions," which concluded that governments and third parties are legally bound to achieve "workable accommodations" with aboriginal people and interests if they seek to benefit from exploitation of indigenous resources. And yet, to this day, most logging operations in Canada still lack any degree of consent and completely fail to accommodate Aboriginal Title and rights. (*See also Chapter 14 by Terri-Lynn Williams-Davidson.*)

Canada's Fiduciary Responsibility

The Canadian Supreme Court has ruled that the Canadian constitution enshrines a "fiduciary responsibility" on the part of the government to protect lands held under Aboriginal Title. Any revenues that the government collects by granting rights to loggers—such as stumpage fees—or to other resource developers on indigenous lands qualify as a collective proprietary interest of indigenous peoples that the government is under a fiduciary obligation to protect and account for. If the government and companies do not take Aboriginal Title into account, and make no payments to compensate for the takings of real property, the Canadian government is violating its fiduciary obligations.

Thus, it is especially surprising and appalling that in the submissions to the World Trade Organization in the softwood lumber dispute with the United States, the Canadian government tried to defend its practices by arguing that corporations have a "quasi-proprietary interest" in Canada's public and Aboriginal Title forests. This despite the clarity of the constitutional protection of Aboriginal Title, the rulings of the Supreme Court of Canada, and the obligation to "accommodate" aboriginal interests. The government of Canada refuses to change its unconstitutional policy aiming at the extinguishment of Aboriginal Title so as to be able to grant global resource corporations "free" access to indigenous lands.

IV. VALUING INDIGENOUS ECONOMIES

Acceptance of the indigenous submissions by major international trade tribunals has put a focus on some related questions, such as how to value indigenous economies. Mainstream economists tend to value development strategies solely in terms of their wealth generation potential for industry and government. Resources are viewed strictly in monetary terms. But indigenous peoples consider the value of land and resources in far broader, more integrated terms, including cultural, social, spiritual and environmental values, as well as sustainability. Among indigenous peoples, decisions about caring for resources and the environment are usually made as part of a collective process, where the community takes into account a full spectrum of values and benefits beyond short-term economic gain.

Mainstream economics tend to ignore indigenous values about land and resources, and usually have no means of quantifying such relatively subjective impacts. Mainstream development sees profit as the only goal. Indigenous nations take very seriously issues of sustainability and depletion of habitat—such as salmon spawning grounds —or the potential loss of an important food staple with direct economic and health implications for indigenous communities and families.

It is important that indigenous nations bring together elders, youth, political leaders, land users, lawyers and economists to determine the factors to be included in any economic evaluation of forest or other resources, rather than leaving value to be determined strictly by industrial developers.

Nor do mainstream economics recognize the value of the indigenous knowledge base about how to successfully use indigenous lands and resources in a sustainable manner. This knowledge has been gathered over centuries by indigenous peoples and is the densest and most reliable long-term data available anywhere. This knowledge and experience should be a benchmark for future sustainable land and resource management, as a precondition for fair and sustainable flow of international trade.

But even in strictly economic terms, when indigenous peoples have received some compensation for development on their lands, government agencies in Canada, the United States and elsewhere have performed poorly when supposedly acting on behalf of indigenous interests. The U.S. courts are filled with cases where indigenous peoples are citing the inadequate payment they have received for valuable resources—far below market value and far below amounts offered to non-indigenous communities for the same resources.

One notable case now working its way through the U.S. court system is *Cobell v. Norton, the American Indian Trust Case.* In that class action case, some 500,000 American Indians are suing to recover funds that were supposed to be managed on their behalf for over a century by the U.S. Bureau of Indian Affairs. The courts have consistently found in the Indians' favor during the nine years the case has been litigated, citing a level of mismanagement that one court called "the gold standard of malfeasance" by the government. Tens of billions of dollars remain undistributed to the Indian trustees and unaccounted for.

These matters have gained the attention of leading economists, including Professor Joseph E. Stiglitz, winner of the Nobel Prize in Economics in 2001, former chair of the Council of Economic Advisors under President Bill Clinton and former chief economist and senior vice president of the World Bank. Stiglitz provided expert advice and independent economic analysis to the Seneca tribe in the 1980s, when a lease they had given settlers expired and they did not want to renew it. Professor Stiglitz calculated that the difference between what was paid and a fair market rent was enormous, amounting to billions of dollars. As a result, the federal government passed a bill ordering back compensation and increasing future payments from $57,000 to $800,000 to be increased over time.

During his tenure at the White House Council of Economic Advisors, Stiglitz followed the U.S.-Canada Softwood Lumber Dispute. The failure of the indigenous peoples to receive remuneration for the resources—including the lumber—on land in which they had had a long-standing interest was not only unacceptable but also destructive to the economy, lives, and livelihoods of the indigenous peoples. But the failure also raised serious and complicated questions for assessing the impact of Canadian softwood lumber management policies, including potentially those at issue in the Softwood Lumber Dispute. If the lumber companies benefitted from the failure to provide remuneration to the indigenous peoples, then issues of fair trade could not be ignored.

Stiglitz concluded that it will be important in the future to provide just compensation to the indigenous peoples. This will require looking at the core economic, environmental, social, and cultural values that indigenous peoples associate with their land, determining the true economic worth of the land and its resources, and valuing both current and cumulative infringements.

In any case, the arguments submitted by indigenous peoples in the WTO's U.S.-Canada Softwood Lumber Dispute have demonstrated that aboriginal peoples' interests and rights must be part of any macro-economic decision-making. Now that we are in the game, we have the opportunity to ultimately ensure better government policies and legislation, and better enforcement of aboriginal land rights, via the rules of international trade.

Of all categories of international law, trade law has the most readily available enforcement mechanisms. If a nation ignores WTO rules, for example, powerful economic and political sanctions can be applied. Until now, indigenous peoples have always had to make arguments in "softer" venues that deal with human rights or environmental law but cannot easily enforce rulings. Becoming an active party to a WTO trade dispute gives us access to these more effective, "harder" sanctions and mechanisms, which can better protect aboriginal and treaty rights for us and other indigenous nations around the globe.

(The author wishes to acknowledge the assistance of Nicole Schabus, international legal advisor, Dr. Joseph Stiglitz, and Anton Korinek, senior research assistant of Dr. Stiglitz, in developing these arguments.)

Indigenous peoples throughout the world are now mobilized and increasingly unified in their efforts to establish their sovereign rights, control resources and development, and share in the benefits of any economic projects. They have become active on regional and national levels, in the Philippines and in the international scene as well, as they try to allay the powers of global economic bureaucracies.

CHAPTER 26

The Prospect Ahead

Victoria Tauli-Corpuz

(Igorot)

Tebtebba (Indigenous Peoples' International Centre for Policy Research and Education)

THE YEAR 2004 WAS THE LAST in the United Nations International Decade of the World's Indigenous People. Both indigenous organizations and the United Nations have tried to evaluate the achievements of this decade. In my opinion we made significant progress on the international front, and I was invited to present my opinions on these achievements to the UN Commission on Human Rights in July 2004. This article is a partial summary of some of the gains I cited, but also some disappointments and continuing roadblocks. Finally, I suggest ways that I believe we can move forward from here.

The United Nations is now launching its Second Decade of the World's Indigenous Peoples (2005–15.) In a rapidly evolving international political climate, and with a greatly expanded capacity for effective organizing by indigenous people and nonindigenous supporters, we have a good chance over the next ten years to achieve some fundamental demands: confirmed sovereign rights to our traditional lands, resources and livelihoods; greater protections for our cultures, knowledge, and languages; and self-determination with respect to all aspects of our existence.

❀   ❀   ❀

In addition to the advances we have made within global and national bureaucracies, there have been important shifts in the awareness of indigenous peoples' rights and issues on both the international and national levels. Our struggle for *self-determination* and to confirm our *prior rights* to our territories and resources was not confined to our ranks. It is significant that we received help in these causes from allies in civil society and government.

Ten years ago the level of awareness of, and inclusion of our rights and issues in broader dialogues was far lower than what we witness today. Now, whenever constitutions, policies or projects are discussed, especially in countries where indigenous peoples live, the indigenous question can not be avoided. The environmental and human rights movements, the women's movement, the antiglobalization and global justice movements, and even liberation or revolutionary movements now have to grapple with the issues raised by indigenous peoples. This has opened the way for new alliances and the formation of complex new networks and coalitions among ourselves, and with allies and supporters. These new alliances are shaped along geographic and transnational lines, ethnic lines, and around gender and thematic issues. All of these give shape to what can now be seen as an international indigenous peoples' movement. Our struggles extend beyond the boundaries of the state, the market and the various movements for change. In spite of our limited numbers and capacity, we have managed to challenge and disturb racist and discriminatory mind-sets of people in government, corporations and NGOs. And we take credit for significantly influencing the debates and decisions in intergovernmental bodies such as the UN Commission on Human Rights, the Commission on Sustainable Development, the Convention on Biological Diversity, and the Organization of American States.

Among the most important achievements of the past decade is a burgeoning recognition that indigenous peoples should enjoy not only *individual* rights but also *collective human rights*. There is now an active discourse on collective human rights never seen before. Several countries in Latin America made new amendments to their constitutions to acknowledge that they have multicultural and multiethnic "plurinational" societies. The Philippines has passed the Indigenous Peoples' Rights Act (1997), which was strongly influenced by the United Nations Draft Declaration on the Rights of Indigenous Peoples. These developments bring increased possibilities for mutual coexistence between indigenous and nonindigenous cultural, social, economic, political, and knowledge systems.

But all of that having been said, one great failure of the period is that we did not achieve final adoption of the UN Draft Declaration, which still founders in the UN subcommittee that created it. This is largely due to the continued intense opposition by the United States and Great Britain, who oppose the idea of collective human rights, as well as the rights of indigenous peoples

to sustain both *internal* and *external* self-determination and to control resources on our lands.

I. UPDATE ON PROGRESS IN INTERNATIONAL VENUES

Box H in this chapter lists som policies, laws, and programs addressing indigenous peoples that were adopted by intergovernmental bodies, international financial institutions, and national governments within the past decade. The list is by no means exhaustive, but it indicates new efforts to formulate effective policies and laws specifically addressing indigenous peoples' issues. While many of those have not yet been implemented, they are tools and instruments we can use.

Following are brief descriptions of progress in some important categories within global agencies that relate to indigenous concerns.

1) Human Rights Issues

The establishment of the United Nations Permanent Forum on Indigenous Issues and the appointment of the United Nations Special Rapporteur on the Situation of Human Rights and Fundamental Freedoms of Indigenous Peoples are two important new instruments that emerged over the last decade. The Permanent Forum is a unique body within the United Nations because it allows for the selection of eight indigenous experts from seven indigenous regions and eight representatives from government, creating an unusually balanced body.

The UN Permanent Forum on Indigenous Issues is a subsidiary body under the United Nations Economic and Social Council (ECOSOC). Its mandate is to provide expert advice to UN programs, agencies and funds, to raise awareness and promote the integration of indigenous issues within the United Nations system, and to disseminate information. It focuses on economic and social development, education, environment, culture, health, and human rights. In its past three sessions (2002–4), Secretary General Kofi Annan has personally attended the opening or closing sessions. (I was chosen by the Asian indigenous organizations to represent them from 2005 to 2007.)

The Special Rapporteur is mandated to investigate human rights and fundamental freedoms of indigenous peoples and make recommendations on how to protect and respect them. Since 2001 he has conducted missions to Guatemala, the Philippines, Chile, Colombia, Mexico and Canada. Recommendations from these country missions are used to push governments to respect the basic human rights of indigenous peoples. (*Note:* Tebtebba Foundation has published a very useful guide to help other indigenous peoples who would like to invite the Special Rapporteur to visit them and their countries: *Engaging the Special Rapporteur on the Situation of Human Rights and Fundamental Freedoms of Indigenous Peoples.* The book contains the rapporteur's mandate, a guide to his methods, and ideas for how indigenous peoples can use this opportunity, as well as testimonials by other indigenous groups. *Available at tebtebba@tebtebba.org.*)

2) *Traditional Knowledge*

As has been repeatedly mentioned in this book, the traditional knowledge of indigenous peoples—concerning medicinal plants, aspects of biodiversity, and other cultural domains—is increasingly targeted by corporations seeking to appropriate that knowledge for commercial purposes, usually without the informed consent of the indigenous communities, and without them receiving any benefits.

Many indigenous organizations are engaged in intergovernmental processes that seek to reverse this dire trend. Such bodies as the UN Convention on Biological Diversity deal with issues such as biopiracy, access and benefit sharing of biodiversity, and protection and uses of traditional

knowledge of indigenous communities. Other processes that address these issues include the Working Group on Access and Benefit Sharing, the World Intellectual Property Organization's (WIPO) Intergovernmental Committee on Intellectual Property, Genetic Resources and Traditional Knowledge, and the WTO's Agreement on Trade-Related Aspects of Intellectual Property Rights, which permits corporations to patent life forms, a situation that indigenous peoples oppose.

As discussed elsewhere in this report, the outcome of these processes has been mixed. We had some gains in some venues, but the overall results too often involve unfavorable compromises, particularly on issues of benefit sharing and the uses of "common property." (*More extended discussion on this can be found in Box D on "Whose Common Property" as well as Chapter 7 by Victor Menotti, and Chapter 8 by Debra Harry, and elsewhere.*)

3) *Agriculture*

Regarding the World Trade Organization, the Agreement on Agriculture (AoA) and the negotiations on investment liberalization—part of the so-called "Singapore Issues"—most of our negative forecasts for the impact on indigenous peoples from these agreements have been realized. They facilitate invasion of indigenous lands by plantation farmers and agribusinesses and "biopiracy" and export dumping by rich countries, thus threatening many indigenous peoples. In my own region, the Cordillera, we have seen massive destruction of indigenous livelihoods because of the dumping of highly subsidized cheap agricultural products, as wealthy countries get around antisubsidy stipulations of WTO agreements. Between 2002 and 2003, livelihoods of about 250,000 indigenous farmers were destroyed by dumping of vegetables from Australia, New Zealand and China, among others. Meanwhile, in Mexico, Colombia and Guatemala, livelihoods of indigenous coffee farmers were adversely affected because of massive coffee plantations developed in Vietnam. With the increase of plantations in the Central Highlands, indigenous peoples of the region were deluged with migrants and settlers from the lowlands seeking jobs. Thousands of indigenous peoples were driven from their ancestral lands. Ironically, coffee prices soon collapsed because of overproduction. But the social and environmental costs of this kind of globalization—destruction of livelihoods, displacement of peoples, and increase in conflict situations between indigenous peoples and new settlers—are high. This remains an area of grave concern and increased activity, with little gain so far.

4) Gender

The last decade has seen the formation of several important new indigenous women's networks and organizations. Among these are the Asian Indigenous Women's Network, the African Indigenous Women's Organization, the Intercontinental Network of Indigenous Women in the Americas and the Arctic Indigenous Women's Forum. The 1995 Fourth World Women's Conference produced the Beijing Indigenous Women's Declaration, and the Second Asian Indigenous Women's Conference produced the Baguio Declaration, later included among the official documents of the Third Session of the UN Permanent Forum, on "indigenous women." The issue of violence against women in situations of armed conflict is important to indigenous women, and attempts are under way to engage the UN Special Rapporteur on Violence Against Women to develop effective responses to militarization of indigenous women.

5) "Free, Prior Informed Consent"

The year 2005 is the last for the adoption of a revised version of the World Bank's Operational Directive 4.10, which includes principles and rights of indigenous peoples to "free, prior informed consultation." The text of this revised version is much weaker than the *original* policy,

since it does not explicitly recognize our rights to our ancestral territories and resources. Also, the principle and right of indigenous peoples to free, prior and informed *consent* (FPIC) for all activities on all lands—notably mining—is now reduced to free, prior informed *consultation*, a substantial reduction in the power of the resolution. Obtaining the free, prior and informed *consent* of indigenous peoples before an extractive industry is allowed to enter communities was strongly recommended by the World Bank's own extractive industries review (WB-EIR) process, but the report was not favorably received by the Bank's Executive Board. Similarly, the Bank has refused to be bound by the recommendations of the World Commission on Dams.

Meanwhile, the final 2004 report of another body, the World Commission on the Social Dimension of Globalization further affirmed the right of indigenous peoples to their lands and territories and to free, prior and informed consent. Also, the United Nations General Assembly session in October 2004 passed a resolution in support of rights to free, prior and informed consent and urged the various UN bodies to implement the recommendations. The International Labor Organization (ILO) plays the lead role in ensuring that the proposals from the report are taken on board by the various multi-stakeholders. Of course, we will continue to battle in all venues for "free, prior and informed consent," including the fundamental right to say no to development we don't want.

6) UN Draft Declaration on Indigenous Rights

As mentioned earlier, a key failure of the decade is that the UN has not yet adopted a Universal Declaration on the Rights of Indigenous Peoples. The Draft Declaration on the Rights of Indigenous Peoples was adopted by the Sub-Commission on Human Rights in 1993 but still remains a draft. The last working session ended on December 3, 2004 without adopting anything. At this time only two of forty-five operative articles have been adopted. The delegations of the United States and the United Kingdom maintained hard-line positions on all articles related to recognition of the right to self-determination and rights to lands, territories and resources. The U.S. delegation remained firm in its position that it can only accept *internal self-determination* and not *external self-determination*. Indigenous peoples are likewise firm that self-determination is both internal and external and cannot be separated. Meanwhile, the U.K. delegation continued to argue against *collective human rights*. The United Kingdom recognizes collective rights but not collective *human* rights, since human rights are only individual rights. Many legal experts have shown overwhelming evidence that collective human rights are recognized in international law, but this has not changed the position of the U.K. delegation.

Even though the draft remains only a draft, it already has served as a key reference point on indigenous peoples' rights. Its evolution is unique in the history of the United Nations because it involves rights beyond those of the member-states of the UN. With indigenous peoples and governments sitting side by side in the process, the Draft Declaration has guided the formulation of many national and international laws (e.g., the 1997 Indigenous Peoples' Rights Act of the Philippines and the United Nations Development Program Policy of Engagement with Indigenous Peoples).

Although the measure has not been adopted, the prospects are still hopeful. There is an emerging consensus for the *provisional* adoption of around 50 percent of the original draft, which includes some revised articles. The Working Group has recommended that this commission be extended for several years until the declaration is adopted. This would then be forwarded to the UN General Assembly for adoption. I believe we eventually will achieve this.

II. REALITIES ON THE GROUND

In spite of some important gains in the past decade, the grim reality for most indigenous peoples is still increasing marginalization, impoverishment, and violation of their most basic human rights. Neoliberal globalization, undoubtedly, is the key factor in the worsening situation of many indigenous peoples. The pressure on us to play by the rules and logic of the globalized market economy increases each day, although we largely succeeded in demolishing the myths of development. We have resisted full assimilation into the dominant society, as well as the assaults of modernization and development on our existence as distinct peoples and cultures. Still, we face a multifaceted juggernaut. For example:

▲ The language and concept of "sustainable development," first introduced at the Earth Summit in Rio in 1992, has been increasingly hijacked and distorted by the market. The mining industry tried to sell the bizarre concept of "sustainable mining," even though mining was not discussed at all in Rio in 1992, because it was (and is) inconceivable to think of mining as a sustainable activity. Similar conceptual distortions have appeared in proposals for ecotourism, forest certifications, and proposals that claim to "protect" traditional knowledge and genetic resources within regimes that actually do the opposite: commercial monopolization of the common intellectual property of indigenous peoples, as in the TRIPS agreement of the WTO. Even such neutral-sounding concepts as "access and benefit sharing," supposedly created to protect indigenous and Third World interests against global corporations, have now been distorted by the CBD to serve countries that are economically rich but poor in biodiversity over Third World and indigenous communities. Thus, it is imperative that we stay alert to both the tactics and language being used against us, and that we do not fall into the trap of trying to define our interests and future through concepts and frameworks that are inevitably biased toward global market considerations.

Now, indigenous groups are direct participants in the UN Commission on Sustainable Development. Ten years after Rio, at the World Summit on Sustainable Development in Johannesburg, we issued the Kimberley Declaration and the Johannesburg Indigenous Peoples' Implementation Plan for Sustainable Development to define our interests in our own terms. *(See Appendix.)*

▲ For those of us who still live in our traditional territories, we must persist in defending our rights to our lands and resources. All threats of forced displacement and land alienation by extractive industries have to be squarely confronted. And we need to prevent the incursions that mega-development projects of all kinds bring into our territories, with adverse impacts. As for those who have already been displaced, they can still make strenuous claims to recover lands and territories they traditionally occupied. Of course, a crucial step in securing our territories is to finally *institutionalize* the concept of free, prior and informed consent for all those who are affected by development projects. As we have discussed, important work toward that end is under way within the World Bank and various bodies of the United Nations.

▲ Liberalization of trade, investment, and finance within global bureaucracies like the WTO is rapidly leading to further alienation of our lands and resources and the destruction of our traditional livelihoods. There is an inherent tension between the claims of nation-states to *eminent domain* and national sovereignty, and those of indigenous peoples who assert their rights to their traditional lands and permanent sovereignty over surface and subsurface resources. *There is no question that we have inherent and prior rights to our territories and lands, since our ancestors occupied these places long before nation-states came into existence.*

We have also been the protectors of these places over centuries and longer, keeping the resources and ecosystems intact. If we do not fight destructive development projects, such as logging, mining, oil and gas exploration, dam-building, what remains now will be gone. Claims of eminent domain by nation-states are both immoral and preposterous, a clear legal fiction. Such claims against our lands must always be contested.

The international and national systems, which are heavily influenced by the global market, will continue to do everything they can to subordinate indigenous peoples. But we have now advanced to the point where they can no longer blithely concoct their development schemes without taking our interests into account. We have seen how they co-opt and distort concepts and processes to ensure the perpetuation of their political and economic dominance. We have also seen the ways state and industry collude to undermine our rights. The official balance of power between indigenous peoples and the state and market is very skewed in favor of the latter. *But our ultimate power is the profound legitimacy of our causes, the strength of our struggles, and the foundation of our organized communities and formations, combined with the renewed support of our allies.*

In the so-called First World (Canada, the United States, Australia, New Zealand, and Europe) many indigenous peoples have succeeded in forging treaty agreements with their former colonizers. They have demanded recognition of these treaties by the states, and this has led to national legal recognition of indigenous rights. Numerous cases have been brought to court by indigenous peoples, and even to the treaty-monitoring bodies of the United Nations. Nevertheless, though we push for the creation of national and international laws to recognize and respect our rights, *we have not conceded that our rights are solely defined by any of these agreements. We believe that our rights are mainly defined by our own customary laws, indigenous governance systems and resource management and land tenure systems.*

III. FUTURE STRATEGIES

As for the future, the challenges for indigenous peoples are tremendous and daunting, especially in the face of brutal globalization and increasing competition over resources and knowledge. We have to enhance the capacity of our movements to constantly challenge the states, the market and civil society to respect and uphold our individual and collective rights. This means we have to build upon and use wisely the gains we achieved through the years. The spaces we have successfully carved at the local, national, regional and global levels must be effectively occupied and utilized by us. Sometimes we open or build these spaces and then abandon them to be manipulated by the government and corporations, and even by unscrupulous members of our own community.

The UN Permanent Forum on Indigenous Issues is an example of one space where we should put our best activists and diplomats. This is one of the newest bodies within the UN. It came about as a result of our serious efforts to make the UN more responsive to our needs and views. In that body, we are equal partners with governments and with the UN in evolving the Permanent Forum's capacity to appropriately address our issues. But beyond attending the meetings, we have to ensure that the recommendations are implemented by the UN agencies and the governments in partnership with us.

We also have to make wise use of the mechanism of the Special Rapporteur on Human Rights and Fundamental Freedoms of Indigenous Peoples. To do an official mission, he or she has to be invited by a government. Since time to do a mission is limited, indigenous peoples must prepare well so the visit can accomplish many things. Documentation and research of violations of human rights and fundamental freedoms has to be done meticulously. Organizing visits to communities to talk with the indigenous peoples is crucial. Since governments would like to confine and control these visits, we have to struggle to shape a program that will permit visits to indigenous communities suffering from militarization and oppression. After the report comes out, we have to work out a national process toward implementation. It is also important that we share these experiences with indigenous peoples from other countries to build a broad base of knowledge and experience.

At the local and national levels, we should push to strengthen the new spaces we created. In some countries the indigenous peoples' movements formed their own political parties, such as the Pachakutik in Ecuador and the Coordinadora Defensa del Agua y la Vida of Bolivia. In some cases indigenous peoples join or make alliances with mainstream political parties though they are not always successful in influencing such parties to take on indigenous issues. Some countries have existing national bodies that deal with indigenous peoples, such as the Bureau of Indian Affairs in the United States, the Bureau of Aboriginal Affairs in Canada, the National Commission on Indigenous Peoples in the Philippines, and FUNAI (Fundacao Nacional do Indio) in Brazil. While the track records of these bodies are not good from the perspective of indigenous peoples, we have to make them work for us as much as possible. If there seems no hope they will work on our behalf, we need to replace them or reorient them.

It is customary for local and sectoral indigenous organizations to create national coalitions or federations. In some cases there are several national and regional formations and sometimes there is a tendency to compete instead of collaborate. We need to build unity among formations so that we can be more effective. Our guiding framework in our relations with each other should be to ensure that what one formation does reinforces or supplements what others are doing. Indigenous formations are now focusing in such different areas as human rights, sustainable development, forests, biodiversity, tourism, trade, ancestral land delineation, and indigenous knowledge. If we spread our influence more widely and come together occasionally to collectively assess where we are and plot how to get farther ahead, the chances of more victories will improve. As long as we are clear that what underpins these efforts is the promotion of indigenous peoples' rights and the reinforcement of their perspectives on development, we cannot go astray.

Multilateral agencies and donor bodies have allotted part of their budgets for projects in indigenous peoples' territories. We now have to increase the awareness and knowledge of indigenous peoples about these existing instruments and to equip our own community members to *assert their right to be involved* in designing and deciding what projects should be implemented and evaluated. The biggest challenge is to get these bodies to implement *their own policies and standards to protect our rights*.

IV. HUMAN RIGHTS-BASED APPROACH

Many indigenous peoples are now discussing alternatives to our intensely negative experiences with unsustainable mainstream development and globalization. A vibrant debate within indigenous communities focuses on what development projects should be promoted; emerging concepts include human rights-based development, sustainable human development, ethnodevelopment, and life projects. But all indigenous communities consistently express the desire to maintain their traditional values, practices, and identity as part of *any* development strategy. Indigenous peoples believe they *already* constitute a viable alternative to globalization, underpinned by the fundamental values of reciprocity, respect for the earth and nature, community solidarity and collectivity.

The so-called human rights–based approach to development offers advantages for indigenous peoples. This approach asserts that basic human rights must be respected in all development projects, including our rights to our territories and resources, to our culture and knowledge, and to internal and external self-determination, based on free, prior and informed consent. All development is contingent on these rights, whether in dealing with the nation-state or the global market or civil society institutions. This approach is one of our priorities in engagement with UN agencies, donor bodies, governments and market forces.

During more than fifty years of the United Nations' existence, many human rights instruments and standards have been created. Even if the Draft Declaration on the Rights of Indigenous Peoples has not yet been adopted, there are many treaty bodies that indigenous peoples can use. Among these are the Human Rights Committee of the UN Covenant on Civil and Political Rights, the Committee on the Elimination of Racial Discrimination of the International Convention on the Elimination of Racial and All Forms of Discrimination, and the Committee on the Rights of the Child of the Convention on the Rights of the Child. In spite of the limitations of these monitoring bodies, we can still use them. Legal opinions of the expert members of these committees can be important, especially if they acknowledge and further support the rights of indigenous peoples.

The use of regional courts like the Inter-American Human Rights Court is another option for indigenous peoples in the Americas. The recent victory by the Sumo peoples of the Atlantic Coast in the Awas Tingni Indigenous Land Rights Case filed at the Inter-American Human Rights Court is a positive example. The court ruled that "the State of Nicaragua is actively responsible for violations of the right to property" embodied in Article 21 of the American Convention on Human Rights, by granting a concession to a company, SOLCARSA, to carry out road construction and logging on Awas Tingni lands, *without the consent of the Awas Tingni community.*

Many governments are signatories to international human rights instruments and have obligations to implement them. We can pressure governments to implement these instruments in their own countries and in countries to which they give loans and grants. Governments in the First World practice a double standard. The environmental and human rights standards they implement in their own countries are not the same ones they follow for corporations in the Third World. They even use donor bodies like USAID (Agency for International Development) and CIDA (Canadian International Development Agency) to pry open access into indigenous communities for global corporations. We have many examples of this in the Philippines, for instance the CIDA contribution to a Canadian mining company (Toronto Ventures Incorporated). The Canadian Embassy in the Philippines is pushing Toronto Ventures into indigenous land, even though the company is blatantly violating the rights of indigenous peoples in Mindanao. Such examples are, of course, not unique to the Philippines.

It is important for indigenous peoples in the Philippines to link with NGOs and indigenous peoples in Canada to put pressure on the Canadian government and the mining company. But this must be the process everywhere: links between NGOs and indigenous communities in both the victimized country and the source country. That is the challenge of solidarity. A basic question is how to strengthen the linkages with indigenous peoples in other countries and NGOs to provide support to each others' struggles?

Finally, there is a need to share experiences among indigenous peoples and NGOs, UN agencies like UNDP, the International Fund for Agricultural Development (IFAD), UNICEF, and donor bodies to promote and enhance indigenous life projects. There are many lessons for all of us from these experiences. Many lessons can be found in reports and publications, but somehow they do not often get to the indigenous peoples.

CONCLUSION

The United Nations Second Decade of the World's Indigenous Peoples will last from 2005 to 2015. The objectives and program for this decade are being presented at the Fourth Session of the Permanent Forum. Indigenous peoples need to create a vision of where we would like to be in 2015 and how we propose to get there. Of course, there will be different objectives for indigenous peoples coming from different countries. So apart from the global vision, there must be a variety of visions, goals and programs at national and regional levels.

There is no slowing down. We have managed to survive against all odds in the past millennium. We contributed in reshaping discourses on human rights, development and environment. The terrains of our struggles range from our own communities to the national, regional and global arenas. And because of these struggles it is now imperative for governments, corporations, intergovernmental bodies, and even social movements and revolutionary groups to deal with the indigenous question if they operate in indigenous territory. While we engaged with intergovernmental bodies that are addressing areas of concern, we tried to ensure that our interventions were always informed by human rights and indigenous perspectives on development. This new millennium should finally witness the creation of a world where indigenous peoples do not just aim for survival. This millennium should create a world where more respectful and equal relationships between us and the rest of humanity will prevail.

Box H:
Partial List of Institutional Gains, 1994–2004

Creation of *UN Draft Declaration on the Rights of Indigenous Peoples* (adopted by the Sub-Commission on Human Rights in 1993). *(See Appendix.)*

Addition of *Article 8(j) and other related provisions* of the Convention on Biological Diversity, which recognize the need to protect the traditional knowledge of indigenous and local communities.

Establishment of *UN Permanent Forum on Indigenous Issues*, as well as appointment of *UN Special Rapporteur on the Situation of Human Rights and Fundamental Freedoms of Indigenous Peoples*. These bodies investigate, raise awareness and promote the interests and integration of indigenous issues within all UN bodies and in participating countries.

Asian Development Bank: *The ADB Policy on Indigenous Peoples* (April 1998)

Inter-American Development Bank: *Indigenous Peoples and Sustainable Development, The Role of the Inter-American Development Bank* (1997)

Commission of the European Communities: *Working Document on Support for Indigenous Peoples in the Development Co-operation of the Community and the Member States*

The European Council of Ministers of Development Cooperation: *Resolution on Indigenous Peoples within the Framework of the Development Cooperation of the Community and Member States*

Denmark: *Strategy for Danish Support to Indigenous Peoples* (July 1994)

Netherlands: National Advisory Council for Development Cooperation's *Recommendation on Indigenous Peoples* (26 Jan. 1993)

Germany: *Policy for Development Cooperation with Forest-Dependent Peoples (1994) and Policy for Development Cooperation for Indigenous Peoples in Latin America* (1996)

United Kingdom: *Guidance on Ethnicity, Ethnic Minorities and Indigenous Peoples* (1995)

Spain: *Strategy for Co-operation with Indigenous Peoples in Latin America* (1997)

Philippines: *Indigenous Peoples' Rights Act* (1997)

India: *Panchayat Extension to Scheduled Areas Act* (PESA), recognizes traditional governance systems of adivasis (original peoples)/tribal/indigenous peoples

Nepal: *Act on the National Foundation for Development of Indigenous Nationalities* (NFDIN, 2003), recognizes 59 groups as indigenous nationalities

Proposed American Declaration on the Rights of Indigenous Peoples (approved by the Inter-American Commission on Human Rights, 26 Feb., 1997)

United Nations Development Programme (UNDP) *Policy of Engagement with Indigenous Peoples* (2001)

UNDP Regional Bureau of Asia and the Pacific: *Regional Initiative on Strengthening Policy Dialogue on Indigenous/Highland and Tribal Peoples' Rights and Development* (RIPP)

Report of the African Union's Working Group of Experts on Indigenous Populations and Communities (2003)

Photo of Sonja Holy Eagle, a young activist from Honor the Earth, a Native American national environmental advocacy organization, including a combined constituency of more than two hundred grassroots groups.

CHAPTER 27

Epilogue: Summary and Final Comments

Jerry Mander
International Forum on Globalization

MANY OF THE PREVIOUS CHAPTERS have described harsh global realities that could easily lead to despair. Had there been ample space we could have added dozens more examples. But most amazingly, despite the assaults upon indigenous peoples, the technologies of development and militarism that are arrayed against them, and a global economic system that has conspired in every possible way to undermine indigenous rights, indigenous peoples are now everywhere resistant, well organized, and optimistic about eventual success. As Victoria Tauli-Corpuz puts it, "The ultimate power we have is the profound legitimacy of our causes, the strength of our struggles, and the foundation of our organized communities."

Of course the problem remains daunting. Indigenous nations of the world sit on much of the planet's remaining natural resources. In itself, this is a clear expression of the long-term viability of their traditional values and practices of stewardship, reciprocity, and integration with nature. It also confirms a highly advanced knowledge of how to be in this world—the rules, limits and practices of sustainability. But at a time of disappearing resources, the continued indigenous

presence on their own lands outrages global corporations, who live by other priorities. The global development model and worldview make corporations feel they have a right or entitlement to these lands, and they want to push native peoples off and continue global dominance for a few more years.

In the face of such tremendous pressures, it would be understandable if indigenous peoples acquiesced or compromised to try and fit in at the margins of the dominant system. Some have had to. But as every preceding chapter has shown, millions of native peoples are declining to take that stance, and their numbers and achievements are growing.

In this book, while discussing problems, we have also tried to show the size, energy, and drive of the resistance that is now under way. It has a diversity, reach and impact that has never before existed. Throughout the world, the surge of activity is large-scale, organized and focused. Now it is also becoming broadly collaborative. Native peoples are joining together regionally and globally, as well as with compatible non-native groups.

Beverly Bell's report on the gathering of indigenous peoples of South America, for example, could have been written about similar gatherings in dozens of other places around the world—among Arctic peoples, Pacific Islanders, or North American peoples. Many of the declarations in the Appendix are the result of such gatherings, and we could have made an entire book of such statements. In fact, Tebtebba Foundation has recently published such a book, *We, Indigenous Peoples,* comprising fifty declarations on subjects including economic development, culture, human rights, health and environment *(available at www.tebtebba.org).*

In this new age of electronic communications, nonindigenous activists are also finding common cause with indigenous struggles, especially on issues of environmental sustainability, human rights, democracy, equity, self-determination and sovereignty. The word is out. Collective action is possible. This is not the sixteenth century anymore.

REGIONAL SHIFTS

I believe a few closing words on the importance of the South American experience are particularly relevant right now, because of the very high percentage of indigenous peoples on that continent, and also their new level of organization, assertiveness and success! Several chapters have described aspects of the remarkable revolutionary changes in Bolivia, for example, where an estimated 70 percent of the population is indigenous. Other countries in Latin America also have very large indigenous populations, including Guatemala (49%), Peru (40%), Ecuador (35%), Mexico (13%), Chile (10%), and Panama (8%). Most of these countries have also been significantly impacted by rising indigenous demands for autonomy, recognition and codification of their rights, as described in this book.

In a recent report from the Center for Economic Justice, *Indigenous Movements and Latin America* (available from www.econjustice.net), co-authors Juan Houghton and Beverly Bell detail the breadth and complexity of the resistance activities in that region. They range from huge mass mobilization, to direct interventions in electoral politics; from political lobbying to the establishment of "parallel governments"; and, in places like southern Mexico, the achievement of a high degree of control and self-determination. These movements have successfully operated at the level of local, provincial and national councils, as well as in collaboration with other indigenous movements opposing the privatization or export of natural resources. They are also strongly resisting incursions by global corporations and the new multilateral and bilateral trade agreements, such as the Central American Free Trade Agreement (CAFTA), the proposed Free Trade Area of the Americas (FTAA), and development projects like Plan Puebla Panama. Meanwhile, they advocate for full recognition of sovereign territories and rights to their traditional lands and resources and their cultural, political and legal practices.

INTERNATIONAL PROGRESS

All this activity has led to the recent very surprising political changes in South America, where new governments have been installed in Brazil, Argentina, Bolivia, Ecuador, Uruguay and Venezuela, all in the last decade. It is fair to say that South America has become the first continent in the world where a majority of countries and populations have turned away from the neoliberal development model and toward local self-determination. Though you would not know it from the reports in the American media, indigenous movements have played a strong and possibly decisive role in that shift.

As mentioned earlier, in May 2005 it was announced in New York that the newly established UN Permanent Forum on Indigenous Issues—comprised of an equal number of representatives from nation-states and indigenous regions—had elected its new chairperson, by consensus: Victoria Tauli-Corpuz. This is, first of all, a magnificent recognition of her tremendously significant work over the last decade, but also a clear sign of the progress that has generally been made on indigenous issues within the international community. In the chapter before this one, she eloquently described the significant gains of the last decade, as indigenous peoples apply increasing pressure upon global bureaucracies and institutions to codify fundamental rights of indigenous peoples. Most of these rights are included in the Draft Declaration on the Rights of Indigenous Peoples, which is working its way through the United Nations process, but I think it is useful to summarize the key goals here:

▲ Recognition and codification of indigenous rights to self-determination and cultural identity in all forms, including economic, cultural, political, legal and religious rights;

▲ Recognition and codification of the right to both internal and external sovereignty (now primarily opposed by the United States);

▲ Recognition and codification of Aboriginal Rights, (or "prior rights") to full ownership of traditional lands and the resources on and in them;

▲ Recognition and codification of the right to collective ownership and collective human rights (now primarily opposed by the United Kingdom);

▲ Recognition and codification of the absolute right to *free, prior and informed consent* to any development project that infringes on indigenous lands or resources, or any other fundamental rights and options of indigenous peoples; this, of course, includes the absolute right to say no without further explanation;

▲ Final passage and enforcement of the UN Declaration on the Rights of Indigenous Peoples.

Victoria Tauli-Corpuz is optimistic that these rights, and quite a few others specifically related to culture, religion, language, collectivity, and traditional systems of education and governance, among others, will finally achieve a full degree of international institutional protection over the next several years.

Other authors in this volume have tackled legal issues; we have seen good ideas from Debra Harry, Terri-Lynn Williams-Davidson and Victor Menotti, among others. Arthur Manuel has articulated a particularly creative idea, I think, in that he proposes to use currently existing trade law against itself, as it were, showing how the refusal of nation-states to enforce Aboriginal Title to land and resources, combined with nonremuneration for those stolen resources, amounts to "illegal trade subsidies" under WTO rules. If successful, this approach may have a profound long-term effect in a variety of interesting ways. Meanwhile, such cases as *Cobell v. Norton* in the United States have the potential to recover billions of dollars of Indian Trust funds that have been irresponsibly managed by the U.S. government *(see Chapter 21)*.

These are not minor instances. If one added up the numbers, we would see that millions of indigenous peoples are involved. It would be a major understatement to call this hopeful, inspiring, promising.

WHAT CAN WE DO NOW?

Clearly, any ultimate victory in these matters will require a broad movement that can bridge cultures, issues, and nations; reach out to leaders, public officials and mass media; and leverage resistant global institutions. The progress that this document has described in South America,

North America, the Philippines, and among international and domestic bureaucracies, needs active protection and support to be solidly realized. Indigenous peoples need partners from the outside—not leadership but supporters and collaborators, especially from the environmental and antiglobalization movements, the global justice movement, the human rights movement, the women's movement, and the democracy movement among others, and also from individuals becoming active on a broader scale.

Perhaps a few simple suggestions are appropriate. First of all, for people for whom this is a new subject, we suggest that you start by educating yourself on the details. The Appendix lists some seventy outstanding indigenous and nonindigenous organizations that are active on the kinds of issues we describe here. It is by no means an exhaustive list—there are dozens of other good organizations—but it will be a good beginning. Go to their Web pages, gather their materials, go to their events if you can, volunteer time, try to respond to their requests. Give money. It will also be worthwhile to check out the indigenous declarations that we have included at the back of the book (and those in the boxes). They are all excellent. They clearly articulate the main issues in play, and offer the precise indigenous viewpoint on those subjects. By acquainting yourselves with these efforts and seeking an increased level of personal attachment, you will discover new avenues. The most important act is the first one: seeking connection.

If you are already affiliated with an engaged organization working in one of the areas we listed above, perhaps the best thing you can do is to persuade your group to bring indigenous issues to the front burner since they directly affect all our movements. Earlier, I described the indigenous rights movement as dealing with "frontier issues" in the sense that indigenous peoples live on the geographic frontier of the advancement of the Western development juggernaut. But more to the point, it is also because indigenous people embody a worldview that is vastly different from the dominant Western worldview, with rare exceptions, and it has a proven potential for better outcomes for both human beings and the natural world.

For example, for those involved in the antiglobalization movement, it is crucial that we recognize that as we speak of alternatives to globalization (one of the most important subjects the IFG and other groups are working on these days), we need to celebrate the clear reality that indigenous societies are a *living alternative* to the current economic, political and philosophical models of our time—and a successful one. In fact, given the terrible incursions they have withstood over centuries, their continued presence on Earth is itself proof of the validity of their social, political and spiritual choices.

As we have reported over and over in this book, the dominant global economic system can thrive only by constant economic expansion, constantly expanding exploitation of scarce resources, constantly expanding consumerism, privatization of all elements of the natural commons, export-oriented production—involving ecologically disastrous long-distance shipping—and the homogenization of global cultures within a commodified, commercialized, and yet individualistic ("Look-out-for-Number-One") worldview. It is a system that measures its success purely by the achievement of short-run economic goals. *That is the formula that is killing the world.*

Indigenous societies, though diverse in many ways, have traditionally shared an opposite set of paradigms and values from those of the larger society. As we have discussed, these include: shared natural commons; collective land ownership; philosophies of reciprocity, exchange, sharing and balance; religions integrated with nature; the primary virtue of sacred ancestral lands; consensus decision-making on economic and political matters; and the long-term viability of locally based, self-sufficient, subsistence-oriented economies. Most of all there is a nearly universal commitment to social, political, economic and spiritual values that sustain strong, coherent land-based communities.

"The people belong to the land," not vice versa, said Winona LaDuke in Chapter 3. And in Chapter 4, Jeannette Armstrong put it this way: "The soil, the water, the air, and all the other life forms contributed parts to be our flesh. We are our land."

In fact, indigenous people bring something new to the table in discussions of how we should live now. Many environmentalists today—as well as activists of other stripes—hesitate to say that such prevailing paradigms as economic growth, corporatism, capitalism, and the ideologies of the global market and consumerism are to varying degrees the root causes of the grave environmental and social crises of our time.

Those paradigms are now so dominant, and the mass media so willing to amplify them for their own purposes, that we have become enveloped by them and may skirt the central issues. We are willing to accept that some kind of "clean growth" may eventually be achieved, thus preserving our present overconsumptive lifestyles. Or that giant corporations may eventually exhibit more moral and responsible behavior, as if there was nothing intrinsic in the model based on resource use,

economic growth, and short-term profit that must invariably lead to environmental and social catastrophes. Or that the "free market" equates with "freedom."

Very few indigenous peoples are attached to such ideas. They have shown little interest as a group, and only rarely as individuals, in the deification of private property or the expansion of short-term growth as an ideal development model. The goals of the vast majority of indigenous peoples, certainly those involved in the kinds of struggles we have discussed here, are nearly always to sustain the ability to live in a traditional manner, in direct relationship to their lands, maintaining healthy communities within healthy environments, free of all outside domination and control, while emphasizing full rights to autonomy and self-determination in their political, legal, economic and spiritual practices.

In Chapter 3 John Mohawk said: "All [indigenous peoples] are asking for is to be able to maintain the life they have been living in the environment they found, where they became conscious of themselves as Peoples and Nations. . . . In many ways it is the indigenous cultures' relationships to the earth that represent the only real hope for the long-term survival of the people, on any scale in the world. They are here to maintain survival as a still plausible goal." Indeed. And so it is obvious to me that whatever our movements can do to further the indigenous cause, in its many struggles and forms, also furthers our own and our children's.

APPENDIXES

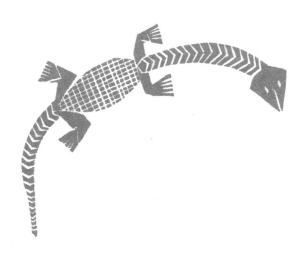

Active Groups and Resources

INDIGENOUS ORGANIZATIONS

'Aha Punana Leo

96 Pu'uhonu Place
Hilo, HI 96720 USA
Tel: 808-935-4304
Fax: 808-969-7512
E-mail: contact@ahapunanaleo.org
Web site: www.ahapunanaleo.org

The 'Aha Punana Leo is dedicated to the reestablishment of Hawaiian as a daily, living language in Hawaii. The organization assists Native Hawaiians and indigenous peoples worldwide in maintaining and developing traditional languages and cultures for life today. 'Aha Punana Leo has been a key force in changing legislation in the state of Hawaii, and at the federal level, to lift the bans that formerly existed regarding the use of Hawaiian in schools. From a pioneer group of "language nest" immersion preschools, the 'Aha Punana Leo has evolved into a nonprofit Native Hawaiian family-based educational organization serving students and family members of all ages with numerous programs and functions.

Asian Indigenous Women's Network

c/o Tebtebba Foundation
No. 1 Roman Ayson Rd., 2600
Baguio City, Philippines
Tel: 63-74-4447703
Fax: 63-74 4439459
E-mail: tebtebba@skyinet.net
Web site: www.tebtebba.org

Works to improve the lives of indigenous women and give them a greater voice in their communities by increasing their consultation on political matters impacting them, providing greater involvement in actual decision-making, and promoting activities in the defense of their land, life and resources.

The Center for Economic and Political Research of Community Action (CIEPAC)

Calle de la Primavera No. 6
Barrio de la Morced 29240
San Cristóbal, Chiapas, Mexico
E-mail: ciepac@laneta.apc.org
Web site: www.ciepac.org

Conducts research, analysis and publishing on the economic, political, social, and human rights conditions of indigenous and rural peoples in Mesoamerica. Has been a catalyst in the fight against poverty and marginalization of indigenous and rural peoples in Mesoamerica. Provides training to civil society groups as they engage in national and international struggles for greater social and economic justice.

The Civic Council of Popular and Indigenous Organizations of Honduras (COPINH)

Barrio Lempira
Intibuca, Honduras
Tel: 504-783-0817
Fax: 504-239-2927
E-mail: copinh@hondutel.hn
Web site: www.rds.org.hn/copinh

A federation of 400 Maya Lenca indigenous communities committed to strengthening and unifying indigenous communities in Honduras and in other countries of Central America. Builds a stronger indigenous voice in political and economic policy-making—both locally and globally. COPINH generates debate and analysis concerning the national and international climate, especially as it affects indigenous people and their land and environments, and advocates for recognition of political, cultural, and socio-economic rights of its members.

Confederation of Indigenous Nationalities of Ecuador (CONAIE)

Av. Los Granados E10-275 y Av. 6 de Diciembre
Quito, Ecuador
Tel: 593-2-245-2335
E-mail: reincon@uio.telconet.net
Web site: www.conaie.org

CONAIE was formed in 1986 to provide broad representation for the indigenous communities of Ecuador. Composed of regional indigenous organizations throughout Ecuador, it works to recover ownership of indigenous lands and to rescue indigenous language and culture. The organization promotes unity among indigenous nations, and is at the forefront of one of the most powerful indigenous movements in Latin America against oil development in the Amazon.

Confederation of Indigenous People of Bolivia (CIDOB)

Casilla No. 6135
Santa Cruz, Bolivia
Tel: 591-3-3460714
Fax: 591-3-3498494
E-mail: cidob@scbbs.com.bo
Web site: www.cidob-bo.org

A national confederation of regional and local indigenous groups throughout Bolivia. Assists indigenous people in the systematization of juridical information on the legalization process and helps lobby for their rights at national and international levels. CIDOB developed an information system (database and Web site) to track the process of land-right claims for indigenous groups in Bolivia. Information is used to keep regional indigenous groups informed about the status of land right claims and to lobby for action at national government and international levels.

The Confederation of the Nationalities Indigenous to the Amazon of Ecuador (CONFENIAE)

Av. 6 de Diciembre 159 y Pazmino Of. 408
Apdo. 17-01-4180
Quito, Ecuador
Tel: 593-2-543-973
Fax: 593-2-220-325
E-mail: confeniae@applicom.com
Web site: www.unii.net/confeniae

CONFENIAE is an umbrella organization for indigenous communities located in the Ecuadorian Amazon, and is a major component of CONAIE, Ecuador's nationwide indigenous confederation. It comprises thirteen federations, and is aligned with similar confederations in Venezuela and Brazil. The federation includes the Quechua, Shuar, Achuar, Siona, Secoya, Cofán and Huaorani peoples. The main objectives of CONFENIAE are the defense and legal titling of indigenous territories, as well as preservation of the environment of the Amazon. CONFENIAE promotes the cultural and economic development of indigenous communities. The organization constituted the Indigenous Parliament of the Ecuadorian Amazon in 1993, as a means of strengthening unity among the Amazonian indigenous communities.

Continental Network of Indigenous Women

c/o CONAMUIP
Apartado 6-1626
Panama
Tel: 502-227-4130
E-mail: conamuip@cableonda.net

The network serves to strengthen the capacity of indigenous women from grassroots organizations on issues that affect them—in particular, intellectual property rights for traditional designs and patterns, and militarization. It also works to promote the voice of indigenous women inside the international arena.

Coordination of the Indigenous Organizations of the Amazon Basin (COICA)

Calle Sevilla N24 - 358 y Guipuzcoa
La Floresta, Quito, Ecuador
Tel: 593-2-2236-658
Fax: 593-2-281-2098
E-mail: com@coica.org
Web site: www.coica.org

COICA is composed of nine national Amazon native organizations. The organization brings more than four hundred indigenous peoples together to help them defend their rights, and fight for the survival of their culture and for indigenous peoples' self-determination. COICA has a congress that meets every four years to create policies and find new authorities. They have been successful in securing the right of indigenous peoples to be educated in their native languages. They also founded Amazon Indigenous University.

Coordination of Indigenous Organizations of the Brazilian Amazon (COIAB)

Ave. Ayrao, 235-Presidente Vargas
Manaos, Brazil C.P. 69-025-290
Tel: 55-92-233-05-48
Fax: 55-92-233-02-09
E-mail: coiab@coiab.com.br
Web site: www.coiab.com.br

COIAB is a coalition of over 100 indigenous groups. It defends and promotes indigenous rights and supports alternative income-generating initiatives. COIAB also supports health and education projects with indigenous communities and raises awareness among the nonindigenous community of the customs, language, beliefs, and traditions of indigenous peoples.

Coordination of Mayan Peoples' Organizations of Guatemala (COPMAGUA)

10a Calle No. 5-35, Zona 11
Guatemala City, Guatemala
Tel: 502-472-48-28
Fax: 502-472-48-28

COPMAGUA is a coordinating group made up of five Mayan umbrella organizations: the Council of Guatemalan Mayan Organizations (COMG), the Academy of Mayan Languages of Guatemala (ALMG), the Coordination of Mayan Unity and Consensus (IUCM), the Union of Mayan People, and the Mayan Council Tukum Umam. COPMAGUA has been especially active concerning the implementation of the Indigenous Rights Accord within the Guatemalan Peace Accords of 1996. (The organization is also known by its Mayan language initials, SAQB'ICHIL.)

Cordillera Peoples Alliance

P.O. Box 975
2600 Baguio City, Philippines
Tel: 63-74-442-2115
Fax: 63-74-443-7159
E-mail: cpa@cpaphils.org
Web site: www.cpaphils.org

A federation of indigenous peoples' grassroots organizations at the forefront of indigenous peoples' struggles for the defense of land, life, and resources in the Cordillera Region of the Philippines. The alliance has launched sustained information drives, advocacy activities, campaigns and direct actions on indigenous peoples' rights and related issues. These activities were implemented alongside organizing work among various indigenous communities in the region, helping build their capacity through education seminars, trainings and various types of assistance.

Cultural Conservancy

P.O. Box 29044
San Francisco, CA 94129-0044 USA
Tel: 415-561-6594
Fax: 415-561-6482
E-mail: mknelson@igc.org
Web site: www.nativeland.org

An indigenous rights organization dedicated to the preservation and revitalization of native languages, arts, cultures, communities and ancestral lands. Provides mediation, legal assistance, information referral, and audio recording services. Also produces educational programs and materials and technical trainings on issues of native land conservation, land rights, cultural and ecological restoration, and traditional indigenous arts and spiritual values.

En'owkin Centre

Lot 45 Green Mountain Road
RR#2, site 50, comp 8
Penticton, BC, V2A 6J7 Canada
Tel: 250-493-7181
Fax: 250-493-5302
E-mail: enowkin@vip.net
Web site: www.enowkincentre.ca

The En'owkin Centre is an indigenous cultural, educational, ecological and creative arts postsecondary institution that articulates and promotes indigenous knowledge, systems, and culture. En'owkin provides students with a strong cultural and academic foundation for success in further postsecondary studies.

Environmental-Aboriginal Guardianship through Law and Education (EAGLE)

Semiahmoo Reserve
16541 Beach Road
Surrey, BC, V3S 9R7 Canada
Tel: 604-536-6261
Fax: 604-536-6282
E-mail: eagle@eaglelaw.org
Web site: www.eaglelaw.org

An aboriginal-environmental organization that combines aboriginal and environmental law in support of aboriginal efforts to protect land and environment. Responds to requests from aboriginal peoples for legal assistance and advice concerning a broad range of issues, including forests, mining, sacred sites, fishing, oil and gas development, toxins and water. EAGLE envisions a future in which lands and resources are protected and restored, aboriginal rights and title protected, and inclusive processes are developed by which sustainable development can co-exist with the protection of aboriginal rights and title.

First Nations Development Institute (FNDI)

2300 Fall Hill Avenue, Suite 412
Fredericksburg, VA 22401 USA
Tel: 540-371-5615
Fax: 540-371-3505
E-mail: info@firstnations.org
Web site: www.firstnations.org

First Nations Development Institute was founded to assist indigenous peoples in controlling and developing their assets and, through that control, building the capacity to direct their economic futures in ways that fit their cultures. To meet the needs of Native American communities, FNDI created the Native Assets Research Center, a research and policy center dedicated to promoting indigenous knowledge and assisting tribal communities in building sound, sustainable reservation economies. The program's main goal is to help native peoples conduct independent research projects on asset development, analyzing culturally appropriate practices, policies and theories affecting self-sufficiency and building national policy initiatives.

Gwich'in Steering Committee

122 First Avenue, Box 2
Fairbanks, AK 99701 USA
Tel: 907-458-8264
Fax: 907-457-8265
E-mail: gwichin@alaska.net
Web site: www.alaska.net/~gwichin

A leading traditional community in Alaska focused on protecting the Arctic National Wildlife Refuge, traditional indigenous economic and political practice, and the Gwich'in community itself. The committee has been a leader in the campaign against oil development in the Arctic.

Honor the Earth

2104 Stevens Avenue South
Minneapolis, MN 55404 USA
Tel: 612-879-7529
Fax: 612-813-5612
E-mail: honorearth@earthlink.net
Web site: www.honorearth.org

Creates awareness of and support for native environmental and cultural issues and develops innovative financial and political strategies for the survival of sustainable native communities. Addresses the economic issues posed by energy development choices in Native America, and challenges tribal governments to move toward a renewable energy agenda. Also supports grassroots native buffalo restoration initiatives and has formed a program to improve the self-esteem of indigenous youths by involving them in environmental issues in their communities, reinforcing their cultural identities and developing their management and outreach skills.

Indian Law Resource Center

602 North Ewing Street
Helena, MT 59601 USA
Tel: 406-449-2006
E-mail: mt@indianlaw.org
Web site: www.indianlaw.org

A nonprofit law and advocacy organization established and directed by American Indians. It provides legal assistance to Indian and Alaska native nations working to protect their land, resources, human rights, environment, cultural integrity, and national sovereignty. The principal goal of the center is the preservation and security of Indian and other native nations and tribes. The organization also helps indigenous leaders and Indian communities to develop the capacity to advocate for and protect their own interests.

Indigenous Environmental Network (IEN)

P.O. Box 485
Bemidji, MN 56619 USA
Tel: 218-751-4967
Fax: 218-751-0561
E-mail: ien@igc.org
Web site: www.ienearth.org

Advocates and organizes to support indigenous communities and tribal governments in developing mechanisms and campaigns to protect their sacred sites, land, water, air, natural resources, and the health of their people while protecting traditional economic practice. IEN convenes local, regional, and national meetings on environmental and economic justice issues, and provides support, resources and referral to indigenous communities and youth throughout North America.

Indigenous Network on Economies and Trade (INET)

Dominion Building, Suite 714
207 West Hastings Street
Vancouver, BC, V6B 1H7 Canada
Tel/Fax: 604-608-0244
E-mail: amanuel@telus.net

The Indigenous Network on Economies and Trade is working with indigenous peoples in the Americas and around the world toward a new global interdependence that respects their inherent rights and indigenous economies. INET has submitted *amicus curiae* briefs to the WTO and NAFTA on the U.S.-Canada softwood lumber dispute.

Indigenous Peoples Council on Biocolonialism

P.O. Box 72
Nixon, NV 89424 USA
Tel: 775-574-0248
Fax: 775-574-0345
E-mail: ipcb@ipcb.org
Web site: www.ipcb.org

Fights to protect indigenous genetic resources, knowledge, and cultural and human rights from the negative effects of biotechnology and global corporate intrusion, as well as WTO rules. Provides educational and technical support to indigenous peoples in the protection of their biological resources, cultural integrity, knowledge and collective rights.

Indigenous Tourism Rights International

366 North Prior Avenue, Suite 205
Saint Paul, MN 55104 USA
Tel: 651-644-9984
Fax: 651-644-2720
E-mail: info@tourismrights.org
Web site: www.tourismrights.org

Indigenous Tourism Rights International is dedicated to collaborating with indigenous communities and networks to help protect native territories, rights and cultures. They work to facilitate the exchange of local experiences in order to understand, challenge and take control of the ways tourism affects native community life. Supports the right to prevent invasive tourism imposed from outside the community and the right to control community-based tourism in a culturally appropriate and environmentally sustainable way.

International Alliance of Tribal and Indigenous Peoples of the Tropical Forests

International Technical Secretariat
6/1 Moo 1, Suthep Rd.
Suthep Subdistrict, Muang District
Chiang Mai 50202 Thailand
Tel: 66-1-885-2212
Fax: 66-53-277-645
E-mail: iait@loxinfo.co.th
Web site: www.international-alliance.org

The International Alliance of Indigenous and Tribal Peoples of the Tropical Forests is a worldwide network of organizations representing indigenous and tribal peoples living in tropical forest regions (Africa, the Asia-Pacific and the Americas). Promotes full recognition of the rights and territories of indigenous and tribal peoples, as well as their participation in decision- and policy-making. Also works to establish effective networks between indigenous peoples at regional and international levels.

International Indian Treaty Council

2390 Mission St., Suite 301
San Francisco, CA 94110 USA
Tel: 415-641-4482
Fax: 415-641-1298
E-mail: alberto@treatycouncil.org
Web site: www.treatycouncil.org

Organization of indigenous peoples from the American continent and the Pacific; works for their sovereignty and self-determination and the recognition and protection of indigenous rights, traditional cultures, and sacred lands. Objectives include: promoting and building official participation of indigenous peoples in the United Nations and its specialized agencies, as well as other international fora, and seeking international recognition for treaties and agreements between indigenous peoples and nation-states.

International Indian Treaty Council—Guatemala office

19 Avenida 3-17, Zona 7
Colonia Villas de San Juan, #203
Guatemala City, Guatemala
Tel: 502-474-1805
Fax: 502-474-1808
E-mail: defemaya@guate.net

The Central American office creates indigenous community-based tourism projects, as well as certification and standards for ecotourism.

Inuit Circumpolar Conference (ICC)

P.O. Box 2099
1084 Aeroplex Building
Iqaluit, NU, X0A 0H0 Canada
Tel: 867-979-4661
Fax: 867-979-4662
E-mail: icccan@baffin.ca
Web site: www.inuitcircumpolar.com

The ICC works to strengthen unity among Inuit of the circumpolar region, promote Inuit rights and interests on an international level, develop and encourage long-term policies that safeguard the Arctic environment, and secure full and active partnership in the political, economic, and social development of circumpolar regions. Currently the lead campaigner on the effects of climate change on Arctic peoples.

Mexican Indigenous, Economic, and Social Development Civil Association (DESMI)

Calle Flavio A. Paniagua No. 79
Barrio Guadalupe, 29230
San Cristóbal de las Casas, Chiapas, Mexico
Tel: 01-9-678-1248
E-mail: desmiac@laneta.apc.org
Web site: www.laneta.apc.org/desmiac

Supports economic and social development in indigenous communities, mainly by strengthening cooperatives. DESMI has provided credit and technical assistance to over 300 grassroots groups in Chiapas; it is also helping to build a network of community-based production and consumer cooperatives that will enable indigenous communities to trade with one another and gain economic self-sufficiency.

Mutawintji Aboriginal Land Council

E-mail: Mutawintji@bigpond.com
Web site: www.austlii.edu.au/au/special/rsjproject
/remote/mutawintji

Represents the traditional aboriginal owners of Mutawintji National Park and Mutawintji Nature Reserve, which was the first national park to be returned to aboriginal ownership in New South Wales, Australia, in 1998. The council runs all tours to the national park.

National Congress of American Indians (NCAI)

1301 Connecticut Ave. NW, Suite 200
Washington D.C. 20036 USA
Tel: 202-466-7767
Fax: 202-466-7797
E-mail: ncai@ncai.org
Web site: www.ncai.org

The oldest and largest tribal government organization in the United States. Serves as a forum for consensus-based policy development among its membership of over 250 tribal governments from every region of the country. Its mission is to inform the public and federal government on tribal self-government, treaty rights, and a broad range of federal policy issues affecting tribal governments.

National Indigenous and Campesino Coordination (CONIC)

8a Calle No. 3-18, Zona 1
Guatemala City, Guatemala
Tel: 502-251-02-78
E-mail: conic1@c.net.gt

CONIC´s work focuses primarily on land rights for indigenous Mayan peasant farmers and respect for human rights to specifically support economic, social and political development in Guatemala. It was formed by campesinos working on different plantations in order to fight for an increase in the minimum wage and for access to land. CONIC has recovered land through occupation of territory that has historically belonged to indigenous communities or that is state or national lands. It has about 80,000 members in Guatemala, 95 percent of them indigenous.

National Indigenous Organization of Colombia (ONIC)

Calle 13 No. 4-38
Bogotá, Colombia
Tel: 57-1-2842168
Fax: 57-1-2843465
E-mail: onic@onic.org.co
Web site: www.onic.org.co

A national umbrella organization that represents and works with the indigenous peoples of Colombia. ONIC strives to strengthen indigenous unity and to fight for indigenous peoples' rights to land, culture and autonomy within Colombia.

The Organization of Forest Production Ejidos of the Mayan Zone, Quintana Roo (OEPFZM)

F. Carrillo Puerto
Quintana Roo, Mexico
Tel/Fax: 52-9-834-0675

OEPFZM is part of a network of community forest organizations that manage over 2.5 million acres of tropical forest and agricultural land in central and southern Quintana Roo. The OEPFZM communities are composed of Yucatec Mayans who settled the forests, which now comprise 23 *ejidos* (agrarian reform units) on over 1 million acres of tropical forest and agricultural land in central Quintana Roo; 366,660 acres have been declared permanent forest areas.

Permanent Coordination of Indigenous Peoples of Peru (COPPIP)

Av. San Eugenio 981
Urbanización Santa Catalina, La Victoria
Lima 13, Peru
Tel: 51-1-266-1573
Fax: 51-1-472-4605
Email : coppip@amauta.rcp.net.pe
Web site: www.rcp.net.pe/coppip

COPPIP was created by the First National Congress for Human Rights and Indigenous People in Peru. Its purpose is to serve as an indigenous and communal collective with rotating leadership. COPPIP aims to create space for meetings and dialogue for Peruvian indigenous organizations from the coast, the forest, and the Amazon.

RICANCIE

Av. El Chofer y Cuenca
Tena-Napo, Ecuador
Tel/Fax: 593-6-2888-715
E-mail: ricancie@hotmail.com
Web site: www.ricancie.nativeweb.org

Comprising nine Quechua communities in the Sumaco Biosphere Reserve in Ecuador, the organization offers an ecotourism program focused on preserving the forest and generating an alternative source of income and employment in the communities. The ecotourism program is based on traditional respect for the culture and environment, and represents a "low impact" alternative path of development for current and future generations.

Russian Association of Indigenous Peoples of the North (RAIPON)

P.O. Box 110
Moscow 119415 Russia
Tel: 7-095-780-8727
Fax: 7-095-432-9992
E-mail: raipon@online.ru
Web site: www.raipon.org

Represents the cultural, economic, environmental, political, and social interests of the thirty-one indigenous peoples of the Russian North. The organization deals with such issues as self-government, the safeguarding of rights, and the preservation of identity and the environment. The main objectives of the association are: promoting the unification of the aboriginal peoples of the North, defending their rights and interests, and resolving problems relating to the socio-cultural and economic development of these peoples.

Saami Council

Seitatie 35
99980 Ohcejohka, Finland
Tel: 358-0-16-677-351
Fax: 358-0-16-677-353
E-mail: saamicouncil@saamicouncil.net
Web site: www.saamicouncil.net

The primary aims of the Saami Council are to promote Saami rights and interests in the four countries where the Saami live, to consolidate the feeling of affinity among the Saami people, to attain recognition for the Saami as a nation and to maintain the economic, social and cultural rights of the Saami in the legislation of the four states: Norway, Sweden, Russia and Finland.

Sarstoon Temash Institute for Indigenous Management (SATIIM)

124 José Maria Nuñez St.
Punta Gorda, Toledo District, Belize
E-mail: satiim@btl.net

In 1994, the government of Belize established the Sarstoon-Temash National Park without consulting or considering the zone's indigenous inhabitants. Shortly thereafter the five indigenous villages located in and around the park established a comanagement arrangement with the national government, resulting in the nonprofit Sarstoon-Temash Institute for Indigenous Management (SATIIM). SATIIM's approach is widely regarded as innovative and has been hailed by organizations like the World Conservation Union (IUCN) as a model for community-based conservation.

Seventh Generation Fund

P.O. Box 4569
Arcata, CA 95518 USA
Tel: 707-825-7640
Fax: 707-825-7639
E-mail: of7gen@pacbell.net
Web site: www.7genfund.org

The Seventh Generation Fund manages and supports numerous innovative native community projects throughout the Western Hemisphere that raise awareness of and gain national and international attention for vital indigenous peoples' issues. Their work includes rebuilding native sustainable communities, promoting traditional economies, developing alternative energy, protecting sacred sites and traditional spiritual practices, pressuring the United Nations to recognize the rights of indigenous peoples, and establishing national and international coalitions and linkages for social justice around the world.

Tebtebba (Indigenous Peoples Global Research and Education Network)

No. 1 Roman Ayson Rd., 2600
Baguio City, Philippines
Tel: 63-74-4447703
Fax: 63-74 4439459
E-mail: tebtebba@skyinet.net
Web site: www.tebtebba.org

An indigenous peoples' organization that seeks the recognition, promotion and protection of indigenous peoples' rights and aspirations while building unity so as to uphold indigenous knowledge systems, social and environmental justice, and sustainability. Works locally and internationally through multiple fora, including the United Nations.

Toledo Ecotourism Association

P.O. Box 157
Punta Gorda, Belize
Tel: 501-722-2096
Fax: 501-722-2199
E-mail: ttea@btl.net
Web site: www.southernbelize.com/tea.html

A community-based organization helping indigenous groups benefit directly from ecotourism. Ten villages participate in the program, which is owned and operated by an association of Mopan, Kek'chi, and Garifuna villages in Belize.

Ulew Che'Ja

c/o Ecologic Development Fund
25 Mt. Auburn St., #203
Cambridge, MA 02138 USA
Tel: 617-441-6300
Fax: 617-441-6307
E-mail: info@ecologic.org
Web site: www.ecologic.org

Ulew Che'Ja (which means Earth, Trees and Water) is an indigenous-led, community-based organization composed of fifty-two Maya Quiche villages in Totonicapán, Guatemala. It was founded to help communities sustain the communal land rights of local people and implement community development and conservation projects. It operates in the most densely populated rural area of Guatemala to effectively protect over 50,000 acres of old-growth forest. Through their efforts, much of the Totonicapán forest has remained intact for centuries.

Union of Indigenous Communities in the Northern Zone of the Isthmus (UCIZONI)

Hombres Illustres No. 505, Matias Romero
Oaxaca, Mexico
Tel: 52-9-722-1646
E-mail: ucizoni@laneta.apc.org
Web site: www.redindigena.net/organinteg/ucizoni.html

A network of Mixe, Zapoteca, Zoque, Chinanteca, Barreña, Mixteca, and Mestiza communities in the isthmus region of Oaxaca that works on issues relating to indigenous rights, poverty, and gender equality. Leading player in the citizens' resistance to Plan Puebla Panama.

The Unrepresented Nations and Peoples Organization (UNPO)

P.O. Box 85878
2508 CN The Hague
The Netherlands
Tel: 31-0-70-3646504
Fax 31-0-70-3646608
E-mail: unpo@unpo.org
Web site: www.unpo.org

UNPO is a democratic, international membership organization of groups not represented in major international fora, such as the United Nations. Its members are indigenous peoples, occupied nations, minorities and independent states or territories who have joined together to protect their human and cultural rights, preserve their environments, and find nonviolent solutions to conflicts that affect them. UNPO provides a legitimate and established international forum for member aspirations and assists its members in effective participation at the international level. UNPO is dedicated to the five principles enshrined in its charter: Nonviolence, Human Rights, Self-determination and Democracy, Environmental Protection, and Tolerance.

U'wa Defense Project (UDP)

Presidio P.O. Box 29457
San Francisco, CA 94129 USA
Tel: 415-561-4518
Fax: 415-561-4521
E-mail: udp@mindspring.com

The U'wa Defense Project provides legal, community development, advocacy and research support to the indigenous U'wa people in Colombia as they work to defend their life, land and cultural autonomy, particularly in defense of the lethal effects of petroleum extraction. UDP is currently focused on building the leadership and technical capacity of U'wa youth and establishing a legal defense program to stop drilling on U'wa land. All of UDP's projects are created under the guidance of the U'wa Traditional Authorities—the legal and community-elected representatives of the U'wa.

Western Shoshone Defense Project

P.O. Box 211308
Crescent Valley, NV 89821 USA
Tel: 775-468-0230
Fax: 775-468-0237
E-mail: wsdp@igc.org
Web site: www.wsdp.org

Works to affirm Newe (Western Shoshone) jurisdiction over Newe Sogobia (Western Shoshone homelands) by protecting, preserving, and restoring Newe rights and lands for present and future generations based on cultural and spiritual traditions. Leads the campaign against Yucca Mountain nuclear dumpsite, as well as the campaign for recognition of treaties guaranteeing land ownership.

White Earth Land Recovery Project

32033 E. Round Lake Rd.
Ponsford, MN 56575 USA
Tel: 218-573-3448
Fax: 218-573-3444
E-mail: info@welrp.org
Web site: www.welrp.org

Facilitates recovery of the original land base of the White Earth Indian reservation, while preserving and restoring traditional practices of sound land stewardship, language fluency, and community development, and strengthening the spiritual and cultural heritage. Advocates recovery of traditional agriculture practices and the promotion of innovative sustainable economic practices.

The Woodfish Institute

P.O. Box 29044
San Francisco, CA 94129-0030 USA
Tel: 415-263-0423
E-mail: lgray@woodfish.org
Web site: www.woodfish.org

Provides education and services to the general public for the purpose of bridging core indigenous ways of knowing and transindigenous healing methodologies with modern multidisciplinary approaches to human problem-solving, mindbody healing, and ecopsychology.

NONINDIGENOUS ORGANIZATIONS

Amazon Alliance

1367 Connecticut Ave. NW, Suite 400
Washington D.C. 20036 USA
Tel: 202-785-3334
Fax: 202-785-3335
E-mail: amazon@amazonalliance.org
Web site: www.amazonalliance.org

Works to defend the rights, territories and environment of indigenous and traditional peoples of the Amazon Basin. The alliance was born out of the partnership between indigenous and traditional peoples of the Amazon and groups and individuals who share their concerns for the future of the Amazon and its peoples.

Amazon Watch

1 Haight St., Suite B
San Francisco, CA 94102 USA
Tel: 415-487-9600
Fax: 415-487-9601
E-mail: amazon@amazonwatch.org
Web site: www.amazonwatch.org

Amazon Watch works to defend the environment and rights of the indigenous peoples of the Amazon Basin in the face of large-scale industrial development, including oil and gas pipelines, power lines, roads, and other mega-projects. They have four key programs: 1) monitoring mega-projects (track and publicize controversial mega-projects in early planning stages to catalyze local and international response); 2) supporting rainforest peoples (mobilize direct support to affected communities and generate media and public pressure on decision-makers); 3) influencing investors (pressure financial institutions and corporations to shift their investments to more sustainable alternatives); and 4) sponsoring the Amazon Communication Team (provide media and communications training and equipment to increase the capacity of Amazonian partner groups to defend their rights).

Arctic Peoples Alert
Zusterstraat 58 B
2512 TN The Hague
The Netherlands
Tel: 070-4020943
Fax: 070-3882915
E-mail: arctica@planet.nl
Web site: www.arctica.nl

Focuses on matters concerning the Arctic from the perspective of indigenous organizations; attempts to inform and mobilize Dutch and European politicians and the public in its efforts to support indigenous peoples in Arctic and Sub-Arctic regions, and to enhance the protection of the Arctic environment and the sustainable development of the Arctic.

Center for Economic Justice
202 Harvard Dr. SE
Albuquerque, NM 87106 USA
Tel: 505-232-3100
Fax: 505-232-3101
E-mail: info@econjustice.net
Web site: www.econjustice.net

Helps strengthen international movements fighting corporate-driven globalization and promotes just policy alternatives. Supports groups struggling for environmentally healthy, human-centered and sustainable economies by helping them gain political power, as well as supplying technical and funding assistance. One of the center's main programs focuses on indigenous peoples and globalization.

Center for Native Lands
Environmental Law Institute
2000 L Street NW, Ste 620
Washington D.C. 20036 USA
Tel: 202-939-3864
Fax: 202-939-3868
E-mail: nativelands@eli.org
Web site: www.nativelands.org

Native Lands works to protect biological and cultural diversity in Latin America, with a focus on Central America and southern Mexico. Assists indigenous peoples in developing and carrying out their agendas for the preservation of the region's natural and cultural heritage through a combined program of applied research, training, and the facilitation of conferences, workshops, and technical exchanges.

Cultural Survival
215 Prospect Street
Cambridge, MA 02139 USA
Tel: 617-441-5400
Fax: 617-441-5417
E-mail: culturalsurvival@cs.org
Web site: www.cs.org

Promotes the rights, voices, culture and visions of indigenous peoples. Publishes *Cultural Survival Quarterly,* a leading journal of indigenous affairs in the United States.

Earth Rights International
U.S. office
1612 K St. NW, Suite 401
Washington D.C. 20006 USA
Tel: 202-466-5188
Fax: 202-466-5189
E-mail: infousa@earthrights.org
Web site: www.earthrights.org

Earth Rights International is an organization comprising activists, organizers, and lawyers with expertise in human rights, the environment, and corporate and government accountability. They document human rights and environmental abuses in countries where few other organizations can safely operate, and litigate in U.S. courts on behalf of people around the world whose rights have been violated by governments and transnational corporations. They were particularly active in the U.S. lawsuit against UNOCAL for human rights violations in Burma.

Forest Peoples Programme
1c Fosseway Business Park
Stratford Road
Moreton-in-Marsh, GL56 9NQ, UK
Tel: 44-0-1608-652893
Fax: 44-0-1608-652878
E-mail: info@forestpeoples.org
Web site: www.forestpeoples.gn.apc.org

Supports forest peoples' rights to determine their own future, to control the use of their land and to carry out traditional and sustainable use of their resources. Helps to create space for forest peoples to negotiate their demands through their own representative institutions and to determine their own future. Provides technical, fundraising, capacity-building and policy advice to local forest communities and indigenous peoples.

Forest Trends
1050 Potomac Street NW
Washington D.C. 20007 USA
Tel: 202-298-3000
Fax: 202-298-3014
E-mail: amartin@forest-trends.org
Web site: www.forest-trends.org

Forest Trends works in partnership with local communities to conserve forests by promoting more diverse trade in the forest sector, moving beyond an exclusive focus on lumber and timber to a broader range of products and services. To further these goals, Forest Trends has sponsored three initiatives: the Katoomba Group, dedicated to advancing markets for ecosystem services provided by forests; the Katoomba Group's Ecosystem Marketplace, the first global information resource on ecosystem service markets; and the China/Asia-Pacific Initiative, which seeks to build a knowledge base on the Chinese forest market and the industry and export trade of China's Asia Pacific supplying countries.

International Development Exchange (IDEX)

827 Valencia Street, Suite 101
San Francisco, CA 94110-1736 USA
Tel: 415-824-8384
Fax: 415-824-8387
E-mail: info@idex.org
Web site: www.idex.org

IDEX promotes economic empowerment and social change in Africa, Asia and Latin America. It partners with community-based organizations to support their initiatives by providing grants, fostering regional and international alliances, and engaging U.S.-based constituencies. Their partners' programs promote economic development and the alleviation of poverty; rights for women, workers and indigenous peoples; youth empowerment; and sustainable agriculture. IDEX also actively educates U.S. citizens about the challenges facing these communities.

International Forum on Globalization (IFG)

1009 General Kennedy Avenue #2
San Francisco, CA 94129 USA
Tel: 415-561-7650
Fax: 415-561-7651
E-mail: ifg@ifg.org
Web site: www.ifg.org

The International Forum on Globalization is a north-south research and educational institution composed of leading activists, economists, scholars, and researchers providing analyses and critiques on the cultural, social, political, and environmental impacts of economic globalization. IFG's Indigenous Peoples and Globalization project examines and publicizes the multiple impacts of the globalization process on native peoples. This project works with indigenous and nonindigenous activists from around the world to develop a broader understanding of the ways in which corporate globalization is impacting native communities. IFG also seeks to identify opportunities to alter those forces at various levels, from local to international.

International Rivers Network (IRN)

1847 Berkeley Way
Berkeley, CA 94703 USA
Tel: 510–848–1155
Fax: 510–848–1008
E-mail: info@irn.org
Web site: www.irn.org

Works to halt the construction of destructive river development projects and to promote sound river management worldwide. Has collaborated with many indigenous communities, particularly in China, India and elsewhere, in fighting big dams. Works to protect their rivers and watersheds, and encourages equitable and sustainable methods of meeting needs for water, energy, and flood management.

The International Work Group for Indigenous Affairs (IWGIA)

Classensgade 11 E
DK 2100 Copenhagen, Denmark
Tel: 45-35-27-05-00
Fax: 45-35-27-05-07
E-mail: iwgia@iwgia.org
Web site: www.iwgia.org/sw617.asp

IWGIA supports indigenous peoples' struggle for human rights, self-determination, right to territory, control of land and resources, cultural integrity, and the right to development. Collaborates with indigenous peoples' organizations all over the world and documents indigenous affairs by publishing books, periodicals and a yearbook about indigenous peoples.

KWIA Support Group for Indigenous Peoples

Breughelstraat 31-33
2018 Antwerpen, Belgium
Tel: 32-0-3-218-8488
Fax: 32-0-3-230-4540
Web site: www.kwia.be

Provides support to indigenous organizations in their lobbying efforts vis-à-vis national governments and international institutions. Encourages and supports indigenous efforts in the sustainable management of fragile ecosystems, including deserts, through protection of traditional land rights.

Minority Rights Group International

54 Commercial Street
London, E1 6LT, UK
Tel: 44-0-20-7422-4200
Fax: 44-0-20-422-4201
E-mail: minority.rights@mrgmail.org
Web site: www.minorityrights.org

Minority Rights Group International works to secure the rights of ethnic, religious and linguistic minorities and indigenous peoples worldwide, and to promote cooperation and understanding between communities. Activities include promoting the active participation of minorities and indigenous peoples in decisions affecting their lives, securing the implementation of international standards, advancing conflict resolution and reconciliation initiatives, and advocating for the integration of minority rights into development policies.

Netherlands Centre for Indigenous Peoples

P.O. Box 94098
1090GB Amsterdam, The Netherlands
Tel: 31-0-20-693-8625
Fax: 31-0-20-665-2818
E-mail: info@nciv.net
Web site: www.nciv.net

The Netherlands Centre for Indigenous Peoples has been supporting the promotion and protection of the rights of indigenous peoples worldwide since 1969, and pays special attention to the role and position of indigenous women. The centre attempts to raise awareness on indigenous peoples' issues in Dutch society and beyond.

Pachamama Alliance

P.O. Box 29191
San Francisco, CA 94129-9191 USA
Tel: 415-561-4522
Fax: 415-561-4521
E-mail: info@pachamama.org
Web site: www.pachamama.org

Pachamama Alliance works to halt the destruction of the Earth's tropical rainforests and the loss of its indigenous cultures and to contribute to the creation of a new global vision of equity and sustainability for all. The organization has two distinct program areas: social and economic development projects in the South and education and awareness building in the North. Pachamama has been collaborating with the Achuar in Ecuador, providing access to technical expertise and funding to support them with the design and implementation of a variety of projects, such as developing sustainable economic enterprises based on the renewable resources of the land.

Pacific Environment

311 California Street, Suite 650
San Francisco, CA 94104-2608 USA
Tel: 415-399-8850
Fax: 415-399-8860
E-mail: info@pacificenvironment.org
Web site: www.pacificenvironment.org

Strives to protect the living environment of the Pacific Rim by strengthening democracy, supporting grassroots activism, empowering indigenous communities, and redefining international policies. Provides direct support to over one hundred grassroots organizations throughout Siberia, the Russian Far East, China, and Japan in an effort to stop the harmful effects of trade, especially on Pacific Rim forests.

Rainforest Action Network (RAN)

221 Pine St., Suite 500
San Francisco, CA 94104 USA
Tel: 415-398-4404
Fax: 415-398-2732
E-mail: rainforest@ran.org
Web site: www.ran.org

Collaborates with environmental, indigenous and human rights groups around the world to protect the earth's rainforests and support the rights of their inhabitants through education, grassroots organizing, anticorporate activism, and nonviolent direct action. Programs include promoting a halt to old-growth logging and organizing to force corporate accountability.

Rainforest Foundation

Suite A5, City Cloisters
196 Old Street
London, EC1V 9FR, UK
Tel: 44-0-20-7251-6345
Fax: 44-0-20-7251-4969
E-mail: rosemaryb@rainforestuk.com
Web site: www.rainforestfoundationuk.org

Supports indigenous people and traditional populations of the world's rainforests in their efforts to protect their environment and fulfill their rights. The foundation assists in securing and controlling the natural resources necessary for their long-term well-being, and in managing these resources in ways that do not harm the indigenous environment or compromise their future.

Research Foundation for Science, Technology, and Ecology

A-60, Hauz Khas
New Delhi, India 110016
Tel: 91-11-26968077
Fax: 91-11-26856795
E-mail: rfste@vsnl.com
Web site: www.vshiva.net

Works on biodiversity conservation and protecting agricultural and tribal people's rights to their livelihoods and environment threatened by centralized systems of monoculture in forestry, agriculture, and fisheries. Projects include seed saving, impacts of trade liberalization on agriculture, and "no patents of life."

Survival International

6 Charterhouse Buildings
London, EC1M 7ET, UK
Tel: 00-44-20-7687-8700
Fax: 00-44-20-7687-8701
E-mail: info@survival-international.org
Web site: www.survival-international.org

An international organization supporting tribal peoples and their right to decide their own future; calls for the protection of indigenous lives, lands, and human rights. Works in three complementary ways: education, advocacy and campaigns. Also makes use of letter-writing campaigns directed not only at governments, but also at companies, banks, missionaries, guerrilla armies, and others who violate tribal peoples' rights.

Third World Network (TWN)

121-S, Jalan Utama, 10450
Penang, Malaysia
Tel: 60-4-2266728
Fax: 60-4-2264505
E-mail: twnet@po.jaring.my
Web site: www.twnside.org.sg

The Third World Network is an extensive network of developing-country NGOs that articulates a Southern perspective on economic, social, and environmental issues pertaining to the South. Their programs cover trade issues and developments, global financial institutions, biotechnology, biodiversity and indigenous rights, biopiracy, tourism, and women's rights and gender issues. TWN's Biodiversity, Access, Indigenous Knowledge and Intellectual Property Rights program works to protect indigenous and traditional knowledge; the Tourism program focuses on issues affecting local communities and the natural environment and strives to provide communities with an opportunity to influence policy-making structures.

Via Campesina

Apdo. Postal 3628MDC
Tegucigalpa, Honduras
Tel: 504-2394679
Fax: 504-2359915
E-mail: viacampesina@multivisionhn.net
Web site: www.viacampesina.org

An international movement that coordinates peasant organizations of small and middle-scale producers, agricultural workers, rural women, youth, landless movements, and indigenous communities from Asia, Africa, America, and Europe to develop alternative proposals to the present neoliberal model. Advocates agrarian reform, farmers' rights, food sovereignty, and indigenous self-determination.

World Rainforest Movement

Maldonado 1858 - 11200
Montevideo, Uruguay
Tel: 598-2-413-2989
Fax: 598-2-410-0985
E-mail: wrm@wrm.org.uy
Web site: www.wrm.org.uy

An international network of Northern and Southern citizens' groups involved in efforts to defend the world's rainforests. Works to secure the lands and livelihoods of forest peoples and supports their efforts to defend the forests from commercial logging, dams, mining, plantations, shrimp farms, colonization, and settlement.

GOVERNMENTAL ORGANIZATIONS

Bureau of Indian Affairs (BIA)

Department of the Interior
1849 C Street NW
Washington D.C. 20240 USA
Tel: 202-208-3710
E-mail: webteam@ios.doi.gov
Web site: www.doi.gov/bureau-indian-affairs.html

The Bureau of Indian Affairs is responsible for the administration and management of 55.7 million acres of land held in trust by the United States for American Indians, Indian tribes, and Alaska Natives. Developing forestlands, leasing assets on these lands, directing agricultural programs, protecting water and land rights, developing and maintaining infrastructure, providing for health and human services, and encouraging economic development are all part of this responsibility in cooperation with the American Indians and Alaska Natives. BIA is the target of voluminous critisim by American Indian tribes for its failure to fulfill its trust obligations or account for its finances.

Department of Indigenous and Northern Affairs (INAC)

Ottawa, Ontario
K1A 0H4 Canada
Tel: 1-800-567-9604
E-mail: InfoPubs@ainc-inac.gc.ca
Web site: www.ainc-inac.gc.ca/index_e.html

The department is charged with fulfilling the lawful obligations of the federal government to aboriginal peoples arising from treaties, the Indian Act and other legislation. It administers Indian reserve lands and elections of First Nation councils; registers entitlement to Indian status and First Nation membership; administers First Nation funds and the estates of certain individual Indians; and negotiates the settlement of accepted land claims. Some of INAC's responsibilities include: recognition of greater program and political authority of First Nations and territorial governments by establishing a framework for the effective implementation of the inherent right of self-government; specific initiatives to implement self-government; continued devolution to territories of program administration; and assisting First Nations and Inuit peoples in strengthening their communities.

Inter-American Commission on Human Rights

1889 F St. NW
Washington D.C. 20006 USA
Tel: 202-458-6002
Fax: 202-458-3992
E-mail: cidhoea@oas.org
Web site: www.cidh.org

An autonomous organ of the Organization of American States working for the promotion and defense of human rights. Administers the inter-American legal instruments in defense of and to promote the human rights of the indigenous peoples. In 1989 the Commission began preparing an American declaration on the rights of indigenous peoples, which led to the creation of the Proposed American Declaration on the Rights of Indigenous Peoples. Approved in 1997, the declaration defines the term "indigenous peoples," and proclaims that these people possess all human rights, including the right to belong to an indigenous community and freedom from forced assimilation or discrimination.

International Labor Organization (ILO)

4, Route des Morillons
CH-1211 Geneva 22
Switzerland
Tel: 41-22-799-6111
Fax: 41-22-798-8685
E-mail: ilo@ilo.org
Web site: www.ilo.org

A UN specialized agency that promotes social justice and internationally recognized human and labor rights. The ILO formulates international labor standards in the form of conventions and recommendations setting minimum standards of basic labor rights: freedom of association, the right to organize, collective bargaining, abolition of forced labor, equality of opportunity and treatment, and other standards regulating conditions across the entire spectrum of work-related issues. The ILO is responsible for two international conventions concerning indigenous and tribal peoples: Convention No. 107 of 1957 concerning Indigenous and Tribal Populations, and Convention No. 169 of 1989 concerning Indigenous and Tribal Peoples. Convention 169 recognizes the existence of indigenous peoples' governments, territories, and legal systems, and their rights to prior informed consent for any intrusive developments on indigenous lands.

National Commission on Indigenous Peoples

2nd Floor N. dela Merced Building
Cor. West and Quezon Avenues
Quezon City, Metro Manila, Philippines
Tel: 63-2-373-97-87
Fax: 63-2-373-97-65
E-mail: resource@ncip.gov.ph
Web site: www.ncip.gov.ph

The primary government agency that formulates and implements policies, plans and programs for the recognition, promotion and protection of the rights and well-being of indigenous peoples regarding their ancestral domains and lands, self-governance and empowerment, social justice and human rights, and cultural integrity.

National Foundation for Indians (FUNAI)

SEPS Quadra 702/902 Projeção A
Ed. Lex 70-390-025
Brasília, DF, Brazil
Tel: 61-313-3500
Web site: www.funai.gov.br

The official Brazilian agency in charge of protecting indian interests and culture.

United Nations Economic and Social Council (ECOSOC)

Department for Economic and Social Affairs
United Nations, 2 UN Plaza
New York, NY 10017 USA
Tel: 212-963-4628
Fax: 212-963-1712
E-mail: ecosocinfo@un.org
Web site: www.un.org/docs/ecosoc

ECOSOC established the Permanent Forum on Indigenous Issues, and is the principal organ to coordinate the economic, social, and related work of the UN's fourteen specialized agencies, ten functional commissions and five regional commissions. The council serves as the central forum for discussing international economic and social issues, and for formulating policy recommendations addressed to member states and the United Nations system. It is responsible for promoting higher standards of living, full employment, and economic and social progress; identifying solutions to international economic, social and health problems; facilitating international cultural and educational cooperation; and encouraging universal respect for human rights and fundamental freedoms.

United Nations Office of High Commissioner for Human Rights

United Nations Office at Geneva
1211 Geneva 10, Switzerland
Fax: 41-22-917-9011
E-mail: ngochr@ohchr.org
Web site: www.ohchr.org

The High Commissioner is mandated to ensure that the human rights of all are fully respected and enjoyed in conditions of global peace. It does so by encouraging the international community and its member states to uphold universally agreed human rights standards. It alerts governments and the world community to the daily reality that these standards are too often ignored or unfulfilled, and is a voice for the victims of human rights violations everywhere. Presses the international community to take steps to prevent violations, including support for the right to development.

United Nations Permanent Forum on Indigenous Issues

United Nations, 2 UN Plaza
Room DC2-1772
New York, NY 10017 USA
Tel: 917-367-5100
E-mail: IndigenousPermanentForum@un.org
Web site: www.un.org/esa/socdev/unpfii

Reports and makes recommendations to the UN Economic and Social Council on economic and social development, culture, the environment, education, health and human rights. The Forum also raises awareness, promotes the integration and coordination of activities relating to indigenous issues within the UN system, and prepares and disseminates information on indigenous issues. The Permanent Forum was created to give indigenous peoples a unique voice within the United Nations system.

United Nations Voluntary Fund for Indigenous Populations

Office of the High Commissioner for Human Rights
CH-1211
Geneva 10, Switzerland
Tel: 41-22-917-9145
Fax: 41-22-917-9066
E-mail: eortado-rosich@ohchr.org
Web site: www.unhchr.ch/html/menu2/9/vfindige.htm

A program of the UN High Commissioner for Human Rights. Established to help representatives of indigenous communities and organizations participate in the deliberations of the Working Group on Indigenous Populations of the Sub-Commission on the Promotion and Protection of Human Rights. Provides them with financial assistance, funded by means of voluntary contributions from governments, nongovernmental organizations and other private or public entities.

United Nations Draft Declaration on the Rights of Indigenous Peoples

As Agreed upon by the Members of the Working Group on Indigenous Populations at its Eleventh Session—1993

AFFIRMING that indigenous peoples are equal in dignity and rights to all other peoples, while recognizing the right of all peoples to be different, to consider themselves different, and to be respected as such,

AFFIRMING ALSO that all peoples contribute to the diversity and richness of civilizations and cultures, which constitute the common heritage of humankind,

AFFIRMING FURTHER that all doctrines, policies and practices based on or advocating superiority of peoples or individuals on the basis of national origin, racial, religious, ethnic or cultural differences are racist, scientifically false, legally invalid, morally condemnable and socially unjust,

REAFFIRMING also that indigenous peoples, in the exercise of their rights, should be free from discrimination of any kind,

CONCERNED that indigenous peoples have been deprived of their human rights and fundamental freedoms, resulting, *inter alia*, in their colonization and dispossession of their lands, territories and resources, thus preventing them from exercising, in particular, their right to development in accordance with their own needs and interests,

RECOGNIZING the urgent need to respect and promote the inherent rights and characteristics of indigenous peoples, especially their rights to their lands, territories and resources, which derive from their political, economic and social structures and from their cultures, spiritual traditions, histories and philosophies,

WELCOMING the fact that indigenous peoples are organizing themselves for political, economic, social and cultural enhancement and in order to bring an end to all forms of discrimination and oppression wherever they occur,

CONVINCED that control by indigenous peoples over developments affecting them and their lands, territories and resources will enable them to maintain and strengthen their institutions, cultures and traditions, and to promote their development in accordance with their aspirations and needs,

RECOGNIZING ALSO that respect for indigenous knowledge, cultures and traditional practices contributes to sustainable and equitable development and proper management of the environment,

EMPHASIZING the need for demilitarization of the lands and territories of indigenous peoples, which will contribute to peace, economic and social progress and development, understanding and friendly relations among nations and peoples of the world,

RECOGNIZING in particular the right of indigenous families and communities to retain shared responsibility for the upbringing, training, education and well-being of their children,

RECOGNIZING ALSO that indigenous peoples have the right freely to determine their relationships with States in a spirit of coexistence, mutual benefit and full respect,

CONSIDERING that treaties, agreements and other arrangements between States and indigenous peoples are properly matters of international concern and responsibility,

ACKNOWLEDGING that the Charter of the United Nations, the International Covenant on Economic, Social and Cultural Rights and the International Covenant on Civil and Political Rights affirm the fundamental importance of the right of self-determination of all peoples, by virtue of which they freely determine their political status and freely pursue their economic, social and cultural development,

BEARING IN MIND that nothing in this Declaration may be used to deny any peoples their right of self-determination,

ENCOURAGING States to comply with and effectively implement all international instruments, in particular those related to human rights, as they apply to indigenous peoples, in consultation and cooperation with the peoples concerned,

EMPHASIZING that the United Nations has an important and continuing role to play in promoting and protecting the rights of indigenous peoples,

BELIEVING that this Declaration is a further important step forward for the recognition, promotion and protection of the rights and freedoms of indigenous peoples and in the development of relevant activities of the United Nations system in this field,

SOLEMNLY PROCLAIMS the following United Nations Declaration on the Rights of Indigenous Peoples:

PART I

Article 1
Indigenous peoples have the right to the full and effective enjoyment of all human rights and fundamental freedoms recognized in the Charter of the United Nations, the Universal Declaration of Human Rights and international human rights law.

Article 2
Indigenous individuals and peoples are free and equal to all other individuals and peoples in dignity and rights, and have the right to be free from any kind of adverse discrimination, in particular that based on their indigenous origin or identity.

Article 3
Indigenous peoples have the right of self-determination. By virtue of that right they freely determine their political status and freely pursue their economic, social and cultural development.

Article 4
Indigenous peoples have the right to maintain and strengthen their distinct political, economic, social and cultural characteristics, as well as their legal systems, while retaining their rights to participate fully, if they so choose, in the political, economic, social and cultural life of the State.

Article 5
Every indigenous individual has the right to a nationality.

PART II

Article 6
Indigenous peoples have the collective right to live in freedom, peace and security as distinct peoples and to full guarantees against genocide or any other act of violence, including the removal of indigenous children from their families and communities under any pretext.

In addition, they have the individual rights to life, physical and mental integrity, liberty and security of person.

Article 7
Indigenous peoples have the collective and individual right not to be subjected to ethnocide and cultural genocide, including prevention of and redress for:
   (a) Any action which has the aim or effect of depriving them of their integrity as distinct peoples, or of their cultural values or ethnic identities;
   (b) Any action which has the aim or effect of dispossessing them of their lands, territories or resources;
   (c) Any form of population transfer which has the aim or effect of violating or undermining any of their rights;
   (d) Any form of assimilation or integration by other cultures or ways of life imposed on them by legislative, administrative or other measures;
   (e) Any form of propaganda directed against them.

Article 8
Indigenous peoples have the collective and individual right to maintain and develop their distinct identities and characteristics, including the right to identify themselves as indigenous and to be recognized as such.

Article 9
Indigenous peoples and individuals have the right to belong to an indigenous community or nation, in accordance with the traditions and customs of the community or nation concerned. No disadvantage of any kind may arise from the exercise of such a right.

Article 10
Indigenous peoples shall not be forcibly removed from their lands or territories. No relocation shall take place without the free and informed consent of the indigenous peoples concerned and after agreement on just and fair compensation and, where possible, with the option of return.

Article 11
Indigenous peoples have the right to special protection and security in periods of armed conflict.

States shall observe international standards, in particular the Fourth Geneva Convention of 1949, for the protection of civilian populations in circumstances of emergency and armed conflict, and shall not:
   (a) Recruit indigenous individuals against their will into the armed forces and, in particular, for use against other indigenous peoples;
   (b) Recruit indigenous children into the armed forces under any circumstances;
   (c) Force indigenous individuals to abandon their lands, territories or means of subsistence, or relocate them in special centres for military purposes;
   (d) Force indigenous individuals to work for military purposes under any discriminatory conditions.

PART III

Article 12
Indigenous peoples have the right to practise and revitalize their cultural traditions and customs. This includes the right to maintain, protect and develop the past, present and future manifestations of their cultures, such as archaeological and historical sites, artifacts, designs, ceremonies, technologies and visual and performing arts and literature, as well as the right to the restitution of cultural, intellectual, religious and spiritual property taken without their free and informed consent or in violation of their laws, traditions and customs.

Article 13
Indigenous peoples have the right to manifest, practise, develop and teach their spiritual and religious traditions, customs and ceremonies; the right to maintain, protect, and have access in privacy to their religious and cultural sites; the right to the use and control of ceremonial objects; and the right to the repatriation of human remains.
States shall take effective measures, in conjunction with the indigenous peoples concerned, to ensure that indigenous sacred places, including burial sites, be preserved, respected and protected.

Article 14

Indigenous peoples have the right to revitalize, use, develop and transmit to future generations their histories, languages, oral traditions, philosophies, writing systems and literatures, and to designate and retain their own names for communities, places and persons.

States shall take effective measures, whenever any right of indigenous peoples may be threatened, to ensure this right is protected and also to ensure that they can understand and be understood in political, legal and administrative proceedings, where necessary through the provision of interpretation or by other appropriate means.

PART IV

Article 15

Indigenous children have the right to all levels and forms of education of the State. All indigenous peoples also have this right and the right to establish and control their educational systems and institutions providing education in their own languages, in a manner appropriate to their cultural methods of teaching and learning.

Indigenous children living outside their communities have the right to be provided access to education in their own culture and language.

States shall take effective measures to provide appropriate resources for these purposes.

Article 16

Indigenous peoples have the right to have the dignity and diversity of their cultures, traditions, histories and aspirations appropriately reflected in all forms of education and public information.

States shall take effective measures, in consultation with the indigenous peoples concerned, to eliminate prejudice and discrimination and to promote tolerance, understanding and good relations among indigenous peoples and all segments of society.

Article 17

Indigenous peoples have the right to establish their own media in their own languages. They also have the right to equal access to all forms of nonindigenous media.

States shall take effective measures to ensure that State-owned media duly reflect indigenous cultural diversity.

Article 18

Indigenous peoples have the right to enjoy fully all rights established under international labour law and national labour legislation.

Indigenous individuals have the right not to be subjected to any discriminatory conditions of labour, employment or salary.

PART V

Article 19

Indigenous peoples have the right to participate fully, if they so choose, at all levels of decision-making in matters which may affect their rights, lives and destinies through representatives chosen by themselves in accordance with their own procedures, as well as to maintain and develop their own indigenous decision-making institutions.

Article 20

Indigenous peoples have the right to participate fully, if they so choose, through procedures determined by them, in devising legislative or administrative measures that may affect them.

States shall obtain the free and informed consent of the peoples concerned before adopting and implementing such measures.

Article 21

Indigenous peoples have the right to maintain and develop their political, economic and social systems, to be secure in the enjoyment of their own means of subsistence and development, and to engage freely in all their traditional and other economic activities. Indigenous peoples who have been deprived of their means of subsistence and development are entitled to just and fair compensation.

Article 22

Indigenous peoples have the right to special measures for the immediate, effective and continuing improvement of their economic and social conditions, including in the areas of employment, vocational training and retraining, housing, sanitation, health and social security.

Particular attention shall be paid to the rights and special needs of indigenous elders, women, youth, children and disabled persons.

Article 23

Indigenous peoples have the right to determine and develop priorities and strategies for exercising their right to development. In particular, indigenous peoples have the right to determine and develop all health, housing and other economic and social programmes affecting them and, as far as possible, to administer such programmes through their own institutions.

Article 24

Indigenous peoples have the right to their traditional medicines and health practices, including the right to the protection of vital medicinal plants, animals and minerals.

They also have the right to access, without any discrimination, to all medical institutions, health services and medical care.

PART VI

Article 25
Indigenous peoples have the right to maintain and strengthen their distinctive spiritual and material relationship with the lands, territories, waters and coastal seas and other resources which they have traditionally owned or otherwise occupied or used, and to uphold their responsibilities to future generations in this regard.

Article 26
Indigenous peoples have the right to own, develop, control and use the lands and territories, including the total environment of the lands, air, waters, coastal seas, sea-ice, flora and fauna and other resources which they have traditionally owned or otherwise occupied or used. This includes the right to the full recognition of their laws, traditions and customs, land-tenure systems and institutions for the development and management of resources, and the right to effective measures by States to prevent any interference with, alienation of or encroachment upon these rights.

Article 27
Indigenous peoples have the right to the restitution of the lands, territories and resources which they have traditionally owned or otherwise occupied or used, and which have been confiscated, occupied, used or damaged without their free and informed consent. Where this is not possible, they have the right to just and fair compensation. Unless otherwise freely agreed upon by the peoples concerned, compensation shall take the form of lands, territories and resources equal in quality, size and legal status.

Article 28
Indigenous peoples have the right to the conservation, restoration and protection of the total environment and the productive capacity of their lands, territories and resources, as well as to assistance for this purpose from States and through international cooperation. Military activities shall not take place in the lands and territories of indigenous peoples, unless otherwise freely agreed upon by the peoples concerned.

States shall take effective measures to ensure that no storage or disposal of hazardous materials shall take place in the lands and territories of indigenous peoples.

States shall also take effective measures to ensure, as needed, that programmes for monitoring, maintaining and restoring the health of indigenous peoples, as developed and implemented by the peoples affected by such materials, are duly implemented.

Article 29
Indigenous peoples are entitled to the recognition of the full ownership, control and protection of their cultural and intellectual property.

They have the right to special measures to control, develop and protect their sciences, technologies and cultural manifestations, including human and other genetic resources, seeds, medicines, knowledge of the properties of fauna and flora, oral traditions, literatures, designs and visual and performing arts.

Article 30
Indigenous peoples have the right to determine and develop priorities and strategies for the development or use of their lands, territories and other resources, including the right to require that States obtain their free and informed consent prior to the approval of any project affecting their lands, territories and other resources, particularly in connection with the development, utilization or exploitation of mineral, water or other resources. Pursuant to agreement with the indigenous peoples concerned, just and fair compensation shall be provided for any such activities and measures taken to mitigate adverse environmental, economic, social, cultural or spiritual impact.

PART VII

Article 31
Indigenous peoples, as a specific form of exercising their right to self-determination, have the right to autonomy or self-government in matters relating to their internal and local affairs, including culture, religion, education, information, media, health, housing, employment, social welfare, economic activities, land and resources management, environment and entry by non-members, as well as ways and means for financing these autonomous functions.

Article 32
Indigenous peoples have the collective right to determine their own citizenship in accordance with their customs and traditions. Indigenous citizenship does not impair the right of indigenous individuals to obtain citizenship of the States in which they live.

Indigenous peoples have the right to determine the structures and to select the membership of their institutions in accordance with their own procedures.

Article 33
Indigenous peoples have the right to promote, develop and maintain their institutional structures and their distinctive juridical customs, traditions, procedures and practices, in accordance with internationally recognized human rights standards.

Article 34
Indigenous peoples have the collective right to determine the responsibilities of individuals to their communities.

Article 35
Indigenous peoples, in particular those divided by international borders, have the right to maintain and develop contacts, relations and cooperation, including activities for spiritual, cultural, political, economic and social purposes, with other peoples across borders.

States shall take effective measures to ensure the exercise and implementation of this right.

Article 36

Indigenous peoples have the right to the recognition, observance and enforcement of treaties, agreements and other constructive arrangements concluded with States or their successors, according to their original spirit and intent, and to have States honour and respect such treaties, agreements and other constructive arrangements. Conflicts and disputes which cannot otherwise be settled should be submitted to competent international bodies agreed to by all parties concerned.

PART VIII

Article 37

States shall take effective and appropriate measures, in consultation with the indigenous peoples concerned, to give full effect to the provisions of this Declaration. The rights recognized herein shall be adopted and included in national legislation in such a manner that indigenous peoples can avail themselves of such rights in practice.

Article 38

Indigenous peoples have the right to have access to adequate financial and technical assistance, from States and through international cooperation, to pursue freely their political, economic, social, cultural and spiritual development and for the enjoyment of the rights and freedoms recognized in this Declaration.

Article 39

Indigenous peoples have the right to have access to and prompt decision through mutually acceptable and fair procedures for the resolution of conflicts and disputes with States, as well as to effective remedies for all infringements of their individual and collective rights. Such a decision shall take into consideration the customs, traditions, rules and legal systems of the indigenous peoples concerned.

Article 40

The organs and specialized agencies of the United Nations system and other intergovernmental organizations shall contribute to the full realization of the provisions of this Declaration through the mobilization, inter alia, of financial cooperation and technical assistance. Ways and means of ensuring participation of indigenous peoples on issues affecting them shall be established.

Article 41

The United Nations shall take the necessary steps to ensure the implementation of this Declaration including the creation of a body at the highest level with special competence in this field and with the direct participation of indigenous peoples. All United Nations bodies shall promote respect for and full application of the provisions of this Declaration.

PART IX

Article 42

The rights recognized herein constitute the minimum standards for the survival, dignity and well-being of the indigenous peoples of the world.

Article 43

All the rights and freedoms recognized herein are equally guaranteed to male and female indigenous individuals.

Article 44

Nothing in this Declaration may be construed as diminishing or extinguishing existing or future rights indigenous peoples may have or acquire.

Article 45

Nothing in this Declaration may be interpreted as implying for any State, group or person any right to engage in any activity or to perform any act contrary to the Charter of the United Nations.

Indigenous Peoples' Seattle Declaration

on the Occasion of the
Third Ministerial Meeting of the World Trade Organization
November 30—December 3, 1999

We, the Indigenous Peoples from various regions of the world, have come to Seattle to express our great concern over how the World Trade Organization is destroying Mother Earth and the cultural and biological diversity of which we are a part.

Trade liberalization and export-oriented development, which are the overriding principles and policies pushed by the WTO, are creating the most adverse impacts on the lives of Indigenous Peoples. Our inherent right to self-determination, our sovereignty as nations, and treaties and other constructive agreements which Indigenous nations and Peoples have negotiated with other nation-states, are undermined by most of the WTO Agreements. The disproportionate impact of these Agreements on our communities, whether through environmental degradation or the militarization and violence that often accompanies development projects, is serious and therefore should be addressed immediately.

The WTO Agreement on Agriculture (AoA), which promotes export competition and import liberalization, has allowed the entry of cheap agricultural products into our communities. It is causing the destruction of ecologically rational and sustainable agricultural practices of Indigenous Peoples.

Food security and the production of traditional food crops have been seriously compromised. Incidents of diabetes, cancers, and hypertension have significantly increased among Indigenous Peoples because of the scarcity of traditional foods and the dumping of junk food into our communities.

Small-scale farm production is giving way to commercial cash-crop plantations further concentrating ancestral lands into the hands of few agri-corporations and landlords. This has led to the dislocation of scores of people from our communities who then migrate to nearby cities and become the urban homeless and jobless.

The WTO Forest Products Agreement promotes free trade in forest products. By eliminating developed country tariffs on wood products by the year 2000, and developing country tariffs by 2003, the Agreement will result in the deforestation of many of the world's ecosystems in which Indigenous Peoples live.

Mining laws in many countries are being changed to allow free entry of foreign mining corporations, to enable them to buy and own mineral lands, and to freely displace Indigenous Peoples from their ancestral territories. These large-scale commercial mining and oil extraction activities continue to degrade our lands and fragile ecosystems, and pollute the soil, water, and air in our communities.

The appropriation of our lands and resources and the aggressive promotion of consumerist and individualistic Western culture continue to destroy traditional lifestyles and cultures. The result is not only environmental degradation but also ill health, alienation, and high levels of stress manifested in high rates of alcoholism and suicides.

The theft and patenting of our biogenetic resources is facilitated by the TRIPS (Trade-Related Aspects of Intellectual Property Rights) of the WTO. Some plants which Indigenous Peoples have discovered, cultivated, and used for food, medicine, and for sacred rituals are already patented in the United States, Japan, and Europe. A few examples of these are ayahuasca, quinoa, and sangre de drago in forests of South America; kava in the Pacific; turmeric and bitter melon in Asia. Our access and control over our biological diversity and control over our traditional knowledge and intellectual heritage are threatened by the TRIPS Agreement.

Article 27.3b of the TRIPS Agreement allows the patenting of life-forms and makes an artificial distinction between plants, animals, and micro-organisms. The distinction between "essentially biological" and "non-biological" and "microbiological" processes is also erroneous. As far as we are concerned all these are life-forms and life-creating processes which are sacred and which should not become the subject of private property ownership.

Finally, the liberalization of investments and the service sectors, which is pushed by the General Agreement on Trade in Services (GATS), reinforces the domination and monopoly control of foreign corporations over strategic parts of the economy. The World Bank and the International Monetary Fund impose conditionalities of liberalization, deregulation and privatization on countries caught in the debt trap. These conditionalities are reinforced further by the WTO.

In light of the adverse impacts and consequences of the WTO Agreements identified above, we, Indigenous Peoples present the following demands:

We urgently call for a social and environmental justice analysis which will look into the Agreements' cumulative effects on Indigenous Peoples. Indigenous Peoples should be equal participants in establishing the criteria and indicators for these analyses so that they take into consideration spiritual as well as cultural aspects.

A review of the Agreements should be done to address all of the inequities and imbalances which adversely affect Indigenous Peoples. The proposals to address some of these are as follows:

1. FOR THE AGREEMENT ON AGRICULTURE:

a. It should not include in its coverage small-scale farmers who are mainly engaged in production for domestic use and sale in the local markets.
b. It should ensure the recognition and protection of rights of Indigenous Peoples to their territories and their resources, as well as their rights to continue practicing their indigenous sustainable agriculture and resource management practices and traditional livelihoods.
c. It should ensure the food security and the capacity of Indigenous Peoples to produce, consume and trade their traditional foods.

2. WITH REGARD TO THE LIBERALIZATION OF SERVICES AND INVESTMENTS WE RECOMMEND THE FOLLOWING:

a. It must stop unsustainable mining, commercial planting of monocrops, dam construction, oil exploration, land conversion to golf clubs, logging, and other activities which destroy Indigenous Peoples' lands and violate the rights of indigenous peoples to their territories and resources.
b. The right of Indigenous Peoples to their traditional lifestyles, cultural norms and values should likewise be recognized and protected.
c. The liberalization of services, especially in the areas of health, should not be allowed if it will prevent Indigenous Peoples from having access to free, culturally appropriate as well as quality health services.
d. The liberalization of finance services which makes the world a global casino should be regulated.

3. ON THE TRIPS AGREEMENT, THE PROPOSALS ARE AS FOLLOWS:

a. Article 27.3b should be amended to categorically disallow the patenting of life-forms. It should clearly prohibit the patenting of micro-organisms, plants, animals, including all their parts, whether they are genes, gene sequences, cells, cell lines, proteins, or seeds.
b. It should also prohibit the patenting of natural processes, whether these are biological or microbiological, involving the use of plants, animals and micro-organisms and their parts in producing variations of plants, animals and micro-organisms.
c. It should ensure the exploration and development of alternative forms of protection outside of the dominant western intellectual property rights regime. Such alternatives must protect the knowledge and innovations and practices in agriculture, health care, and conservation of biodiversity, and should build upon indigenous methods and customary laws protecting knowledge, heritage and biological resources.
d. It should ensure that the protection offered to indigenous and traditional knowledge, innovation and practices is consistent with the Convention on Biological Diversity (i.e., Articles 8j, 10c, 17.2, and 18.4) and the International Undertaking on Plant Genetic Resources.
e. It should allow for the right of Indigenous Peoples and farmers to continue their traditional practices of saving, sharing and exchanging seeds, and cultivating, harvesting and using medicinal plants.

f. It should prohibit scientific researchers and corporations from appropriating and patenting indigenous seeds, medicinal plants, and related knowledge about these life-forms. The principles of prior informed consent and right of veto by Indigenous Peoples should be respected.

If the earlier proposals cannot be ensured, we call for the removal of the Agreement on Agriculture, the Forest Products Agreements and the TRIPS Agreement from the WTO.

We call on the member-states of the WTO not to allow for another round whilst the review and rectification of the implementation of existing agreements has not been done. We reject the proposals for an investment treaty, competition, accelerated industrial tariffs, government procurement, and the creation of a working group on biotechnology.

We urge the WTO to reform itself to become democratic, transparent and accountable. If it fails to do this we call for the abolition of the WTO.

We urge the member nation-states of the WTO to endorse the adoption by the UN General Assembly of the current text of the UN Declaration on the Rights of Indigenous Peoples and the ratification of ILO Convention 169.

We call on the peoples' organizations and NGOs to support this "Indigenous Peoples' Seattle Declaration" and to promote it among their members.

We believe that the whole philosophy underpinning the WTO Agreements and the principles and policies it promotes contradict our core values, spirituality and worldviews, as well as our concepts and practices of development, trade and environmental protection. Therefore, we challenge the WTO to redefine its principles and practices toward a "sustainable communities" paradigm, and to recognize and allow for the continuation of other worldviews and models of development.

Indigenous peoples, undoubtedly, are the ones most adversely affected by globalization and by the WTO Agreements. However, we believe that it is also us who can offer viable alternatives to the dominant economic growth, export-oriented development model. Our sustainable lifestyles and cultures, traditional knowledge, cosmologies, spirituality, values of collectivity, reciprocity, respect and reverence for Mother Earth, are crucial in the search for a transformed society where justice, equity, and sustainability will prevail.

Declaration by the Indigenous Peoples' Caucus convened and sponsored by the Indigenous Environmental Network, Seventh Generation Fund in alliance with the TEBTEBBA (Indigenous Peoples' International Centre for Policy Research and Education), International Indian Treaty Council, Indigenous Peoples Council on Biocolonialism and the Abya Yala Fund.

INDIGENOUS PEOPLES' ORGANIZATIONS PARTICIPATING IN THE SEATTLE WTO
THAT SIGNED ON TO THIS DECLARATION ARE LISTED BELOW:

Nilo Cayuqueo, Abya Yala Fund, USA

Victoria Tauli-Corpuz, Indigenous Peoples' International Centre for Policy Research and Education, Philippines

Tom Goldtooth, Indigenous Environmental Network, USA/Canada

Antonio Gonzales, International Indian Treaty Council, International

Margarita Gutierrez, Social Commission for the Development of the Nanhu, Mexico

Debra Harry, Indigenous Peoples Council on Biocolonialism, USA

Clemencia Herrera Nemarayema, National Indigena Organization of Colombia, South America

Chief Johnny Jackson, Klickitat Band of Yakama, Elder Committee of Indigenous Environmental Network, USA/Canada

Carol Kalafatic, International Indian Treaty Council, International

Dune Lankard, Eyak Alaska Preservation Council, USA

Chief Arthur Manuel, Interior Alliance of First Nations, Canada

Alvin Manitopyes, Cree Strong Heart Environmental and Wellness Society, Canada

Jim Main Sr., Gros Ventre White Clay Society, USA

Jose Matos, Indigenous Alliance Without Borders, USA/Mexico

Esther Nahgahnub, Anishinaabeg Treaty 1854 Committee, USA

Chris Peters, Seventh Generation Fund, USA

Priscilla Settee, Indigenous Women's Network, USA/Canada

Taita Stanley, Movimiento de la Juventad Kuna, Panama

Chaz Wheelock, Great Lakes Regional Indigenous Environmental Network, USA/Canada

Clemente Ibe Wilson, Movimiento de la Juventad Kuna, Panama

The International Cancun Declaration of Indigenous Peoples

Fifth WTO Ministerial Conference
Cancun, Quintana Roo, Mexico, 12 September 2003

We, the international representatives of Indigenous Peoples gathered here during the 5th WTO Ministerial Conference in Cancun, Mexico 10–14 September 2003 wish to extend our thanks to the Indigenous Peoples of Mexico, particularly the Mayan Indigenous Peoples of Quintana Roo, for welcoming us.

We share the concerns of our Indigenous brothers and sisters, as expressed in the Congreso Nacional Indigena Declaration of Cancun. We join our voices to this CNI Declaration and its conclusions and recommendations.

We wish to especially recognize and honor the sacrifice of our Korean brother, Mr. Lee-Kyung-Hae, made here in Cancun. His act of self-immolation was a dignified cultural expression profoundly reflecting the daily reality of the effects of globalization and liberalized trade on peasants and Indigenous Peoples throughout the world.

We have come to Cancun to address critical issues and negative impacts of the WTO Trade Negotiations on our families, communities and nations.

With the creation of the World Trade Organization (WTO) and with the continuing imposition of the structural adjustment policies of the World Bank and International Monetary Fund, our situation, as Indigenous Peoples, has turned from bad to worse. Corporations are given more rights and privileges at the expense of our rights. Our right to self-determination, which is to freely determine our political status and pursue our own economic, social and cultural development, and our rights to our territories and resources, to our indigenous knowledge, cultures and identities are grossly violated. Some of the prime examples of the adverse impacts of the WTO Agreements on us are the following:

▲ Loss of livelihoods of hundreds of thousands of indigenous peasants in Mexico who are producing corn because of the dumping of artificially cheap, highly subsidized corn from the USA and tens of thousands of indigenous vegetable producers in the Cordillera region of the Philippines because of dumping of vegetables. The contamination of traditional indigenous corn in Mexico by genetically modified corn is a very serious problem for Indigenous Peoples. All these are due to the liberalization of trade in agriculture and the deregulation of laws which protect domestic producers and crops required by the WTO Agreement on Agriculture (AOA). The structural adjustment policies of the World Bank and the

International Monetary Fund are the foundations for liberalization, privatization and deregulation. High export subsidies and domestic support provided to rich agribusiness corporations and rich farmers in the United States and the European Union have also made this possible.

▲ The increasing impoverishment of indigenous and hilltribe farmers engaged in coffee production in Guatemala, Mexico, Colombia, Vietnam, etc. because of the drop in commodity prices of coffee.

▲ The increasing conflicts between transnational mining, gas and oil corporations and Indigenous Peoples in the Philippines, Indonesia, Papua New Guinea, India, Ecuador, Guyana, Venezuela, Colombia, Nigeria, Chad-Cameroon, USA, Russia, Venezuela, among others, and the militarization and environmental devastation in these communities due to the operations of these extractive industries. The facilitation of the entry of such corporations is made possible because of liberalization of investment laws pushed by the TRIMs (Trade-Related Investment Measures) Agreement and WB-IMF conditionalities, regional trade agreements like NAFTA and bilateral investment agreements.

▲ The militarization of Indigenous Peoples' lands and territories, and the many cases of assassination and arbitrary arrests and detention of indigenous activists and leaders and people who are supporting them, as well as the criminalization of Indigenous Peoples' resistance, all significantly increased.

▲ The upsurge in infrastructure development, particularly of mega hydroelectric dams, oil and gas pipelines, roads in Indigenous Peoples' territories to provide support to operations of extractive industries, logging corporations, and export processing zones. The infrastructure development, for instance, under Plan Panama has destroyed ceremonial and sacred sites of Indigenous Peoples in the six states of Southern Mexico and in Guatemala.

▲ The patenting of medicinal plants and seeds nurtured and used by Indigenous Peoples, like the quinoa, ayahuasca, Mexican yellow bean, maca, sangre de drago, hoodia, yew plant, etc. Such biopiracy and patenting of life-forms is facilitated by the TRIPS Agreement.

▲ Soaring prices of pharmaceutical products and inaccessibility of cheaper drugs for diseases like tuberculosis, malaria,

AIDS, which are diseases in Indigenous Peoples' communities, and decreasing public health services in these communities.

▲ Privatization of basic public services such as water and energy in several countries which has spurred massive general strikes and protests such as those led by Indigenous Peoples in Bolivia. The General Agreement on Trade in Services (GATS) whose coverage is being expanded to include environmental services (sanitation, nature and landscape protection), financial services, tourism, among others, allowed for this.

▲ The undermining of international instruments, constitutional provisions, and national laws and policies which protect our rights.

All these developments are alarming. This global situation has undermined self-sufficient economies of Indigenous Peoples, leading to food insecurity, worsening poverty and loss of land, culture and identity. We, Indigenous Peoples' representatives, present in Cancun during the event of the Fifth Ministerial Meeting of the WTO, are asking the governments to do the following:

1. Recognize and protect our territorial and resource rights and our right to self-determination. The human-rights framework should underpin trade, investment, development and anti-poverty policies and programmes. Investment liberalization rules like the TRIMs Agreement, conditionalities by the WB and IMF which push countries to liberalize their investment laws, regional trade agreements and bilateral investment agreements which give more protection and rights to corporations than to Indigenous Peoples should be changed. Many of these facilitate the displacement of Indigenous Peoples and the appropriation of our lands, waters, resources and knowledge. Indigenous peoples who have been displaced from their lands because of militarization, infrastructure projects, extractive industries, export processing zones and other development schemes should be repatriated back to their lands or should be justly compensated. International human rights and environmental standards should be upheld by governments and should guide the way trade agreements are formulated and implemented. The free and prior informed consent of Indigenous Peoples should be obtained before any project is brought into their communities. Article 8j and 10c of the Convention of Biological Diversity that protect traditional knowledge and indigenous systems and practices of land use and land tenure should be the framework for WTO Agreements. Governments should support the immediate adoption of the UN Draft Declaration on the Rights of Indigenous Peoples that will help ensure the recognition and protection of our rights.

2. Stop patenting of life-forms and other intellectual property rights over biological resources and indigenous knowledge. Ensure that we, Indigenous Peoples, retain our rights to have control over our seeds, medicinal plants and indigenous knowledge. We call for an explicit statement for the banning of patents on life-forms in the TRIPS Agreement. We also demand that the patent rights, patent applications and claims of corporations, individuals or governments over indigenous medicinal plants, seeds, and knowledge and even over Indigenous Peoples' human genetic materials should be withdrawn. Biopiracy should be stopped and the free and prior informed consent of Indigenous Peoples should be obtained before access to their resources is granted. The issue of protection of indigenous knowledge should not be dealt with by the WTO TRIPS Agreement because its basic assumptions contradict the concepts, values and ethics underpinning indigenous knowledge systems. This can be best protected under the United Nations and we therefore urge the UN Permanent Forum on Indigenous Issues to convene a technical meeting to explore how the UN can address the issue of protection of indigenous knowledge.

3. Ensure Indigenous Peoples' basic right to health. The right of countries to take measures to protect public health and promote access to medicines should take precedence over their obligations to protect intellectual property rights of corporations. The patent protection asked by pharmaceutical and biotechnology corporations should be limited in order to protect public health and safety and ensure production and easy access to cheap essential medicines. Health is a basic human right and Indigenous Peoples should enjoy this right. Governments should be allowed to use the flexibilities allowed in the TRIPS Agreement which are reflected in the Doha TRIPS and Public Health Declaration. An amendment to TRIPS should be done to simplify and clarify the procedures for compulsory licensing and parallel importation and to remove the unnecessary obstacles to the import and export of medicines needed to provide affordable medicines to the poor.

4. No new issues should be negotiated in this 5th Ministerial Conference. We support the position of some developing countries to stop the launching of a new round or to expand the WTO by negotiating on new issues such as investments, competition, transparency in government procurement and trade facilitation. The WTO should not pursue any negotiation on investment and should change its existing investment rules which provide excessive rights to corporations and allow for their unregulated behavior. Those rules which prevent governments from pursuing rights-based development and environmentally sustainable policies should be abandoned.

5. Prevent the expansion of the GATS Agreement and amend the existing agreement to stop the privatization and liberalization of health, education, water, energy, and environmental services. The liberalization and privatization of services in environmental services (e.g., parks and landscape services), the commercialization of indigenous cultures and the increasing monopoly control of the tourism industry in the hands of international and national travel and tour agencies should be stopped. We must be allowed to be the managers of protected areas, parks, forests and waters found in our territories. We should be able to continue practicing our own indigenous natural management practices in forest, water, biodiversity and ecosystem management.

6. Stop the negotiations on agriculture which will push for further import liberalization of agricultural products. Drastically end the export and domestic subsidies of the US and the EU for their agribusiness corporations and rich farmers. States

must take decisive measures to promote and protect food sovereignty and food security, and stop the dumping and smuggling of artificially cheap and highly subsidized agricultural products from the US, EU, Canada, Australia and New Zealand. Ensure the right of indigenous farmers to sustain their indigenous agricultural systems and to plant and reproduce their traditional seeds. States must not include indigenous agriculture systems in the scope of international trade rules. The rights of Indigenous Peoples to their traditional livelihoods and to food should be recognized and protected, thus trade and investment rules which undermine these rights should be repealed or appropriately amended.

7. End the militarization of Indigenous Peoples' communities and stop the criminalization of protest and resistance actions of Indigenous Peoples against destructive industries, projects and programs. There should be meaningful and effective investigation of the many cases of assassinations, arbitrary arrests and detentions, rapes committed against Indigenous Peoples and their supporters. Justice should be accorded to the victims and their families, and the perpetrators punished for their crimes.

8. Support and strengthen the sustainable trading systems which have existed for centuries between the Indigenous Peoples of the Americas. Trade routes between the various Indigenous Peoples within the Americas (USA, Canada, Mexico) have been existing for centuries and trading between them is still practiced. Militarization of borders and other destructive practices have greatly limited their scale and utility for Indigenous Peoples. Trade between Indigenous Peoples should be sustained and promoted.

The ministers at this Fifth Ministerial meeting of the WTO have the responsibility to represent not only commercial interests but all of the people of their States, including Indigenous Peoples. Existing human rights, environmental, social and cultural conventions and covenants developed within the United Nations system continue to be the states' legal if not moral obligation. All international law including human rights law binds them.

Indigenous peoples are the subjects of many of these covenants and conventions and their jurisprudence. Our rights cannot be ignored, nor can their observance be diminished or compromised by trade agreements and regimes. We as Indigenous Peoples have the right to participate as peoples and actors in our own development, consistent with our own vision and tradition. Our free and informed consent, free of fraud or manipulation, must be secured through our own traditional means of decision-making. State sponsored development cannot just be imposed upon us. Our rights as peoples to our lands and territories and natural resources must be recognized, respected and observed. Our survival as peoples depends upon it.

The Mataatua Declaration

On the Cultural and Intellectual Property Rights of Indigenous Peoples

June 1993

In recognition that 1993 is the United Nations International Year for the World's Indigenous Peoples:

The Nine Tribes of Mataatua in the Bay of Plenty Region of Aotearoa New Zealand convened the First International Conference on the Cultural and Intellectual Property Rights of Indigenous Peoples (12-18 June 1993, Whakatane).

Over 150 Delegates from fourteen countries attended, including indigenous representatives from Ainu (Japan), Australia, Cook Islands, Fiji, India, Panama, Peru, Philippines, Surinam, USA and Aotearoa.

The Conference met over six days to consider a range of significant issues, including: the value of indigenous knowledge, biodiversity and biotechnology, customary environmental management, arts, music, language and other physical and spiritual cultural forms. On the final day, the following Declaration was passed by the Plenary.

PREAMBLE

Recognizing that 1993 is the United Nations International Year for the World's Indigenous Peoples;

Reaffirming the undertaking of United Nations Member States to:

▲ Adopt or strengthen appropriate policies and/or legal instruments that will protect indigenous intellectual and cultural property and the right to preserve customary and administrative systems and practices. United Nations Conference on Environmental Development; UNCED Agenda 21 (26.4b);

▲ Noting the Working Principles that emerged from the United Nations Technical Conference on Indigenous Peoples and the Environment in Santiago, Chile, 18-22 May 1992 (E/CN.4/Sub.2/1992/31); and

▲ Endorsing the recommendations on Culture and Science from the World Conference of Indigenous Peoples on Territory, Environment and Development, Kari-Oca, Brazil, 25-30 May 1992;

We Declare that Indigenous Peoples of the world have the right to self-determination and in exercising that right must be recognized as the exclusive owners of their cultural and intellectual property;

▲ Acknowledge that Indigenous Peoples have a commonality of experiences relating to the exploitation of their cultural and intellectual property;

▲ Affirm that the knowledge of the Indigenous Peoples of the world is of benefit to all humanity;

▲ Recognize that Indigenous Peoples are capable of managing their traditional knowledge themselves, but are willing to offer it to all humanity provided their fundamental rights to define and control this knowledge are protected by the international community;

▲ Insist that the first beneficiaries of indigenous knowledge (cultural and intellectual property rights) must be the direct indigenous descendants of such knowledge;

▲ Declare that all forms of discrimination and exploitation of Indigenous Peoples, indigenous knowledge and indigenous cultural and intellectual property rights must cease.

1. RECOMMENDATIONS TO INDIGENOUS PEOPLES

In the development of policies and practices, Indigenous Peoples should:

1.1 Define for themselves their own intellectual and cultural property.

1.2 Note that existing protection mechanisms are insufficient for the protection of Indigenous Peoples' Intellectual and Cultural Property Rights.

1.3 Develop a code of ethics which external users must observe when recording (visual, audio, written) their traditional and customary knowledge.

1.4 Prioritize the establishment of indigenous education, research and training centres to promote their knowledge of customary environmental and cultural practices.

1.5 Re-acquire traditional indigenous lands for the purpose of promoting customary agricultural production.

1.6 Develop and maintain their traditional practices and sanctions for the protection, preservation and revitalization of their traditional intellectual and cultural properties.

1.7 Assess existing legislation with respect to the protection of antiquities.

1.8 Establish an appropriate body with appropriate mechanisms to:

(a) preserve and monitor the commercialism or otherwise of indigenous cultural properties in the public domain;

(b) generally advise and encourage Indigenous Peoples to take steps to protect their cultural heritage;

(c) allow a mandatory consultative process with respect

to any new legislation affecting Indigenous Peoples' cultural and intellectual property rights.

1.9 Establish international indigenous information centres and networks.

1.10 Convene a Second International Conference (Hui) on the Cultural and Intellectual Property Rights of Indigenous Peoples to be hosted by the Coordinating Body for the Indigenous Peoples Organizations of the Amazon Basin (COICA).

2. RECOMMENDATIONS TO STATES, NATIONAL AND INTERNATIONAL AGENCIES

In the development of policies and practices, States, National and International Agencies must:

2.1 Recognize that Indigenous Peoples are the guardians of their customary knowledge and have the right to protect and control dissemination of that knowledge.

2.2 Recognize that Indigenous Peoples also have the right to create new knowledge based on cultural traditions.

2.3 Note that existing protection mechanisms are insufficient for the protection of Indigenous Peoples' Cultural and Intellectual Property Rights.

2.4 Accept that the cultural and intellectual property rights of Indigenous Peoples are vested with those who created them.

2.5 Develop in full co-operation with Indigenous Peoples an additional cultural and intellectual property rights regime incorporating the following:

▲ collective (as well as individual) ownership and origin
▲ retroactive coverage of historical as well as contemporary works
▲ protection against debasement of culturally significant items
▲ co-operative rather than competitive framework
▲ first beneficiaries to be the direct descendants of the traditional guardians of that knowledge
▲ multi-generational coverage span

Biodiversity and Customary Environmental Management

2.6 Indigenous flora and fauna is inextricably bound to the territories of indigenous communities and any property right claims must recognize their traditional guardianship.

2.7 Commercialization of any traditional plants and medicines of Indigenous Peoples must be managed by the Indigenous Peoples who have inherited such knowledge.

2.8 A moratorium on any further commercialization of indigenous medicinal plants and human genetic materials must be declared until indigenous communities have developed appropriate protection mechanisms.

2.9 Companies, institutions both governmental and private must not undertake experiments or commercialization of any biogenetic resources without the consent of the appropriate Indigenous Peoples.

2.10 Prioritize settlement of any outstanding land and natural resources claims of Indigenous Peoples for the purpose of promoting customary, agricultural and marine production.

2.11 Ensure current scientific environmental research is strengthened by increasing the involvement of indigenous communities and of customary environmental knowledge.

Cultural Objects

2.12 All human remains and burial objects of Indigenous Peoples held by museums and other institutions must be returned to their traditional areas in a culturally appropriate manner.

2.13 Museums and other institutions must provide, to the country and Indigenous Peoples concerned, an inventory of any indigenous cultural objects still held in their possession.

2.14 Indigenous cultural objects held in museums and other institutions must be offered back to their traditional owners.

3. RECOMMENDATIONS TO THE UNITED NATIONS

In respect for the rights of Indigenous Peoples, the United Nations should:

3.1 Ensure the process of participation of Indigenous Peoples in United Nations fora is strengthened so their views are fairly represented.

3.2 Incorporate the Mataatua Declaration in its entirety in the United Nations Study on Cultural and Intellectual Property of Indigenous Peoples.

3.3 Monitor and take action against any States whose persistent policies and activities damage the cultural and intellectual property rights of Indigenous Peoples.

3.4 Ensure that Indigenous Peoples actively contribute to the way in which indigenous cultures are incorporated into the 1995 United Nations International Year of Culture.

3.5 Call for an immediate halt to the ongoing Human Genome Diversity Project (HUGO) until its moral, ethical, socio-economic, physical and political implications have been thoroughly discussed, understood and approved by Indigenous Peoples.

4. CONCLUSION

The United Nations, International and National Agencies and States must provide additional funding to indigenous communities in order to implement these recommendations.

The Kimberley Declaration

International Indigenous Peoples Summit on Sustainable Development, Khoi–San Territory
Kimberley, South Africa, 20–23 August 2002

We, the Indigenous Peoples, walk to the future
in the footprints of our ancestors.
— *Kari–Oca Declaration, Brazil, 30 May 1992*

We the Indigenous Peoples of the World assembled here reaffirm the Kari-Oca Declaration and the Indigenous Peoples' Earth Charter. We again reaffirm our previous declarations on human and environmental sustainability.*

Since 1992 the ecosystems of the earth have been compounding in change. We are in crisis. We are in an accelerating spiral of climate change that will not abide unsustainable greed.

Today we reaffirm our relationship to Mother Earth and our responsibility to coming generations to uphold peace, equity and justice. We continue to pursue the commitments made at Earth Summit as reflected in this political declaration and the accompanying plan of action. The commitments which were made to Indigenous Peoples in Agenda 21, including our full and effective participation, have not been implemented due to the lack of political will.

As peoples, we reaffirm our rights to self-determination and to own, control and manage our ancestral lands and territories, waters and other resources. Our lands and territories are at the core of our existence—we are the land and the land is us; we have a distinct spiritual and material relationship with our lands and territories and they are inextricably linked to our survival and to the preservation and further development of our knowledge systems and cultures, conservation and sustainable use of biodiversity and ecosystem management.

We have the right to determine and establish priorities and strategies for our self-development and for the use of our lands, territories and other resources. We demand that free, prior and informed consent must be the principle of approving or rejecting any project or activity affecting our lands, territories and other resources.

We are the original peoples tied to the land by our umbilical cords and the dust of our ancestors. Our special places are sacred and demand the highest respect. Disturbing the remains of our families and elders is desecration of the greatest magnitude and constitutes a grave violation of our human rights. We call for the full and immediate repatriation of all Khoi-San human remains currently held in museums and other institutions throughout the world, as well as all the human remains of all other Indigenous Peoples. We maintain the rights to our sacred and ceremonial sites and ancestral remains, including access to burial, archaeological and historic sites.

The national, regional and international acceptance and recognition of Indigenous Peoples is central to the achievement of human and environmental sustainability. Our traditional knowledge systems must be respected, promoted and protected; our collective intellectual property rights must be guaranteed and ensured. Our traditional knowledge is not in the public domain; it is collective, cultural and intellectual property protected under our customary law. Unauthorized use and misappropriation of traditional knowledge is theft.

Economic globalization constitutes one of the main obstacles to the recognition of the rights of Indigenous Peoples. Transnational corporations and industrialized countries impose their global agenda on the negotiations and agreements of the United Nations system, the World Bank, the International Monetary Fund, the World Trade Organization and other bodies which reduce the rights enshrined in national constitutions and in international conventions and agreements. Unsustainable extraction, harvesting, production and consumption patterns lead to climate change, widespread pollution and environmental destruction, evicting us from our lands and creating immense levels of poverty and disease.

We are deeply concerned that the activities of multinational mining corporations on Indigenous lands have led to the loss and desecration of our lands, as exemplified here on Khoi-San territory. These activities have caused immense health problems, interfered with access to and occupation of our sacred sites, destroyed and depleted Mother Earth, and undermined our cultures.

Indigenous Peoples, our lands and territories are not objects of tourism development. We have rights and responsibilities towards our lands and territories. We are responsible to defend our lands, territories and indigenous peoples against tourism exploitation by governments, development agencies, private enterprises, NGOs, and individuals.

Recognizing the vital role that pastoralism and hunting-gathering play in the livelihoods of many Indigenous Peoples, we urge governments to recognize, accept, support and invest in pastoralism and hunting-gathering as viable and sustainable economic systems.

We reaffirm the rights of our peoples, nations and communities, our women, men, elders and youth to physical, mental, social, and spiritual well-being.

We are determined to ensure the equal participation of all Indigenous Peoples throughout the world in all aspects of planning for a sustainable future with the inclusion of women, men, elders and youth. Equal access to resources is required to achieve this participation.

We urge the United Nations to promote respect for the recognition, observance and enforcement of treaties, agreements and other constructive arrangements concluded between Indigenous Peoples and States, or their successors, according to their original spirit and intent, and to have States honor and respect such treaties, agreements and other constructive arrangements.

Language is the voice of our ancestors from the beginning of time. The preservation, securing and development of our languages is a matter of extreme urgency. Language is part of the soul of our nations, our being and the pathway to the future.

In case of the establishment of partnerships in order to achieve human and environmental sustainability, these partnerships must be established according to the following principles: our rights to the land and to self-determination; honesty, transparency and good faith; free, prior and informed consent; respect and recognition of our cultures, languages and spiritual beliefs.

We welcome the establishment of the United Nations Permanent Forum on Indigenous Issues and urge the UN to secure all the necessary political, institutional and financial support so that it can function effectively according to its mandate as contained in ECOSOC Resolution E/2000/22. We support the continuation of the United Nations Working Group on Indigenous Populations based on the importance of its mandate to set international standards on the rights of Indigenous Peoples.

We call for a World Conference on Indigenous Peoples and Sustainable Development as a culmination of the United Nations International Decade for the World's Indigenous Peoples (1995–2004) and as a concrete follow-up to the World Summit on Sustainable Development.

We continue to meet in the spirit of unity inspired by the Khoi-San people and their hospitality. We reaffirm our mutual solidarity as Indigenous Peoples of the world in our struggle for social and environmental justice.

*Including the Draft Declaration on the Rights of Indigenous Peoples; the Charter of the International Alliance of Indigenous and Tribal Peoples of the Tropical Forests; the Mataatua Declaration; the Santa Cruz Declaration on Intellectual Property; the Leticia Declaration of Indigenous Peoples and Other Forest Dependent Peoples on the Sustainable Use and Management of All Types of Forests; the Charter of Indigenous Peoples of the Arctic and the Far East Siberia; the Bali Indigenous Peoples Political Declaration; and, the Declaration of the Indigenous Peoples of Eastern Africa in the Regional WSSD Preparatory Meeting.

About the Contributors

JEANNETTE ARMSTRONG (*Okanagan*) is executive director of the En'owkin Centre, a native creative writing school. She is also a teacher, artist, sculptor and activist. She writes poetry, fiction, essays and children's literature and was the first native woman novelist from Canada. Armstrong is the recipient of a Buffet Award (2003) for Indigenous Leadership; she often speaks to international audiences on traditional native values, native education and indigenous rights.

BEVERLY BELL is director of the Center for Economic Justice. She has collaborated for more than two decades with justice movements throughout Latin America, the Caribbean, Southern Africa, and the United States. Her work has focused on human rights, democratic participation, just economies, and women's empowerment. Bell is the author of *Social Movements and Economic Integration in the Americas*.

DR. ZOHL DÉ ISHTAR is an Irish-Australian sociologist with the University of Queensland who works in collaboration with indigenous Australian and Pacific Island peoples on opposing the nuclearization and colonization of the Pacific region and promoting cultural revitalization. She is editor of the 1998 *Pacific Women Speak Out for Independence and Denuclearization*. Dr. Ishtar was nominated for the Nobel Peace Prize 2005 as part of the 1000 Women for the Nobel Peace Prize, a global project drawing attention to women's peace-building initiatives in 150 countries.

ORONTO DOUGLAS (*Ijaw*) is a leading human rights attorney in Nigeria, the founder and deputy director of Environmental Rights Action/Friends of the Earth, Nigeria, and was on the defense team for the Ogoni leader Ken Saro-Wiwa, later executed by the military rulers for his campaigns against Shell Oil. Douglas is also cofounder of Operation Climate Change, a nonviolent protest and civil disobedience movement in Nigeria that stopped as much as half of Chevron's oil production there, during 1998. He is co-author with Ike Okonta of the book *Where Vultures Feast: Shell, Human Rights and Oil*.

MARK DOWIE teaches science reporting at the University of California, Berkeley. A former editor of *Mother Jones*, Dowie is the author of numerous books on the environmental movement, including *Losing Ground: American Environmentalism at the Close of the Twentieth Century*. He is now writing a history of the relationship between conservation and indigenous peoples for the Orion Society. Dowie is the recipient of sixteen journalism awards, including three National Magazine Awards.

DR. LESLIE GRAY (*Oneida*) is executive director and founder of the Woodfish Institute, and a Native American psychologist who has studied with medicine people and elders from various tribal backgrounds. She advocates a new vision of health care integrating ancient healing and modern medicine. Dr. Gray consults with individuals and organizations on ecopsychology, and her work has been featured in such periodicals as *East-West Journal* and *Re-Vision Journal*, as well as in the book *Ecopsychology: Restoring the Earth, Healing the Mind*.

DEBRA HARRY (*Northern Paiute*) is an activist from Pyramid Lake, Nevada, and executive director of the Indigenous Peoples Council on Biocolonialism. She is a leader in the international movement to expose the impact of new genetic technologies on indigenous peoples, and advocates for indigenous rights at the Permanent Forum on Indigenous Issues and the Convention on Biological Diversity. In 1994, Harry received a Kellogg Foundation leadership fellowship, and recently produced a film on biotechnology called *The Leech and the Earthworm*.

ANTONIA JUHASZ is a former project director for IFG and was coordinator of IFG's report *Does Globalization Help the Poor?* Her writing has appeared in the *New York Times*, *Los Angeles Times*, *Cambridge University Review of International Relations*, the *Star* (South Africa), *Tikkun* magazine, and elsewhere. She recently completed a book on the Iraq war, *The Bush Agenda: Invading the World, One Economy at a Time.*

KEVIN KOENIG is the Northern Amazon Campaign Coordinator for Amazon Watch. He works with indigenous and *campesino* communities affected by oil extraction and infrastructure development in Ecuador, Colombia, and Peru. Koenig collaborated closely with Ecuador's southern indigenous peoples, the Shuar and Achuar, to stop oil extraction by ARCO on their traditional lands.

WINONA LADUKE (*Anishinaabeg*) is a leading indigenous activist, program director of Honor the Earth, and founding director of White Earth Land Recovery Project, which is reintroducing traditional wild rice production on White Earth reservation. She has written extensively on Native American and environmental issues, including *All Our Relations: Native Struggles for Land and Life.* LaDuke received the Reebok Human Rights Award in 1989, and was 1997 *Ms.* Woman of the Year. She was the Green Party candidate for vice president in 1996 and 2000.

JANET LLOYD has a PhD in political anthropology from the Institute of Latin American Studies at the University of Liverpool in England. As part of her PhD dissertation, she spent several years working with indigenous organizations in the Ecuadorian highlands around issues of capacity building, organizational strengthening, indigenous rights and the environment.

LUIS MACAS (Quechua) is a long-time indigenous leader, former agriculture minister, and the first indigenous person elected to Ecuador's National Congress. Macas recently assumed the presidency of the Confederation of Indigenous Nationalities of Ecuador (CONAIE), the country's most prominent indigenous peoples' organization. He also heads the Institute for the Knowledge of Indigenous Culture

and has served as a national deputy for the Pachakutik movement.

JERRY MANDER is founder and board member of the IFG, senior fellow at the Public Media Center, and author or coeditor of the best-selling books *In the Absence of the Sacred: The Failure of Technology and the Survival of the Indian Nations, The Case against the Global Economy and for a Turn toward the Local, Four Arguments for the Elimination of Television,* and *Alternatives to Economic Globalization: A Better World Is Possible.*

ARTHUR MANUEL (*Neskonlith Band of the Secwepemc Nation, British Columbia*) is spokesperson for the Indigenous Network on Economies and Trade, a network of indigenous organizations who are achieving recognition for Aboriginal and Treaty Rights at the international level. He has had three *amicus curiae* submissions successfully accepted at the World Trade Organization and one accepted by the North American Free Trade Agreement on the Canada-U.S. softwood lumber dispute.

VICTOR MENOTTI is the director of IFG's Environment Program, the author of IFG's publications *Free Trade, Free Logging: How the WTO Undermines Global Forest Conservation* and *The WTO and Sustainable Fisheries,* and a contributing author of *Environmental Impacts of Globalization.*

JOHN MOHAWK (*Seneca*) is the former editor of *Akwesasne Notes* and *Daybreak* magazines. He is also the author of *Utopian Legacies: A History of Conquest and Oppression in the Western World.* Mohawk is an associate professor at the Center for the Americas, codirector of that center and director of indigenous studies at the State University of New York at Buffalo.

IKE OKONTA (*Ijaw*) is a Research Fellow in the Department of Politics and International Relations, Oxford University. Okonta was a cofounder of *Tempo,* an underground newspaper in Lagos, Nigeria, that played a crucial role in ousting the dictator General Ibrahim Babangida in 1993. In addition to co-authoring *Where Vultures Feast: Shell, Human Rights and Oil* with Oronto Douglas, he worked with the late Ken Saro-Wiwa and Environmental Rights Action in opposition to oil company domination of the Niger Delta. Okonta now writes a weekly column for the Lagos daily newspaper, *This Day*. His collection of short stories, *The Expert Hunter of Rats*, won the Association of Nigerian Authors Prize in 1998.

E. KOOHAN PAIK is a Hawaii-based writer, filmmaker and educator. She is currently media literacy coordinator for Kauai's public access television station Ho`ike, where she is organizing a student film festival featuring the first all-Hawaiian-language category. Paik is also completing a feature documentary film on traditional agricultural practices in Hawaii, Korea and Sicily. She is a faculty member at the University of Hawaii, Kauai.

The late DARRELL ADDISON POSEY was former director of the Programme for Traditional Resource Rights at Mansfield College, Oxford University, and one of the world's leading anthropologists fighting for indigenous rights. He was founder and past president of the International Society for Ethnobiology and author of many books, including *Cultural and Spiritual Values of Biodiversity* and *Beyond Intellectual Property Rights: Toward Traditional Resource Rights for Indigenous Peoples and Local Communities.*

VANDANA SHIVA is founder and director of the Research Foundation for Science, Technology, and Natural Resource Policy in New Delhi, and an IFG board member. She received the Right Livelihood Award in 1993, and in 2001 was named one of the top five "Most Important People in Asia" by *AsiaWeek* magazine. She is author of more than three hundred papers in leading journals and numerous books, including *Monocultures of the Mind: Biodiversity, Biotechnology, and the Third World.*

ATOSSA SOLTANI is the founder and executive director of Amazon Watch, a nonprofit organization dedicated to defending the environment, territories, and rights of the region's indigenous peoples. Since the mid 1990s Soltani has been closely tracking extractive industries and mega-projects in the Amazon Basin. She serves on the board of directors of Social and Environmental Entrepreneurs, on the Steering Council of the Amazon Alliance and on the Advisory Board of International Funders for Indigenous Peoples.

VICTORIA TAULI-CORPUZ (*Igorot*) is an indigenous activist from the Cordillera region in the Philippines. She is head of the Tebtebba Foundation (Indigenous Peoples' International Centre for Policy Research and Education) in the Philippines. She helped organize and convene the UN's fourth World Conference on Women. Tauli-Corpuz is also chairperson of the UN Voluntary Fund for Indigenous Populations, convenor of the Asian Indigenous Women's Network, and a board member of the IFG. She is one of the leading indigenous activists lobbying for UN adoption of the Declaration on the Rights of Indigenous Peoples and was recently elected chairperson of the UN Permanent Forum on Indigenous Issues.

SHEILA WATT-CLOUTIER (*Inuk*) is chair of the Inuit Circumpolar Conference, representing Inuit communities in Canada, Greenland, Alaska, and Russia, especially in opposition to climate change. She has contributed to ICC Canada's 1996–2000 Institution-Building Project for Northern Russian Indigenous Peoples' Project (INRIPP-1), and to the ongoing second phase of this project focusing on economic development and training in remote northern communities.

TERRI-LYNN WILLIAMS-DAVIDSON (*Haida*) is executive director of EAGLE (Environmental-Aboriginal Guardianship through Law and Education). She has lectured and published on aboriginal law, particularly as it relates to cultural heritage, environmental protection, and forestry and has taught environmental law at the Centre for Indigenous-Environmental Research in Winnipeg, Manitoba.

SUZANNE YORK is research director for IFG. She was primary researcher on the Indigenous Peoples and Globalization map and IFG's publication *Globalization and the Environment*. She also researched and helped produce an IFG map depicting areas of the world that have been impacted by GMO crops.

About the International Forum on Globalization

THE INTERNATIONAL FORUM ON GLOBALIZATION (IFG) is a North-South research and educational institution composed of leading activists, economists, scholars, and researchers providing analyses and critiques on the cultural, social, political, and environmental impacts of economic globalization. Formed in 1994, the IFG came together out of shared concern that the world's corporate and political leadership was rapidly restructuring global politics and economics on a level that was as historically significant as any period since the Industrial Revolution. Yet there was almost no discussion or even recognition of the impacts of this new "free market" or "neoliberal" model, or of the institutions and agreements enforcing this system—the World Trade Organization (WTO), the International Monetary Fund (IMF), the World Bank, the North American Free Trade Agreement (NAFTA), and other such bureaucracies. In response, the IFG undertook a series of events and publications to stimulate new thinking, joint activity and public education about this rapidly rising economic paradigm.

Unique in its diversity, depth, and breadth, the IFG works through an active international board of key citizen movement leaders; a small, dedicated staff; and a network of hundreds of associates representing regions throughout the world on a broad spectrum of issues. Our work is closely linked to social justice and environmental movements, providing them with critical thinking and frameworks that inform campaigns and activities on the ground.

The IFG produces numerous publications; organizes high-profile, large public events; hosts many issue-specific seminars; coordinates press conferences and media interviews at international events; and participates in many other activities that focus on the myriad consequences of globalization. During the last few years, the IFG has launched a pioneering program that focuses on alternative visions and policies to globalization that are more just, equitable, democratic, accountable, and sustainable for people and the planet.

IFG BOARD MEMBERS

MAUDE BARLOW
Council of Canadians, Canada

WALDEN BELLO
Focus on the Global South, Thailand & the Philippines

AGNÈS BERTRAND
Institute for Economic Relocalisation, France

JOHN CAVANAGH
Institute for Policy Studies, U.S.

TONY CLARKE
Polaris Institute, Canada

TEWOLDE BEHRAN GEBRE EGZIABHER
Institute for Sustainable Development, Ethiopia

EDWARD GOLDSMITH
The Ecologist, U.K.

CANDIDO GRZYBOWSKI
IBASE, Brazil

MARTIN KHOR
Third World Network, Malaysia

ANDREW KIMBRELL
International Center for Technology Assessment, U.S.

SARA LARRAIN
Chile Sustainable, Chile

CAROLINE LUCAS
Member, European Parliament, U.K.

JERRY MANDER
Public Media Center, U.S.

HELENA NORBERG-HODGE
International Society for Ecology and Culture, U.K.

VANDANA SHIVA
Research Foundation for Science, Technology & Natural Resource Policy, India

VICTORIA TAULI-CORPUZ
Tebtebba (Indigenous Peoples' Int'l Centre for Policy Research & Education), the Philippines

LORI WALLACH
Public Citizen—Citizen's Trade Campaign, U.S.

EX-OFFICIO:
Randall Hayes, Executive Director